Poverty and Charity in
Middle Eastern Contexts

SUNY series in the Social and Economic History of the Middle East

Donald Quataert, editor

POVERTY AND CHARITY IN MIDDLE EASTERN CONTEXTS

Edited by
Michael Bonner
Mine Ener
Amy Singer

STATE UNIVERSITY OF NEW YORK PRESS

Cover illustration: An Ottoman bey giving alms to the poor, from a sixteenth-century miniature commissioned by Sulton Ahmed I. (B. 408, fol. 6b). Courtesy of Topkapi Palace Library, Istanbul, Turkey.

Published by
State University of New York Press, Albany

For information, address State University of New York Press,
90 State Street, Suite 700, Albany, NY 12207

Production by Kelli Williams
Marketing by Jennifer Giovani

Library of Congress Cataloging-in-Publication Data

Poverty and charity in Middle Eastern contexts / edited by Michael Bonner, Mine Ener, Amy Singer.
    p. cm. — (SUNY series in the social and economic history of the Middle East)
    Based on papers presented at a conference held at University of Michigan Center for Middle Eastern and North African Studies in May 2000.
    Includes bibliographical references and index.
    ISBN 0-7914-5737-0 (alk. paper) — ISBN 0-7914-5738-9 (pbk. : alk. paper)
    1. Poverty—Middle East—Congresses. 2. Charity—Middle East—Congresses. 3. Islam—Charities—Congresses. I. Bonner, Michael David. II. Ener, Mine, 1965– III. Singer, Amy. IV. University of Michigan. Center for Middle Eastern and North African Studies. V. Series.

HC415.15.Z9 P67 2003
362.5'0956—dc21   2002042629

10 9 8 7 6 5 4 3 2 1

Contents

List of Illustrations

Note to the Reader

This volume includes articles that rely on sources written in the Arabic, Ottoman Turkish, and modern Turkish languages and that discuss different regions of the Middle East. The result is that the text contains terms and names from these languages and regions, some of them not familiar to readers of English. In addition, Arabic and Turkish each use words from the other language, but with modifications in pronunciation and spelling. Authors in this volume have used the transliteration that is correct for the language they work with (in the case of Arabic and Ottoman Turkish), or cited words in Turkish (modern Turkish uses a modified Latin alphabet since 1928).

The editors have taken a number of measures to make the texts easily accessible and similar words recognizable. First, each foreign term is defined at first use in each chapter. Second, foreign terms are all defined briefly in the index, and similar words are cross-referenced there. Third, a modified system of transliteration from Arabic and Ottoman Turkish has been adopted, eliminating under-dots on consonants and macrons on vowels.

The following characters are used in modern Turkish:

c = "j" as in jam
ç = "ch" as in chat
ğ = soft g, silent, but lengthening the sound of the preceding vowel
ı = undotted "i," sounds like the "e" of shovel
ş = "sh" as in ship

Throughout the notes, the *Encyclopaedia of Islam,* 2nd ed. (Leiden: Brill, 1960–), will be abbreviated as *EI²*.

Introduction

Ideas and practices of poverty and charity relate to one another in many and complex ways, in the Middle East as well as elsewhere. The contributors to this volume explore ideas about the poor and poverty, the ideals and practices of charity, and state and private initiatives of relief to the poor over a period of fourteen centuries. Their research spans the Middle East, introducing new sources and re-exploring familiar ones with new questions. The volume offers methodological insights and historical analyses in a field that has come into existence only recently. All of the chapters presented here evolved from working papers presented at a four-day conference, funded by the National Endowment for the Humanities (NEH), which took place at the University of Michigan Center for Middle Eastern and North African Studies (CMENAS) in May 2000. The intention of the conference was to fill a serious gap in the study of the Islamic Middle East. For until recently there has been hardly any analysis of the means by which Middle Eastern families, communities, and states have cared for the destitute and needy. Similarly, few questions have been posed concerning the religious and social precepts guiding such actions.

Charity *(sadaqa)* is a signal characteristic of Islamic societies. The alms tax *(zakat)* is one of every Muslim's five fundamental obligations. Alongside this duty, the Quran and traditions *(hadith)* constantly recommend that believers practice voluntary charity. Charitable practices have shaped various institutions and structures throughout Islamic history, so that beneficence has become an important force of social cohesion and has worked as a kind of cultural glue to bind communities together. Beneficent undertakings may be inspired by a number of motivations, including comprehensive social vision or self-seeking ambition. Students, religious figures, artists, and family members may be targets of beneficence, even to the detriment of the truly destitute.

The language of charitable giving, which has permeated written texts and popular speech throughout the Islamic world, is an element of continuity in the history of Islamic societies. Beneficence takes many forms and is effected by various agents. Individuals, communities, institutions, and states all operate as benefactors. What any of them gives may depend on the needs of the recipient or the will of the donor. At times, the poor are a rhetorical necessity, as "taking care of the poor" justifies individual, community or state action. The welfare of the poor can be invoked to further the interests of one person, one neighborhood, one religious group, one town, or one nation. Definitions of *poor* are often flexible enough to allow benefactors to decide how inclusive or exclusive they wish to be.

The concept of *need* is also understood and articulated in different ways. Charitable giving does not take its inspiration only from a desire to relieve suffering or to end want. The desire for personal redemption or salvation is another motivation for beneficence, as are the struggle for political power and social standing, the wish to honor someone, the hope for financial gain or advantage, and the desire to assert social control. Charity, as the conference participants argued repeatedly, can never be removed from political, social, or economic contexts. The relationship between the ideals and acts of beneficence and the condition and definitions of poverty is subtle and complex.

To highlight some of the key themes that emerge from the study of charity and poverty, and their interrelationship in Middle Eastern contexts, the chapters have been organized into five parts designed to identify and explore some of the problematics of this field of study. In part 1, "Entitlement and Obligation," the chapters discuss how poverty and the poor were defined. They analyze the ways in which need was determined, the notion of 'deserving poor,' and the moments at which the state intervened to forestall deprivation and famine. In these and other ways, charity served to elaborate and reinforce social and communal hierarchies. Michael Bonner discusses how elements of generosity and competition over leadership from pre-Islamic Arabia survived (chapter 1), in a new guise, in the charitable practices of early Islam. Ingrid Mattson shows the early Muslim jurists grappling with the definitions of who does and who does not deserve charity (chapter 2), recognizing the baselines of need and the imperatives of providing for the most needy. Mark Cohen, in his reading of documents from the Cairo Geniza, similarly deals with the problem of determining who are the deserving poor, in this case among the Jews of medieval Egypt. Here (chapter 3) we see, with precision and clarity, how communities were forced to prioritize among the poor: Families and kin, together with the "known" poor, were the first to receive assistance, whereas strangers or the "foreign" poor carried less weight. Rulers were also guided by social norms and rules designed to protect the poor from privation. Adam Sabra discusses the question of price-fixing (chapter 4), as articulated by Muslim jurists and as practiced by Mamluk rulers seeking to protect the poor in times of famine and hoarding of food.

Under the rubric of "Institutions," several authors explore the formalization of beneficence in part 2. First and foremost among the institutions that evolved in early Islamic society was the endowment or *waqf*. Waqf was a long-lived and ubiquitous, although also quite varied and malleable, means of reserving the revenues from property for beneficent purposes. It became, in Marshall Hodgson's words, "a vehicle for financing Islamic society."[1] Indeed, the institutions funded and maintained through waqf—including mosques, schools, hospitals, various public works, libraries, and tombs—sustained the foundations of Islamic societies. The chapters in part 2 explore endowed institutions within a variety of social contexts. Yasser Tabbaa examines one such set of institutions: the hospitals of the Islamic Middle Ages (chapter 5). He traces transformations in their uses and the practical and intellectual challenges that they generated. Although Tabbaa points to a gradual decline in the hospitals and the practice of medicine in general, Miri Shefer claims that hospitals retained their importance (chapter 6), both in regard to the motivations for their establishment and the individuals who made use of them. Miriam Hoexter, in her analysis of the distribution of alms (chapter 7), focuses on the targets of benefactors, exploring the social standing of the various recipients of charity originating in Ottoman Algiers. She demonstrates that the destitute, both in the Arabian Holy Cities and in Algiers itself, were only one of several social groups who benefited from endowments.

Because the rhetorical emphasis in Islamic writings tends to fall on the role of the individual benefactor, the state usually has not been perceived as a charitable actor. Yet some discussion of the state as a charitable actor is implicit in most of the chapters in this volume. With a more explicit consideration of "The State as Benefactor," part 3 examines the ways in which rulers and governments assumed or avoided roles in the distribution of beneficence. Eyal Ginio's analysis of eighteenth-century Salonica (chapter 8) explores the ways the poor managed to survive in a provincial setting devoid of imperial benevolence. Both in the provincial capitals of the Ottoman Empire and at its center, subsequent efforts at administrative centralization, together with economic and political transformations, resulted in an increase in state welfare projects. The studies by Mine Ener (chapter 9) and Nadir Özbek (chapter 10) both "bring the state back in" with analyses of state-funded projects. Ener discusses the extent to which the inhabitants of Egypt sought state assistance in the nineteenth century, while Özbek looks at the means by which acts of benevolence were publicly orchestrated to demonstrate a ruler's concern for his subjects.

The chapters in part 4, examine "Changing Worlds"—new uses for and articulations of beneficence and poverty. At the same time, beneficence remained important as an element of cohesion, both rhetorically and practically. Reformers such as Rifaʿa al-Tahtawi sought to understand the reasons for poverty. This Egyptian intellectual, as Juan R. I. Cole demonstrates (chapter 11), posited that the state has maintained primary responsibility for the poor since earlier eras of Islamic history. In contrast (chapter 12), Beth Baron discusses the religious and nationalist motivations of one woman—Labiba Ahmad—to analyze how members of the elite in a country such as Egypt assumed a commitment to bettering the condition of the poor. Articulating the question of who should take responsibility for needy children (chapter 13), Kathryn Libal introduces the growing number of actors in the field of child welfare during the crucial first years of the Turkish Republic, their critiques of one another and the state, and the programs they designed.

The chapters in part 5, "Welfare as Politics," look at how older ideas and practices related to poverty and charity have made the transition to the contemporary era. Timur Kuran analyzes ongoing debates on the institution of zakat in contemporary Islamic societies and the successes and failures of efforts to reinstate this tax as a means of alleviating poverty (chapter 14). Amy Singer explores the centrality of waqf within the Ottoman Empire (chapter 15), the historical critiques made against endowments, and the ways contemporary Turkey continues to bear witness to the legacy of imperial endowments.

"Middle Eastern contexts" is the geographical boundary of these studies. Recurring questions, posed from the outset, have been to what extent was or is there anything particularly Islamic about approaches to poverty and charity in the Middle East, and to what extent do attitudes and practices found in the Middle East share features common to other cultures and societies? For it may seem unclear whether or in what way the Middle Eastern framework of this subject contributes any particular insights into the understanding of poverty or the formulation of beneficent responses. Much writing on Islamic history essentializes 'Islam' across vast dimensions of time and space to produce largely meaningless and baseless generalizations. Yet it is also impossible to study the Middle East, in any period, without taking into account the ideologies and practices that have evolved in part under the influence of religious doctrine and belief. The forms of charitable assistance and attitudes to poverty that evolved in western Christian, Byzantine, and Jewish communities, for example, all resulted from the combined influence of religious ideology, cultural practices and specific communal needs, political goals, and economic conditions; much the same is true of the Islamic Middle East. Therefore, some authors in this volume consciously chose to identify the role played by ideologies based in Islamic theology and belief, together with the impact of processes of state formation, large-scale political and social transformations, and economic crises.

One subject this volume does not address is "voluntary poverty," including ascetic and mystical (Sufi) doctrine and social practice. These have received attention elsewhere, though the focus there, at least until recently, has been mainly textual and phenomenological. Although "voluntary" and "involuntary" aspects of poverty often cannot be considered in isolation from one another, the chapters in this volume concentrate on involuntary poverty, discussing voluntary poverty only as it pertains to other issues in any one chapter.

The authors all draw on sources that until now have not been used to elucidate arguments and ideas regarding poverty, private charitable initiatives, the conditions of the poor, and the roles of the state and the ruling elites in charitable endeavors. These include religious texts, literary compositions, historical narratives, newspapers, and private and official documents. Moreover, each scholar comes to the broader topic from a different problematic and methodological perspective, so that together they offer diverse insights into and explore avenues of research in philosophical, religious, cultural, economic, social, political, and anthropological history.

A methodological discussion runs throughout the entire volume, with two main aspects: First, each chapter demonstrates the practical possibilities and limitations of working with the existing literary and documentary sources in this field. Because of the broad chronological and geographical distribution of the chapters, the source materials used by the group as a whole constitute a representative spectrum of the sources available to scholars interested in poverty and charity in Middle Eastern societies. Many of these sources are particular to and generated only within Islamic societies, such as the Quran, the traditions of the Prophet *(hadith),* legal commentaries and juridical texts, the protocols *(sijillat)* of Muslim judges, and the opinions *(fatawa)* issued by Muslim jurisconsults. Of course, these types of sources have parallels in other traditions, and some authors also consider non-Muslim traditions that flourished within Muslim societies, in particular those of the Jewish communities.

Second, the methodological discussion also considers the place of poverty and charity within society as a whole and the theoretical frameworks available for their study. Although the contributors are mainly historians, the conference compelled them to engage with the ideas and methods of participating scholars from economics, anthropology, politics, and sociology. Furthermore, because studies from Western cultures comprise the majority of existing scholarship on poverty and charity, scholars of Middle Eastern societies must test critically the applicability of frameworks articulated in other fields, particularly with regard to private charity and the role of the state in the creation of social welfare systems.

It is only in the last decade or so that the detailed, systematic study of poverty and the poor in the Middle East has been undertaken in essays and monographs and has begun to draw attention. It has been mainly the modern period for which poverty and the poor have been considered as a separate subject. There, they have been regarded in conjunction with other situations such as social disturbances, disease, or political unrest. Charity, on the other hand, has been more extensively discussed in studies focusing on the institutions of zakat and waqf. Waqf, in particular, has received serious consideration. However, endowments have been studied mostly as individual institutions, as expressions of imperial patronage and beneficence, or with regard to property law and usage. They have not been examined in an attempt to elucidate the nature of public and private charity in Islamic or Middle Eastern societies.

Influenced by historical inquiries in other regions of the world and seeking to understand what might be unique to the experience of poverty in the Middle East and to the development and role of private and state-sponsored charity there, historians of the Middle East have now begun to explore the history of poverty and charity. A growing number have chosen to investigate broad questions of social welfare, relief, and the nature of poverty, relying on a wide variety of rich source materials to pursue these questions. Over the past twenty years, scholars such as Said Arjomand, Michael Dols, Robert McChesney, Carl Petry, Norman Stillman, and the authors in this volume have addressed the uses of philanthropy, the meaning of charity, and the numerous institutions that provide social, economic, and cultural assistance. Another group of contemporary researchers—including Randi Deguilhem, Abdulkarim Rafeq, Amira Sonbol, Mahmoud Yazbak, and others—is examining related questions in a forthcoming volume on poverty and wealth. Altogether, these recent studies demonstrate the possibilities for research, the importance of considering the motivations behind charitable acts, and the role of the poor as integral, though marginalized, members of society. This increasing interest in aspects of poverty and charity is no surprise given the urgency and persistence of these questions in our own contemporary world, including the Middle East.

The conference that led to this volume began as a collaboration among the editors that produced a series of conference panels at annual meetings of the Middle East Studies Association of North America from 1996 to 1998. However, because these panels could not provide for extensive discussion, and because each year more scholars of all generations appeared to be studying poverty and charity as historical aspects of Middle Eastern and Islamic societies, it seemed worthwhile to hold a meeting devoted to these topics alone. Thus, the conference in 2000 brought together some of the most active scholars in this field in an intensive workshop atmosphere. This was the first extended opportunity for them to meet to assess the significance of their achievements, both for understanding these particular topics and for assessing their contribution to the present and future study of states and societies in the Middle East.

All the participants agreed that the structure of the conference contributed measurably to the meeting's success. The combination of commentators from the field of Middle Eastern studies and from the study of poverty and charity in other cultures ensured an ongoing comparative and cross-cultural discussion. Altogether, the discussions identified areas and questions as yet unaddressed and articulated the problematic aspects of those under study, thus producing agendas for future research. Finally, the explanation and critique of methodologies helped to hone existing research tools to further ongoing scholarly work and encourage other scholars to pursue related topics.

Over three and one-half days, successive discussions built on and informed each other. The small, focused workshop structure has repeatedly proved to be a stimulating and productive mode of engaging a particular topic. Papers were submitted well in advance of the conference and were distributed to all authors and commentators. During the conference, each presentation comprised a brief comment by the author, stressing the main ideas of the paper and reflecting further on the topic. An invited commentator then spoke for a further fifteen to twenty minutes. Following this, general discussion continued for another hour.

In discussion, a number of comments and questions were collected from participants before returning to the author for his or her response. This procedure was repeated several times for each paper, a strategy allowing for a maximum number of comments and questions, as well as responses from the authors. The result was a rich, multilateral discussion instead of a series of limited dialogues between author and individual questioners. It is difficult to capture this dynamic on paper, in a linear fashion, but the people, subject, format, and setting created an intense, lively, and continuous exchange of ideas, comments, critiques, and stories that sent the participants home to rethink and rewrite.

The success of the conference was due equally to the commentators themselves. Many of them treated the initial invitation to the conference with skepticism, unconvinced that they could contribute substantially to a discussion "not in their field." The proceedings proved otherwise. The commentators helped to explore extensively the implications of each paper on substantive and theoretical grounds. Their "remoteness" allowed them to see and question the underlying assumptions that often become invisible to those who are closest to the material.

The commentators' critiques and comments have been incorporated into the papers during the process of revision and are not included here separately. However, because these commentators shaped the final product so profoundly, it would be ungrateful not to name them here. They are:

Sandra Cavallo (Department of History, Royal Holloway College), author of *Charity and Power in Early Modern Italy: Benefactors and Their Motives in Turin, 1541–1789* (Cambridge: Cambridge University Press, 1995).

Natalie Zemon Davis (Departments of History, Princeton University and the University of Toronto), author of *The Gift in Sixteenth-Century France* (Madison: University of Wisconsin Press, 2000) and *Society and Culture in Early Modern France* (Stanford: Stanford University Press, 1977). Professor Davis's summation provided a thought-provoking conclusion to the conference, just as her valuable concluding chapter in this volume brings together its main themes in comparative perspective.

Lori D. Ginzberg (Department of History, Pennsylvania State University), author of *Women and the Work of Benevolence: Morality, Politics, and Class in the Nineteenth-Century United States* (New Haven: Yale University Press, 1990).

Fatma Müge Göçek (Department of Sociology, University of Michigan), author of *Rise of the Bourgeoisie, Demise of Empire: Ottoman Westernization and Social Change* (New York: Oxford University Press, 1996).

Seth Koven (Department of History, Villanova University), coeditor of *Mothers of a New World: Maternalist Politics and the Origins of Welfare States* (New York: Routledge, 1993).

Adele Lindenmeyr (Department of History, Villanova University), author of *Poverty Is Not a Vice: Charity, Society, and State in Imperial Russia* (Princeton: Princeton University Press, 1996).

Zachary Lockman (Department of Middle Eastern Studies, New York University), author of *Workers on the Nile: Nationalism, Communism, Islam, and the Egyptian Working Class, 1882–1954* (Princeton: Princeton University Press, 1987).

Leslie P. Peirce (Departments of History and Near Eastern Studies, University of California at Berkeley), author of *The Imperial Harem: Women and Sovereignty in the Ottoman Empire* (New York: Oxford University Press, 1993).

Jenny B. White (Department of Anthropology, Boston University), author of *Money Makes Us Relatives: Women's Labor in Urban Turkey* (Austin: University of Texas Press, 1994).

All these scholars contributed their time and thoughtful consideration of the research presented here. Their experience in generating numerous and varied theoretical approaches and methodologies helped us assess our achievements thus far and define an agenda for future research. We thank them for their generosity.

At the same time, the editors hope and expect that research on poverty and charity in the Middle East will contribute to the work of those who are interested in other societies, just as we benefited so obviously from their scholarship and their presence at this conference. Until now, the history of Middle Eastern and Islamic societies, on the whole, has been marginalized, or at any rate not readily accessible to those working outside its boundaries. Yet this field is enormously important both from the perspective of world history and from that of contemporary policy.

This conference was generously funded by an NEH Collaborative Research Grant, which we recognize with gratitude. We also owe thanks for the support of our home institutions: the University of Michigan, Villanova University, and Tel Aviv University. In particular, we recognize the institutional backing of the University of Michigan Center for Middle Eastern and North African Studies and International Institute. At CMENAS, Jeanie Lebak, Esther Meima, and Rob Haug provided invaluable time and effort with the logistics of organizing the conference. Valerie Carey, Karen Kron, and Maya Jordan provided expert assistance in the final stages of editing and production. Betsi Ojalvo at Tel Aviv University was an efficient and accurate editorial assistant. We also express our thanks to the State University of New York Press, to Professor Donald Quataert, Dr. Michael Rinella and Kelli Williams, and to the anonymous readers for their insightful critiques.

Note

1. Marshall G. S. Hodgson, *The Venture of Islam,* 3 vols. (Chicago: University of Chicago Press, 1974), 2:124.

Part I

Entitlement and Obligation

CHAPTER ONE

Poverty and Charity in the Rise of Islam

MICHAEL BONNER

The "Return of Wealth" / I~ TRO Background

Each generation of Muslims in the Middle East has used charitable practices to alleviate suffering and to maintain balance and order in society. At the same time, a set of concepts clustering around poverty and charity have remained essential elements for understanding and expressing the norms that have governed much of Middle Eastern life. Poverty and charity thus were, and to some extent still are, focal points and ways of understanding for Muslims as they have thought about the creation and distribution of wealth and as they have established and sustained a wide variety of institutions.

One element of what we might call the Islamic "economy of poverty"[1] has to do with the concept of return. Historical narratives regarding the earliest period of Islam inform us that as the Prophet Muhammad sent out his administrators of the *zakat* (obligatory alms) for the nascent Islamic polity, he instructed them to "take the possessions *(amwal)* of the rich and return them to the poor"; or to inform the donors that "God has laid the obligation of alms *(sadaqa)* on their possessions, to be taken from the rich among them and returned to the poor";[2] and similar formulations. (The Arabic words for this are usually *radd* and its derivatives, less often *ruju'* and other words). Similarly, in the *hadith* (narrative accounts of sayings and deeds ascribed to the Prophet),[3] *return* often means "give," as in: "Return (i.e., give to) the beggar, even if it is only the head of a sandgrouse."[4] It can also be argued, on the basis of the hadith, that as wealth returns from the rich to the poor it must never return from the rich to the rich. The original donor of an item must afterward never retrieve it.[5]

These are not the only ways in which the early Islamic texts conceptualize charity or the circulation of wealth. But at the same time, the calls for return are not merely casual metaphors. We see this already in the Quran where in an important passage (59:7) we read: "That which God has returned *(ma afa'a llahu)* to His Messenger from the [conquered] people of the towns is for God and the Messenger and those close [to the Messenger] and for the orphan and the pauper and the traveler, so that it does not become something which circulates *(dulatan)* among the rich among you." This passage sets forth vividly the precept of good circulation of wealth (never from the rich to the rich). At the same time it provides one of the foundations of early fiscal theory: from this passage of the Quran the jurists derived the concept of *fay* (another word for return), which came to refer technically to the wealth accruing constantly to the community of believers from the lands they have conquered and from the labor of the conquered, non-Muslim "protected people" *(ahl al-dhimma)*, in a never-ending cycle or return.[6]

More generally, the Quran makes constant admonitions and demands for almsgiving—*zakat/sadaqa* here the context often seems to be that of prodding reluctant believers into making contributions, whether toward the conduct of warfare or the maintenance of the poor—these two being much the same thing. "If you fear destitution, God will make you wealthy [give you surplus] out of His *fadl* [surplus], if He wills" (9:28). Hoarding and greed are roundly condemned,[7] broadly in harmony with a conception of return (since hoarded goods cannot move). And the Quran insists upon a *haqq* (plural: *huquq*), a right or claim, which inheres in property. Of course persons have huquq, but we also find the haqq in the property itself. Thus the community of true believers consists of "those upon whose property there is an agreed right *[haqq ma'lum]* for the beggar and the destitute" (70:24, cf. 51:19). And in the Quran we also find *riba*, generally understood to refer to the forbidden "usury." It is difficult to say what riba actually means in the Quran (rather than in mature Islamic law). However, one passage where it occurs (30:39) clearly contrasts some kind of bad circulation (riba) with good circulation (zakat or almsgiving).

Although this notion of return occurs repeatedly in foundational Islamic texts, it has largely escaped the notice of modern scholarship. Notable exceptions include the Egyptian radical reformer Sayyid Qutb, especially in his commentary on the Quran,[8] and the anthropologist Christian Décobert in his controversial *Le mendiant et le combattant*. There Décobert identified an *économie aumônière* or economy of alms as the basis of exchange in the early Islamic conquest polity. In his view the early Islamic economy forms, ideally, a system in which goods circulate perpetually within the community through constant almsgiving. The poor recipient of alms becomes rich so that he may then reimpoverish himself by giving, in a never-ending eleemosynary chain. However, he is not, again ideally, a producer of the goods that circulate. These enter the system from outside—as this is, after all, a conquest polity and economy. What the Muslim eats has ideally been produced by others; and gain is perceived as separate from the activities of production and exchange.[9]

Even if Décobert overstated his case, he identified Islamic notions of charity that feature the notion of return. Later I will try to show that this is largely an Arabian inheritance. In different terms, we may say that Islamic charity is, in part, an extension or descendant of an older Arabian economy of gift. First, however, comes a broader look at poverty and charity within the context of the history and historiography of the rise of Islam.

The Literary Sources for Poverty and Charity in Arabia

Any thesis about the role of charity and poverty in Islamic societies must take us back to the origins of Islam. And, indeed, poverty and charity were never more important in the history of Islam than they were then, at the very beginning. Zakat, the obligatory poor-rate, and sadaqa, voluntary alms, both appear prominently in the Quran and in other foundational texts, as we have just seen. (It should be remembered, however, that this distinction between compulsory zakat and voluntary sadaqa does not apply systematically in the Quran and in the earliest period of Islam.) In the old Arabic narratives about the early Muslim community and its conquests and quarrels, zakat and sadaqa loom large at several moments of crisis. These include the beginning of Muhammad's prophetical career in Mecca, when what appear to be the earliest pieces of scripture insist on almsgiving more than any other human activity. These moments of crisis also include the wars of the *ridda* or apostasy in C.E. 632–634, just after Muhammad's death. At that time most of the Arabs throughout the peninsula refused to continue paying zakat (now a kind of tax) to the central authority in Medina; Abu Bakr, upon assuming the leadership, swore he would force them all to pay this zakat, "even if they refuse me only a [camel's] hobble of it," and sent armies that subdued these rebels or "apostates" in large-scale battles that were soon followed by the great Islamic conquests beyond the Arabian peninsula itself.[10]

By the same token, in recent years some of the most influential historical accounts of the rise of Islam have attributed considerable importance to these charitable practices and to the structures that are supposed to have grown out of them. However, as we try to identify and describe charitable practices in pre-Islamic and early Islamic Arabia with historical accuracy, we encounter serious problems in the source materials available to us.

We have no direct, contemporary, documentary evidence for the rise of Islam in the Hijaz (west central Arabia). Archaeological evidence, now marshaled by some researchers,[11] remains incomplete and difficult to interpret. Modern ethnography and travel literature provide insights and parallels but no hard evidence for the political and moral economy of seventh-century Arabia. We continue to rely, for the most part, on a large corpus of narratives written during the Islamic period, in Arabic, and relating to pre-Islamic and early Islamic Arabia. These writings have been preserved through a process of literary transmission, in such a way that texts mostly do not survive from before around A.H. 150 (C.E. 767). In the form in which we have them, the majority of these texts are the products of scholars who lived later than that, often much later. These scholars worked with earlier sources that have since then become lost, and it may well be that their work reproduces those earlier sources faithfully. However, some modern analysts have argued that the Arabic historical narratives contain parallel and contradictory versions of events, and that in both content and form they are the products of long processes of literary stereotyping.[12] Others have countered that the narratives do contain a significant core of accurate historical information. This debate has absorbed much of the time and effort of specialists in early Islam, especially in the latest generation.

Within this larger controversy, poverty and charity have received some attention. In the 1950s, W. Montgomery Watt argued that Muhammad's activity as a prophet in Mecca took place within a larger context of a "weakening social solidarity [in Arabia] and . . . growth of individualism." According to Watt a crisis, both economic and spiritual, beset the Hijaz, expressed in a new vocabulary of poverty and wealth: "While it seems unlikely that there had been any increase in absolute poverty in Mecca, it is probable that the gap between rich and poor had widened in the last half-century. The Qur'an implies an increasing awareness of the difference between rich and poor. . . . The rich were showing less concern for the poor and uninfluential, even among their own kin."[13] In this crisis the Quran offered a "new basis for social solidarity," in an idiom already familiar to the Meccans and their Arab neighbors. So even though many scholars, following Ignaz Goldziher, saw a deep gulf between pre-Islamic Arabian *muruwwa* (manly heroism, *virtus*) on the one hand, and Islamic *din* (religion) on the other hand,[14] Watt saw continuity between pre-Islamic and earliest Islamic society, between "old Arab ideals" and the new monotheist solution proposed in the earliest parts of the Quran. This continuity resided in the old Arab ideal of generosity, which now acquired powerful monotheist sanctions through the doctrine and practice of almsgiving: Watt described the creation of new fiscal institutions in the Islamic community that Muhammad established at Medina in 1/622. Although the institutions provided for the needs of the new circumstances, they were still built around the concept of generosity.[15] Poverty, charity, and generosity thus provide keys to the transition between *jahiliyya* (Arabia before Islam) and early Islam.

The crisis in social solidarity in early-seventh-century Mecca had to have a context and an explanation, which Watt located in the larger commercial history of western Arabia. Mecca had turned its unpromising, barren site to advantage by seizing control over the peninsular caravan trade, including the lucrative trade in spices and aromatics from South Arabia to the Mediterranean world. As Mecca's merchants, especially the dominant tribe of Quraysh, quickly accumulated riches, they wove the Meccans and the surrounding tribes into their "financial net."[16] The result was an increasing and unprecedented inequality. In this way, Meccan poverty and Meccan generosity both resulted directly from the rapid growth of Meccan trade. The story of Meccan trade, which has been told with increasing refinement down to the present day,[17] has received far more attention than the poverty and charity that were the original centerpieces of Watt's carefully constructed biography of Muhammad. All the same, Watt's work has had enormous influence, as has his approach to the Arabic sources for the life of Muhammad, which may briefly be described as commonsensical: accepting the general narrative framework of *sira* (prophetical biography) and *akhbar* (historical narratives), while sifting individual details and contradictory accounts for an acceptable narrative in accordance with criteria of plausibility.[18]

In 1987 Patricia Crone aimed a devastating critique at Watt's propositions (as Crone put it) that Mecca was an entrepôt of peninsular and international trade; that the Quraysh were the "bourgeois" entrepreneurs controlling that trade; and that "the Qurashi transition to a mercantile economy undermined the traditional order in Mecca, generating a social and moral malaise to which Muhammad's preaching was the response."[19] Crone arrived instead at the following negative conclusions: Mecca never was the favorable location for trade that modern scholars have made it out to be. In fact it made no sense as a commercial site. In late antiquity the incense trade and the transit trade in luxury goods from India did not usually take the overland route from Yemen to Syria. (The Mediterranean market for incense, in any case, had collapsed by the third century.) Mecca never dominated Arabian commerce with other countries and failed even to attract their notice. Meccan trade did not extend much beyond local distribution of such items as leather, cheap cloth, and livestock.

Guiding all this demolition work is a running critique of the Islamic sources, in which "apparently sober accounts of separate events turn out to be nothing but elaborations on a single theme."[20] "The tradition asserts both A and not A, and it does so with such regularity that one could, were one so inclined, rewrite most of Montgomery Watt's biography of Muhammad in the reverse."[21] Crone shows little interest in Watt's themes of poverty and wealth, generosity and almsgiving. The assumption is that once Watt's premise of large-scale Meccan trade before Islam has been removed, his entire edifice crumbles.

Several contributions made since Crone's *Meccan Trade* have sought to transcend the conflict between the older view of the sources,[22] whereby history emerges as a residue of the "right" texts, and what has been called the "revisionist school,"[23] according to whom the defectiveness of the textual tradition makes history unrecoverable, or nearly so. None of these, however, has fully answered the objections made by Crone against Watt. Historiographical problems still prevent us from understanding the role of poverty and charity in the rise of Islam.

Yet another obstacle lies in scholars' almost exclusive concentration on sadaqa and zakat. These two words, which denote alms in the earliest Islamic Arabic texts, both have close cognates in other Semitic languages, including Hebrew and Aramaic, throughout their broad semantic ranges. So for instance, zakat in Arabic carries the connotation of "a payment on property in order to purify it and, hence, cause for it to be blessed and multiply." This sense of "purification," plus that of "exemption from taxes," occurs in other Semitic languages.[24] How and when did these terms enter the Arabic language and the Arabian peninsula? It seems that sadaqa and zakat occur rarely, if at all, in Arabic texts relating to Arabia before Islam or at the time of the beginning of Islam, *other than in specifically Islamic contexts.*[25] This indicates that sadaqa and zakat are relatively recent borrowings from the outside; or in other words, that they belong to the Near Eastern heritage of early Islam, at least as much as to the Arabian.

Several explanations have been offered for how these terms, and the practices associated with them, might have gained currency in the Hijaz in the early seventh century. These have included the idea that Muhammad witnessed these practices during his youthful travels to Syria, or else that Jewish or Christian practices became familiar in Mecca, despite the town's lack of a Jewish or Christian community. However, most of these explanations and theories have been philological in method on the one hand; while on the other hand, they have viewed the early history of these practices and doctrines through the history of the Islamic community, and through the use of Islamic texts.[26] But there cannot have been such a chasm between the redistributive practices of the jahiliyya and those of Islam.

Décobert's *Le mendiant et le combattant* constitutes one of the few attempts so far to go beyond the familiar discussion of sadaqa and zakat. He compresses a complex argument into his composite figure of "the beggar and the warrior." He begins with the historiographical problem, trying to view it sociologically. He distinguishes between the "preaching" *(prédication)* of Muhammad, a moment of crisis in early-seventh-century Arabia, and the "teaching" *(enseignement)* that came afterward.[27] However, Décobert's critique of the revisionist authors[28] fails to produce a countertheory in favor of the validity of those sources. He does not base his argument on close reading of Arabic sources, especially regarding Arabia before Islam. All the same, Décobert brings up an important point, namely, that the gift provides a key to the political economy of old Arabia and earliest Islam. The connected concepts of poverty and warfare were central to the formation of Muslim identity and have remained so ever since.

Trajectories /method

In Arabia before the rise of Islam there was a wide variety of distributive and redistributive practices, many of them now obscure to us. I am working to identify some of these to recover certain aspects of the political economy of old Arabia. Then I propose to trace the evolution, rebirth, or death of these practices under the new dispensation of Islam. The source material available for this is fragmentary. However, we can identify themes of economic relevance among the writings, including poetry, that relate to pre-Islamic and early Islamic Arabia. We cannot simply accept these narratives at face value: this especially applies to the stories in prose that provide narrative context to the poetry. However, once we have identified a recurring and/or underlying theme, we must seek its trajectories in time and space.

As for time, we may find a practice of jahiliyya recurring in Islam, under different circumstances and possibly under different names, but still recognizably itself. In this case, the Islamic sources—above all the hadith[29]—may allow us to reconstruct a trajectory over time.[30]

As for space, we need to discover networks and to plot them, with emphasis on the constant movement and "connectivity" of the Arabian environment.[31] These ought to include networks of trade and pilgrimage, but also the tribal matrix itself, with its intensive and shifting occupation of space.[32] Even though the "biases" of some of our Arabic sources can complicate the matter, these biases may also correlate to region or locality.[33] Moreover, even though the Arabic sources have been accused of rhetorical embellishment, stereotyping, party spirit, local bias, and so on, they show remarkable consistency of detail in their description of networks, or at least in providing pieces that we may then reassemble into networks. Patricia Crone has demonstrated this in relation to the early Islamic polity,[34] while her book on Meccan trade shows that accounts of jahiliyya also show consistency of detail that we can use to reconstruct networks of trade and pilgrimage.[35]

Rather than focusing on the dilemma of Meccan trade, we should take a broader view of Arabia as a whole. In what follows I will point to two aspects of the pre-Islamic economy, which coexisted even though they seem to contradict one another. One of them is the Arabian background of the Islamic return of wealth, which I mentioned toward the beginning of this chapter. The other, discussed first, is its seeming opposite: nonreturn, noncirculation, waste of surplus through competition over leadership.

Generosity, Competition, and Waste

In Arabic writings pertaining to pre-Islamic Arabia, we find a recurring motif. A man of means has a camel slaughtered to provide a feast to the members of a kin-based group of moderate size, called *"qawm"* or *"hayy."* Another man then becomes angry and has one of his camels slaughtered and its meat distributed. The first donor counters with another camel, the second donor retaliates, and soon a pile of dead beasts accumulates, far beyond the capacity of the group to consume. The first of the contestants who runs out of camels or who gives up, must leave in disgrace. This competitive and self-destructive display, known by various names[36] and related to the poetic contests called *"tafakhur"* and *"mufakhara,"* was discussed briefly by Julius Wellhausen and Ignaz Goldziher more than a century ago, and then not much until recently. The parallel with the self-destructive feasting or potlatch of the Pacific Northwest is fairly clear.[37]

Variations occur on the motif. Hatim al-Ta'i, the paragon of Arab generosity not long before Islam, had a reputation both as a poet and as the lord of his people *(sayyid qawmihi)*. Once when al-Hakam b. Abi l-'As was passing through on his way from the Hijaz to al-Hira, he asked Hatim for protection *(jiwar)*, in the area controlled by the Tayyi', Hatim's tribe. Hatim agreed and provided lavish hospitality in the form of slaughtered camels. Hatim's right to obligate all of Tayyi' in a matter of jiwar was then challenged by his relatives the Banu Lam, another branch of the Tayyi'. The two sides came briefly to blows but then agreed to settle the matter with a competitive feast *(mijad)* at the market *(suq)* of al-Hira. The opponents marshaled their resources. Hatim made sure of the loyalty of various "cousins" and allies who pledged their wealth *(mal)*—meaning numbers of camels for slaughter. Hatim's side attained such superiority that the Banu Lam had to admit defeat before the contest even began. This was good news both for the local camel population and for Hatim, whose fame and preeminence within his own qawm were now assured.

This practice of hamstringing and/or sacrificing of camels, most often expressed by the verb *'aqara/'aqr* and its derivative *ta'aqur* (competitive feasting) connects both with ancient practices of camel sacrifice and with questions of leadership. Not only must a prospective *sayyid* or *shaykh* show prowess in war, he also must nourish the group he seeks to lead, if need be in self-destructive competition. The consumers are not described as needy or poor, but they have a right to the camel feasts whenever these take place.

One of the fullest descriptions we have of ta'aqur comes from the early days of Islam, during the caliphate of 'Ali (c.e. 656–661).

> Ghalib [b. Sa'sa'a, father of the poet al-Farazdaq] slaughtered a female camel *['aqara naqatan]* and distributed [its meat] among the tents of the clan *[buyut al-hayy]* [of Tamim]. A portion was brought to Suhaym [b. Wathil al-Riyahi], who became angry and returned it, and then slaughtered a camel of his own. Ghalib then slaughtered another one, and so they vied with one another *[fa-ta'aqaru]* until Suhaym ran out [of camels]. Afterward, when Suhaym arrived at al-Kufa, his people chided him. He tried to excuse himself by saying that he had been away from his own herd. Then he sent for a hundred camels, which he slaughtered over the refuse dump *[kunasa]* of al-Kufa. Whereupon 'Ali [b. Abi Talib, then caliph]

said, This has been consecrated for the worship of something other than God, so don't eat it *[inna hadha mimma uhilla biha li-ghayr Allah fa-la ta'kuluhu]*. And so it remained where it was until the wild beasts and the dogs ate it.[38]

Here we see ta'aqur surviving into the early Islamic period, despite the existence of a caliph and a centralized administration. Objections to it are stated on religious grounds because of the association with pagan sacrifice. Other statements of disapproval and prohibition include the hadith "there is no *'aqr* in Islam."[39] These prohibitions lack historical context, though interestingly, it is often 'Ali who condemns the practice on religious grounds, as in the passage just quoted. All the same, we find veiled allusions to the practice in other early Islamic contexts, including the Quran (the hamstringing by Thamud of the *naqat Allah* [God's camel]) and the famous Battle of the Camel of A.H. 36 (C.E. 656), which culminated in a hamstringing. But this will have to be taken up elsewhere. For now we see that in ancient Arabia there existed a trend toward competitive and sometimes self-destructive feasting, connected to contests over leadership. This trend seems to correlate to an archaic condition of society, where camels represent the main form of surplus and wealth. In this situation, surplus is given away, consumed, or simply destroyed. It does not circulate and does not return to its original owner.

Were these merely acts of generosity pushed to an extreme? The best discussion so far of generosity in pre-Islamic Arabia has been M. M. Bravmann's essay "The Surplus of Property."[40] Bravmann saw a basic identity between the generosity of old Arabia and the charity of early Islam, with some adjustment of vocabulary and practice. Although there are difficulties in this approach and conclusion,[41] Bravmann showed that acts of generosity among individuals in old Arabia followed certain patterns. The Arabs thought and said that property (mal) has a surplus (fadl, or *'afw*), which its owner must give away. Indeed, that surplus carries a right or claim (haqq) within itself, which occurs in the Quran (see the opening section to this chapter, "The Return of Wealth"). The owner of surplus does not have to destroy it and may give it to someone who needs it. This needy recipient then enters into or continues a relationship with the donor, as protected guest *(jar)*, client *(mawla)*, or ally *(halif)*. In other words, donor and recipient know each other—even if, as often, they do not belong to the same kin group—and the relationship between them is one of inequality. Now, most likely the recipient can never reciprocate this gift fully. He will be frustrated in his expectation (familiar to us from Marcel Mauss)[42] that the gift must be returned in some way and at some time. More specifically, the donor's act of benefaction traps the recipient into a relationship of clientage, or worse. The fact that the ta'aqur is a contest over dominance within the group,[43] in which the consumers of the feast can never reciprocate, indicates that this Arabian destructive potlatch is indeed only an an extreme point on a spectrum of acts of generosity.

Markets and Trade

I stated at the beginning of this chapter that an Islamic notion of return of wealth had its roots in pre-Islamic Arabia. At first glance this appears not to be so, since the Arabic texts relating to Arabia before Islam, including the poetry, do not literally insist on a return of wealth, at least not with the same clarity as do the texts relating to Islam. However, the main connection does not lie where Bravmann thought it did, in acts of individual generosity, which, as we have seen, were associated with the acquisition and maintaining of power by individuals, with unequal relationships, and, in the extreme case, with dramatic waste of resources. Instead, we may look at two larger-scale types of exchange connected with trade and war.

Trade assumed a wide variety of forms in Arabia, as did its focal points, which we call markets. Róbert Simon worked out a typology of these markets, with the purpose of explaining the ultimate triumph of Mecca and Quraysh.[44] But the focus on Meccan trade may, as elsewhere, divert our attention from some important points. In the years before Islam, the Arabs developed a sense that goods traveled around the Arabian peninsula in an annual cycle. We see this in a narrative tradition about the "markets of the Arabs" *(aswaq al-'Arab).*[45] This tradition describes only a fraction of the markets that actually existed. More precisely, it describes a sequence of from ten to fourteen, whereas the early-fourth/tenth-century writer al-Hamdani, in his *Sifat Jazirat al-'Arab* (Description of the Arabian Peninsula), lists more than fifty.[46] Moreover, even though these markets of the Arabs included sites of obvious importance, such as Aden and San'a', they also include some that are utterly obscure. Meanwhile, some famous market towns, such as al-Hira, are lacking in the tradition altogether. The purpose of this tradition on the markets of the Arabs, in its various versions, is, therefore, not simply to provide a list and description of the most important Arabian places of exchange; instead, two main themes emerge.

First, the tradition on the markets describes a sequence of places, beginning in Dumat al-Jandal in north central Arabia on the confines of the Byzantine and Persian Empires, then moving east to al-Mushaqqar, near Hajar, not far from the coast of al-Bahrayn; from there to coastal 'Uman, then on to Hadramawt, Yemen, and the market-fairs of 'Ukaz and its environs, and (in some versions) including the pilgrimage of 'Arafa and Mina. The course continued north to Khaybar and then east to al-Yamama. In other words, the tradition traces the contours of Arabia and the approximate limits of Arab habitation. It includes a remarkable variety of political conditions, including the protectorate of the great empires, tribal control, and control by no one at all. It also describes an even more remarkable variety of types of merchandise and economic arrangements. So we have prostitution and slavery in Dumat al-Jandal, "goods of the sea" arriving from India and China at

Suhar and Daba at the entrance to the gulf, and elsewhere various local goods, all being traded with a number of distinct and colorful techniques. With all this movement and variety, including contact with the outside world, the dominant fact is still the outline of Arabia traced by this long itinerary.

Second, the tradition on the markets of the Arabs describes a constant motion of persons and goods along this clockwise path. Now, in reality this is difficult to believe: The route traced in this way seems only tangentially related to the trade routes familiar to us from our textbooks and from some of the books discussed earlier in this chapter. Yet the transmitters of this tradition insist on this movement, which has much in common with some of the conceptions of circulation of wealth current in the early Islamic period: not strictly circular,[47] but with goods and persons moving in the same direction and returning year after year.

The most fully described of these markets of the Arabs is its culminating point, the market-fair of ʿUkaz, with its extensions in nearby al-Majanna and Dhu l-Majaz (all of these two or three days' journey from Mecca). ʿUkaz was especially known for its contests of boasting and poetry. By some accounts it was also a place where one gave things away more than where one bought and sold.[48] The episodes of generosity at ʿUkaz have much in common with the potlatch episodes just described, except that they involve less waste, they are not restricted to camel feasts, and they take place in this one locale within a repeating, seasonal pattern. While there were still kings in Yemen (presumably in the fifth and sixth centuries C.E.), these would send fine swords, mounts and clothing to ʿUkaz, and have a messenger announce: "Let the most valiant of the Arabs take it!" In this way the Yemeni rulers would find out whom they needed to cultivate in the tribal hinterland.[49] Again, the emphasis is on generosity and competition. But despite this mention of kingship, ʿUkaz is described as outside political or tribal control, or as Wellhausen put it: "here no one was master of the house."[50] Although other accounts describe the Quraysh of Mecca as extending their influence within the fairs of ʿUkaz, the fairs of ʿUkaz took place outside Mecca and apparently beyond Meccan control.[51]

These traditions are difficult to reconcile with other information (also derived from a process of literary transmission) regarding trade routes. But taken together, the traditions on the markets of the Arabs point to a conception of circulation in Arabia that tended in a different direction from that of the wasteful generosity discussed in the previous section. Things move in a repeating pattern that defines Arabia and the Arabs as a geographical unity. The itinerary embraces a wide variety of political and economic arrangements. Above all, whatever the reason for existence of the itinerary may be, it is not the acquiring and maintaining of power and domination. It points instead to a growing sense of collective identity among the Arabs, as well as to a notion of return that prefigures the later Islamic notion of return of wealth.

Warfare and Brigandage

Bravmann noted that "the surplus which is given away" was often the result of "acquisition" *(kasb)*, or in other words, of raiding.[52] Indeed, prowess in warfare was always associated with generosity, as the one could hardly exist without the other. With so much raiding taking place, one could at least conceive of goods being constantly taken and then recirculated, always through violence. In these ways, Arabian warfare provided some of the elements of the Islamic return of wealth.

In the period just before Islam, the ideal of warfare as an extension or counterpart to generosity seems to have come under some pressure. We see this in the genre of poetry associated with the Arabian *sa'alik* (singular: *su'luk*). Su'luk in this literature[53] is usually understood to mean "brigand" or "wretch." It can also be one of many terms meaning poor, lacking. But while some of the sa'alik humbly accept crumbs from the great, wealthy men (sayyids), others are famous for courage, solitude, and familiarity with death. And some individuals associated with the category, such as Hatim al-Ta'i, are legendary not for deprivation but rather for abundant generosity. Their typical activities are raiding and distributing spoils among their followers. One of the things making a coherent category of the sa'alik is their conservatism, their outrage at the shifting values all around them.

'Urwa b. al-Ward provides a fine example: "Let me strive for riches, for I have seen that the worst of the people is the poor man *[al-faqir]*, and the most shameful and despicable among them, even though he may have had good birth and fortune and attained the utmost in generosity: his wife despises him and his children chase him away."[54] For the embittered 'Urwa, the old values of good birth and generosity have been upended by a new distinction between rich and poor. The villains here are Arabian (not necessarily Meccan) nouveaux riches, arrogantly displacing the old sayyids who have struggled so long to acquire and maintain their reputation for valor and generosity. In any case, 'Urwa was not the enemy of those in need. He was known as "'Urwa of the *sa'alik*" because "in harsh years" he would gather together a band of the sick and weak from his own tribal group *('ashira)* to whom he provided rough shelter and leadership in raids. Interestingly, he does not seem to have taken the fourth or fifth of the spoils, which (we think) customarily went to the leader (sayyid or shaykh) in war.[55] And after a season of raiding, his companions would return to their homes. We may infer from all this that the old ways of conducting war and of choosing leaders, and above all of generosity, have come under stress. 'Urwa carries on in the old fashion, but for all his efforts he cannot halt a threatening and encroaching distinction between rich and poor. Arabia had always been a harsh country where most people could eke out only a marginal existence. But if there was always, to our mind, "objective" poverty in Arabia, the existence of a category of "poor," defined in part by their lack of protection and their lack of connection to the social system around them, seems to predate Islam by not very long.

In the early Islamic period we again find sa'alik. These are unruly, violent, urban riffraff, especially in frontier outposts, the predecessors of the *'ayyarun* (urban gangs) and *ahdath* (urban militias of young men) of the great medieval cities. Their connection with the swashbuckling heroes of the jahiliyya is little more than that of a name. However, the old Arabian, pre-Islamic sa'alik do set a precedent for Islam: self-deprivation and self-marginalization as moral and political protest, a story that begins with the revolt of Abu Dharr al-Ghifari in the early years of the caliphate.[56]

Conclusion

In this chapter I have sketched the outlines of a thesis for which present and future work will provide fuller substance. But some conclusions already emerge. There existed in the medieval period, and to some extent there still exists in the Islamic world, an economy of poverty in which the idea of a return of wealth had a key role. This may be traced in part to the heritage that Islam shared with other monotheist traditions of the Near Eastern and Mediterranean worlds. But much of it goes back to Arabia itself.

For thousands of years Arabia had existed on the margins of wealthier societies. Even though its trade routes brought goods and people from outside the peninsula and fostered contact among the Arabs themselves, the peninsula lagged behind its neighbors in acquiring new technologies of metallurgy, toolmaking, and so on.[57] An archaic sense of economy and society survived in Arabia, as if the outside world of the great empires and trade were not there—even though the Arabs knew perfectly well of the existence of that world and often came into contact with it.

From the sources available to us we may identify two main articulations of that archaic economy. The first has to do with competition and waste, of giving away and even, on occasion, destroying one's wealth, in order to maintain or improve one's position within a group. Here the main resource in circulation is the camel. Most important, however, is that questions of leadership and power are decided in these or similar ways: The sayyid or shaykh must be the most valiant and the most generous.

The second articulation of the archaic economy is a larger-scale economy of return. Here there are many goods in circulation—the camel is only mentioned in these contexts as a means of transport—which follow in an annually repeated movement circumscribing the entire peninsula. If the economy of waste reminds us of the potlatch of the American Pacific Northwest, the economy of return reminds us of the *kula*, the twin cycles of exchange described by Malinowski in the western Pacific.[58] Although this return was connected with generosity and gift-giving, it did not require that the participants know one another and did not easily allow for any individual to establish or express domination over others. Despite the apparent contradiction between return and waste, these two must have coexisted for a long time.

There is reason to believe that the notion of return was gaining strength in the centuries just before Islam. In those same years a new group was emerging—the poor—both a cause and an effect of dislocation and the weakening of old ties. On the one hand, the sa'alik poets object, in words and actions, to this state of affairs; while on the other hand, it seems (though it remains to be proved) that the acts of generosity in Arabia just before Islam, as described by Bravmann, are aimed increasingly at recipients outside the donors' own groups.

One thing to emerge from all this is the importance of the annual fairs at 'Ukaz and neighboring locales. There the wasteful and return trends came together, with minimal violence, beyond the domination of any individual or group, and on a pan-Arab basis. In these and other ways the annual fairs were precursors of Islam.

This brings us back to the historiographical dilemma of Meccan trade. Even though I cannot resolve that dilemma, I can suggest that the rise of Islam brought together two things that had been hatching more or less independently of one another for some time. One of these was the growing idea of circulation as return, receiving its geographical expression in an idealized, constantly moving cycle of markets culminating in the fair of 'Ukaz and the pilgrimage. The second was a change in the way goods and power were distributed locally, resulting in the brutal fact of poverty: not that there was any more or less objective need in Arabia than before, but rather that this new category was now growing for a number of reasons that remain to be spelled out. This category of poor had counterparts in the settled societies of the Mediterranean and Fertile Crescent, and so we see the entrance into Arabia of such concepts as 'sadaqa' and 'zakat.' Meanwhile, older Arab concepts relating to distribution and redistribution underwent a transformation that resulted in the charitable practices and in the broader economy of poverty, including the return of wealth, which have characterized Islamic societies ever since.

Notes

1. The phrase is borrowed from the European medievalist G. Todeschini. See his "'Quantum valet?' Alle origini di un'economia della povertà," *Bullettino dell'Istituto Storico Italiano per il Medioevo* 98 (1992): 173–234; and his *Il prezzo della salvezza. Lessici medievali del pensiero economico* (Rome: La Nuova Italia Scientifica, 1994). See also L. K. Little, *Religious Poverty and the Profit Economy in Medieval Europe* (Ithaca: Cornell University Press, 1978).

addresses question of why there's a continuity between pre-Islamic gift exchange and Islamic charity?

2. M. Bonner, "Definitions of Poverty and the Rise of the Muslim Urban Poor," *Journal of the Royal Asiatic Society* 3rd series, 6 (1996): 339–340. For a critique of this article, see Ingrid Mattson's contribution to this volume (chapter 2).

3. The hadith may be more closely defined as authoritative sayings and deeds attributed to the Prophet Muhammad, but also in some cases going back to those around the Prophet (the Companions) and to authoritative figures of the next generations (the Successors). These were transmitted orally, from quite early on with the support of written texts. After a few generations these written collections of hadith became numerous and voluminous.

4. *Ruddu l-sa'il wa-law bi-ra's al-qata.* Muhammad b. Isma'il al-Bukhari, *Jami'* (Leiden: Brill, 1862–1908), 1:352, zakat 2; 1:369, zakat 41; 1:380, zakat 63; Bonner, "Definitions," 339, n. 16.

5. Malik, *Muwatta'* (Cairo: 'Isa al-Babi al-Halabi, 1370/1951), 2:282, zakat 26, nos. 49, 50; Bukhari, *Jami'* 1:379, zakat 59; Ahmad Ibn Hanbal, *Musnad* (Bulaq: al-Matba'a al-Amiriyya, 1313; reprint, Beirut, 1389/1969), 1:25, 2:55.

6. F. Løkkegaard, "Fay'," *EI²*, 2:870; and his *Islamic Taxation in the Classic Period* (Copenhagen: Branner and Korch, 1950); W. Schmucker, *Untersuchungen zu einigen wichtigen bodenrechtlichen Konsequenzen der islamischen Eroberungsbewegung* (Bonn: Selbstverlag des orientalischen Seminars der Universität, 1972),

7. At 69:7–9, 74:11–15, and numerous other places.

8. O. Carré, *Mystique et politique: lecture révolutionnaire du Koran par Sayyid Qutb* (Paris: Editions du Cerf, 1984), 152f.

9. C. Décobert, *Le mendiant et le combattant. L'institution de l'islam* (Paris: Editions du Seuil, 1991), esp. 238f.

10. On calls for almsgiving in the earliest layer of the Quran, see M. W. Watt, *Muhammad at Mecca* (Oxford: Clarendon Press, 1953), 72f. On the ridda wars, see E. Shoufani, *Al-Riddah and the Muslim Conquest of Arabia* (Toronto: University of Toronto Press, 1973); translation of Tabari's chronicle covering the ridda is by F. Donner, *The Conquest of Arabia* (Albany: State University of New York Press, 1993).

11. G. W. Heck, "Gold Mining in Arabia and the Rise of the Islamic State," *Journal of the Economic and Social History of the Orient* 42 (1999): 364–395.

12. A. Noth, *Quellenkritische Studien* (Bonn: Selbstverlag des orientalischen Seminars der Universität, 1973); new version, based on a translation by M. Bonner and in collaboration with L. Conrad, entitled *The Early Arabic Historical Tradition: A Source-Critical Study* (Princeton, N. J.: Darwin Press, 1994).

13. Watt, *Muhammad at Mecca*, 72–73.

14. Ibid., 75, 82, referring to volume 1 of I. Goldziher's *Muhammedanische Studien* (Halle: M. Niemeyer, 1888). A translation of this book has been published: *Muslim Studies*, ed. Stern, trans. S. M. Stern and C. M. Barber (London: Allen and Unwin, 1966).

15. W. M. Watt, *Muhammad at Medina* (Oxford: S.M.: Clarendon Press, 1956), 250–260.

16. Watt, *Muhammad at Mecca*, 3.

17. M. Rodinson, *Mahomet* (Paris: Editions du Seuil, 1968). A translation of this book has been published: A. Carter, trans. *Muhammad* (New York: Pantheon, 1971); R. Simon,

Meccan Trade and Islam: Problems of Origin and Structure (Budapest: Akademiai Kiadó, 1989); M. Ibrahim, *Merchant Capital and Islam* (Austin: University of Texas Press, 1990), with observations on Meccan poverty within the context of capital accumulation by the Meccan leadership. Earlier work on Meccan trade, going back to Lammens, is summarized by Watt, *Muhammad at Mecca*, 3, and by P. Crone in *Meccan Trade and the Rise of Islam* (Princeton: Princeton University Press, 1987), 231.

    18. Set out in *Muhammad at Mecca*, xi–xvi.

    19. Crone, *Meccan Trade*, 231.

    20. Ibid., 90.

    21. Ibid., 111; see also 203–230.

    22. These include Ibrahim, *Merchant Capital*; J. Chabbi, *Le seigneur des tribus. L'Islam de Mahomet* (Paris: Noêsis, 1997); Décobert, *Le mendiant;* and M. Bamyeh, *The Social Origins of Islam: Mind, Economy, Discourse* (Minneapolis: University of Minnesota Press, 1999).

    23. The term *revisionist*—used by J. Koren and Y. Nevo in "Methodological Approaches to Islamic Studies," *Der Islam* 68 (1991): 87–101, as well as by Décobert and others—has acquired currency, even though the revisionists themselves mostly have not adopted the term.

    24. S. Bashear, "On the Origins and Development of the Meaning of *Zakat* in Early Islam," *Arabica* 40 (1993): 84–113. See also the articles in EI^2 on "Sadaka" (A. Zysow), 9:708–716, and "Zakat" (A. Zysow), 11:406–422; and Timur Kuran's contribution to this volume (chapter 14).

    25. Sadaqa and zakat do not appear in the massive concordance by M. Arazi and S. Masalha (*Six Early Arab Poets: New Edition and Concordance* [Jerusalem: Hebrew University of Jerusalem, Max Schloessinger Memorial Series, 1999]); nor in the important essay by M. M. Bravmann ("The Surplus of Property: An Early Arab Social Concept," *Der Islam* 38 [1962]: 28–50, also in *The Spiritual Background of Early Islam* [Leiden: Brill, 1972]: 229–253). On the other hand, see E. Landau-Tasseron, "Asad from Jahiliyya to Islam," *Jerusalem Studies in Arabic and Islam* 6 (1985): 13; Bamyeh, *Social Origins of Islam;* and Ibrahim, *Merchant Capital.* However, references to pre-Islamic sadaqa in the latter two do not hold up to scrutiny.

    26. These two trends appear in the article by the late Bashear ("On the Origins and Development").

    27. Décobert, *Le mendiant*, 28–29.

    28. Ibid., 33f., 181–185.

    29. See note 3 above.

    30. For an example, see M. Bonner, "*Ja'a'il* and Holy War in Early Islam," *Der Islam* 68 (1991): 45–64; and his *Aristocratic Violence and Holy War: Studies in the Jihad and the Arab-Byzantine Frontier* (New Haven, Conn.: American Oriental Society, 1996), 11–42.

    31. A strategy along these lines has been suggested by J. E. Wansbrough in *Lingua Franca in the Mediterranean* (Richmond, U.K.: Curzon Press, 1996), 55–58; see also his reviews of Crone's *Meccan Trade* in *Bulletin of the School of Oriental and African Studies* 52 (1989): 339–340, and of Robert Simon's *Meccan Trade* in *Bulletin of the School of Oriental and African Studies* 53 (1990): 510–511.

32. Modern reworkings of tribal data extracted from medieval Arabic genealogical sources include Werner Caskel, *Ǧamharat an-nasab. Das genealogische Werk des Hišam ibn Muhammad al-Kalbi* (Leiden: Brill, 1966); T. Nishio et al., *A Dictionary of Arab Tribes* (Tokyo: Institute for the Study of Languages and Cultures of Asia and Africa, 1999). For a dense description of tribal occupation of territory and local networks, see M. Lecker, *The Banu Sulaym* (Jerusalem: Magnes Press 1989).

33. On this see Noth, *Early Arabic Historical Tradition.*

34. P. Crone, *Slaves on Horses: The Evolution of the Islamic Polity* (Cambridge: Cambridge University Press, 1980).

35. For a less optimistic view, see G. R. Hawting's review of Lecker's *Banu Sulaym* in *Bulletin of the School of Oriental and African Studies* 54 (1990): 359–362; and his *The Idea of Idolatry and the Emergence of Islam* (Cambridge: Cambridge University Press, 1999), 111–129.

36. *Taʿaqur, taʿati, munajada, tanajud, mumajada, mijad.*

37. I discussed this practice in a paper, "God's Camel: Competitive Feasting in Ancient Arabia and Early Islam," at the American Oriental Society in Philadelphia, March 1996. J. Stetkevych has also taken up this topic, noting the parallel with the potlatch in *Muhammad and the Golden Bough: Reconstructing Arabian Myth* (Bloomington: Indiana University Press, 1996). On sacrifice, the main authority is still J. Chelhod, *Le sacrifice chez les Arabes: recherches sur l'évolution des rites sacrificiels en Arabie occidentale* (Paris: Presses Universitaires de France, 1955). In referring to the "classic" potlatch of the Pacific Northwest, I mean the idea that is commonly held about that potlatch as the exemplar of self-destructive, competitive feasting and gift-giving. Much recent research indicates otherwise.

38. Yaqut, *Buldan*, ed. F. Wüstenfeld (Leipzig: F. A. Brockhaus, 1866–1877), 3:430–431; Ibn Habib, *al-Muhabbar*, ed. I. Lichtenstadter (Hyderabad: Matbaʿat Jamiyat Daʾirat al-Maʿarif al-ʿUthmaniyah, 1942), 142; J. Wellhausen, *Reste arabischen Heidentums* (Berlin: De Gruyter, 1927), 90; Goldziher, *Muslim Studies*, 1:62; M. J. Kister, "Ghalib b. Saʿsaʿa," *EI²*, 2:998.

39. A. J. Wensinck, *Concordance et indices de la Tradition musulmane* (Leiden: Brill, 1962), 4:296.

40. Bravmann, "The Surplus of Property."

41. Bonner, "Definitions," 337.

42. M. Mauss, "Essai sur le don. Forme et raison de l'échange dans les sociétés archaïques," *Sociologie et anthropologie* (Paris: Presses Universitaires de France, 1950), 30–186.

43. An important question is whether the challenger in taʿaqur is a member of the group. As far as I can tell, sometimes he is and sometimes he is not.

44. Simon, *Meccan Trade*, 78–91.

45. Abu ʿAli Ahmad al-Marzuqi, *Kitab al-azmina wal-amkina* (Hyderabad: Daʾirat al-Maʿarif al-ʿUthmaniyya, 1332/1914), 2:161–170; Ibn Habib, *al-Muhabbar*, 263–268; Ahmad al-Yaʿqubi, *Taʾrikh* (Beirut: Dar Sadir lil-tibaʿa wal-nashr, 1379/1960), 1:270–171; S. al-Afghani, *Aswaq al-ʿArab fi l-jahiliyya wal-Islam* (Damascus: Dar al-Fikr, 1960); Simon, *Meccan Trade*, 78–91; Crone, *Meccan Trade*, 170–175, 183.

46. Abu Muhammad al-Hasan al-Hamdani, *Sifat Jazirat al-ʿArab* (Leiden: Brill, 1884–1901; reprint, 1968), 179–180.

47. The tradition on the markets does not make the Arabs and their merchandise complete the circle by going back to the starting point of Dumat al-Jandal in the north.

48. Yaqut, *Mu'jam al-buldan*, s.v. "'Ukaz"; Wellhausen, *Reste*, 88–91.

49. al-Marzuqi, *Kitab al-azmina wal-amkina*, 2:165.

50. Wellhausen, *Reste*, 92; "niemand war hier Herr im Hause."

51. On the relation between Mecca, the pilgrimage, and the fairs, see Crone, *Meccan Trade*, 170ff.

52. Bravmann, "Surplus," in *Spiritual Background*, 237.

53. See A. Arazi's article *"Su'luk"* in *EI²*, 9:863–868, and literature cited there.

54. 'Urwa b. al-Ward, *Diwan* (Cairo: n.p., 1966), 91; Abu l-Faraj al-Isfahani, *Kitab al-aghani* (Cairo: Matba'at Dar al-Kutub al-Misriyya, 1927–1958), 3:75; 'A. 'A. Salim, *Ta'rikh al-'Arab fi 'asr al-jahiliyya* (Beirut: Dar al-Nahda al-'Arabiyya, n.d), 439–440.

55. Abu l-Faraj, *Kitab al-aghani*, 3:78. At 3:81, when the Banu 'Abs cried out to him, "O father of the *sa'alik*, help us!" 'Urwa "had mercy on them and went out raiding with them," again without taking the fourth or fifth of the spoils. On the sayyid's share, see A. Morabia, *Le ǧihâd dans l'Islam médiéval* (Paris: A. Michel, 1993), 40; Løkkegaard, "Fay'," 2:1005.

56. Ibrahim, *Merchant Capital*, 145–146.

57. G. Garbini, "Preistoria e protostoria," in *I primi arabi*, ed. B. Chiesa et al. (Milan: Jaca Book, 1994), 11–18.

58. B. Malinowski, *Argonauts of the Western Pacific* (New York: Routledge, 1922).

CHAPTER TWO

Status-Based Definitions of Need in Early Islamic *Zakat* and Maintenance Laws

INGRID MATTSON

In early Islamic society, Muslims were expected to support and assist others who were poor and in need. As political and legal institutions developed over the first few centuries of Islam, some of these duties became legally binding, others remained social obligations or moral imperatives. Among the duties that became obligatory and enforceable by the state were the yearly payment of alms (*zakat al-mal*) and the support and maintenance of dependents (*nafaqa*). Although some individuals had a right to receive zakat or maintenance even if they were not poor—for example, zakat administrators in the former case and wives in the latter case—eliminating or satisfying need was the primary goal of both institutions.

To enforce such laws in a consistent and systematic manner, Muslim jurists needed to find workable definitions of *need* and *poverty*. In this chapter, I will examine a variety of definitions offered by some of the earliest jurists in the second century of Islam (eighth century of the Common Era)[1] and compare these definitions with those proposed by some later jurists, including those who lived after the formation of the dominant schools (*madhahib, s. madhhab*) of Sunni law in the fourth and fifth Islamic centuries (tenth and eleventh centuries C.E.). What we shall see is that the various definitions almost always included a combination of what might be considered relative and absolute factors. Relative factors included, for example, the subjective feeling of need experienced by an individual; absolute factors included, among other things, the minimum amount of food needed by an average person to support life.

First, I will examine these issues with respect to zakat laws. What will be discovered is that over time jurists seem increasingly to have related the subjective feeling of need to the social and economic context in which individuals had been raised. Here, I will not argue that the majority of Muslim jurists emphasized this context above all other factors in determining need; however, I will argue that this was a tendency present in Islamic legal discourse from the early period, and that this tendency may have increased over time. I will argue that jurists increasingly may have resorted to status-based definitions of need in zakat laws because this was the dominant norm that had been set in the area of maintenance laws. Although the two areas of law are rarely related by the jurists themselves, they both require a definition of need, and certain concepts such as *al-maʿruf* (what is customary, or what is fair) and *al-kifaya* (sufficiency) are found in both places.

Who Are the Poor and How Much Zakat Are They to Be Given?

The Quran (9:60) lists eight categories of potential recipients of alms: "Alms are for the poor *[al-fuqara]*, and the indigent *[al-masakin]*, for those who work to administer them, for those whose hearts are to be won over, for those in bondage, for debtors, for those who are in the cause of God, and for wayfarers." Because al-fuqara' and al-masakin[2] are both listed in this verse, most early Muslim scholars believed that these must represent two different kinds of poor people. Resorting to various *hadith* (sayings of the Prophet Muhammad) and customary expressions of the Arabs led to numerous definitions—many of them completely contradictory.[3] For example, some scholars argued that the difference between the two terms had to do with the severity of poverty. Thus, while some defined the poor as those who were worse off than the indigent—having no possessions at all—other scholars reversed this definition. In other cases, the two categories were distinguished by whether the poor person resorted to begging. Finally, some scholars thought that there was no significant difference between the two terms, but, they argued, like a number of other terms used to indicate poverty generally, each term was sometimes used in different contexts. These other terms included *al-muʿattar*, which could be translated as "the unfortunate," *al-baʾis*, which could be translated as "the wretched," and *al-ʿani*, which was said to specify a poor person one knew well enough that he or she could easily ask for help—perhaps a neighbor or relative. In the end, any distinctions among such terms were irrelevant to legal scholars for, as the early Iraqi scholar Abu ʿUbayd said, "all of them are recipients of charity and feeding."[4]

What was relevant and important in these definitions, however, were those things that distinguished the poor and the indigent from others who did not have this legal status. The two major criteria that one can broadly distinguish in early legal literature are "need" and "excess wealth." In the first case, a poor person is defined as someone who is in a state of need *(al-haja)*. Of course, such a definition is incomplete until need is defined. In the second case, a poor person is defined as someone who does not possess a specific amount of wealth in surplus of what is needed to support and protect life; this amount is called the *nisab*.

That there were significant consequences resulting from favoring one of these definitions over the other becomes obvious when we see how jurists decided the amount of charity that the poor were to be given. In general, those who defined poverty as need did not place a monetary limit on this amount, since needs vary among individuals. On the other hand, jurists who defined poverty in absolute financial terms generally allowed no more than a specified amount of zakat to be given to any one individual. The majority of Sunni schools—the Malikis, Shafi'is, and Hanbalis—took the former position, while the Hanafis took the latter position. Because a comprehensive comparison of the schools is beyond the scope of this chapter, I will limit my discussion to the positions articulated by those prominent individuals later considered to be founders of the dominant Sunni schools. Possibly the earliest systematic discussion of zakat is found in the writings of the Iraqi jurist Abu 'Ubayd al-Qasim ibn Sallam, a scholar whose ideas never gave rise to a school but, nonetheless, were influential in this early period. In the following section, I examine his writing in some detail.

Abu 'Ubayd and His Critique of the Iraqi School

Like many scholars of the second century, Abu 'Ubayd (c. 154/770–224/838) was the descendent of non-Arab converts to Islam. His father had been a slave of an Arab tribe who lived in the eastern Islamic province of Khurasan, and like other freed slaves, Abu 'Ubayd's father retained ties of loyalty to and mutual support with his former masters after his manumission and, henceforth, carried the title "client" *(mawla)* of the tribe. The success of his son in the world of scholarship was not uncommon for such clients and is proof of the relative openness of Islamic society at the time. Abu 'Ubayd completed the majority of his studies in Iraq and lived in Baghdad most of his life.[5] He is best remembered in Muslim tradition for his philological works, but he was also a legal scholar and worked as a judge for two decades. Although some later biographers tried to place him in one school of law or another, in fact, he lived before the dominant Sunni schools had taken firm shape.[6] Unlike many of his contemporaries, however, Abu 'Ubayd never did become strongly affiliated, in retrospect, with one particular school of law. This likely made Abu 'Ubayd's work more resistant to redaction and reformulation by later scholars to "fit" a school profile. This may be one reason why Abu 'Ubayd seems to stand out among his contemporaries for drawing equally on the earlier legal traditions of the Hijazi (Medinan) scholars—who provided the foundation for the Maliki, Shafi'i, and Hanbali schools—and the Iraqi scholars—who provided the foundation for the Hanafi school. It may also be that Abu ʿUbayd's strong training in philology, especially in the rare usage of terms in hadith,[7] allowed him to exercise relative independence in choosing which interpretations of sources he preferred. In any case, all these factors make Abu ʿUbayd's books valuable sources.

In his *Kitab al-amwal* (Book of Wealth), Abu ʿUbayd describes the various kinds of alms, land, and property taxes that are incumbent upon Muslims.[8] He discusses zakat in great detail, and presents a clear argument for what he considers the proper guidelines for zakat distribution. He begins his argument with a survey of most of the well-known Prophetic hadith that define poverty and need. After this survey, Abu ʿUbayd acknowledges that some of the hadith seem to restrict greatly the amount of zakat that can be given to any one person, while others seem to allow much more to be given to the poor. Abu ʿUbayd says that the most unrestricted of the hadith states that the Prophet said:

> Begging is not permissible except for three kinds of people: a man who has incurred debt, for him begging is permissible until he pays that off, then he must refrain [from begging]; a man who has been afflicted by a natural disaster which destroys his wealth, and he asks for charity so he can have what will support him, or will provide him subsistence for life, then he must refrain [from begging]; and a person who has been smitten by poverty and three sound members of his community witness that he has been so smitten, for him begging is permissible until he acquires what will support him, or will provide him subsistence to live on, then he must refrain [from begging].[9]

Abu ʿUbayd says that this hadith is the most unrestricted *(awsaʿuha)* in terms of how much charity is permissible to give to a person because no limit is put on "what will support," such a person, or what his "subsistence" entails. The most restricted of the hadith *(adyaquha)*, on the other hand, states that the Prophet said that asking for charity is not permitted when people have enough food for themselves and their dependents for a day and a night.[10] Abu ʿUbayd seems to accept that this hadith is likely authentic, but he argues that it only prohibits individuals who have food for a day and a night from *asking* for charity; the hadith does not prohibit such persons from *taking* charity if they possess nothing more than food for a day and a night. The rule Abu ʿUbayd derives from this hadith, then, is that no one should continue asking for charity once he has enough and it relieves him *(mā yakfīhi wa yaʿfīhi)*.[11]

Among all the hadith, Abu ʿUbayd prefers the report in which the Prophet says that anyone who asks for charity when they possess an *awqiyya* (a unit of value that is equivalent to forty dirhams) has asked importunately. Abu ʿUbayd favors this hadith, he says, because it has the strongest chain of transmitters *(isnad)* among the group.[12] Further, the ruling in this hadith is corroborated by other reports from the Prophet and the caliphs. Nevertheless, Abu ʿUbayd says that the meaning of this hadith is that the awqiyya to be taken into account is what is left over *(fadl)* after accounting for the dwelling people need for themselves and their dependents, and after taking into account their clothes to the extent that there is no luxury (*ghina'*) in them, and after taking into account their slaves, "if they need them (*in kanat bihim ilayhi haja*)" (735–737).

The important distinction Abu 'Ubayd makes, then, is between an absolute limit on surplus wealth, beyond which asking for charity is not permissible, and the relative needs of individuals. Obviously everyone needs food, clothes, and shelter, and as long as such belongings are not luxurious, beyond ordinary needs, then individuals who possess them can still be given alms. Some people even have a need for slaves (an issue I will discuss further), and if they do, they can still take alms if they do not have surplus wealth beyond forty dirhams.

The limit of forty dirhams, therefore, is not a limit on the amount of money one can give a person in need—whether it be voluntary charity or zakat. Abu 'Ubayd's opinion is that the amount of zakat that is given to any one person in need has no fixed limit and it is up to the giver to decide how much to give. He offers the following example as proof for his position:

> A man, who has a lot of money, notices a family of good Muslims who are poor and destitute. Those people have no house to shelter them and to safeguard their privacy, so he buys a house from his zakat al-mal to protect them from the biting cold of winter and the heat of the sun. Or they are naked—they have no clothes, so he clothes them to cover their bodies for their prayer and to shield them from the heat and the cold. Or he sees a slave who has an evil master who mistreats him and abuses his ownership of him, so he rescues him from his enslavement by buying him and freeing him. Or a wayfarer, far from his family, mourning the home that is cut off from him passes by him, so he carries him back to his land and his family by renting or buying [transportation]. These needs, and others like them, cannot be met except with a lot of money, yet the person who wants to give this money cannot do it as an act of voluntary charity [*nafila*]. However, if he does meet these needs with his zakat al-mal, would he have fulfilled his obligation? Of course! Indeed, he would be, God willing, a righteous person. (750)

Here Abu 'Ubayd is determined to prove that there is no necessary limit on the amount of zakat al-mal that can be used to relieve the suffering of just one needy individual. The passion of his argument makes it evident that he is trying to convince others who hold a contrary view. Most likely those whom Abu 'Ubayd is trying to convince are the majority of Iraqi scholars who did not permit a zakat recipient to be given more than a fixed amount (739–740). This is because these scholars defined wealth and poverty in absolute economic terms. Some of them, basing their definition on a statement of the Prophet, defined *rich* as having fifty dirhams surplus wealth. Other scholars drew the poverty line at the nisab, in livestock, produce, or cash, above which one had to pay zakat; for cash, the nisab is two hundred dirhams. This latter position became dominant among the Iraqi scholars and was adopted by Abu Hanifa (80/699–150/767), the eponym of the Hanafi school. Abu Hanifa is reported to have "placed a ceiling of two hundred dirhams or twenty gold dinars on what may be given to the poor and needy, which must not be reached so that they are not required to pay zakat on the charity they receive."[13]

In their arguments, the Iraqis seem compelled by a highly legalistic outlook to draw clear categories and to create a logical and objective system for zakat distribution. Their general argument can be paraphrased in the following manner: Because the Prophet said to take zakat from the rich and give it to the poor, and because people who possess the nisab above their needs have to pay zakat, those who possess the nisab therefore must be rich, and the opposite of rich being poor, those without the nisab must be poor. Consequently, if poor people are given more than the nisab, they would automatically enter the category of the rich and would have to pay zakat on the money they received.

It is not surprising that such an argument, grounded heavily in logic, should have come out of the Iraqi school. Indeed, the jurists of Iraq were known, above all, for their extensive reliance on this kind of logical discourse.[14] Therefore, it is likely that their position was derived more from their legal methodology than from their view of the proper social and economic order. At the same time, even if the Iraqis, and later the majority of Hanafis, based their views of zakat distribution on a possibly flawed but plausible logic, did they not realize the social implications of their position? Did this limit not hurt the very poor, above all?

Michael Bonner has argued that at least the hadiths narrated by Iraqi scholars demonstrate their "conservative" stance regarding the obligations of the wealthy toward the poor.[15] This conservative stance, argues Bonner, encompasses the following views: A poor person is simply one who has no surplus wealth; poor people should not beg, but be patient with their condition; only the disabled or those unable to work should get alms; and family should be taken care of first. Bonner argues that in contrast to this position, a "radical" version of poverty, embodied in hadith of mostly Medinan origin, is "about entitlement." In this view, there is no need for the poor to work, wealth is brought into the community from the outside, and the wealthy are entitled to receive alms if they ask, even if they have a house or a servant.

Now, although Bonner's article is important for the issues it raises, a number of his conclusions are flawed because of methodological problems. One serious problem is the way he splits up and groups the hadith according to broadly "Iraqi" and "Medinan" narrators. Without providing a detailed analysis of the isnads, it is unclear that the hadith really can be separated in this manner. Grouping the decontextualized hadith back into "radical" and "conservative" views of poverty is even more problematic. In doing so, Bonner does not show how he can prove that the people who narrated the hadith at any time in history meant or implied

*my complaint about
the connection between
"theories" and reality*

what he says they did. Anticipating this objection, Bonner argues that by taking the hadith out of context, he can identify an "ideal type" (338). But does not this come perilously close to a fundamentalist reading of texts? Without knowing what any of the narrators meant by their words, how can we understand what ideal they had in mind?

Another problem is that Bonner makes no distinction between voluntary and obligatory alms. As we have seen, the Iraqi jurists limited the amount of zakat that could be given to any one person because they relied on a logical distinction between rich and poor as technical legal terms in the context of the zakat institution. There is no evidence, however, that these scholars discouraged unlimited voluntary alms to the poor.

Bonner resorts to decontextualized hadith because, he says, "we find few discussions which are at all discursive or complete from before the time of the fourth *fitna* and the siege of Baghdad (197/812–813). A notable exception is the discussion of alms by Muhammad ibn Idris al-Shafi'i (150/767–204/820). But even here it turns out that al-Shafi'i's text, as we have it, may be largely the product of later jurists (338). Bonner's skepticism about al-Shafi'i's *Kitab al-Umm* is based on the claims of Norman Calder, who assigned a much later date to all the earliest works of Islamic jurisprudence.[16] Calder's claims, however, have been strongly refuted by a number of scholars of early Islamic law who have pointed out serious problems with his assumptions about the development of Islamic legal thought, as well as his ignorance or inattention to manuscript evidence that contradicted his arguments.[17] In his research, Bonner also overlooked the extensive discussion of poverty by Abu 'Ubayd cited here. For that reason, he missed, among other things, the distinction Abu 'Ubayd made between receiving charity and begging for charity.

Finally, as we shall see, the social implications of other hadith Bonner mentions are often clearly different from what he claims. Despite these shortcomings, Bonner has drawn attention to important differences among early Muslim scholars regarding poverty, and it was his article that provided the inspiration for this study.

Zakat Should Be Given according to Relative Needs, but There Is an Upper Limit to Need

In determining whether an individual with property is eligible to receive zakat, Abu 'Ubayd, like other early jurists, uses the term *surplus* (fadl). Surplus property includes those possessions for which an individual and his or her dependents do not have a need (haja). Beyond specifying a house and clothes that fall short of luxury (ghina'), Abu 'Ubayd does not go into much detail about how such needs should be defined. He does say, however, that some people may need a slave, and such persons, therefore, should not necessarily be excluded from receiving zakat.

Abu 'Ubayd's position is close to that found in the earliest juridical text of the Maliki madhhab, the *Mudawwana* of Sahnun (240/854). Here, is it reported that Malik ibn Anas (93/711–179/796), the eponym of the school, when asked if a man with a house and a slave can be given zakat replied, "Houses vary. If it is a house whose value would not yield a surplus if it were sold so that with its price he could buy another house and still have a surplus that he could live on, then it is my opinion that he is given (zakat) and should not sell his house." If there would be enough of a surplus, however, Malik said that such a man is not to be given zakat. It is the same if he owns a slave.[18]

In determining need, we see, then, that both Abu 'Ubayd and Malik are reported not to have allowed any housing or other property essential for life (food, clothes, slaves) to be excluded from consideration as surplus. Someone who has more property than he really needs should sell it to take care of his essential needs, rather than take zakat.

Ahmad ibn Hanbal (164/780–241/855), the eponym of the Hanbali school, is reported to have taken a similar position. When asked what amount should be given to each person who has a right to receive zakat, he replied that everyone is given "what removes his need without excess *(ghayr ziyada)*" and that no one should be given more than enough to remove his need.[19] Thus, Ahmad, Abu 'Ubayd, and Malik, unlike the Hanafis, rely on a relative concept of need in defining poverty, yet also set a limit that nothing excessive should be given.

In this respect, these jurists also seem to differ on the position that is reported to have been taken by the early and influential Iraqi scholar al-Hasan al-Basri (d. 110/798). Al-Hasan is considered by later jurists to be one of the best informed and most reliable sources of information about authentic early Islamic practice (the *sunna*). Therefore, it is significant that some sources record him as saying that the first generations of Muslims "used to give zakat to a person whose horse, weapons, servant and home were worth ten thousand dirhams."[20] However, in other reports, including the report transmitted by Abu 'Ubayd, this statement is qualified by the words "if he needs it" *(in ihtaja)*.[21] Basing his understanding of this report on another report about the "rightly guided" caliph 'Umar ibn 'Abd al-'Aziz (d. 101/719), Abu 'Ubayd argues that this means, for example, that if what the man owns is sufficient *(al-kafaf)*, without affluence, he can be given zakat to pay off a debt.[22] In this case, the man with relatively valuable possessions is not given zakat because he is poor, rather, because he falls under another category of zakat recipients, that of debtors.

It is not likely that we will ever be able to know what al-Hasan al-Basri really said or meant about this situation. It is possible that he really did advocate the more "radical" position that Bonner believes was held by some early Muslims—especially to the extent that this position involved both giving some kinds of alms to anyone in the community who asked for it and expecting these recipients to return it to the community through self-impoverishment.[23] Malik, Abu 'Ubayd, and Ahmad, however, do not seem to have accepted this model of zakat distribution. Nevertheless, it seems clear that they were rejecting one interpretation of zakat distribution that allowed some people who possessed valuable property to take zakat because they "needed" it. Was this al-Hasan's interpretation they were rejecting, or that of later scholars? Or were they, perhaps, directing their implicit criticism at state practices?

There are indications that these jurists may have been partially motivated to argue for such limits by a mistrust of state rulers and administrators. This deep mistrust is evident even among those jurists who believed that it was better to work with state officials, at least to try to influence their policies, than to withdraw totally from them. An example of such a jurist is Abu Yusuf (d. 182/798), the prominent student of Abu Hanifa and chief judge of Baghdad during the early part of the caliphate of Harun al-Rashid (d. 193/809). In his *Kitab al-kharaj* (Book of Taxes), Abu Yusuf warns zakat collectors of the great punishment they will incur if they appropriate money or goods for themselves. At the same time, to protect themselves from harm, he argues that individuals should not withhold their zakat from corrupt officials; rather, they should give them the zakat "and seek refuge in God from their evil."[24]

A generation after Abu Yusuf, Abu 'Ubayd also served for many years as a judge under 'Abbasid rule. The fact that he composed the *Kitab al-amwal* is evidence that he was involved in advising state officials on tax collection in general. Nevertheless, it is unclear how involved the state was during his time in collecting and distributing zakat. Indeed, Abu 'Ubayd's argument for the legitimacy of an individual paying a large amount of zakat to just one very needy individual indicates that at least some people in his time may not have been paying their zakat to the state treasury but were distributing it themselves. In this context, at least, Abu 'Ubayd does not seem inclined to discourage such a practice.

Malik and Ahmad were among those jurists who had a less-than-comfortable relationship with the 'Abbasid rulers. Ahmad's deep conviction that the 'Abbasids were thoroughly corrupt, and that their treasuries were filled with prohibited funds which they used in all sorts of illicit ways, is well-known.[25] Malik, too, had a difficult relationship with the 'Abbasid rulers of his time.[26] Although Malik did not advocate withholding zakat from the authorities—his public humiliation by them taught him that such resistance was futile—he is reported to have said, when asked "secretly" by his student Ibn al-Qasim, that each community should distribute among themselves their *zakat al-fitr* (the charity distributed at the end of Ramadan), if they know that the ruler will not distribute it justly.[27] The limits Malik and Ahmad placed on need in the distribution of zakat al-mal may have been, therefore, at least partially based on a concern that impious individuals associated with the state were distributing zakat to their associates on the basis of an illegitimate claim of need.

The arguments of these jurists for the decentralization of zakat collection and distribution could also have been an attempt to limit the loss of these funds to corrupt government officials. The Prophet's words to his governor Mu'adh ibn Jabal that wealth is to be taken from *their* rich and given to *their* poor (my emphasis), is taken by these jurists as evidence that zakat must be redistributed within the area in which it is collected, and not transferred to another area.[28]

Local distribution of zakat has another significance, and that is the importance of building and maintaining a sense of community. I suggest that this is the real significance of the notion of the 'return of wealth' to which Bonner has drawn our attention. When we examine the writings of the early jurists, we find it is al-Shafi'i who argues most explicitly and articulately for the use of local zakat distribution to build and maintain harmonious communal relations.[29] Al-Shafi'i explains that Arabs in the pre-Islamic period shared their wealth with their neighbors to avoid tension and conflict and that the Prophet incorporated this pre-Islamic custom into his own practices (sunna) by ordering local zakat distribution (2:117). However, al-Shafi'i's writings do not suggest that alleviating tension created by material inequities in a community is the only or the most important reason for local zakat distribution. Rather, Shafi'i implies that the requirement to give charity to those to whom one is closest—in a locational or familial sense—is simply the most efficient and effective way to take care of the poor. A rich person should give first to those who live closest to him and to relatives in the area because no one else is in a better position to know that these people are needy (2:118, 2:120). This will save the needy from having to beg, because their neighbors and relatives who know them will take care of them.

Returning to the topic of the way in which early Muslim jurists defined need and poverty, we see that in his book of law al-Shafi'i seems to have somewhat different concerns than the other scholars I have discussed. Nevertheless, al-Shafi'i's position does not seem significantly different from the general concepts of relative need expressed by Malik and Abu 'Ubayd. When we look at the opinions expressed by later scholars associated with the Shafi'i madhhab, however, we see them emphasizing a different kind of relative definition of need. In these later works, relative needs are almost completely determined by social status. I will argue that this is a significant departure from al-Shafi'i's view of zakat distribution. I will also suggest, however, that al-Shafi'i's resort to customary norms in determining wealth may have provided a conceptual framework for the later scholars who applied this framework in a different context. Finally, I will propose that concepts of relative need formed within the context of maintenance law, by al-Shafi'i and other jurists, may have contributed to an apparent increase in status-based definitions of need.

From Communal Obligations toward a Status-Based Definition of Need

Like Malik and Abu 'Ubayd, al-Shafi'i rejects Abu Hanifa's view that the definition of poverty and wealth is related to the nisab. He says, "There could be a wealthy man who does not possess (surplus) wealth on which he has to pay zakat, while there could be a poor man with many dependents who possesses wealth on which he has to pay zakat. Instead, wealth and poverty are what people know by assessing the circumstances of a man," *(al-ghina wal-faqr ma 'arafa al-nas bi-qadr hal al-rajul)* (2:131). Providing a more detailed example, al-Shafi'i says,

> How could it be, if one man has a hundred dependents and [only] two hundred dirhams that he is not given [zakat], when this is obvious need, while another—who although he does not have two hundred dirhams and is not wealthy, but has no dependents—is given [zakat]? [How can this be] when people know that this [latter] one, who [they say] is supposed to be given zakat, is closer to wealth, whereas the one who [they say] is not supposed to be given zakat, is farther from wealth? (2:139)

Unlike Malik and Abu 'Ubayd, however, al-Shafi'i does not explicitly address the issue of what limit can be placed on the property that is to be excluded from one's surplus. Rather, al-Shafi'i argues that the zakat administrator must calculate "how much will take [the poor and the indigent] from poverty or indigence to the closest [state] called 'wealth'" (2:110, 2:128). For one poor person, this might be one hundred dirhams, for another, three hundred, for another, six hundred. Each is given enough until he just enters the "first level of wealth" so that if he can become "rich" with one dirham more of his wealth or by his work, no more is given to him (2:111). Therefore, a man's ability to support himself and his dependents by working is taken into consideration. If the zakat administrator has evidence that a man claiming poverty or indigence enriches himself with his work to what is generally recognized to be a state of wealth *(ghinan ma'ruf)*, he is not given anything. However, if the zakat administrator does not have such evidence, he must give zakat to such a man even if it appears that he is capable of supporting himself through his labor. The potential to earn a living, therefore, does not exclude a needy person from receiving zakat; only if such a person is already earning what he needs is he ineligible (2:124–125).

In *Kitab al-umm*, al-Shafi'i provides a subtle and carefully argued definition of need, which includes the recognition that no fixed amount of money or wealth can define poverty; rather, one's obligations toward one's dependents, as well as one's ability to enrich oneself, are taken into consideration. However, al-Shafi'i's definition does recognize that people in a community know what makes someone wealthy, and that someone who has reached this limit is ineligible to receive zakat.

Al-Shafi'i's recognition of the importance of community standards of wealth is significant. This indicates al-Shafi'i's recognition that poverty cannot be defined in absolute material terms; rather, poverty is what is acknowledged to be such by people in a community. It is important to understand that al-Shafi'i is not arguing for an individualistic, subjective definition of poverty. Just because someone feels in need, does not mean that he or she is truly needy. Rather, there is a kind of common wisdom or community knowledge of what poverty is; this knowledge is signified by the term *ma'ruf* (what is known). Since al-Shafi'i believes that one of the main functions of zakat distribution is to alleviate social tensions created by material inequalities, it is natural that he leaves the definition of poverty to the local community.

When we compare al-Shafi'i's discussions of zakat distribution with those of later jurists who claimed him as the eponym of their school of law, we see some significant differences. What is most striking is the emphasis these jurists place on the importance of status, custom, and honor in determining need. Unlike in *Kitab al-umm*, there is little indication in their texts that one of the main purposes of zakat is to lessen the gap between rich and poor in a local community. Rather, zakat exists to alleviate individual needs—needs that are calculated according to the rank and status of individuals. Thus, it is not only one's physical ability to support oneself that is taken into consideration when deciding eligibility for zakat; rather, what is relevant is whether a man claiming poverty can find "work that is appropriate for his status and sense of honor" *(kasb yaliqu bi-halihi wa-muruwwatihi)*.[30] Al-Ghazali (d. 505/1111) was reportedly asked about "a strong man from a distinguished family *(min ahl al-buyutat)* whose custom *('adat)* was not to engage in manual labor: could he take zakat from the share for the poor and the indigent?" "Yes," al-Ghazali replied (6:202).

In this model of zakat distribution, we see a new understanding of relative and absolute need. Here, needs are relative to a person's social and economic status, which themselves are absolute factors. One is raised within a family that lives a certain lifestyle, and that is the lifestyle one continues to "need" indefinitely. In general, one's profession is assumed to be an absolute factor in determining need. Thus, according to the Shafi'i scholar Abu Ishaq al-Shirazi (d. 476/1083), a merchant is given the kind of merchandise that he needs to make a business that will rectify his situation and make a good business for him—even if that means giving him "a lot of money *(mal kathir)*" (6:198). Later Shafi'i scholars take this idea even further, saying, "If [a man's] custom *('adat)* is to practice a trade, he is given enough so he can buy his merchandise or the tools of his trade, whether that is a small amount or large . . . the amount should be enough so that he can make a profit that will for the most part give what is sufficient *(kifaya)* for him. This will vary among different trades, regions, times and people" (6:204).

Given the fact that in the medieval Islamic Near East it was not easy to move from one trade to another, this seems like a rather sensible long-term approach to meeting the needs of individuals. However, the implications of this position are that the purpose of zakat is not to reduce the material gap between different social groups; rather, need is fully relative to one's status and, therefore, the humble street merchant will never need, nor should be given, enough zakat to bring his lifestyle closer to a man from a distinguished family. This idea is quite clear in the statement al-Nawawi (d. 676/1277) attributes to some Shafi'i scholars: "Someone who sells vegetables is given five or ten dirhams, while someone whose trade is to sell jewels is given ten thousand dirhams, for example, if he cannot attain what is sufficient for him with less than that" (6:203).

When trying to compare this view of zakat distribution with the views of early scholars, it is difficult to claim definitively that this status-based definition of need was not present in earlier Muslim jurisprudence. Indeed, it is the very ambiguity and relativity of terms such as *need* and *sufficiency* that make so many conflicting interpretations possible. Perhaps the later Shafi'i scholars differed from al-Shafi'i himself only in that they provided specific examples of what different kinds of needs could exist and should be met. However, I think that this is unlikely. Based on al-Shafi'i's statements *in Kitab al-umm*, it seems to me that he viewed zakat primarily as a way to lessen the gap between rich and poor in any particular region. Similarly, it seems unlikely that Malik and Abu 'Ubayd, with the limits they placed on property that could be exempt from surplus, would have agreed with these later Shafi'i scholars. It is also interesting that although the term *sufficiency* can be found in earlier works,[31] it seems to have been used more by later scholars. As I have discussed elsewhere, this idea of sufficiency was used by some scholars to allow believers to determine subjectively how many worldly goods they really needed, in opposition to those who argued for an absolute standard of asceticism.[32] In any case, given the fact that the status-based definition of need formulated by the Shafi'i school could lead to a jeweler being given ten thousand dirhams on the same day that a vegetable seller received five dirhams, one wonders in retrospect if there had not been some wisdom in defining poverty in relation to the nisab as the Hanafis had done.

Although I have argued that there is a distinction between the views of poverty and zakat distribution held by early jurists—such as Malik, Abu 'Ubayd, and al-Shafi'i—and the views of many later scholars, I also believe that the status-based definition of need articulated by these later scholars did not originate with them. Indeed, I believe that the notion of ma'ruf which we came across in al-Shafi'i's definition of need, may have provided an important conceptual framework for these scholars. Ma'ruf, which literally means "what is known," became a technical term in Islamic law to signify customary standards of fairness, particularly in the context of maintenance (nafaqa) laws. Although the two areas of law are rarely related by the jurists, it is my suspicion that the concepts formulated within the area of maintenance laws had an effect—perhaps an increasing effect over time—on some jurists' conceptions of need in their models of zakat distribution. Although I will not be able to provide an extensive comparison here, I will suggest some of the possible influences and differences between the two areas of law.

Maintenance Laws

Zakat has an interesting relationship to maintenance because, as a general rule, jurists do not permit individuals to pay zakat to any persons they are responsible for maintaining. Some early Iraqi scholars are an exception to this rule. These scholars allowed zakat to be given to needy relatives outside the immediate family. Unlike other jurists, they also required individuals to provide maintenance for these relatives.[33] In contrast, the other schools of law limit the obligation for maintenance to immediate family members (parents and children); wives; women and children who are under a man's guardianship; and slaves.

Another difference between zakat and maintenance is that most scholars say that the latter is an obligation for men alone, although some argue that a wealthy woman has a responsibility toward her parents. However, such a woman is never considered to have an obligation to provide maintenance for her own children— that is the responsibility of the father, other male relatives, or, in the absence of such relatives, the state.[34]

Another important difference between zakat and maintenance is that whereas zakat is ideally collected and distributed by the political rulers of an area, maintenance is provided directly by a man to his dependents. Maintenance becomes a concern of the state only when a man is suspected, or accused, of not providing what is sufficient for his dependents. This kind of dispute seems to have arisen most commonly after a divorce, when, in most cases, a woman has a right to maintenance for a certain period of time. These are the maintenance issues specifically addressed by the Quran (2:233) and most frequently discussed by early jurists.[35] A related issue is the maintenance obligation of a man toward his children when they are in the custody of the mother. Less common, and perhaps mostly apocryphal, are stories that some women were so frustrated with their stingy husbands that they took them to court.[36]

Because most discussions about maintenance in legal texts involve the obligations of men toward their wives, I will focus on this issue while exploring how Muslim jurists understood need and poverty. What must be kept in mind is that the obligation of a man to provide full maintenance for his wife is absolute—it does not depend on her ability to provide for herself through her labor or wealth. Even a rich woman has a right to full maintenance from her husband. For this reason, we see that early jurists were required to determine a wife's needs in a manner quite different from how they determined need in zakat distribution.

In the *Mudawwana, Malik* is reported as saying that the general principle for maintenance is that the wife should be maintained according to "what is customary for someone like her" *(bi-'adat amthaliha)*. Other early Maliki jurists qualify this, saying that her maintenance should depend on both "his means and her status" *(bi-qadar was'ihi wa-haliha)*.[37] Both of these principles can be found in the Quran (2:233), where it is written that men are ordered to maintain their divorced wives who are nursing their children according to "customary standards of fairness" *(al-ma'ruf)*, but that "no one shall have a greater burden placed on them than they can bear" *(la tukallafu nafsun illa wus'aha)*.

Al-ma'ruf also appears in the Quran (4:6) where it is written that poor guardians of orphans are given permission to support themselves with some of the orphans' wealth to the extent that it is ma'ruf. Not surprisingly, Muslim jurists frequently cite this Quranic term as the standard for determining maintenance in general. Although sometimes considered by later jurists to be synonymous with custom *('urf)*, most early Quran commentators and jurists understood al-ma'ruf to include also a notion of fairness or kindness. For this reason I have translated it as "customary standards of fairness." The tendency to interpret ma'ruf as simple custom is possible, however, because it is an ambiguous term. Elsewhere I have shown that the interpretation of ma'ruf as custom alone may have been used to weaken the impact of some hadith, which seemed to require that slaves be maintained on an equal level with their masters.[38] It is perhaps to avoid such ambiguity that Malik, rather than relying on the term *al-ma'ruf*, uses another term for what is customary, *'adat*, and qualifies it with the words "for someone like her."

One of the most important factors in determining proper maintenance for a woman, then, is what *kind* of woman she is. The use of the phrase *someone like her* naturally brings to mind the concept of 'equivalent dower' *(mahr mithl)*, which was applied in cases of disputed dower.[39] In both cases, when there are disputes—in maintenance and in dower—what is a fair sum is determined by considering the status of the family in which the woman was raised. Although some other factors, like age and beauty, are considered, above all, it is the family's social and economic status that will determine what maintenance is sufficient and fair for her. On this point, there seems to be a complete consensus among early jurists. Abu Yusuf, Malik, al-Shafi'i, and Ahmad all agree that if a woman is not accustomed to serving herself, then her husband should provide her with a servant.[40] Later, al-Mawardi agreed that the husband must provide a servant to his wife if this is customary for "someone like her" *(mithluha)*. He explained in detail how this was to be determined:

> The consideration given to custom ('urf) here is from two principles: [First,] the custom of "rank and station" *(al-qadr wal-manzila)*, because the custom of those

who are in a position of nobility *(sharaf)* or affluence *(yasar)* is to have people other than themselves serve them, and not to serve themselves, while those who have a low rank and whose station is decreased is to serve themselves, and not to be served. . . . [Second,] the custom of the region: for the common practice ('adat) of urban people *(ahl al-amsar)* is to be served and not to serve, while the common practice of the rural people *(ahl al-sawad)* is to serve, and not to be served.[41]

Therefore, from the time of the earliest Muslim jurists, maintenance laws assumed a social structure in which there were women who served and those who were served. As I have shown elsewhere, servants were not necessarily slaves; indeed, slave women themselves could have servants. Some jurists even argued that, depending on their upbringing and status, concubines, like free wives, could have a right to be provided with servants.[42] Al-Mawardi seems to carry this assumption over to men as well. Recall that even Malik and Abu 'Ubayd, when discussing zakat, allowed that some men might "need" a slave. Did they have only the ill and the elderly in mind in making this allowance, or were they also making concessions to notions of social status? We cannot know for certain, but it is evident that from an early time maintenance laws contained some of the rather rigid notions of social structure that we find in some later discussions of zakat.

This correlation is even more apparent when we see how different terms signifying economic status and financial means are used in relation to the maintenance of wives. The Hanafi jurist al-Khassaf (d. 261/874), in discussing the details of this maintenance obligation, generally classifies women as poor or rich.[43] This classification, however, has nothing to do with how much wealth a woman actually possesses during her marriage. Rather, a "rich" woman is one who lived a wealthy lifestyle before marriage; a "poor" woman is one who lived a poor lifestyle before marriage.

It may also be significant that, although al-Khassaf sometimes applies the classifications of rich and poor to men, more often he refers to husbands in a way that suggests a more temporal financial state. Thus, men are either "in straightened financial circumstances" *(mu'sir)*, "well-off" *(musir)*, or "excessively well-off" *(musir mufrit al-yasar)*. These terms signify the man's financial capacity *(wus')*, which, as indicated by the Quran, must also be taken into consideration when determining maintenance. The final calculation for maintenance, therefore, is a balance between the status of the woman, which is absolute, and the means of the husband, which can vary. Consequently, a man of limited means may be required to pay less to his rich wife than what she was accustomed to having, unless there was a specific contractual obligation at the time of marriage. This concession is made so that the man will not be unduly burdened financially. This also means, however, that a man who is well-off should provide more to his poor wife than what she normally had before marriage. This is required because men are ordered by the Quran (4:19) to live "kindly" with their wives, and it would not be kind to have a large material gap between the lifestyle of a man and his wife.

What we might characterize as a gap between rich and poor within a household is something al-Khassaf was concerned to lessen. Nevertheless, neither he nor most other early jurists were willing to argue that an affluent man must provide his poor wife with all the luxuries he himself enjoyed.[44] Similarly, as I have mentioned, these jurists argued that it was not required for all slave owners to feed and clothe their slaves as they did themselves—despite their acceptance of hadith which explicitly stated this. A wealthy man, they argued, only had to provide for slaves according to what was customary for them—which, they said, was obviously much less than what a wealthy man spent on himself. Their "proof" for their positions was nothing more than a notion of ma'ruf that seems to have become increasingly restricted to signify the status quo, rather than fairness or equity. The social or economic group into which individuals were born was a major factor, perhaps decisive, in determining what would be accepted as a legitimate need.

Conclusion

In this chapter, I have examined a variety of conceptions of need found in early Islamic texts dealing with zakat and maintenance laws. I have shown that a combination of relative and absolute factors have been used differently to determine need. The implications of these definitions were by no means apparent without an exploration of the particular application of these definitions by scholars over the centuries. In the earlier period, for example, absolute definitions of need seemed to disfavor the poor; in the later period, relative definitions of need seemed to reinforce rather rigid status designations even more. Nevertheless, lack of documentary evidence for actual practices and social change makes it impossible to draw firm conclusions on the basis of different legal theories. However, I conclude that at the very least a careful study of religious and legal texts needs to be conducted before arguments about the possible social or economic implications of the norms found within these texts can be made.

I have also shown that it is difficult, given the ambiguous terminology used by early jurists and the lack of detailed examples in their works, to determine that later scholars deviated from their predecessors' conceptions of need and models of zakat distribution. Nevertheless, there are some indications that there was an increasing tendency over time to recognize the social and economic context into which one was born as the most important factor in determining legitimate need.

I have also argued that the concepts underlying maintenance laws may have contributed to the way in which need and poverty were understood in the context of zakat distribution. I argue that this is likely, given the fact that the same scholars were dealing with both issues on a theoretical level, and that, on a practical level, maintenance law was always within the jurisdiction of judges. This was not always the case with the distribution of zakat. Perhaps the details provided in the context of maintenance law, therefore, indicate some of the underlying assumptions present in the early jurists' less detailed discussions about zakat. This is also suggested by the fact that, although zakat was initially collected and distributed at the state level, in later centuries, individuals often distributed their own zakat to those they considered deserving. In this respect, the payment of zakat came to resemble the way maintenance was provided by individuals toward their dependents: with little intervention of the state.

Finally, I would argue that caution needs to be exercised in concluding that later models for zakat distribution—models that do not seem to have been primarily aimed toward alleviating the gap between rich and poor—were of no benefit. Even though this may have been a negative consequence of placing too much emphasis on individuals' subjective feeling of need and deprivation, nevertheless, this feeling must be taken into account in any system of poor relief. A consideration of the previous lifestyle of those who have suffered the sudden loss of wealth or a provider can be a necessary and compassionate aspect of a system of charity. However, if such status-based definitions of need are dominant, to the extent that those born into poverty (the "structurally poor") are neglected, this discourse will contribute to reinforcing the material gap between rich and poor. Such definitions can result in a system of charity in which those who are born wealthy are maintained in this position, while those who are born poor are not considered deserving of more resources to help them attain a higher standard of living.

In making such an observation, I am not assuming that dispensing charity is the best way to diminish structural poverty. Indeed, it is likely that the structurally poor are better served by political stability and an economy based on vigorous trade—both of which were strongly advocated by Muslim jurists of the classical period. It is also possible that charity is most effective when it is directed toward the incidental poor: the elderly, widows, orphans, and others who have "fallen" from more secure financial circumstances for a variety of reasons. Nevertheless, any system of charity and poor relief reflects and affects greater perceptions of the proper distribution of resources within a society. Consequently the way in which Muslim jurists define need is significant not only for what this discourse tells us about distribution of charity but also what it tells us about possible limits to their vision of changing the world around them.

Notes

1. The Islamic calendar begins in C.E. 622 with the emigration *(hijra)* of the Prophet Muhammad and his companions to the city of Medina. Because it is comprised of lunar months, the Islamic year is approximately thirteen days shorter than the solar year. Islamic

dates are signified by the letters "A.H." (after hijra). In this chapter, all dates will be given first according to the Islamic calendar and then the Gregorian calendar.

2. Because the two terms were distinguished in different ways by early Muslim scholars, but both indicated some kind of poor person, it seemed that the best solution was to translate the two terms with two different, but synonymous, English words.

3. A discussion of this issue can be found in most books of Quran commentary *(tafsir)* and positive law *(fiqh)*. Some of the sources consulted for this chapter include Abu 'Ubayd al-Qasim ibn Sallam, *Kitab al-amwal*, ed. Muhammad Khalil Haras (Cairo: Maktabat al-Kuliyyat al-Azhariyya, 1388/1968), 727ff. Abu Ja'far Muhammad ibn Jarir al-Tabari, *Jami' al-bayan fi tafsir al-Qur'an* (Cairo: Dar al-Ma'arif, 1955), 9:109–111; Abu Sulayman al-Khattabi, *Ma'alim al-sunan*, published with *Mukhtasar Sunan Abi Da'ud*, 2 vols., ed. Ahmed Shakir and Muhammad Hamid al-Faqi (Baghwali Sanqlah Hal, Pakistan: al-Maktaba al-Athariyya, 1979), 227–233; Abu Zakariyya Muhyi al-Din ibn Sharaf al-Nawawi, *al-Majmu': Sharh al-Muhadhdhab* (Cairo: Zakariyya 'Ali Yusuf, n.d), 6:204–210. A helpful examination of classical zakat law and modern applications is Yusuf al-Qaradawi's *Fiqh al-Zakat*, 2 vols (Beirut: al-Resalah Publishers, 1977).

4. Ibn Sallam, *Kitab al-amwal*, 793.

5. H. L. Gottschalk, "Abu 'Ubayd al-Qasim b. Sallam," *EI²*, 1:157; Christopher Melchert, *The Formation of the Sunni Schools of Law, 9th–10th Centuries, C.E.* (Leiden: Brill, 1997), 76–78.

6. As Christopher Melchert has demonstrated, at the turn of the third/ninth century, the authority of individual scholars was becoming more important than the earlier regional schools, but independent and self-sufficient schools of law, named after a great scholar and equipped with their own institutions and curriculum, had not yet developed. It is not unusual, therefore, to find a scholar like Abu 'Ubayd to be claimed later by both the Shafi'is and the Hanafis, since each school found that many of Abu 'Ubayd's opinions and his methodology were similar to theirs.

7. Abu 'Ubayd al-Qasim ibn Sallam, *Gharib al-hadith*, ed. Husain Muhammad Sharaf (Cairo: al-Hay'ah al-'Ammah li-Shu'un al-Matabi' al-Amiriyah, 1984).

8. Interestingly, the manuscript states that this copy of the text was verified by the well-known female scholar Shahida bint Abi Nasr al-Dinawari in the year 564/1168 in Baghdad.

9. Ibn Sallam, *Kitab al-amwal* 727–728; narrated by Qabisa ibn al-Makhariq.

10. Ibid., 731; reported from Sahl ibn al-Hanzaliyya.

11. Cf. al-Nawawi, *al-Majmu'*, 6:204.

12. Even though it is narrated by an unnamed "man." Abu 'Ubayd says that despite this, the hadith is strong because it was narrated by Malik (Ibn Sallam, *Kitab al-amwal*, 737).

13. Abu'l-Hasan 'Ali ibn Muhammad ibn Habib Al-Mawardi, *Al-Ahkam al-sultaniyya wal-wilayat al-diniyya*, translated as *The Ordinances of Government* by Wafaa H. Wahba (Reading, U.K.: Center for Muslim Contribution to Civilization; London: Garnet Publishing, 1996), 136.

14. Melchert, *Formation of the Sunni Schools*, 36–37.

15. Michael Bonner, "Definitions of Poverty and the Rise of the Muslim Urban Poor," *Journal of the Royal Asiatic Society*, series 3,6 (1996): 335–344.

16. Norman Calder, *Studies in Early Muslim Jurisprudence* (Oxford: Oxford University Press, 1994).

17. Among Calder's critics are Jonathan Brockopp in his "Early Islamic Jurisprudence in Egypt: Two Scholars and Their *Mukhtasars*," *International Journal of Middle East Studies* 30 (1998): 167–182. At the University of Utah Islamic legal theory conference in 1999, Brockopp elaborated on his criticism of Calder saying that the latter's fundamental methodological mistake—and the mistake of a number of others who have wanted to redate legal texts—is that they have assumed that there was a linear development in the development of Islamic legal theory, wherein the reliance on the opinions of scholars gave way to the reliance on sacred texts. For example, Calder argued that the *Mudawwana*, which relies almost solely on Malik's opinions, is earlier than the *Muwatta,* which contains a relatively large amount of hadith and Qur'an. Brockopp argues that Sahnun cites Malik in the *Mudawwana*, rather than prophetic hadith, because he attributed charismatic authority and knowledge to Malik himself—so that Malik is the most reliable source for the sunna. This resort to the authority of earlier scholars is, in fact, a characteristic of the institution of the madhhab, an institution which obviously arose after the classical compilations of hadith.

18. Sahnun ibn Sa'id al-Tanukhi, *al-Mudawwana al-kubra lil-Imam Malik,* 7 vols. (Beirut: Dar Sadir, n.d.), 1:295.

19. Abu Muhammad 'Abdullah ibn Ahmad ibn Qudama, *Al-Mughni* (Cairo: Maktabat al-Jumhuriyya al-'Arabiyya, n.d.), 2:670.

20. Al-Qaradawi, *Fiqh al-Zakat,* 553.

21. Ibn Sallam, *Kitab al-amwal,* 737.

22. Al-Khattabi, *Ma'alim al-sunan,* 738.

23. Bonner, "Definitions of Poverty," 340.

24. Ya'qub ibn Ibrahim Abu Yusuf, *Kitab al-kharaj* (Beirut: Dar al-Ma'arif, n.d.), 81–84.

25. See Ingrid Mattson, "A Believing Slave is Better than an Unbeliever: Status and Community in Early Islamic Society and Law" (Ph.D. diss., University of Chicago, 1999), 219.

26. "Malik ibn Anas," *EI²,* 6:262–265.

27. Al-Tanukhi, *al-Mudawwana,* 1:358.

28. Ibn Sallam, *Kitab al-amwal,* 588.

29. Muhammad ibn Idris al-Shafi'i, *Kitab al-umm,* 8 vols. (Cairo: Dar al-Ghada al-Arabi, 1409/1989), 2:118, 2:133.

30. Al-Nawawi, *al-Majmu',* 6:198.

31. Ibn Sallam, *Kitab al-amwal,* 739–740.

32. Mattson, "A Believing Slave," 51–60.

33. Ibn Sallam, *Kitab al-amwal,* 776.

34. Al-Tanukhi, *al-Mudawwana,* 2:367; al-Mawardi, *Al-Ahkam,* 205.

35. For example, almost all of the questions asked of Malik in the *Mudawwana* regarding maintenance have to do with divorced women (al-Tanukhi, *al-Mudawwana,* 2:, 470–475).

36. There is a widely cited hadith that Abu Sufyan's wife Hind complained to the Prophet that her husband was stingy and did not provide well for her and her children.

Because Abu Sufyan was the father of the early Umayyad caliphs, no doubt this story was popular within anti-Umayyad circles. See *Sahih Muslim,* trans. Abdul Hamid Siddiqui, 4 vols. (Beirut: Dar al-Arabia, n.d), 3:928.

37. Shams al-Din Muhammad 'Arafa al-Dasuqi, *Hashiyyat al-Dasuqi 'ala l-Sharh al-kabir,* 4 vols. (Aleppo: 'Isa al-Babi, n.d.), 2:509.

38. Mattson, "A Believing Slave," 107–113.

39. Jamal J. Nasir, *The Islamic Law of Personal Status,* 2nd ed. (London: Graham and Trotman, 1990), 90–91.

40. Al-Tanukhi, *al-Mudawwana,* 2:218, al-Shafi'i, *Kitab al-umm,* 5:125; Mattson, "A Believing Slave," 191–199.

41. Al-Mawardi, *Al-Ahkam,* 45.

42. Mattson, "A Believing Slave," 203–204.

43. Al-Shaybani, Abu Bakr Ahmad b. 'Amr al-Khassaf (d. 261), *Kitab al-Nafaqat,* with commentary by Husam al-Din Abu Muhammad 'Umar ibn 'Abd al-'Aziz al-Bukhari (d. 536), ed. Abu'l-Wafa' al-Afghani (Beirut: Dar al-Kitab al-Arabi, 1984), 29, 36.

44. Al-Khassaf, 36-37; al-Shaf'i, *Kitab al-umm,* 5:125, al-Mawardi, *Al-Ahkam,* 59–61.

CHAPTER THREE

The Foreign Jewish Poor in Medieval Egypt

MARK R. COHEN

I heard, my brother, what happened to you at sea. May God be with you, my brother, in accordance, my brother, with the many prayers I invoke for you. May He look out for you, being a foreigner *(fi l-ghurba)*, and be with you and me, and may He look out for all your affairs. Do not be stingy with me, my brother, because I would not be pressing family except at a time like this when I, my brother, am in a foreign country *(fi balad al-ghurba)* without a dinar or dirhem.

> —A Yemenite Jew, a newcomer to Fustat, the capital of Egypt, suffering
> from poverty, writing to his brother in Alexandria for help.[1]

Needy Jewish Foreigners in Medieval Egypt

Egypt, as is well-known, was a major crossroads in the Islamic Middle Ages. Naturally, Alexandria, the main seaport, and Fustat, the main riverport and hub of the country, saw vast numbers of foreigners enter their gates; but the Egyptian countryside abounded in foreigners as well. The influx of Jewish newcomers to all parts of Lower Egypt is seen, among other ways, in the preponderance of foreigners in positions of intellectual and judicial leadership in the capital, in Alexandria, and in the countryside. Maimonides, the most illustrious immigrant serving the Egyptian community in the twelfth century, had his counterparts in the eleventh. As I have written elsewhere, since the second half of the eleventh century, nearly all the chief communal personalities in the Egyptian capital had been newcomers or descendants of recent immigrants, and this had seminal significance for the transfer from Palestine to Egypt of Jewish central self-government at that time.[2] We may surmise, too, that the attitudes of at least the leadership in Fustat toward the foreign poor were influenced by their own initial experience as newcomers.

Our main source for Jewish life in medieval Egypt, the Cairo Geniza documents, contains scores of letters written by the foreign poor or on their behalf, as well as hundreds of alms-lists and records of charitable donations, wherein the foreign poor and their benefactors are generously represented.[3] Like the newcomer from Yemen I quoted, most of these foreigners had left families back home and thus lacked in their new locale that most important source of succor in traditional societies: the kinship group. To be separated from home and family meant to be vulnerable to destitution. This sentiment crops up dramatically as a theme in a very long formulary letter of recommendation for a "foreigner 'So-and-So.'" In addition to elaborate phrases of gratitude, the missive describes a famine "that impoverished the rich, humbled the strong and cast out people from their homelands, causing them disquiet, scattering them and destroying their unity (with family), sending them far away from their homelands and from the sight of their children."[4]

The foreign Jewish presence in Egypt was not restricted to judges and celebrated scholars; it crossed the entire gamut. Elementary school teachers, for example, were to a large extent foreigners, whether refugees from war or persecution, or others who, for one reason or another, had lost their livelihood. Many of the European Jews in the Geniza, whether they resettled in Egypt or the Holy Land, experienced economic hardship, either before leaving their homelands or after their long journeys.[5]

Most foreigners in Egypt are identifiable as such in our documents by geographical place-names ("the Damascene," "the Syrian," "the Maghrebi," "the Rumi" [from Byzantium or simply from Christian Europe]), and so forth.[6] Or, we encounter them under the rubric *gharib* (stranger) or *tari'* (newcomer).[7] The word *gharib* in Islamic literary sources, as Franz Rosenthal has shown, usually represents "everybody who left his original place of residence and went abroad," including both merchants and beggars. Experiencing loneliness as well as the loss of prestige gained from nearby family and friends, the "stranger in Islam" typically suffered from poverty, which as a rule he or she was unable to overcome. The association of poverty with being a stranger is also an ancient trope in the Near East, mirrored already in their linkage in the Hebrew Bible.[8] Not surprisingly, too, Gharib is the name given to the trickster–beggar from the Islamic "underground" in a shadow play written in fourteenth-century Egypt.[9]

When writing their own letters, foreigners in the Geniza often identify themselves as coming from afar, for example, Ephraim, a refugee from Morocco, who, in a letter soliciting help, uses Hebrew and Arabic to call himself "the poor, poor foreigner" *(al-faqir al-'ani al-gharib).*[10] A common Hebrew locution for foreigners is "wayfarer" *('over va-shav).* I will discuss the special significance of this term further on.

Needy Wayfarers

Needy foreigners fell roughly into four categories, though the boundaries separating them were somewhat fluid: wayfarers, poor immigrants (temporary or long-term), captives, and refugees (the latter including Christian proselytes fleeing to safety in the Muslim orbit). The captives and refugees formed a group whose deservedness for charitable assistance was obvious and unquestionable, requiring little, if any, verification.[11]

We encounter wayfarers abundantly in letters of appeal, though many more of them are doubtless subsumed under the designation "newcomer" *(tari')* in the alms-lists.[12] Travelers from such faraway places as Morocco, Sicily, Muslim Spain, Christian Spain, France, Kiev–Rus, Syria and Mesopotamia, and Iraq often carried letters bearing multiple signatures, in effect vouching for their neediness in anticipation that communities or individuals might be reluctant to support unknown persons from distant locales.[13]

The itinerant foreign poor also included travelers from closer by. Indigents living in the small towns of the Egyptian countryside would journey to the capital in search of charity.[14] It worked the other way, too: Some wayfarers wished to leave the capital for better pickings in the countryside and for that purpose obtained letters of recommendation from a Jewish dignitary in Fustat.[15]

Indigent foreigners often wanted, simply, to go home. Pathetic to read is the letter from a poor mother with an infant daughter who needed money to cover the expenses of traveling home to Palestine. Her husband there had divorced her and she had come to Egypt, leaving a grown daughter behind. Now she wished to return home and rejoin her daughter. She secured a letter of recommendation from the Nagid (Abraham Maimonides) in Fustat requesting travel assistance for her from the community of Alexandria, which was on her route home.[16]

Settling in or making a pilgrimage to Jerusalem was highly valued and could be exploited by wayfarers to obtain charity, especially in the light of a *halakha* (law) that privileged charitable giving to the poor of Eretz Israel over the poor living outside the Holy Land.[17] A letter from Ashkelon, Palestine, from the judge Nathan ha-Kohen b. Mevorakh (end of the eleventh century) to the *parnas* (social welfare official) Eli b. Yahya in Fustat asks the latter to assist Solomon b. Benjamin, the bearer of the letter. He, too, was formerly well-off (and also generous) but had become destitute as a result of difficulties. He was a refugee from war and now wished to settle in Jerusalem and needed money for that purpose. Significantly, the information that Solomon's goal was to settle in Jerusalem after collecting sufficient funds in Egypt was an afterthought, inserted interlinearly in the text. The supplicant, or perhaps his intercessor, the letter writer, knew that this fact would have a compelling impact on would-be benefactors and did not wish to leave it out.[18] At the same time, needy travelers arriving in Egypt from the Holy Land, especially Jerusalem, could expect a favorable reception.[19] There was even a special pious trust in Fustat for the Jews of Jerusalem, a property called "the Compound of the Jerusalemites," and its rental income was earmarked to assist indigents in and from the holy city.[20]

Immigrants

Wayfarers normally were transients who, as individuals, did not represent an on-going burden on private or public charity. More problematic were the immigrants proper: people who had come to Egypt from other countries, or from the Egyptian provinces to the capital, and settled there on a long-term basis, ostensibly seeking to improve their lot.[21] They did not always succeed, as the following from a letter in Arabic characters, reveals. The writer had lived for six years in Alexandria and another in Fustat. His family, including a widowed daughter and a three-year-old grandson, was suffering from hunger and sickness. The addressee had paid the writer's poll tax in the past (the annual "tribute" levied on non-Muslims in return for protection of religious observance, life, and property). Now he appeals to him "for the ship's fare to travel," one imagines to return to his original home.[22]

Far more than in letters of appeal we find immigrants on the communal dole, registered in the alms-lists. Foreigners, indeed, constitute "by far the most numerous" category of persons on the lists of beneficiaries, S. D. Goitein writes.[23] As newcomers, they were slow finding work, let alone work that paid a living wage. Many of the people who streamed into Egypt were chronically poor to begin with. Other reasons, too, forced these "strangers" to resort to public charity.

Foreigners and the "Deserving Poor"

The Geniza documents afford a unique opportunity to explore the relationship between normative halakha and actual practice. Here I will examine this for the case of charitable obligations toward foreigners, with particular reference to the issue of the deserving poor. This matter, which was of considerable concern to authorities in medieval and early-modern Europe and, in turn, has attracted the attention of modern scholars, had occupied minds centuries earlier in Jewish society.[24]

The biblical laws of charity, mainly agricultural in keeping with the agrarian character of Israelite society, give prominence to the foreigner, or stranger, *ger* in biblical Hebrew—a resident alien who attached himself to the Israelite people. Typically needy because separated from family, the stranger is grouped with widows and orphans (fatherless children), the classical paradigms of the deserving poor in many societies (e.g., Lev. 23:22; Deut. 24:19–22).[25] These laws, indeed the biblical laws of agriculture in general, held sway only in the Holy Land and would come into force once again at the time of the Messiah, when all Jews living in exile would return to live in Israel and the land would be restored to Jewish sovereignty.

While the issue of "foreignness" faced Jews living in the late antique and medieval Diaspora, the biblical privileging of the resident alien (*ger* now had the meaning of proselyte) did not carry over. Rather, an ancient halakha potentially impinged on the acceptance of foreign Jews as worthy recipients of assistance. It rules that the poor of one's family take precedence in charity over the poor of one's city, and both take precedence over the poor of another city.[26]

As quoted in the Geniza letters, the halakha takes the following form: "The poor of your household have priority over the poor of your city, and the poor of your city have priority over the poor of another city." "The poor of another city" could, of course, apply either to indigents writing from another city to request assistance from a benefactor in the Egyptian capital, or to foreigners from another city sojourning in Fustat. The alms-lists in the Geniza are peppered with the names of poor people who had come to Fustat from another place. The letters of appeal offer examples of both: foreigners writing from outside the capital as well as foreigners already living there, whose "outsider" origins could continue to have an unfavorable affect on them even after their arrival in a new place.

The biblical basis for the halakha is a passage in Deuteronomy dealing with charitable loans:

> If there is a needy person among you, one of your kinsmen in any of your settlements in the land that the Lord your God is giving you, do not harden your heart and shut your hand against your needy kinsman. Rather, you must open your hand and lend him sufficient for whatever he needs. . . . For there will never cease to be needy ones in your land, which is why I command you: open your hand to the poor and needy kinsman in your land. (15:7–8, 11)

The Talmud, in the tractate Bava Mesi'a, which deals with aspects of civil law, derives the order of priorities from a verse in Exodus, in a section pertaining to loans (the law also appears in the early *halakhic midrash, Mekhilta de-R. Ishmael*).

> If you lend money to my people, to the poor who is in your power, do not act toward him as a creditor; exact no interest from him (Exod. 22:24). [This teaches:] *My people* take precedence over a Gentile. *The poor* take precedence over the rich. *Your* poor (*'aniyyekha*) take precedence over the poor of your city (*'aniyyei 'irkha*). The poor of *your* city take precedence over the poor of another city (*'aniyyei 'ir aheret*).[27]

The concept appears, again in the context of loans, but generalized to encompass charitable gifts to the poor as a whole, in the early halakhic midrash, *Sifrei Deuteronomy*, interpreting Deuteronomy 15:7–8.[28]

Maimonides, the first to codify the dispersed Jewish laws of charity, drew from biblical, Talmudic, and post-Talmudic sources in his systematic, fourteen-volume comprehensive code of Jewish law, the *Mishneh Torah*, completed in Egypt circa 1180. Both as a private person and in his capacity as head of the Jewish communities of the Fatimid Empire from around 1171 to 1177 and again from around 1195 until his death in 1204, Maimonides dealt extensively with social welfare. With careful attention to nuances in his code we are able to make some suggestive observations about the relationship between law and practice at that time.

Maimonides split the law in Bava Mesi'a into two parts. He incorporated the statement limiting the amount of interest chargeable to Gentiles to what was necessary to make a living into the section on the laws of lending ("Creditor and Debtor"), a section that opens with the commandment to lend to the poor of Israel.[29] But since free loans are a form of charity, he transferred the part about prioritization in lending to Jews to the section called "Gifts for the Poor" *(Mattenot 'aniyyim)*, in the division on agricultural legislation, "The Book of Seeds." And he gave it a new topic sentence. "A poor man who is one's relative has priority over all others *('ani she-hu qerovo qodem le-khol adam)*, the poor of one's household has priority over the other poor of his city, and the poor of his city have priority over the poor of another city, as it is said, 'to the poor and needy kinsman, in your land'" (Deut. 15:11).[30]

By severing the matter of prioritization from its original context among the Talmudic laws of lending and transplanting it to the laws of charity, Maimonides confused some readers searching for the codifier's sources.[31] This may have been his own, original move, consistent with his overarching socioethical and metaphysical doctrine of charity as expressed, for instance, in the *Guide of the Perplexed*,[32] or it may stem from an earlier codificatory step (unknown to us) by the Geonim or by his teachers in Spain. Whatever the case, it reflects real-life conditions in the world in which he lived.[33]

For example, Maimonides' topic sentence, "a poor man who is one's relative has priority over all others," is not found in that form in the Talmud. To be sure, it reflects the more broadly inclusive sweep of kinship implied by the word *'aniyyekha* in Bava Mesi'a (translated above as "the poor of your household"). But, more important, it fits well the mobile society in which Maimonides lived, where Jews moved more freely from city to city than in the mostly sedentary, predominantly agricultural Jewish world of the Talmudic period. In the medieval Mediterranean many people had relatives in other cities, and at times, travelers found kin in the foreign cities they traversed. Thus, Maimonides' introduction encompasses the case of a poor relative from "another city" who is eligible for immediate assistance despite being a foreigner.

In actuality, however, most foreigners lacked local kinship ties, and, for them, the halakha about "the poor of another city" could pose difficulties. Newcomers sensed that they were competing for local philanthropic resources preferentially earmarked for resident indigents or for local and visiting relatives.[34] This awareness finds expression, for instance, in an Arabic Geniza letter from a man in need of financial assistance. He was under house arrest for failing to pay his poll tax as well as that of his two sons. Though not a relative of the man to whom he appealed, he exhorts him (quoting the halakha in the original Hebrew): "'the poor of your household have priority over the poor of your city, and the poor of your city have priority over the poor of another city,'" then adds: "*Count me among 'the poor of your household.'*"[35] Similarly, in a finely penned petition a man thanks a benefactor for "these two nights," that is, for paying for his and his companions' overnight stay (in an inn, apparently). He then asks for an extension, adding, "may you put us in the place of the *people of your household.*"[36]

The occasional, or at least potential, unwillingness to assist foreigners is mentioned specifically or by inference in letters of appeal. A foreigner complains about the bad reception he was experiencing in Fustat:

> I have no cover, and n[o] couch, and no work to which I can resort. I am from a faraway place, namely Rahba [a town in Iraq]. Three months I have been here, and none of our coreligionists has paid attention to me or fed me with a piece of bread. So I have turned to God the exalted and to my master to do for me what is appropriate with every wayfarer and give me as charity a little money to raise [my] spirits, for I am miserable and dying from hunger. Dogs get their fill these days with bread, not I.[37]

All of the evidence presented so far and more to be presented elsewhere points to the fact that the itinerant poor—the poor of another city—experienced, at least potentially, the low prioritization in eleemosynary giving prescribed by the ancient halakha. They, more than family and local residents, faced the challenge of proving their deservedness. Moreover, as we have seen, it was not only those writing for assistance from another city—the remote foreign poor—but also foreign indigents living in the capital of Egypt, who experienced discrimination.

Many, if not most, of the foreign needy who wrote letters of appeal, or had them written on their behalf, were seeking private charity to avoid the community dole. For these people, or most of them, poverty arose under specific, intermittent circumstances, the result of what the French *Annalistes* call a "conjuncture." Being in need was also a source of shame. Like those labeled the "shamefaced poor" in early modern Europe, they resisted turning to others for help and certainly the weekly public distributions of bread, not to mention the embarrassment of beggary.[38] They appealed privately, in letters, to limit their shame.

Examining the Foreign Poor for Deservedness

In early modern Europe, methods were put into operation to examine the Christian poor, to establish their legal residence, and to prevent those who did not deserve charity from receiving local assistance.[39] Centuries before, the Babylonian

Talmud had considered circumstances in which the Jewish poor should be examined to verify that their claim was legitimate.

> Rav Huna said: We examine before giving food but not before giving clothing. . . . R. Judah said: We examine before giving clothing but not before giving food. . . . It is taught according to R. Judah: If he said, clothe me, we examine him first; [if he said] feed me, we do not examine him first. . . . It has been taught in agreement with R. Judah: "If a man says 'Clothe me,' he is examined, but if he says 'Feed me,' he is not examined."[40]

Though the foreign poor are not mentioned explicitly, in practice the law about examining the poor had particular relevance to outsiders, who were by nature unknown to the community, at least at first. The Tosefta[41] singles out the foreign poor specifically. It also adds an important nuance that permits donating clothing without examination if the needy individual is "known."

> A poor man traveling from one place to another must not be given less than one loaf of bread that sells for a pondion, when the price is four se'a for one sela. If he lodges for the night, he must be given provisions for the night *(parnasat layla)*, oil and pulse. If he stays over the Sabbath, he must be given food for three meals as well as oil, pulse, fish, and vegetables. This applies to a situation when he is not known. *If he is known, however, then he must also be given clothing.* If he goes begging from door to door, one is not obligated to give him anything.[42]

A variant of this passage adds the words, "all, according to his dignity" *(ve-hakol lefi kevodo),* after the words italicized in the quotation above.[43]

Maimonides' codification of this halakha appears to echo realities of identifying the deserving poor in his time and place. He follows the Babylonian Talmud and resolves the disagreement between Rav Huna and R. Judah in favor of the latter, but he goes further regarding clothing the poor, seemingly on the basis of the Tosefta (with the variant reading just cited).

> If a poor man unknown to anyone comes forth and says, "I am hungry; give me something to eat," he should not be examined as to whether he might be an impostor—he should be fed immediately. If, however, he is naked and says, "Clothe me," he should be examined as to possible fraud. *If he is known, he should be clothed immediately according to his dignity, without any further inquiry.*[44]

In choosing the Tosefta's nuance to the Talmudic halakha about examining the poor, Maimonides seems to have had contemporary circumstances in mind. Poor newcomers to Egypt, let alone needy people writing for help from abroad, were usually not connected with the Egyptian Jewish commercial class, not "known" to local Jews, and so suffered a disadvantage. The halakha in the Talmud does not mention the nuance about being known—that is found only in the Tosefta. Following the Tosefta, Maimonides takes the position that, if the person was known, his deservedness, even for clothing, could easily be determined, and he adds, "without further inquiry."

Systematic ways were found in Maimonides' Egypt to verify the deservedness, especially of foreigners, and to weed out those whose claim to alms was fraudulent. Knowing the person, or at least obtaining the testimony of someone who knew him or her, was an important key in the verification "system," employed in both public and private charity. A frequent notation in the poor lists, one that has not been fully understood, illustrates this system for public assistance. The phrase is *ma'rifat X*. It is found in dozens of lists, all but one of them registers of alms recipients. Goitein rendered the phrase *the acquaintance of X* and thought it was simply an informal way of designating people, somewhat like another term, *the relative (qaraba) of X*.[45] I believe, however, that the term has a different and technical meaning and was employed chiefly for the poor, particularly the foreign poor, and for the specific purpose of verifying their deservedness.[46] Local Jews vouched for people if they knew them, or after they came to know them. When, in one bread list, we find *ma'rifatay Azhar* (the two ma'rifas of Azhar), Azhar is certifying the deservedness of two unknown indigents.[47] Maimonides, himself originally a foreigner from the West, wrote a letter vouching for an acquaintance of his, a newcomer from Morocco ("he is an acquaintance of mine," *min ma'arifina*), and asked the community of Minyat Zifta in the Nile Delta to arrange a collection toward the payment of his poll tax.[48]

The clerks who compiled the alms-lists often did not know the names of needy newcomers (or at least, not yet)—only that they were known to someone in the community who could be trusted to vouch for their genuine need. The scribes entered these strangers in the lists as the ma'rifa of the person who knew them, and they might continue to record them as such even after they learned their names. I have even found one case in which a ma'rifa continued to keep that identifying (and we may add, reassuring) marker even after the death of his patron.[49] Perhaps a better translation of the phrase would be "the person known by X."

A fascinating notation in two tiny Geniza fragments alludes, I believe, to another facet of the process of determining need.[50] The fragments seem to belong to one and the same alms-list. The notation, hitherto unremarked in the Geniza documents, says, in one of the two fragments: "[The wif]e (or widow) of Barakat: she should be investigated," *yukshaf 'anha*; the same notation seems to appear a second time on the other side of that list.[51] The second fragment mentions "the ma'rifa of the son of Da'ud: he should be investigated" *(wa-yukshaf 'anhu)*, followed immediately by "the [ma]'rifa of the son of the dayyan of Barqa: [he] should be investigated" *[wa-yu]kshaf 'anhu*.[52] I believe this seemingly innocuous remark represents instructions to verify the deservedness of the recipients. I surmise, further, that the vast majority of the alms-lists give the names of applicants who have already come to be known and been judged deserving.

Verification of deservedness was the very purpose of all those letters of recommendation written on behalf of needy individuals or families seeking private
charity, and this holds true not only of letters from Europe and from distant Islamic lands but also for the scores of petitions and letters from places closer by.[53]
Some are very explicit about verification. A letter of recommendation carried
by a Maghrebi heading for Fustat contains signatures attesting to his unfortunate
saga and vouches for his deservedness with the words: "He is a deserving person,
worthy of charity" *(wa-annahu rajul mahquq wa-huwa ahlan lil-khayr)*. A phrase
added above the line, praising the poor man's philanthropy prior to his misfortune, notifies the addressee: "Perhaps some of the elders in Fustat know him."[54]
Similarly, a poor woman with a blind child writes to the head of the Jews in
Egypt, the Gaon Masliah ha-Kohen b. Solomon (1127–1139), recommending
herself for charitable assistance and adds in a postscript: "The people of al-
Mahalla know how weakened my situation is and how very poor I am *(shiddat
faqriha)*."[55]

The leaders of the community of Alexandria, in 1253, featured "deservedness"
in their writ of authorization for one Elazar b. Solomon to receive money from the
pious trust to pay his poll tax and also bread from the *quppa* (breadbasket). "We
know and verify the des[ervednes]s *(isti[hqa]q)* of the [e]lder Abu Man[su]r . . . and
his impoverishment and family burden. Since we know about his deservedness *(is-
tihqaqhu)*, we have written and signed for him." And they add further on that they
have done this "by reason of his old age and his noble family, which is famous for
its knowledge and piety."[56] The term *mustahiqq* was still being used in police registers in nineteenth-century Egypt to designate Muslims deemed worthy of
charitable assistance, as Mine Ener shows.[57]

Countering Reluctance to Give to the Foreign Poor

A frequent refrain in letters to Egypt regarding indigent Jews from afar calls on a
Hebrew phrase associated in the Talmud and the midrash with Abraham's generosity toward "every wayfarer" *(kol 'over va-shav)*. The Hebrew locution, richly
resonant with echoes of the revered biblical forefather's hospitality toward visitors
and encouraging would-be benefactors to imitate his good deeds, would be employed even when the letter was written in Arabic. In a typical example, a writer
recommends for charity a poor cantor who was exiled from Spain: "I am asking
you to deal with him as is your beautiful habit with regard to every wayfarer."[58]
This oft-encountered appeal to philanthropy for the wayfarer, with its echoes of
Abraham's munificence, should not be dismissed as mere rhetoric. I believe it was
used with purpose, to counteract the reluctance to give to the foreign poor, in keeping with the halakha that underprivileged the poor of another city.

The political leadership in Fustat and other local influential notables—many of them immigrants themselves—also took measures to counter the potential discrimination against foreign indigents. They regularly responded to petitions from foreigners for charity. Of the head of the Jews, the Nagid Samuel b. Hananya (1140–1159), a petitioner says, "it is well known that you are the patron of every wayfarer *(kol 'over va-shav)*."[59] Two centuries later, when the Jewish community of Egypt (like the society around it) was in economic decline, we find the Nagid and head of the Jews, Joshua (d. 1355), the great-great-grandson of Maimonides, who lived in Cairo, frequently addressing letters of recommendation to the community of Fustat on behalf of needy foreigners, who carried the letters with them.[60]

Still, foreigners knew the power of traditional priorities expressed in the halakha about the poor of another city. Thus, a woman in need describes her plight in detail to the same head of the Jews, Samuel b. Hananya, and, at the end, in a postscript written in a different hand (suggesting it was written some time after the rest of the letter), adds: "Your slave has a family relationship *(hurma ahliyya)* with your excellency. Your excellency's father and my father are the children of your excellency's maternal aunt. Your excellency is the patron of foreigners, all the more so those who are his slaves and his family."[61]

A Comparison with the Foreign Poor in Pagan Antiquity, Early Christianity, and Islam

The situation of the foreign Jewish poor in medieval Egypt calls for comparison with the position of the foreign poor in the pagan and early Christian worlds as well as in Islam. Generally, in pagan antiquity, pity did not figure as a factor in philanthropy. Individual public benefactors (Greek *euergetai*), or the state itself, gave to citizens, regardless of whether they were in need, or built public buildings, to enhance their own prestige and, ultimately, to receive some sort of return from the beneficiaries of their largesse.[62] The ancient Greek and Hellenistic–Roman worlds also knew the institution of the hostel for foreigners and other comers: the *pandocheion*, the etymological cognate of Aramaic *pundaq* and Arabic *funduq*. Itinerants moving from place to place were often poor, but poverty was not a criterion for admission to these shelters (in fact, fees were usually collected to stay and eat there). Often enough, travelers were sick, though that, too, was not a requirement for staying in facilities for transients.

The pre-Christian ancient world thus had a formal institution for dealing with foreigners, but only incidentally with the poor among them. Judaism was different in this respect, for as early as biblical times it associated help for the stranger with help for the needy. There is some archaeological and (not entirely conclusive) Talmudic evidence that Jews in late antiquity provided shelter for the needy in the synagogue compound,[63] and more explicit proof from the letters of Pope Gregory the Great (590–604) with regard to Sicily.[64] Some Geniza texts indicate that a community-sponsored hostel (called *funduq*) and sometimes the synagogue itself offered shelter for homeless and needy foreigners in medieval Fustat.[65] Whatever restraining effect the Talmudic law about the poor of another city, especially as codified in our period by Maimonides in his laws of "Gifts for the Poor," might have had on the private philanthropic instincts of Jews, the Geniza documents, especially the alms-lists, show that foreigners were cared for in some manner or another by the public charity of the community.

Early Christianity, heir to the Old Testament and born during the rabbinic period, inherited Judaism's attitude toward the needy foreigner, and this and other factors led to the introduction, following the Christianization of the Roman Empire, of the *xenodocheion* or *xenon* (in Greek), *hospice* (in Latin), a charitable hostel for needy Christian wayfarers.[66] Thereafter these shelters evolved into real hospitals for the treatment of the ill—who could be foreigners or local, poor or economically self-sufficient. The transition to the hospital began first in fourth-century Byzantium and much later in western Latin Europe.[67]

Islam has similar notions about the wayfarer. The Quran enumerates eight categories of people who are eligible for the benefits of the compulsory alms tax, the *zakat*, a loan word from Hebrew and Aramaic and carrying the meaning "charity" as transmitted to Islam by Judaism and Christianity.[68] One of the eight is *ibn al-sabil* (the wayfarer).[69] This fit the circumstances of the very early Islamic community and the pre-Islamic Bedouin society on which it was founded. It is possible that Jews in the Islamic world, as we observe them in the Geniza, were, in turn, influenced by Muslim insistence on providing charity for the wayfarer.

The letters of appeal I have examined, it must be reiterated, came mainly from supplicants for private charity, most of whom were "conjuncturally" poor, people who would not go on the public dole if they could help it. Their anxiety about possible neglect rose in proportion to their dependence on private philanthropy—hence their concerted attempts in the rhetoric of their letters to counter the presumed tendency of some to favor family or the local poor with their charity. We may assume that most people had their pleas answered and that many more received private charity without having to write special requests when they arrived in Fustat.

The Geniza documents, especially the alms-lists but also the plethora of letters of appeal, reveal that the problem of the foreign poor reached enormous proportions in eleventh–thirteenth century Egypt. This resulted from geographic mobility, local economic factors, man-made and natural forces, and the reputation of Fustat Jews for munificence. Whether they arrived as wayfarers, immigrants, captives, or refugees, foreigners sorely tried the pity of the resident population, for there were many deserving indigents closer to home and especially in the immediate and extended family. Though in theory the halakha privileged "the poor of your household" and "the poor of your city" over "the poor of another city," our Geniza data show that by and large the Jewish foreign poor, like the indigent ibn al-sabil in the surrounding Muslim society, found charitable relief among their coreligionists. Moreover, given the masses of needy foreigners in Egypt, the examination of the poor stipulated by the Talmud was kept simple, based on a system of personal vouching that the newcomers were deserving.

Notes

The following abbreviations are used throughout the notes:

BM = British Museum (now: British Library) Collection

BNUS = Bibliothèque Nationale et Universitaire de Strasbourg

Bodl. = Bodleian Library Collection, Oxford University

BT = Babylonian Talmud

CUL = Cambridge University Library Collection

ENA = Elkan Nathan Adler Collection, Jewish Theological Seminary of America, New York

GW = Richard Gottheil and William H. Worrell, *Fragments from the Cairo Genizah in the Freer Collection* (New York: Macmillan, 1927)

Mosseri = Jacques Mosseri Geniza Collection, Paris (photographic reproductions at Institute of Microfilmed Hebrew Manuscripts, Jewish and National University Library, Jerusalem)

PT = Palestinian Talmud

TS = Taylor Schechter Genizah Collection, Cambridge University Library, Cambridge, England

1. TS 12.13, lines 11–14. The letter is a kind of palimpsest and difficult to decipher because the text beneath shows through quite prominently. The expressions *fi l-ghurba* and *fi balad al-ghurba* are spelled with an *alif* at the end in place of *ta' marbuta*, as in other places in this letter and commonly in Judaeo-Arabic. In the first instance, I understand *ghurba* as "the state of being foreign (or a stranger)." This meaning is clear in GW 9r, margin, "may God the exalted bring you relief *fi ghurbatika*, in your state of being a foreigner" (the root of the word was misunderstood by the translators R. Gottheil and W. H. Worrell, *Fragments from the Cairo Genizah in the Freer Collection* [London: Macmillan, 1927], 55, and corrected by Joshua Blau, *Judaeo-Arabic Literature: Selected Texts* [Hebrew] [Jerusalem: Magnes Press, 1980], 273). Cf. also *ruhi fi l-shidda wal-ghurba wal-wuhda*, written to a father by a man away from his home; ENA 2808.17v, lines 2–3. Cf. also *fi balad gharib*, which S. D. Goitein translates as "in a town where I was a stranger" in *A Mediterranean Society*, 5 vols. (Berkeley: University of California Press, 1967–1988), 3:197 (TS 13 J 8.19) and 5:26 ("feeling as a stranger") and 511n. 77. Reflecting the sentiment of a foreigner, a wandering scholar writes to his kinsmen in his native Egypt: "In spite of my blindness and weakness, which afflicted me in this foreign place (or: this state of being a foreigner)" *(fi hadha al-ghurba)*, I have not perished, for my situation is very good, praised be God, who assures

me sustenance through his kindness"; see TS Arabic Box 53.37, lines 5–8, ed. S. D. Goitein, "The Jewish Communities of Saloniki and Thebes in Ancient Documents from the Cairo Geniza" (Hebrew), *Sefunot* 11 (1971–1977): 11–22. See also a letter from an India trader to a friend, expressing, among other things, his loneliness due to their separation, ENA 2560.193, line 14: *ana fi l-ghurba wa-diq al-sadr wal-wuhda* (I am a foreigner, anxious and alone) and again, verso, line 4, *min shiddat al-ghurba* (this letter was the centerpiece of a seminar paper by my student Judith Shapero, in the fall of 2000). My student Roxani Eleni Margariti, now at Emory University, suggested to me that the Arabic usage in the letter quoted above might parallel Greek *xeniteia*. The second instance in the letter is similar to the expression *f[i] balad al-ghurba* in TS 10 J 10.4, ed. Menahem Ben-Sasson, *Yehudei Sisiliya 825–1068: te'udot u-meqorot* (The Jews of Sicily 825–1068: Documents and Sources) (Jerusalem: Makhon Ben-Zvi, 1991), 22–24 (cf. Goitein, *A Mediterranean Society*, 1:314): "I remained *in a foreign country* without a dinar or dirhem." It is possible to read *ghuraba'* in the second instance above and hence as "in a city of foreigners," but the writer's meaning would not be changed.

2. Mark R. Cohen, *Jewish Self-Government in Medieval Egypt* (Princeton: Princeton University Press, 1980), esp. chap. 3.

3. I am engaged in a larger study of poverty and poor relief in the Jewish community of medieval Egypt during the "classical Geniza period" (eleventh–thirteenth centuries), to be published by Princeton University Press. For an introduction to the Geniza, see Stefan C. Reif, *A Jewish Archive in Old Cairo* (Richmond, U.K.: Curzon, 2000).

4. TS Box H 3.81r, left-hand page, lines 24–26: *afqarat al-aghniya' wa-adhallat al-aqwa' wa-hajjajat dhawi al-awtan min mawatinihim wa-balbalathum wa-shattatat shamlahum wa-ab'adathum 'an mawatinihim wa-nazar awladihim.* I am assuming that the word *hajjajat* is a dittographic mistake for *hajjarat.*

5. See Alexandra Cuffel, "Call and Response: European Jewish Emigration to Egypt and Palestine in the Middle Ages," *Jewish Quarterly Review* 90 (1999–2000): 61–102, esp. 65–77.

6. Examples are TS Box K 15.48; cf. Goitein, *A Mediterranean Society*, 2:444, App. B 25 (1100–1140), two lists of receivers of clothing (a few names recur in both), including from Syria–Palestine, the wife of 'Imran al-Tarabulsi (from Tripoli, Syria, or perhaps Tripoli in North Africa), the wife of Karim al-Tabarani (from Tiberias), Yahya al-Banyasi (from Banyas), the wife of al-Hayfi (from Hayfa), Yahya the in-law of al-'Akawi (from Acre); from Byzantium or elsewhere in Europe, R. Isaac al-Rumi; from the Egyptian countryside, the household (possibly "wife," *bayt*) of al-Maliji (from Malij), al-Malijiyya (the woman from Malij), the *parnas* from Damietta; from Iraq, the son of al-Baghdadi, and the daughter of al-Baghdadi; from North Africa, Khaluf al-Jerbi (from Jerba, Tunisia); from the Mediterranean islands, the parnas Iqritas (from Crete).

7. TS Arabic Box 52.247, cf. Goitein, *A Mediterranean Society*, 2:459, App. B 72 (1150–1190), a list of about sixty-eight persons receiving clothing, among them six designated as "foreigner," for instance, an orphan foreigner (m.) *(yatim gharib)*, a foreigner (f.) *(ghariba)* living in the inn, Ya'ish the foreigner (m.) *(gharib)*, and a proselyte foreigner (f.) *(ghariba giyyoret).* TS Box K 15.96, col. II, line 24: Joseph b. Khalaf the newcomer *(al-tari)*; cf. Goitein, *A Mediterranean Society*, 2:441, App. B 8.

8. Franz Rosenthal, "The Stranger in Islam," *Arabica* 44 (1997): 35–75.

9. Clifford E. Bosworth, *The Medieval Islamic Underworld: The Banu Sasan in Arabic Society and Literature* (Leiden: Brill, 1976), 1: 121; see also Adam Sabra, *Poverty and Charity in Medieval Islam: Mamluk Egypt, 1250–1517* (Cambridge: Cambridge University Press, 2000), 48–49.

10. TS 8 J 20.24, line 14.

11. This chapter will consider only the wayfarers and poor immigrants—two categories of people whose need had to be established before they were given assistance.

12. On aid to travelers see Goitein, *A Mediterranean Society*, 2:135–136. On the knotty issue of whether transient wayfarers received food from a daily "soup kitchen" (the talmudic *tamhui*) as distinct from the *quppa*, the weekly collections/distributions for resident poor, see, for the time being, Mark R. Cohen, "The Voice of the Jewish Poor in the Cairo Geniza," in *Semitic Papyrology in Context*, ed. Lawrence Schiffman (Leiden: Brill, 2003).

13. See the documents listed in Mark R. Cohen, "Four Judaeo-Arabic Petititions of the Poor from the Cairo Geniza," *Jerusalem Studies in Arabic and Islam* 24 (2000): 446–447n. 6, to which add, from Morocco: TS 12.192 (written and signed by Maimonides), ed. R. J. H. Gottheil, *M. Gaster Jubilee Volume* (London: n.p., 1936), 173ff, and reedited with facsimile by Simha Assaf, *Meqorot u-mehqarim* (Texts and Studies in Jewish History) (Jerusalem: Mosad Ha-Rav Kuk, 1946), 163ff, translated into English by Joel L. Kraemer, "Two Letters of Maimonides from the Cairo Genizah," *Maimonidean Studies*, ed. Arthur Hyman (New York: Yeshiva University Press, 1990), 1:87–92; Morocco and Sicily: TS 16.287, ed. Eliyahu Ashtor (Strauss), *Toledot ha-Yehudim be-Misrayim ve-Surya tahat shilton ha-mamlukim* (History of the Jews in Egypt and in Syria under the Mamluks) (Jerusalem: Mosad Ha-Rav Kuk, 1970), 3:101–103 (date should be corrected to 1208 as per Goitein, *A Mediterranean Society*, 2:136 and 548n. 59); Syria and Mesopotamia (Aleppo, Mosul): CUL Add. 3348 (refers to other letters, with signatures).

14. TS 8.143: a Jew in distress leaves his family in the provincial town of Bilbays and travels to the capital hoping to obtain assistance from the Nagid.

15. TS 16.253, a letter from a needy person addressed to the head of the Jews, the Nagid Mevorakh b. Saadya, requesting a letter the writer could use to appeal for charity throughout the Rif (the countryside). Actually, he requests two recommendations, the second from the notable Abu l-Mufaddal. Cf. Cohen, *Jewish Self-Government*, 261. The supplicant wants people to know that his rank *(darajati wa-manzilati)* has not diminished.

16. CUL Or 1080 J.34. Cf. Goitein, *A Mediterranean Society*, 2:136.

17. TS 8 J 17.13, which Goitein summarizes: "For a scholarly person on his way to Jerusalem the Fustat community was instructed to arrange a collection without delay so as to enable him to join a caravan which was about to leave" (*A Mediterranean Society*, 5:35). The halakha: Louis Finkelstein, ed., *Sifrei Deuteronomy*, Piska 116, 2nd printing (New York: Jewish Theological Society, 1969), 175; Reuven Hammer, trans., *Sifrei Deuteronomy* (New Haven: Yale University Press, 1986), 161. See also Cuffel, "Call and Response," 61–102.

18. TS 18 J 4.4, supralinear and sublinear addition at line 21, Alexander Scheiber, ed., *Geniza Studies* (Hildesheim: G. Olms, 1981), 79–81. Cf. M. R. Cohen, "Poverty as Reflected in the Genizah Documents," to be published in the Proceedings of the Seventh

International Conference of the Society for Judaeo-Arabic Studies held at the University of Strasbourg, July 2–5, 1995, ed. Paul Fenton.

19. CUL Or 1080 J 4.

20. See Moshe Gil, *Documents of the Jewish Pious Foundations from the Cairo Geniza* (Leiden: Brill, 1976), 116.

21. On the "incessant exodus from the Rif to the cities," see Goitein, *A Mediterranean Society*, 4:10.

22. TS Arabic Box 40.187.

23. Goitein, *A Mediterranean Society*, 1:56.

24. For Jewish society, however, the issue has been taken up only recently, for the Ashkenazic world in particular, in a pioneering article on Jewish poverty and charity by Elimelech (Elliott) Horowitz, "'(Deserving) Poor Shall be Members of Your Household': Charity, the Poor, and Social Control in the Jewish Communities of Europe between the Middle Ages and the Beginning of Modern Times" (Hebrew), in *Dat ve-kalkala: yahasei gomlin* (Religion and Economy: Connections and Interactions), ed. Menahem Ben-Sasson (Jerusalem: Merkaz Zalman Shazar, 1995), 209–231.

25. See also Jer. 7:5–6 and Zech. 7:9–10, rebuking those who oppress the stranger, the orphan, and the widow.

26. Declarations of the priority of family over strangers can be found in early Christian and early Islamic writings, as well. See Natalie Davis's conclusion in this volume.

27. BT Bava Mesi'a 71a. Cf. *Mekhilta de-R. Ishmael*, Mishpatim 19, 2nd ed., ed. Shaul Horovitz and Yisrael Abraham Rabin (Frankfurt am Main: J. Kaufmann, 1931), 315–316.

28. Finkelstein, *Sifrei Deuteronomy*, Piska 116, 174–175; Hammer, *Sifrei Deuteronomy*, 161. Cf. also S. Buber, ed., *Tanhuma Exodus*, Misphatim 8 (1913; reprint Jerusalem: Ortsel, 1964), 85

29. Mishneh Torah, Malveh ve-loveh 5:2; cf. 1:1.

30. Mishneh Torah, Mattenot 'aniyyim 7:13; English trans. Isaac Klein, *The Code of Maimonides*, Bk. 7 (New Haven: Yale University Press, 1979), 79.

31. The sixteenth-century commentators on the Mishneh Torah (printed in the margins) differed in their attempts at identifying Maimonides' source. Joseph Caro, in *Kesef mishna*, located it in the Talmudic passage just cited. R. David ibn Abi Zimra (Radbaz) turned to *Sifrei Deuteronomy*, Piska 116, but he also cites a more far-fetched source, namely, the comment of Saadya Gaon (tenth-century Baghdad) on Leviticus 25:36, which is based on Rabbi Akiva's view that one's own life takes priority over that of his companion (the parable of the two men in a desert with water enough to save only one of them). See *Sifra* to Leviticus 25:36: *hayyav adam le-haqdim parnasato shene'emar ve-hay ahikha 'immakh hayyekha qodmin le-hayyei ahikha.*

32. See Yonah Ben-Sasson, "The Doctrine of Charity in the Theoretical Teaching of Maimonides" (in Hebrew), in *Sefer ha-zikkaron le-Avraham Spiegelman,* ed. Aryeh Morgenstern (Tel Aviv: Moreshet, 1979), 102–105, 108–109.

33. Maimonides "introduces variations and makes substantive additions to the original formulations that give expression to his independent opinion or interpretations. On occasion he refers to contemporary matters and also suggests that a particular rule is actually still operative." See Aharon Nahalon, "Local Legislation and Independent Leadership

according to Maimonides," in *Maimonides as Codifier of Jewish Law*, ed. Nahum Rakover (Jerusalem: Library of Jewish Law, 1987), 171–172.

34. In *The Guide of the Perplexed* (pt. 3, chap. 42), discussing the laws of property and inheritance, Maimonides speaks associatively about the precedence to be given family in general: "[M]an ought to take care of his relatives and grant very strong preference to the bond of the womb. Even if his relative should do him an injustice and a wrong and should be extremely corrupt, he must nevertheless regard his kinsman with a protective eye. He, may He be exalted, says: 'Thou shalt not abhor an Edomite, for he is thy brother' (Deut. 23:8)." Next Maimonides mentions non-relatives ("foreigners"): "Similarly everyone of whom you have had need some day, everyone who was useful to you and whom you found in a time of stress, even if afterwards he treated you ill, ought necessarily to have merit attaching to him because of the past. He, may He be exalted, says: 'Thou shalt not abhor an Egyptian, because thou wast a stranger in his land' (ibid.). . . . The two last mentioned noble moral qualities do not belong to this seventh class (i.e., the class of laws concerning property). But speaking of the care to be taken of relatives in inheritance, we went on to mention the Egyptian and the Edomite" (trans. Shlomo Pines [Chicago: University of Chicago Press, 1953], 569–570). Professor Gideon Libson directed my attention to this passage.

35. BNUS 4038.9, ed. M. Cohen in the Proceedings of the Seventh International Conference of the Society of Judaeo-Arabic Studies, forthcoming. Also quoted, but loosely and in part only in TS 10 J 25.7, verso, lines 11–12: *'aniyyei beitkha qodem le-'aniyyei ha-'ir.*

36. TS 8.83, line 11.

37. TS 8 J 16.30. Cf. Goitein, *A Mediterranean Society*, 5:90, with partial translation.

38. Cohen, "Poverty as Reflected in the Genizah Documents."

39. With regard to England and the enforcement of settlement laws, see, for instance, Lynn Hollen Lees, *The Solidarities of Strangers: The English Poor Law and the People, 1700–1948* (Cambridge: Cambridge University Press, 1998), 49–51.

40. BT Bava Batra 9a. A similar debate appears in the Palestinian Talmud: "R. Ba Bar Zavda said that Rav and R. Yohanan differed, one saying that we examine before giving clothing, but we do not examine when life (i.e., nourishment) is at stake; the other said, even before giving clothing we do not examine, on account of the covenant with our Father Abraham (i.e., the mark of circumcision)." PT Pe'a 8:6, 21a.

41. This collection, whose contents are often cited by the Talmud, corresponds in structure to the Mishna and was codified perhaps slightly later (early third century of the Common Era).

42. Emphasis added. Tosefta Pe'a 4:8.

43. See Saul Lieberman, *Tosefta Kifshutah* Zera'im (New York: Hotza'at Makhon Rabinovitch al yad Bet ha-Midrash le Rabbanim, 1955), 1:183–184.

44. Emphasis added. Mishneh Torah, Mattenot 'aniyyim 7:6, trans. Klein, *The Code of Maimonides*, Bk. 7, 78. A passage based partly on the Tosefta and partly on the Mishna (Pe'a 8:7) occurs in the Code two sections further on (Mattenot 'aniyyim 7:8). The Mishnaic passage itself deals only with food and with "provisions for the night" but does not mention clothing explicitly. But Maimonides adds "*if he is known, he must be supplied according to his dignity*," a statement that echoes the sentence in the Tosefta regarding

examining the poor for clothing. That Maimonides means by this, clothing, is confirmed by his commentary on this Mishna, where he explains that provisions for the night refer to bedding (as in the Talmud, Bava batra 9a) and then adds: "If this poor person is known to us *[wa-in kana dhalika al-'ani ma'lum 'indana]*, he must be supplied with a wrap *[fa-yu'ta lahu ma yaghtu]*." *Commentary on the Mishna*, ed. Kafah (Jerusalem: Mosad ha-Rav Kuk, 1963), Zera'im, Pe'a 8:7, 128, where Kafah renders the final words *notenim lo kesut*. The printed editions of the Mishna containing Maimonides' commentary (Hebrew only) render imprecisely *notenim lo mah she-yehsar* (what he lacks).

45. Goitein, *A Mediterranean Society*, 2:438. We also find *qarib*, for example, in a fragment of a list of contributors, Musallam *qarib* al-[...], ENA NS 77.209, left-hand page, line 3.

46. I have rarely come across instances of an unknown person on a list of contributors. Obviously, the vast majority of the benefactors were known people, not newcomers. An exception, on a list of people contributing to a pledge drive *(pesiqa)*, are the anonymous "sons of the man" *(banu al-rajul)* who contributed five dirhems, obviously wayfarers, for the next entry is "their boon companion" *(rafiquhum)*, who pledged two. See ENA 4100.9c, line 12.

47. TS Misc. Box 8.9r, line 17 (together they received sixteen loaves, roughly double the highest allotment for a single person). Again in TS NS J.41v, line 1. A "*ma'rifa* of the family of Azhar" appears on a list of beneficiaries that bears some of the same names as lists from around the same time. TS AS 148.14 (a)v, left-hand page, line 3.

48. TS 12.192, line 4, Gottheil, *M. Gaster Jubilee Volume*, 173ff.; Assaf, *Meqorot u-mehqarim*, 163ff.; Kraemer, "Two Letters of Maimonides," 87–92.

49. TS NS 324.132, a list of recipients of clothing dated December 1176/January 1177, includes *ma'rifat Zayn al-khadim* (the beadle), recto, left-hand page, line 10 and *armalat Zayn al-khadim* (his widow), recto, right-hand page, line 9. Cf. Goitein, *A Mediterranean Society*, 2:459, App. B 71. Zayn's mother also appears on the list, recto, left-hand side, line 17.

50. I discovered these fragments while systematically examining a box of crumpled, unconserved fragments at the Jewish Theological Seminary (to which Solomon Schechter could, with justification, have applied the epithet ascribed to him: "rubbish").

51. The fragment is now preserved as ENA NS 77.291. Of the word "wife" only the last letter is present: *[imra'a]t Barakat, yukshaf 'anha*, verso, lines 1–2. On verso, lines 4–5: *[im]ra'at Shabbat, [yukshaf 'an]ha*.

52. ENA NS 77.242.

53. I discuss a sampling of letters of recommendation in my article, "Four Judaeo-Arabic Petitions from the Poor from the Cairo Geniza," *Jerusalem Studies in Arabic and Islam* 24 (2000): 446–471.

54. TS 16.287v, lines 2–3, Ashtor (Strauss), *Toledot*, 3:101 (between lines 27 and 28 there).

55. TS 12.303, margin, Cohen, "Four Judaeo-Arabic Petitions," 456–459.

56. Bodl. MS Heb. d 68.101, Ashtor (Strauss), *Toledot*, 3:10f; reedited Moshe Gil, *Documents of the Jewish Pious Foundations from the Cairo Geniza* (Leiden: Brill, 1976), 477–478 (no. 144). My reading, *'a'ilathu* (family burden), is different from Gil's, and my interpretation of *istihqaq* differs from his as well.

57. See Mine Ener's chapter (9) in this volume, and her "Prohibitions on Begging and Loitering in Nineteenth-Century Egypt, *Der Islam* 39 (1999): 331.

58. TS NS J 120, lines 14–15, *yaf'al ma'ahu ma huwa ahluhu kama jarat 'adatuhu al-jamila ma'a kol 'over va-shav*; cf. Goitein, *A Mediterranean Society*, 5:189. Composite narrative about Abraham's renowned hospitality in Louis Ginzberg, *The Legends of the Jews* (1910–1938; reprint, Philadelphia: Jewish Publication Society of America, 1968), 1:241–243.

59. Mosseri L 9 (IV, 4), line 17.

60. TS NS Box 31.7, S. D. Goitein, trans., *Tarbiz* 54 (1985): 81; TS NS J 258, ibid., 84; TS 6 J 6.21, ibid., 82; TS NS J 336; TS 8 J 13.23, summarized briefly in ibid., 84.

61. TS 13 J 20.27, verso, lines 7–9. For hurma as *famille d'un homme,* see Albert de-Biberstein-Kazimirski, *Dictionnaire Arabe-Français*, 1:415.

62. All of this is discussed in the important book by A. R. Hands, *Charities and Social Aid in Greece and Rome* (Ithaca: Cornell University Press, 1968).

63. A famous inscription from Jerusalem from the first century C.E. describes the donation by Theodotos son of Vettenos of a synagogue and states that the gift also included "a hostel *(xenona)* and rooms and water amenities for the shelter of foreigners *(xe[n]es)* in need." Baruch Lifshitz, *Donateurs et fondateurs dans les synagogues juives*, vol. 7 of *Cahiers de la Revue Biblique* (Paris: J. Gabalda et Cie., 1967), 70–71. Cf. Jean-Baptiste Frey, *Corpus Inscriptionum Judaicarum* (Vatican City: Pontifico instituto di archeologia cristiana, 1952), 1:332–334 (no. 1404), and recent discussion in Lee I. Levine, *The Ancient Synagogue: The First Thousand Years* (New Haven: Yale University Press, 2000), 54–56. Levine also summons the Talmudic evidence, which he accepts as adequate confirmation of use of the synagogue as a place of residence, for instance, a statement in BT Pesahim 100b–101a about "people who eat, drink, and sleep in the synagogue" on Sabbath and holidays (where the word *sleep* does not appear in many manuscripts), and other traditions where lodging in the synagogue is a possibility, though not stated explicitly (ibid., 381–382).

64. Gregory writes regarding the Jews of Palermo (October 598):

> Some time ago, we have written to Victor, our brother and co-bishop, that, whereas some Jews complained in a petition presented to us that synagogues situated in the city of Panormus (Palermo) were occupied by him without reason, together with their hostels *(cum hospitiis suis)*, he should abstain from consecrating them until the case could be adjudged. . . . [He is] obliged to pay the price estimated by our sons, the glorious patricius Venantius and Abbot Urbicus, of the synagogue themselves with the hostels that are within them or adjoined to their walls *(cum his hospitiis quas sub ipsis sunt vel earum parietibus cohaereunt).*

Amnon Linder, *The Jews in the Legal Sources of the Early Middle Ages* (Detroit: Wayne State University Press, 1997), 434–435.

65. Example: CUL 1080 J.31; cf. Goitein, *A Mediterranean Society*, 2:154.

66. See, most recently, Peter Brown, *Poverty and Leadership in the Later Roman Empire* (Hanover, N.H.: Dartmouth College Press, 2002), 33–35.

67. Demetrios J. Constantelos, *Byzantine Philanthropy and Social Welfare* (New Brunswick, N.J.: Rutgers University Press, 1968), 157, 186, 214; Timothy S. Miller, *The Birth of the Hospital in the Byzantine Empire* (Baltimore: Johns Hopkins University Press, 1985); J. H. Mundy, "Charity and Social Work in Toulouse, 1100–1250," *Traditio* 22 (1966): 252ff; Michel Mollat, *The Poor in the Middle Ages: An Essay in Social History*, trans. Arthur Goldhammer (New Haven: Yale University Press, 1986), 146–153. Olivia Remie Constable is writing a book on the *pandocheion* and its successor, the Arab *funduq*, and kindly allowed me to read some of her chapters-in-progress.

68. Franz Rosenthal, "Sedaka, Charity," *Hebrew Union College Annual* 23, pt. 1 (1950–1951): 419–423.

69. For example, Sura 9:60.

CHAPTER FOUR

"Prices Are in God's Hands"

The Theory and Practice of Price Control
in the Medieval Islamic World

ADAM SABRA

In his *Siyasatname*, the famous Seljuk wazir Nizam al-Mulk (d. A.H. 485/C.E. 1092) tells the following story:

> I heard that in the time of King Qubad there was famine in the world for seven years, and blessings [rain] ceased to come down from heaven. He ordered the tax-collectors to sell all the grain which they had, and even to give some of it away as charity. All over the kingdom the poor were assisted by gifts from the central treasury and [local] treasuries, with the result that not one person died of hunger in those seven years—all because the king chid his officers.[1]

Despite the mythic backdrop of this anecdote, it illustrates some important points about the expectation subjects could have of their ruler in the medieval Islamic world. The ancient Persian king, always a paragon of good government, provides an example of how the just ruler in the medieval Islamic world should relieve his subjects' suffering in times of famine. Still, the story is in some ways an ambivalent one. The king intervenes to provide food for his hungry subjects, but the grain he orders distributed has been collected from these very subjects, by the king's tax collectors, who must be chided by their lord. The medieval Muslim state had two faces: that of an overlord and that of a benefactor. The balance between the two could be easily disrupted, especially in hard times. A similar point is exemplified by the famous "Circle of Equity," a schematization of the classes of medieval Muslim society that was popular among medieval Muslim thinkers. On the one hand, the subjects (the flock) are the producers of wealth and thus the source of taxation for the state, while on the other hand, the ruler (the shepherd) has to tend to his flock carefully and rule over them with justice if he wants to guarantee that the commoners (especially the peasantry) will continue to produce. Thus justice, here interpreted as a combination of adherence to Islamic law *(shari'a)* and good state craft, is not only a moral and religious imperative, it is fundamental to the health of the society.

With these facts in mind, it should come as no surprise that famine policy is a major topic for medieval Muslim authors, especially for the jurists and the chroniclers. They exhibit particular interest in urban markets, especially those of capital cities such as Cairo, Baghdad, and Damascus, since food shortages there could be politically destabilizing. An examination of these accounts can be of significance in understanding the economic, political, and ideological bases of medieval Muslim states.

From a very early period, the second/eighth century at the latest, the urban market in foodstuffs attracted the attention of the jurists. As we shall see, their general bias was in favor of allowing the market to regulate itself, or, as they saw it, to leave the matter up to God, whom they considered the true source of the workings of the market. Nonetheless, the jurists did recognize the need for some government regulation of the market in foodstuffs since the harm that could result from shortages, whether natural or man-made, could affect the entire Muslim community. To this end, they developed two legal concepts: price fixing *(tas'ir)* and hoarding *(ihtikar)*. The first concept refers to the policy of state intervention to set prices, especially for certain key commodities during times of shortage. The second refers to the practice of withholding such commodities from the market to drive up the market price—a practice that was not considered illegitimate in itself, but which could have dangerous consequences under certain conditions. In each case, the jurists were careful to balance the right of the property owner to dispose of his property when, where, and at what price he wished, against the need of the Muslim community as a whole, to obtain affordable food.

In this chapter first, I will address the ways in which the legal scholars dealt with these problems. There was no consensus on whether the state had a right to interfere in the market, or on the conditions under which it could do so. I will examine the teachings of the various Sunni schools of law on this subject, beginning in the second/eighth century, and ending in the eighth/fourteenth century, during the period of the Mamluk Sultanate (C.E. 1250–1517) in Egypt, Syria, and the Hijaz. Then I will address the actual application of these principles by the Mamluk state in Egypt. By necessity, this second section will have a narrower scope in time and place. To discuss the policies of a number of Muslim states in different times and places would require a huge body of research and more space than is appropriate here. Still, Mamluk Egypt provides a good test case for examining the policies of medieval Muslim states toward food policy and markets. The period is well represented by numerous contemporary chronicles, and famine policy constituted an important topic in the chroniclers' narratives of state policies.

The Jurists

In his celebrated essay, "The Moral Economy of the English Crowd in the Eighteenth Century," E. P. Thompson identifies at least three different models of the economy of foodstuffs that informed the behavior of eighteenth-century Englishmen.[2] The first of these discourses is the paternalist model, promoted by the gentry, which holds that farmers should sell directly to consumers, that foodstuffs should not be withheld in expectation of rising prices, and that consumers should be protected from dishonest middlemen. Thus, the gentry, while defending their property rights, put forward an economic model that emphasized direct relations between producers and consumers and promoted "fair dealings" between the two. As the century progressed, this model began to give way to the new political economy, which "demoralized" economic relations, replacing the older view that the market was a relation between people with moral claims on one another with a naturalistic model of a self-adjusting economy (193–194, 200–203). The discovery of political economy, with its doctrine of laissez-faire, gradually pushed out the older paternalist model in the minds of the upper classes. Thompson then identifies a third model, the moral economy of the crowd. This moral economy drew on the paternalist model, the favorite of the gentleman class, but adapted that model to suit plebeian interests. According to the plebeians, wheat should be consumed locally, rather than exported in times of dearth, consumers should be protected from cheats; and, when necessary, the people had a right to set prices at just levels by force. According to Thompson, "There is a deeply felt conviction that prices ought, in times of dearth, to be regulated, and that the profiteer put himself outside of society" (229).

Although there are many differences between the society of eighteenth-century England described by Thompson and that of medieval Egypt, a comparison between the two is suggestive. Even though political economy as a discipline was unknown to medieval Muslim thinkers, one can readily identify both paternalist and anti-paternalist arguments about the economy in the writings of the Muslim jurists. Paternalist arguments emphasize the special nature of the trade in grain since grain is the means of subsistence for the majority of the population. The government is expected to intervene if food becomes too expensive, and hoarding is severely condemned. On the other hand, there is a strong anti-paternalist trend. The majority of jurists were opposed to the state setting prices, and they certainly never considered conceding that power to the common people, although, as we will see in the second section, the commoners acted in their own interests. Islamic law fiercely protected property rights and regarded any attempt by the state to restrict or interfere with the right of an individual to dispose of his property as manifest injustice. Although these rights were not always observed in practice in Islamic societies, the jurists never ceased to assert the freedom of the individual (i.e., the free, adult Muslim male) to dispose of his property as he wished, within the limits established by Islamic law. Any attack on the property rights of the individual, as stipulated in the shariʿa, was thus also an attack on God's law. We must keep in mind the theological and legal elements in medieval Muslim ideologies of property and the market when we consider medieval Muslims' responses to social dilemmas.

Of the four Sunni schools of law, it was the Malikis that were the most consistent in their support for government intervention in the market. Indeed, members of other schools who later wished to adopt a pro-interventionist position often relied on the Maliki tradition for proof texts and arguments. The subjects of price-fixing and hoarding first appear in the *Muwatta'* of Malik b. Anas (d.179/796). He cites statements made by the Caliphs ʿUmar b. al-Khattab and ʿUthman b. ʿAffan prohibiting hoarding. ʿUmar said:

> There is no hoarding in our market, and men who have excess gold in their hands should not buy up one of Allah's provisions which he has sent to our courtyard and then hoard it up against us. Someone who brings imported goods through great fatigue to himself in the summer and winter, such a person is the guest of ʿUmar. Let him sell what Allah wills and keep what Allah wills.[3]

Here, ʿUmar is portrayed as the master of the market. He forbids hoarding but makes allowances for importers who have gone to additional effort and expense to make goods available in Medina. In the latter case, the workings of the market are the result of God's will. A second report also shows ʿUmar interfering in the workings of the market, this time to raise prices. He orders Hatib b. Abi Bathaʿa to raise the price of the raisins he is selling, or else "you will be removed from our market."[4] Again, the caliph demonstrates his control of the market, here to prevent an individual from monopolizing the sale of a particular item by underselling. Interestingly enough, it is this very report that is cited by many Maliki authorities to justify government intervention to lower prices during food shortages. Apparently, the salient point was the right of the ruler to fix prices, at whatever level, in the public interest. Finally, Malik cites a prohibition on hoarding by the Caliph ʿUthman.[5] Overall, the picture we get of Malik's Medina is one of a market that is subject to caliphal control, where hoarding is forbidden, and where monopoly is strongly discouraged.

In his commentary on the *Muwatta'*, Abu l-Walid al-Baji (d. 474/1081) differentiates between hoarding (ihtikar) and accumulation *(iddikhar)*. Hoarding is "accumulating in order to sell and seek profit from changes in the market," but, surprisingly, it does not include the accumulation of food, and, therefore, is not illicit.[6] He cites Malik as saying that there is no prohibition on hoarding food in hopes of a dearth *(ghala')*, since everyone who purchases food hopes to profit from such events (5:15–16). We will see that he modifies this view later in his discussion, taking into account the circumstances under which the hoarding of food takes place. As for a person who buys more food than he needs for his own consumption during a period of dearth, if the purchaser is a local, then there is no prohibition on such a sale. If the purchaser is not a local, then, al-Baji reasons that he must be purchasing from an area where food is more plentiful to sell where it is less plentiful. Here he shows an urban bias, citing an epistle of Ibn al-Mawwaz (d. 269/882) (who claims to cite Malik), prohibiting sales from the city *(misr, fustat)* to the country *(rif)*, if this will do harm to the city folk and there is sufficient food available in the country (5:16).

Such sales are not prohibited when food is plentiful in urban areas, but when food is scarce in both places, the country folk may only consume food purchased in the city within the city itself. They are prohibited from removing the food to the countryside for consumption. Villagers may consume from urban supplies "because it is not permissible to surrender them to harm and destruction, but they are to be prevented from weakening the city by removing [food] from it." If one region must suffer, "it is more important to guarantee the preservation of the city" (ibid.). This urban bias appears to originate in the early Islamic conquests, when the Muslim population was predominantly urban and while the subject population was largely rural, and is justified by the theory that food which is stored in cities will be used to feed the surrounding rural areas as well. As Malik is quoted as saying, the city is "the pillar of Islam." If the city is ruined, so will the countryside be ruined; the reverse is not true, in Malik's view. Al-Baji cites one statement in which Malik, cited by Ibn Habib (d. 238/853) from al-Mutarrif b. 'Abd Allah (d. 220/835) and Ibn Majishun (d. 212/827), appears to ban the hoarding of food under any circumstances. Another citation, reported by Ibn al-Qasim (d. 191/806), allows it when there is no "dire need" *(darura)* for the food. According to al-Baji, such a prohibition, if applied under all circumstances, would have to include such substances as oils, honey, butter, and so on, in addition to grains (5:16). He backs up this opinion by quoting a statement by Malik that it is illicit to hoard anything in such a way as to do harm to people and their "interests" *(masalih)*. Clearly al-Baji sympathizes with those who hold that food cannot be hoarded when there is an overwhelming public need for it. He quotes Malik's opinion that during a dearth the Imam may order persons who possess stockpiles of grain to bring their grain to market (5:17). He even quotes some authorities as saying that a person who wishes to repent of having hoarded goods must sell them on the market without receiving a profit.

Finally, al-Baji comes to the topic of price-fixing. He notes that although Malik cites 'Umar as having demanded that Hatib raise his prices, most of the scholars of the school did not think that a small group of sellers could be forced to lower their prices to the level charged by the majority. Al-Baji himself is unsatisfied by this opinion and indicates that the markets should be examined more closely (ibid.). He then mentions the exemptions granted to importers, who may be allowed to sell at a different price, and in a private home, unlike locals who are expected to sell at the market price and in public (5:18). Citing Ibn Habib, he further notes that price-fixing can only be applied to commodities sold by weight or measure, since commodities of differing value *(qima)* cannot be sold at the same price. One cannot expect sellers of fine quality goods to sell at a price set for inferior products. In general, al-Baji notes that it is not permissible to force sellers to accept a specific price for their goods. Here he quotes a report *(hadith)* from the Prophet, which is commonly cited by opponents of price-fixing: "A man came to the Messenger of God, may peace be upon him, and said, 'Fix a price for us, Messenger of God.' He said, 'Rather I will ask for God's aid.' Then a man came to him and said, 'Fix a price for us, Messenger of God.' He said, 'Rather it is God who raises and lowers. I hope to meet God without anyone having a claim against me.'" The import of this hadith is clear: God controls the market; the believer can only pray for relief from distress. Nonetheless, al-Baji notes the opinion of Malik, repeated by Ashhab b. 'Abd al-'Aziz (d. 204/819), that the ruler of the market *(sahib al-suq*, this term is sometimes used for the market inspector) can fix the price of meat. Al-Baji reconciles the opposing opinions by saying that the hadith applies to most circumstances, whereas Ashhab's report indicates that the Imam may set a maximum price in times of dearth, "in the interests of the common people" *(fi masalih al-'amma)*. The Imam may not force the sellers to sell their goods if they choose not to sell at all, and he must set a price that will allow them to make some profit (5:18).

If one accepts Ashhab's report, al-Baji writes, one must then examine the appropriate mechanics of setting the price. The Imam must gather all of the prominent sellers *(wujuh ahl suq dhalika al-shay')* and inquire about their current prices and costs. He should then convince them to accept voluntarily *('an rida)* a price that allows them some profit and is affordable to the commoners. Thus, the interests of both parties (buyers and sellers) will be protected (5:19). One may summarize al-Baji's view by saying that he attempts to find a middle way. He sees a need to balance the needs of all parties and recognizes that the merchants have interests that must be balanced with the needs of the public. Property generates certain interests that the state is bound to protect, but these interests must be balanced against the need of the general population for certain commodities, especially food, that are necessary for human survival. The key criterion is dire necessity, which obligates the state to balance the otherwise sacrosanct rights of property against the needs of the community.

The Shafi'i school took a dimmer view of price-fixing than did the Malikis. Abu Ibrahim al-Muzani (d. 264/878) relates from al-Shafi'i (d. 204/820) the report concerning Hatib and his underpriced raisins, but with additional information. In his version, 'Umar orders Hatib either to raise his prices in expectation of the arrival of a caravan from Ta'if or else to sell privately from his home.[7]

Later on, 'Umar thinks better of it and tells Hatib that he was merely giving his opinion as to what is best for the people of the town, leaving him to sell as he wishes. Here, al-Shafi'i criticizes Malik, saying that he did not narrate the entire hadith as it was narrated by the hadith scholars. He then adds that people are in full control of their property *(musallatuna 'ala amwalihim)*, and no one may interfere with their right to dispose of it without their agreement, except in certain circumstances. By the latter, he presumably means the power of a judge to seize a person's property to pay a debt, provide compensation, and so forth. Thus al-Shafi'i directly responds to the Maliki use of this anecdote to justify state supervision of the market. 'Umar realized the impropriety of his decision, and Malik should have done the same.

According to the great Shafi'i jurist and political theorist al-Mawardi (d. 450/1058), people have complete control over their property; neither the Imam nor anyone else has the right to interfere (ibid.). Anxious to discredit supporters of price-fixing, he quotes a number of supposed proof texts justifying price-fixing. Many of them are totally unfamiliar from the Maliki literature. One statement claims that 'Ali b. Abi Talib burned the goods of those who rejected his prices. We will see later that this hadith was cited by members of al-Mawardi's own school who had Sufi inclinations

In any case, al-Mawardi concludes that price-fixing is forbidden because it denies people control over their property without any cause. He points out that the Imam is obliged to examine everyone's interests, not just those of the buyers. The seller will prefer high prices, while the buyer will prefer low prices (7:81). He does agree that hoarding is forbidden but sees no connection between that and price-fixing. He even argues that price-fixing will have the opposite effect from what is intended. A potential importer will hear that prices have been fixed at a low level and decide not to bring his goods to market, thus decreasing supply and further raising prices. A period of dearth will encourage importers to bring their goods to market, thereby increasing supply and lowering prices (ibid.). Thus al-Mawardi goes beyond the usual juridical defense of property to argue that the market is the best guarantee of affordable food. A free market is in the best interest of the community, not just of the property owners.

Abu Hamid al-Ghazzali (d. 505/1111), on the other hand, is extremely hostile to hoarding food—a practice he sees as corrosive of the Muslim community. He quotes a number of reports in support of his position, including the one about 'Ali that is attacked by al-Mawardi. Another such hadith says that whoever accumulates more than forty days' supply has nothing to do with God, and God has nothing to do with him.[8] Hoarding is an injustice, and one who hoards is subject to the threat of divine retribution in the afterlife. Al-Ghazzali clearly regards hoarding food as forbidden, and notes that some scholars (i.e., some Malikis as we have seen) extend that prohibition to honey, cheese, oil, and so on. Clearly, hoarding foodstuffs is forbidden in times of dearth, but it is also reprehensible in times of plenty because the purchaser is counting on a later crisis to raise prices and provide him with a profit. One is simply profiting from others' misery. Profiting from selling food is like profiting from selling shrouds; in each case one hopes that others will experience misfortune. Al-Ghazzali's attack on hoarding is motivated more by moral concerns than legal proofs. He perceives hoarding as a threat to the Muslim community and thus attacks it on principle. Al-Ghazzali's argument seems rather simplistic. He takes no account of the possibility that one might buy grain where there is a surplus and sell where there is a dearth, hence profiting while performing a socially useful act. His notion of community is purely local and based on ethical considerations that would make sense in a local setting where face-to-face relations among individuals are the norm. It is not clear how major cities would have fed themselves without the grain trade that al-Ghazzali finds so morally repugnant.

The Hanafi sources deal extensively with the problem of habitual hoarders. How, for example, does one deal with someone who has been instructed by the judge to sell his surpluses but who continues to hoard foodstuffs? The second time, the judge should lecture and threaten him; but the third time he can jail him and subject him to discretionary punishment *(ta'zir)*.[9] A number of Hanafi legal works allowed the Imam to sell a hoarder's stocks without his permission, if people's lives were threatened by lack of food. Tatarkhan (d. after 752/1351) even abolishes the privileges possessed by importers under such circumstances. They too may be forced to sell their goods (ibid.). Al-Marghinani (d. 593/1197) concludes his discussion of hoarding in a manner reminiscent of al-Ghazzali by noting, "the upshot is that commerce in food is not praiseworthy."[10] This latter view did not meet with the acceptance of later Hanafis, who defended the trade so long as it did not involve hoarding in times of dearth.

Perhaps the most important Hanafi contribution to the discussion of price control is their treatment of price-fixing as a form of *hajr*. Hajr refers to the right of a judge to sequester a person's property if he or she is legally incompetent. Thus, judges could take control of and manage the property of orphans, the insane, spendthrifts, and so forth. A judge could also use this measure to force a debtor to sell some of his property to repay his creditors. This measure is interpreted by al-Marghinani, and by some other Hanafi jurists, as justifying the forced sale of a hoarder's grain to address a public need.[11] Similarly, price-fixing, although normally forbidden, becomes tolerable when necessary to "protect the rights of the Muslims." This ruling violated the position of Abu Hanifa, who rejected the use of hajr against a free, adult male, although later Hanafis clearly rejected the founder's view.

Al-Marghinani also distinguishes between legitimate profit and "criminal excess" *(ta'addin fahish)*. The latter is defined as "exceeding the value *(qima)*" of the commodity being sold. This distinction between value and price is important because it gives some theoretical coherence to the concept of just price, that is, that a commodity's price should not deviate greatly from its value. In Islamic legal discourse, value denotes a given quantity of a commodity of a certain quality, while prices are determined by the market. Thus, to exchange a product for something of equivalent value means to exchange it for something of a similar quality, which may or may not sell for the same price. Al-Marghinani does not define these terms, but there is some evidence from later works that value is also connected to the rate of profit. Akmal al-Din al-Babarti (d. 786/1384) and Jalal al-Din al-Kurlani (eighth/fourteenth century) give an example of criminal excess in a merchant who buys a *qafiz* (measure of capacity) of a certain product for fifty (of what currency he does not say) and sells for one hundred.[12] A 100 percent profit is clearly unacceptable to al-Babarti and al-Kurlani, but they do not state what a more reasonable profit margin would be. Al-Zayla'i (d. 743/1342) notes that the price of bread (unlike that of meat) is usually well-known *(yazharu)* in a given town.[13] This means that a seller is obliged to turn over a certain quantity of bread, in accordance with custom *(bi-i'tibar al-'ada)*, for the price. Again, the moral economy of the medieval Muslim jurists treats bread, as a subsistence product, differently from a luxury commodity like meat. Custom here does not mean tradition, but rather is synonymous with "convention" *(istilah)*, that is, the common practice of a given locale. Al-Zayla'i is not arguing for a fixed price; he is trying to prevent sellers from cheating buyers by violating a consensus of sellers and buyers as to how much bread the buyer should receive for the price paid. If, for example, a buyer asks for a dirham's worth of bread, he should be certain as to how much bread he will receive for his coin. In medieval Cairo, for example, the standard weight for a loaf of bread was one pound *(ratl)*. Selling underweight loaves was tantamount to cheating the customer. Furthermore, al-Zayla'i does not see forced distributions of grain as a form of hajr; rather, he says, in time of famine this measure is justified by preventing harm to the community.[14] He merely requires that, once the dearth is over, the grain owners be compensated with an equivalent amount of grain to what was seized from them. Here, value seems to win out over price in the moral economy. As long as the grain owners receive an equal quantity of grain as compensation for what they lose, the fact that the price of their goods has dropped is of no concern.

In the case of the Hanbali school, the shift from hostility to government intervention to acceptance of it is even more noticeable, at least in the cases of certain jurists. Ibn Qudama (d. 620/1223), perhaps the greatest representative of the school, strictly forbids price-fixing. He quotes the statement of the Prophet that he does not wish to meet God with a claim against him and echoes al-Mawardi's argument that trying to control prices artificially can cause a dearth if importers are discouraged from selling.[15] Ibn Qudama makes no allowances for emergencies or exceptional cases.

Ibn Qudama is equally opposed to hoarding, citing the usual proof texts. Nonetheless, he narrows the definition of hoarding to "purchasing food in such a way as to cause scarcity to people in a town in which there is a scarcity (2:42)." In another text, he argues that for there to be hoarding of the type that is prohibited, three characteristics must be present: no importation must take place, the good must be a basic foodstuff *(qut)*, by which he seems to mean grain, and a scarcity must result.[16] Here again, he tries to restrict the significance of scarcity. He quotes Ahmad b. Hanbal as saying that such cases are restricted to the shrine cities and frontier towns *(thughur)*, presumably because those towns are dependent on imports for their grain supplies. Thus, he reasons, hoarding is not prohibited in a major city like Baghdad, Basra, or Cairo because such hoarding has no effect on the market on most occasions (5:314). When a town does experience a scarcity, however, the wealthy *(dhawu al-amwal)* are not permitted to meet caravans importing food and buy up their stocks. This practice, he admits, will cause further scarcity for people. The overall thrust of Ibn Qudama's arguments is quite unambiguous: As long as the market remains a public institution, the state should stay out of it and allow buyers and sellers to act as they please.

Later Hanbali activists were not as hostile to state intervention in the market. Ibn Taymiyya and his student Ibn Qayyim al-Jawziyya have very different views from the traditional attitudes of their school. Ibn Taymiyya (d. 728/1328) advocates state involvement in many aspects of public life, with the express purpose of subordinating social interaction to the *shari'a* (sacred law). He thus advocates a *siyasa shar'iyya* (a public policy rooted in the divine law) to govern the society of Mamluk Egypt and Syria. We will see that this idea is based on the increased involvement of the religious scholars in affairs of state, thus reducing their hostility to the state's taking an active role in policing areas of public life that are governed by the law.

Ibn Taymiyya discusses hoarding and price-fixing in his work on *hisba*. This duty included supervision of markets and the maintenance of public morals. Not only did the market inspector *(muhtasib)* keep track of fluctuations in the price of grain, he also punished merchants who sold substandard goods, diluted goods sold by weight or volume, altered scales, or otherwise cheated the public. The muhtasib was frequently a religious scholar, although he could also be a military officer. He was directly responsible to the sultan and was the ruler's eyes and ears in the public markets, baths, and streets. As such, he was usually the first government official to be aware of market fluctuations and the person to whom the merchants and common people turned to ask for action to be taken to prevent hoarding or to fix prices. His role expanded from the twelfth century on, and muhtasibs were important figures in the cities of Egypt and Syria in the fourteenth century.

Ibn Taymiyya begins with a clear denunciation of hoarding of food. Persons who hoard food to cause a dearth should be forced to sell their stocks at a fair value *(qimat al-mithl)*, if people have an overwhelming need for food, such as during a famine.[17] Buyers are not obliged to pay more than the proper price *(si'r)* for such an item. When a price rise results from a diminished supply or increased demand, it indicates that the price has been determined by God, and it is not permissible to tamper with it. If, however, the price rise results from a refusal to sell, one may force hoarders to sell at the equivalent value. This is legitimate price-fixing; indeed, such action is an obligation *(wajib)*. Similarly, it is not permissible to limit buyers to a few persons who are known to the sellers, hence allowing them to profit from being exclusive brokers for items needed by the public. The market must be a public institution, not a private arrangement.

Ibn Taymiyya next addresses the debate on price-fixing. He cites the differences of opinion between Malik and al-Shafi'i, and then follows that up with extensive quotations of al-Baji's discussion of the topic. Even though he does not adopt the position that the ruler or his representative can fix a price arbitrarily, he argues that sellers may be forced to accept the fair value for goods needed by the public, specifically food and clothes. Under those circumstances, the interests of the Muslim community are general, and outweigh the interests of the sellers (27:60). He then quotes the Hanafi discussion of how a judge should treat a habitual hoarder, including the policy of selling the hoarder's goods without his permission. He is careful to note that this practice is not price-fixing because the hadith that forbids price-fixing does not mention that the potential sellers refused to sell their goods. In short, Ibn Taymiyya refuses to permit arbitrary price-fixing because it violates the rights of the seller. Nonetheless, he quotes contrary opinions, especially on the part of the Malikis, and is clearly opposed to any form of hoarding. Because he allows the involuntary sale of a hoarder's goods that are needed by the public, he does give leeway to the state to interfere.

Ibn Qayyim al-Jawziyya (d. 751/1350) expresses similar views. He repeats Ibn Taymiyya's comments that persons who refuse to sell their goods can be forced to do so for the equivalent value, adding, "Here, price-fixing is enforcing the justice commanded by God."[18] He argues that the official in charge of the market (i.e., the muhtasib) must keep close track of the transactions being performed there. He should allow the merchants to make a uniform level of profit but not allow them to increase their prices to increase that profit (262). He attributes this opinion to the Malikis and seems sympathetic to it, although he adds that the merchants must be allowed to make some profit and not forced to sell at a loss (263). He concludes by noting that if a pilgrim needs goods for his journey, the ruler may force those who possess those goods to sell them at the fair price *(thaman al-mithl)*, denying them any increase in price they might be seeking (268). From this passage it appears that "fairness" is associated with the customary price for a commodity, as distinct from its price in times of short supply or increased demand.

With these two thinkers, we reach the period of the Mamluk Sultanate. I now shift from the theories of the jurists to the practices of the Mamluk sultans.

Public Policy in Mamluk Cairo

Centralized control over the market in grain has a long history in Egypt owing to its unique ecology. The narrow strip of agricultural land in the Nile Valley was not only more easily controlled than most agricultural hinterlands in the medieval world, but it was also more closely tied into the urban markets. In particular, Cairo, by far Egypt's greatest population center, was totally dependent on imports of agricultural goods, especially from Upper Egypt. Although medieval Islamic governments never replicated the distribution system of the pharaohs, they did intervene in the urban grain market, dating at least as far back as the Fatimid period. In 414/1023, for example, the caliph ordered his muhtasib to sell grain from his stores at a fixed price and prevent other sellers from charging more.[19] By the Mamluk period, the muhtasib was well established as the official responsible for enforcing the sultan's policies in the market, including price-fixing and preventing hoarding, when the state pursued these policies. In fact, he was in a difficult situation because the amirs who possessed much of the country's grain stores were much more powerful than he. Without the intervention of the sultan, the market inspector was likely to face the refusal of the amirs to cooperate on the one hand, and the anger of hungry crowds demanding affordable bread on the other hand.[20]

Even though the policy of price-fixing answered a public demand that measures be taken in times of shortage, such policies were difficult to enforce, raising the question of why they were employed at all. As we will see, price-fixing was usually just the first step in state intervention in the food market. Given the significance of Cairo as a population center, a vast market, and the political capital, it is not surprising that most of the chroniclers' interest in price-fixing and in economic catastrophes is focused on that city. Like eighteenth-century Paris, Cairo benefited from the desire of the urban-based elite to preserve social peace in the capital.[21] As in Paris, this privilege could cause tension between the capital and the provinces, whose surplus was constantly being drained off for the benefit of the urban market.[22] We are not well informed as to rural conditions in medieval Egypt, but the fact that the state frequently had to send officials to buy up grain from recalcitrant sellers in the countryside shows the "Cairo-first" policy must have been resented in some quarters.

Still, the Mamluk sultans were not irrational in putting the metropolis at the top of their priorities. Not only was this policy politically expedient, it also resulted from an accurate perception that food supply was a major problem in the capital. Egypt had produced agricultural surpluses since antiquity. It had been Rome's granary, then Constantinople's. Under the Ottomans, it would later help to provision Istanbul. Foreign merchants are frequently mentioned as buying Egyptian grain, and Egypt sometimes imported grain from Syria or Sicily. The problem, therefore, was not usually one of an absolute shortage, of an absence of sufficient food to feed the Egyptian population; rather, it was the dependence of a large population on the market economy. The market for foodstuffs was huge, and many amirs, merchants, and even the sultans themselves took advantage of the situation to speculate in grain.[23] During the summer, the Nile rise, the indicator of the size of the prospective harvest, was announced daily or even more frequently. The grain owners watched the market carefully and adjusted their prices, not only in light of present demand but also in expectation of the size of the next year's crop. As a result, prices rose as the period of flooding approached each year, especially if the Nile rise was tardy, only to drop precipitously with the arrival of the "new" grain. These rises and falls in the prices of basic foodstuffs could be frightening, and even disastrous, for much of the urban population, even when no absolute shortfall occurred. As Amartya Sen has suggested, the problem is not so much one of shortage as of entitlement.[24]

In general, the urban elite of Cairo was sheltered from such difficulties. The amirs and sultans had their storehouses, and the state officials received part of their salaries in kind from the treasury. Peasants had a more ambivalent relationship with the fluctuations in price. Landless peasants might face starvation conditions, especially if they were paid in currency to work others' lands. Landed peasants, however, might well profit from the high prices, provided the shortfall was not so great as to deprive them of their crops. It was the urban artisans, religious scholars, and poor who were the worst affected. They had no direct access to foodstuffs and were dependent on their wages to purchase food. A declining exchange entitlement, or worse yet, a complete failure of that entitlement, would leave them in a desperate situation.

It was in this type of circumstances that the jurists envisioned some type of state intervention. There were no local gentry to whom one could appeal; so the sultan was the authority of last resort. Furthermore, as we have seen with Nizam al-Mulk, Islamic political theory placed the responsibility for addressing these situations squarely on the shoulders of the ruler.

The best way to demonstrate these points is to examine the policies of the Mamluk sultans during the crises that afflicted Egypt during their reign. I will not discuss each crisis in detail, since we are principally concerned here with the state's policies.[25] These policies were in place from the very beginning of the Mamluk period.

The first challenge to the Mamluk urban market occurred in Rabi' II 662/February 1264 when the price of grain temporarily went up. Sultan Baybars ordered the price of grain to be fixed.[26] Within a few days, as prices continued to rise and bread disappeared from the market, he realized that his policies were not working and he abolished the measure.[27] He then ordered his chamberlains to take down the names of the poor and divided responsibility for feeding them between the military elite and other wealthy members of society. Thus, price-fixing was the sultan's first response to the crisis. When it did not work, he took more direct action and organized the society's elites to provide for the poor for the length of the dearth, at least three months. According to the sultan's most significant biographer, Baybars's conduct in this crisis became the standard against which all future sultans were compared.

Sometimes such measures were totally insufficient. In the crisis of 694/1295, the rulers were unable to stem the growth of mortality because hunger was accompanied by disease. No attempt was made to fix prices, but the poor were distributed among the wealthy of Cairo and Alexandria, who were expected to feed them.[28] This policy temporarily eliminated hunger, but there was nothing to be done to stop the spread of disease.[29] In the long run, the state's reserves were insufficient to put an end to the famine, and eventually, in 695/1296, there was sufficient agricultural production to bring the problem to an end. Here we can see that not only was price-fixing inadequate, even the state was powerless to stop a long-term shortage from having a disastrous effect on the market.

In another case, in 736/1336, the governor of Cairo did intervene to try to lower prices. Faced with unruly crowds gathering around the bakeries, he had some of the millers and bread sellers beaten to convince them to sell their wares more cheaply.[30] Unfortunately, the amirs, who held some of the biggest grain stocks, hoarded their supplies in hopes of reaping higher profits. When Sultan al-Nasir Muhammad set the price of grain (presumably wheat) at thirty dirhams per *irdabb* (measure of capacity for grain), the amirs closed their storehouses to the public and sold secretly to brokers at twice that price, even though the sultan threatened violators with having their property looted.[31] The sultan then appointed a new market inspector, who kept close records of the amirs' warehouses to make sure they were complying with the sultan's instructions. When a prominent amir, Qusun, tried to evade these measures, he was forced to back down.[32] A few hoarders were even attacked by the people of the market and the poor *(harafish).*[33]

This appears to have been a rare case in which price-fixing actually worked. The success of the policy can be attributed to al-Nasir Muhammad's firmness in forcing the grain suppliers to adhere to his instructions. Such control over the market was rare because it required a powerful sultan who was willing to threaten violence to accomplish his goals. Indeed, even though the legal literature clearly provides a basis for forcing hoarders to sell their stocks in times of need, the use of threats of looting goes well beyond the usual legal discourse on the evils of hoarding food. The threat of loss of one's property was the only measure that would be effective against avaricious grain dealers and amirs. Furthermore, the sultan himself sold his own grain supplies at twenty-five dirhams per *irdabb*, hence underselling the price he himself had fixed.[34] As a major grain seller himself, the sultan had the ability to manipulate the market by his own sales.

Usually the political will necessary to enforce fixed prices did not exist. During a crisis in Jumada I 776/October 1374, for example, the market inspector tried to fix the price of bread, with disastrous results. It disappeared from the markets and prices had to be allowed to rise.[35] Eventually, the amirs were forced to divide the poor among themselves to guarantee that free food would be available. In another crisis, this one in 796–798/1394–1396, the muhtasib once again found himself in the midst of a debate on market policy. Petitions were lodged against Baha' al-Din al-Burji, and the sultan's deputy Sudun ordered the warehouses of Cairo to open and sell at "God's price."[36] Unfortunately, a number of officials, possibly including the sultan himself, were artificially keeping prices up through forced sales *(rimaya)* at high prices. The market inspector resigned in protest but was reappointed by the sultan.[37] Eventually, Sultan Barquq organized the feeding of the poor, which relieved the public's distress.

The limits of state control over the market can also be seen from the events of 819/1415–1416. High prices led to hoarding of grain and widespread looting and rioting in the capital.[38] The market inspector, the Amir al-Taj, banned grain sales to anyone but millers to prevent speculation, and limited the size of sales to one irdabb.[39] This policy led to a sellers' strike, and grain had to be sought outside the city. Eventually, the sultan succeeded in importing grain from Upper Egypt, and this relieved the shortage of bread. Here again, we can see that policies that were intended to prevent speculation only caused food to disappear from the market. It took the importation of grain to lower prices and coax hoarders into selling their stocks.

Furthermore, in some cases, not even the market inspector could escape the temptation to profit from a dearth. In Rabi' II 853/May–June 1449, Sultan al-Zahir Jaqmaq banished an amir for hoarding and eventually had to replace the market inspector for the same reason.[40] Although the sultan tried a variety of measures, such as selling from his own stocks and importing grain, it took years for prices to fall to normal levels. In another crisis, in Safar 875/August 1470, the muhtasib tried to fix prices, but his instructions were ignored.[41] Grain owners preferred to hold on to their stocks in expectation that the price rises would continue.[42] Matters were made worse by the disappearance of the silver currency used to pay many people's wages. A debased copper currency was circulating in its place.[43]

In addition to the examples just cited one could add at least one major crisis in which the government was so weak and divided that it did nothing at all to aid the populace in weathering the storm. We have seen that price-fixing was a common occurrence in Mamluk Cairo. It was generally the first policy attempted by the state to respond to high prices. Yet it was almost always a failure. To make it work, the sultan had to be strong enough to force the amirs and grain brokers to cooperate. This required a threat of force, which can only have alienated the other members of the military elite. So it is not surprising that the policy usually failed. What did work, at least during crises of a few months in duration, was to give food away to the poor. Sultans did do this with some frequency, especially in the first century of Mamluk rule, when the economy was healthier.

These conclusions raise an obvious question: If price-fixing was so unsuccessful, why resort to it so frequently? Indeed, in many cases, price-fixing had the
opposite effect from what was intended, as al-Mawardi and others predicted it
would. Here, I think Boaz Shoshan's use of Thompson's concept of moral economy
is of some help. Shoshan notes that the sultans sometimes presented themselves as
acting on God's behalf when pressuring speculators to bring their grain to market. In 1394, for example, Sultan Barquq ordered hoarders to sell "at God's price"
or have their property exposed to looting.[44] Demanding a fixed price for essential
goods gave the public a moral claim on the rulers to intervene in the market. The
use of this policy by Mamluk sultans and their representatives indicated that they
accepted some responsibility for the effects that market fluctuations had on the
poor. When these measures failed, as they usually did, they then moved on to more
effective, and perhaps more costly, policies like giving away large quantities of food
to the poor.

The debate on price-fixing and hoarding provided the moral framework
around which public policy toward the market and its deleterious effects on society could be discussed. At stake were a number of conflicting interests. There
were the rights of property owners, the needs of the public, and the inscrutable
workings of the market mechanism. As more than one jurist and theologian put
it, citing the Prophet's authority, "prices are in God's hands."[45] Interfering with
the market could be seen as resisting God's authority, a vain and destructive attempt to interfere in God's providence. Nonetheless, not everyone accepted that
God was on the side of property. As the demand that grain be sold at God's price
demonstrates, legal protection of property could be removed if the propertied
went too far in violating the plebeians' expectations of the moral economy. It was
the sultans who were expected to guarantee that food was available to the common people at an affordable price, but if they forgot this duty, commoners used
demonstrations and popular violence to remind them. In the end, the policy of
the Mamluk state was frequently more paternalist than the writings of the jurists
would justify, but then the Mamluk sultans had the Cairene crowd with which
to deal.

Notes

I would like to thank the participants of the conference for their comments on an earlier
draft of this chapter. In particular, I am indebted to Adele Lindenmeyr, who undertook to
provide a formal response to the chapter and to Michael Bonner, Mine Ener, and Amy
Singer for having organized the conference.

   1. Hubert Darke, trans., *The Book of Government for Kings: The Siyar al-Muluk or
Siyasat-nama of Nizam al-Mulk* (London: Routledge and Kegan Paul, 1960), 22–23.

2. See his *Customs in Common* (New York: New Press, 1991), 185–258.

3. Malik b. Anas, *al-Muwatta': riwayat Yahya b. Yahya al-Laythi al-Andalusi*, 2 vols. (Beirut: Dar al-Gharb al-Islami, 1997), 2:179–80; Aisha Abdurrahman Bewley, trans., *al-Muwatta of Imam Malik ibn Anas: The First Formulation of Islamic Law* (Granada: Madinah Press, 1989), 265. The wording is similar in the *riwaya* of Abu Mus'ab al-Zuhri.

4. Malik b. Anas, *al-Muwatta'*, 2:180; Bewley (*Muwatta'*, 265) has a slightly different translation.

5. Ibid.

6. Abu l-Walid al-Baji, *al-Muntaqa sharh Muwatta'* (Cairo: Matba'at al-Sa'ada, A.H. 1331–1322), 5:15.

7. Muhammad ibn Idris al-Shafi'i, *Kitab al-umm*, 8 vols. (Beirut: Dar al-Kutub al-'Ilmiyya, 1993), 9:102.

8. Abu Hamid al-Ghazzali, *Ihya' 'ulum al-din*, 6 vols. (Beirut: Dar al-Khayr, 1990), 2:138.

9. Sultan Alamgir, *al-Fatawa al-hindiyya*, 6 vols. (Cairo: Dar al-Ma'rifa, A.H. 1310), 3:214.

10. 'Ali b. Abi Bakr al-Marghinani, *Hidaya fi sharh bidayat al-mubtadi*, 4 vols. (Beirut: Dar Ihya' al-Turath al-'Arabi, n.d.), 4:377. His views are repeated verbatim by 'Uthman b. 'Ali al-Zayla'i, *Tabyin al-haqa'iq sharh Kanz al-daqa'iq*, 7 vols. (Beirut: Dar al-Kutub al-'Ilmiyya, 2000), 7:60–63. His work is a commentary on a book by Abu l-Barakat al-Nasafi (d. 710/1310). For an example of the opposite point of view, see Badr al-Din al-'Ayni, *al-Binaya sharh al-Hidaya*, 13 vols. (Beirut: Dar al-Kutub al-'Ilmiyya, 2000), 11:215.

11. al-Marghinani, *Hidaya*, 4:378.

12. Ibn Humam, *Sharh Fath al-qadir*, 8 vols. (Cairo: al-Maktaba al-Tijariyya al-Kubra, A.H.1356), 8:127. For al-Kurlani, see the Pakistani edition of Ibn Humam, *Sharh Fath al-qadir*, 9 vols. (Ku'ita: al-Maktaba al-Rashidiyya, n.d.), 8:490.

13. Al-Zayla'i, *Tabyin*, 8:63; this passage is quoted from *Sharh al-Mukhtar*.

14. Ibid. See also the comments of al-Shaykh al-Shalabi in the margin.

15. Ibn Qudama, *al-Kafi fi fiqh al-Imam Ahmad*, 16 vols. (Damascus: al-Maktab al-Islami, 1979), 2:41.

16. Ibn Qudama, *al-Mughni wal-sharh al-kabir*, 16 vols. (Cairo: Dar al-Hadith, 1996), 5:313.

17. Ibn Taymiyya, *Majmu' al-fatawa*, 37 vols. (al-Mansura: Dar al-Wafa' lil-Taba'a wal-Nashr, 1998), 27:47.

18. Ibn Qayyim al-Jawziyya, *al-Turuq al-hukmiyya fi l-siyasa al-shar'iyya* (Cairo: Dar al-Bayan al-'Arabi, n.d.), 253.

19. Boaz Shoshan, "Fatimid Grain Policy and the Post of the Muhtasib," *International Journal of Middle East Studies* 13 (1981): 183–184. For details on this crisis, see Thierry Bianquis, "Une crise frumentaire dans l'Egypte fatimide," *Journal of the Economic and Social History of the Orient* 23 (1980): 67–101.

20. Boaz Shoshan, "Cairo Grain Riots and the 'Moral Economy': Cairo, 1350–1517," *Journal of Interdisciplinary History* 10 (winter 1980): 466.

21. George Rudé, *The Crowd in History: A Study of Popular Disturbances in France and England, 1730–1848* (New York: Wiley, 1964): 47–48.

22. This policy only increased regional antagonisms in France. See R. C. Cobb, *The Police and the People: French Popular Protest, 1789–1820* (Oxford: Oxford University Press, 1970), 284–285.

23. For more information, see Ira M. Lapidus, "The Grain Economy of Mamluk Egypt," *Journal of the Economic and Social History of the Orient* 12 (1969): 1–15.

24. Amartya Sen, *Poverty and Famines: An Essay on Entitlement and Deprivation* (Oxford: Oxford University Press, 1981), 1–8.

25. For further details, see Adam Sabra, *Poverty and Charity in Medieval Islam: Mamluk Egypt, 1250–1517* (Cambridge: Cambridge University Press, 2000).

26. Shihab al-Din Ahmad b. Abd al-Wahhab al-Nuwayri, *Nihayat al-arab fi funun al-adab, 34 vols.* (Cairo: Matba'at Dar al-Kutub, 1923–1998), 30:96; Badr al-Din al-'Ayni, *'Iqd al-juman fi tarikh ahl al-zaman* (Cairo: al-Hay'a al-Misriyya al-'Amma lil-Kitab, 1987), 1:375.

27. Taqi al-Din al-Maqrizi, *Kitab al-suluk li-ma'rifat duwal al-muluk*, 4 vols. (Cairo: Lajnat al-Ta'lif wa al-Tarjama wa al-Nashr, 1956–1973), 1:506–507, and *Kitab al-mawa' iz wal-i'tibar bi-dhikr al-khitat wal-athar*, 2 vols. (Cairo: Bulaq, A.H. 1294), 2:205; Ibn 'Abd al-Zahir, *al-Rawd al-zahir fi sirat al-Malik al-Zahir* (Riyadh: Mu'assasat Fu'ad, 1976), 188; al-'Ayni, *'Iqd*, 1:375, al-Nuwayri, *Nihaya*, 30:96.

28. For an eyewitness account from Alexandria, see Shah Morad Elham, *Kitbugha und Lajin: Studien zur Mamluken-Geschichte nach Baybars al-Mansuri und an-Nuwairi* (Freiburg: Schwarz, 1977) 10 (Arabic).

29. Taqi al-Din al-Maqrizi, *Ighathat al-umma bi-kashf al-ghumma* (Cairo: Matba'at Lajnat al-Ta'lif wal-Tarjama wal-Nashr, 1957), 35; Adel Allouche, *Mamluk Economics: A Study and Translation of al-Maqrizi's* Ighatha (Salt Lake City: University of Utah, 1994), 45.

30. Musa b. Muhammad al-Yusufi, *Nuzhat al-nazir fi sirat al-Malik al-Nasir* (Beirut: 'Alam al-Kutub, 1986), 295; al-Maqrizi, *Kitab al-suluk*, 2:394.

31. Al-Yusufi, *Nuzhat*, 296; al-Maqrizi, *Kitab al-suluk*, 2:394.

32. Al-Yusufi, *Nuzhat*, 297–299; al-Maqrizi, *Kitab al-suluk*, 2:394–395.

33. Al-Yusufi, *Nuzhat*, 300; al-Maqrizi, *Kitab al-suluk*, 2:396.

34. Al-Maqrizi, *Ighathat*, 40; Allouche, *Mamluk Economics*, 48.

35. Al-Maqrizi, *Kitab al-suluk*, 3:231–233.

36. Ibn al-Furat, *Tarikh*, 4 vols. published (nos. 4, 7–9) (Beirut: al-Matba'a al-Amirkaniyya, 1936), 9:387; al-Maqrizi, *Kitab al-suluk*, 3:818; Ibn al-Sayrafi, *Nuzhat al-nufus wal-abdan fi tawarikh al-zaman*, 4 vols. (Cairo: Wizarat al-Thaqafa, 1970–1994), 1:391.

37. Ibn al-Furat, *Tarikh*, 9:427–428; Ibn Hajar al-Asqalani, *Inba' al-ghumr bi-abna' al-'umr*, 9 vols. (Haydarabad: Matba'at Majlis Da'irat al-Ma'arif al-'Uthmaniyya, 1967–1975), 3:280.

38. Al-Maqrizi, *Kitab al-suluk*, 4:332; Ibn Hajar, *Inba'*, 7:186; Ibn al-Sayrafi, *Nuzha*, 2:357.

39. Al-Maqrizi, *Kitab al-suluk*, 4:334; Ibn Hajar, *Inba'*, 7:186; Badr al-Din al-'Ayni, *'Iqd al-juman fi tarikh ahl al-zaman* (Cairo: Matba'at 'Ala', 1985), 243.

40. Shams al-Din al-Sakhawi, *al-Tibr al-masbuk, fi dhayl al-suluk* (Cairo: al-Matba'a al-Amiriyya, 1896), 259, 261.

41. Ibn al-Sayrafi, *Inba' al-hasr bi-abna' al-'asr* (Cairo: Dar al-Fikr al-'Arabi, 1970), 204.

42. Ibid., 205; Shams al-Din al-Sakhawi, *Wajiz al-kalam fi dhayl duwal al-Islam* (Beirut: Mu'assasat al-Risala, 1995), 821.

43. Al-Sakhawi, *Wajiz*, 999.

44. Boaz Shoshan, *Popular Culture in Medieval Cairo* (Cambridge: Cambridge University Press, 1993), 63.

45. Imam al-Haramayn al-Juwayni, *Kitab al-irshad ila qawati' al-adilla fi usul al-i'tiqad* (Cairo: Maktabat al-Khanji, 1950), 367.

Part II

Institutions

CHAPTER FIVE

The Functional Aspects of Medieval Islamic Hospitals

YASSER TABBAA

The importance of the hospital has been largely neglected by most scholars dealing with Islamic urbanism; its significance is, however, indirectly reflected by
the fact that the budget for the Mansuri hospital was the largest of any public
institution in late medieval Cairo.[1]

Introduction

Following a sporadic history that began in Baghdad toward the end of the eighth
century, the hospital became one of the characteristic institutions of most central
Islamic cities. But despite its popularity and relative importance after the twelfth
century, the Islamic hospital has attracted very little scholarly attention, lagging
in this respect behind all other medieval Islamic institutions, including the *madrasa*
(college), the shrine, and the *khanqah* (Sufi convent). Other than the outdated
Tarikh al-bimaristanat fi l-Islam (History of Hospitals in Islam) and the more recent but problematic books by Gönül Cantay and Françoise Cloarec, no serious
book has been written on medieval Islamic hospitals.[2] Both books suffer from narrow geographical focus, perfunctory analysis of the architectural remains, and poor
utilization of the primary sources, whether literary or archival.[3]

The following contribution, part of a larger project on the history of the Islamic
hospital from the eighth to the fifteenth century, attempts a comprehensive and
interdisciplinary approach to hospitals, integrating their institutional and so-
ciomedical histories with their existing architectural remains. In other words, the
charitable or even social function of Islamic hospitals is but one aspect of an institution that fulfilled equally medical and educational purposes, while also having a
distinctive architectural form.[4] In addition to discussing the role of the medieval

Islamic hospital within the contexts of charity and human entitlements, this chapter discusses its early history under the patronage of the 'Abbasid caliphs of Baghdad, its development in the medieval period into a multifunctional institution, and the factors contributing to its gradual decline in the later middle ages. Based on findings in literary, architectural, and a scattering of archival sources, I would suggest that the combined effect of the rise of post-Seljuq city–states in the twelfth century, the creation of alternate sources of patronage in the form of *waqfs* (endowments), and the professionalization of medicine all contributed to the creation of the medieval Islamic hospital as a medical and charitable institution. Thus, the prosperity of these hospitals rested on their continued funding through waqf endowments and on a permissive intellectual atmosphere that tolerated the practice of Galenic or humoral medicine despite its ultimate opposition by most orthodox theologians. Conversely, the hospitals themselves, with their scientific and rationalistic outlook, helped to mitigate the effects of dogmatic theologies and antiscientific trends, preserving ancient medical practices well into the fifteenth century and beyond.

Etymology

The various functions that have historically been fulfilled by hospitals are reflected in the wide-ranging terms applied to this institution throughout its long history. The first hospitals, those developed under Constantine in the early fourth century, were called *nosokomeion* (house of the ill). Those built in Anatolia and the Jazira during the fifth and sixth centuries were generally called *xenodocheion* (house for strangers or travelers). The change in terminology did not necessarily result from a change in function, although it does seem likely that the later institutions, in view of their remote locations, may have been as much hospices as hospitals.[5] Furthermore, despite the greater specificity of the older term, the latter term, *xenodocheion*, was the one that took hold and that was subsequently assimilated into the Persian term *bimaristan* (house of ill), as we learn from a letter by Timothy, the patriarch of the Eastern Church in Baghdad from 780 to 823. In this letter dated 790, Timothy writes to his good friend and doctor Sergius, whom he had previously appointed as metropolitan of Elam (Khuzistan):

> We have built a *ksndwykn* [= *xenodecheion*], that is a *bymrstn [bimaristan]* in the Royal Cities [al-Mada'in or Ctesiphon/Seleucia], and have spent more or less 20,000 [*zuke*]. It has been roofed over already and completed, and pray that our Lord may give in it healing to the sick and to those who are bodily or spiritually sick.[6]

This text is interesting in at least two respects. First, the earliest Eastern word for hospital, bimaristan, is Persian rather than Syriac. This seems to suggest that the institution of the hospital may have been well established in Iran before the eighth century, though not necessarily at or within the region of Jundishapur.[7] Second, the foundation of this Christian hospital very near to Baghdad closely coincides with the foundation of the earliest Islamic hospital, that built by the 'Abbasid caliph Harun al-Rashid in 786 in Baghdad. This temporal and geographic coincidence suggests a kind of competition between Muslims and Christians, a point to which I shall return.

Interestingly, the term *bimaristan* is mainly used in the Arab world, often shortened to *maristan*, whereas in Turkey various terms such as *dar al-şifa* or *şifahane* (house of cure), or even *dar al-'afiya* (house of health) are used.[8] But the terms *bimarhane* and *hastahane* (both variants on bimaristan), and *timarhane* (house of the mentally ill) are also noted. Most recently, the term *mustashfa* (a derivation of the root *shafa* [to cure]) has become the standard Arabic name for modern hospitals.

Therefore, one is led to ask why so many terms were used for a single institution, even during the medieval period. This is all the more curious in view of the fact that the hospital in Islam was not nearly as important as the madrasa, which has just one name in all Islamic countries. In fact, the variety of terms applied to the Islamic hospital, rather than affirming its importance, seems to point in the other direction: toward an institution whose identity never completely coalesced and never became properly rooted in medieval Islamic cities or in an increasingly conservative culture.[9]

The Hospital in Early and Medieval Islam

The premodern history of the Islamic hospital can be divided into three fairly distinct periods: early (785–1000), medieval (1150–1500), and Ottoman (1500–1800). This chapter focuses on the second period, from which the earliest hospitals have survived, while using the first period primarily for comparative purposes. In effect, the first period begins with the 'Abbasids and not the Umayyads (661–750), who did not build any hospitals, with the possible exception of a leprosarium outside Damascus.[10] But soon after the Muslim capital was moved from Damascus to Baghdad, the 'Abbasid caliphs seem to have recognized the importance of medicine and hospitals and built hospitals in their capital city. This took place during the reign of Harun al-Rashid (786–809), apparently under the direct supervision of Syriac-speaking Christian Nestorian physicians, of whom the Bukhtishu' family was by far the most prominent.

No less than eight generations of doctors from the Bukhtishu' family are known to have served as private doctors of 'Abbasid caliphs between the middle of the eighth and the end of the tenth century, and of Buyid sultans well into the middle of the eleventh century.[11] Although some members of this family were occasionally associated with various hospitals in Baghdad, the Bukhtishu' family were primarily court physicians. As such, they were instrumental in the transmission of Syriac–Greek medicine and pharmacology to the 'Abbasid court and from there to the urban populations of Baghdad and Samarra.[12]

Six more hospitals were founded in Baghdad in the ninth and early tenth centuries, culminating in al-'Adudi hospital, built in 978. This large hospital was founded by the Buyid overlord 'Adud al-Dawlah (949–983) on the western bank of the Tigris. It had twenty-four physicians *(tabib* or *taba'i'i)*, a chief physician *(sa'ur)*, and specialists in surgery *(jarrah)* and ophthalmology *(kahhal)*, making it the most illustrious hospital of the 'Abbasid Caliphate. It was partly destroyed by flood in 1045 and substantially rebuilt by the Seljuqs in 1068, when the number of physicians was raised to twenty-eight. It continued to operate under increasingly difficult conditions until its final destruction by the Mongols in 1258.[13]

What led the 'Abbasids and their Buyid overlords to found so many hospitals and to support the greatest physicians of their time? The early 'Abbasids saw themselves as the cultural heirs to the great Sassanian Empire, the first patrons of medicine and hospitals in the Orient. Their capital city Baghdad stood at the physical and spiritual center of the civilized world, and its Neoplatonic form was meant to embody and radiate this centrality and to outshine the glory of the Sassanian kings. Medicine, like poetry, historiography, or architecture, was a direct product of 'Abbasid court culture: It relied on court support and patronage, and its spread and ultimate fate were closely linked to those of the 'Abbasids. By patronizing the great physicians of their time and establishing hospitals in their capital city, the 'Abbasids were claiming for themselves the heritage of earlier civilizations, while also living up to the Muslim ideals of bounty and charity.

It also seems likely that by founding hospitals the 'Abbasids were providing an Islamic alternative to Christian charitable institutions, including hospitals. According to Franz Rosenthal, "Christian intermediaries provided the first and decisive stimulus for Muslims to become aware of medicine's duties to society," adding that such a concept was readily accepted because "Islam was particularly receptive to all ideas concerning the well-being of society."[14]

Finally, one might add that the humoral theory at the foundation of Galenic medicine was not entirely incompatible with Islam, in part because it reaffirmed the unity of body and soul, while leaving a space for God as the Creator and ultimate arbiter of the natural world. Arab medicine, just like Galenic medicine before it, was founded on a view of humans' constitution dominated by the four humors *(amzija)*—blood (sanguine), phlegm (phlegmatic), yellow bile (choleric), and black bile (melancholic)—whose varying mixture within the body determined the organism's health or illness. Physicians hoped to maintain or correct an appropriate balance of humors within their patients through any means at their disposal: medical, pharmaceutical, dietetic, musical, atmospheric, and even spiritual. Overall, physicians were more concerned, and perhaps more successful, in the maintenance of health than in the cure of disease.

The period between 850 and 1100 is rightfully considered to be the peak of Islamic medicine. In many respects, this was the period of the court physician: Although some of these physicians practiced in the hospital, from a shop in the marketplace, or from their own home, the main locus of their activities was the court of the 'Abbasids and Buyids in Baghdad.[15] Numerous anecdotes underline the special favor in which these physicians were held by the caliphs and the familial proximity they enjoyed in their company.[16] It mattered little that most of these early physicians were Christians; what mattered was that they enhanced the prestige of the caliphate while fulfilling an important social service. Correspondingly, by interacting with the privileged culture of the court, Christian physicians and their Galenic medicine became fully integrated in the *adab* or belles-lettres of Islamic culture.

With very few exceptions, hospital building before the twelfth century remained primarily an 'Abbasid phenomenon restricted to their capital in Baghdad. Thus, their political decline in the first half of the eleventh century adversely affected hospitals and even medicine.[17] Such decline is attested to by two main factors: the end of hospital building after the great al-'Adudi hospital; and, more important, the departure from Baghdad of several important physicians to Egypt in the eleventh century and to Syria in the twelfth.

Therefore, it is permissible to speak of a significant disjunction in the history of Islamic medicine, a disjunction most clearly seen between the peak of medical knowledge and the peak of activity in hospital construction. This disjunction is historical: Whereas medicine reached its peak in the ninth and tenth centuries, large-scale hospital building only began in the late twelfth century and reached its height in the thirteenth. It is also geographical: The first center was indisputably Baghdad; subsequently, it was Damascus followed by Aleppo, Cairo, and several Anatolian cities. There was a further disjunction regarding patronage, which was primarily caliphal in the first phase and somewhat more diffuse in the second, involving lesser princes and often their wives or sisters.

Yet this interruption of the 'Abbasid hospitals carried within it the germ of the later revival of this institution—one that began in the middle of the twelfth century in Damascus under the direct impetus of immigrant Baghdadi physicians. According to Max Meyerhof and Joseph Schacht, "the revival of medicine in Syria in the twelfth and thirteenth centuries was ultimately related to the demise of the Ududi hospital."[18] Although medicine in Syria certainly benefited from the demise of the 'Abbasids, it took the personal efforts of the Syrian sovereign Nur al-Din Mahmud ibn Zangi (1146–1174) to lay down its institutional foundations in the form of hospitals. Although primarily known for his military foundations against the Crusaders and for his patronage of Sunni foundations, especially madrasas, Nur al-Din also built several hospitals: two large ones in Aleppo and Damascus, and

smaller ones in Hama, Raqqa, and Harran.[19] Furthermore, his project was continued by Saladin—who built his hospitals in Cairo, Alexandria, Jerusalem, Acre,
and Ramla[20]—and by other dynasts and often their wives or sisters—who built
hospitals in Anatolia, upper Mesopotamia, and Egypt. By the end of the thirteenth
century there were approximately sixty hospitals in the Islamic world, mainly concentrated in the central Islamic world.

Nur al-Din and Saladin's interest in hospitals should ultimately be traced to
their emulation of Baghdad and to their passionate struggle for the Sunni revival.
However, one cannot ignore the element of competition with Christian charity,
both with local Christians and with the new Crusader kingdom and its principal-
ities. Concerning the former, one notes that hospital building in the medieval
period was located in regions (Syria, Palestine, the Jazira, Anatolia, and Egypt) with
still sizable Christian communities who would have received medical care through
the many remaining churches and monasteries. Evidence is scarce, but there are
some indications that Christians frequented those churches or monasteries that
were linked to the healing powers of a particular saint or an ancient cult.[21] For example, the church of Mar Tuma in Mosul was located on an alley named after the
physician Iliyya, who once practiced medicine at the church itself.[22]

Elsewhere in the Jazira, including Nusaybin (Nisibis) and especially Edessa
(Urfa), many churches and monasteries possessed sacred relics that served as places
of magical cure and also contained hospices and even hospitals.[23] Many of these hospices, hospitals, and places of cultic healing continued their earlier mission well into
the medieval period, and they would have served as an example and source of competition for the various petty dynasties that dominated the central Islamic world in
the twelfth and thirteenth centuries. A lack of competition might explain equally
well the absence of hospitals in Islamic India and their rarity in North Africa, two
regions that did not contain large Christian populations in medieval times.

Architectural Form

The renewed activity in hospital construction is heralded by the hospitals of Nur
al-Din, of which only the one in Damascus (1154) is well-preserved.[24] The bimaristan al-Nuri in Damascus stands at an important juncture of the institutional
and architectural history of the Islamic hospital, from where it informs us about its
earlier Baghdadi prototype and provides a model for later Islamic hospitals. As with
nearly all extant pre-Ottoman hospitals, it is a four-*iwan* (a vaulted hall with an
arched opening) structure entered through a single monumental gate (figure 5.1).[25]
The four iwans converge on a large rectangular pool with four corner niches. The
eastern iwan served as a lecture hall, as is evident from several early descriptions
and the presence of niches for books (figure 5.2).[26] The corner rooms were reserved

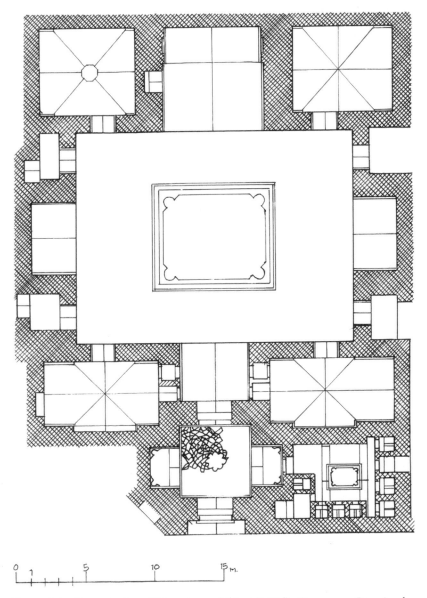

Figure 5.1. Ground plan of Bimaristan al-Nuri (1154), Damascus. Drawing by Yasser Tabbaa.

Figure 5.2. Eastern *iwan* of Bimaristan al-Nuri, Damascus (note inscriptions). Photograph by Yasser Tabbaa.

Figure 5.3. Façade of Bimaristan of Arghun al-Kamili (c. 1285), Aleppo. Photograph by Yasser Tabbaa.

Figure 5.4. First courtyard of Bimaristan of Arghun al-Kamili, Aleppo. Photography by Yasser Tabbaa.

Figure 5.5. Exterior view of Darushifaʾ (or çifte Medrese) al-Ghiyathiyya (1205), Kayseri (note mausoleum of the founder Gevher Nesibe on the right). Photograph by Yasser Tabbaa.

for the patients. The bimaristan was also equipped with a large latrine, with six stalls centered around a pool.[27]

In view of the multidisciplinary nature of this collection of articles, it should suffice to treat the remaining fourteen pre-Ottoman bimaristans as a group, high-lighting their most salient architectural features. Note first that they are centrally located structures, easily accessible from any point in the city.[28] Second, most of them utilize the cruciform four-iwan plan—one used by some contemporary madrasas but one that is also closely linked to palace architecture.[29] Third, they are invariably entered through a single elaborate and controlled entrance, unlike mosques but quite like palaces and madrasas. What in a palace would have been guard rooms flanking the entrance serve here most likely as pharmacies or infir-maries with windows facing the street (figure 5.3). Fourth, they almost always have a single floor consisting of tall iwans and lower enclosed chambers of various sizes (figure 5.4).[30] Fifth, all have at least one central pool with circulating water, and most contain a space for latrines. Sixth, almost none has a mosque, although in some cases a mosque was built at a later point.[31] Seventh, several hospitals contain the mausoleum of the founder and many have Quranic inscriptions (figures 5.5 and 5.2).[32] Generally large, well-built, and amply provided establishments, these hospitals were described by travelers such as Ibn Jubayr in the twelfth century and Evliya Çelebi in the seventeenth in laudatory terms usually reserved for palaces.[33]

The Waqf and Creation of the Functional Hospital

According to Rosenthal, "the noblest expression of the deep concern of medieval Muslim society with matters of public health was a highly developed hospital sys-tem, a network of urban institutions with large staffs, providing numerous services and frequently having teaching facilities attached to them."[34] This view, which is shared by most writers on the subject, is somewhat exaggerated, particularly in its emphasis on the systematic and comprehensive nature of these hospitals.[35] Al-though preceding western European hospitals by several centuries, Islamic hospitals were not built in sufficiently large numbers to serve more than a sample of the urban population. A few examples should suffice. Damascus and Aleppo, with thir-teenth-century populations of 60,000–70,000, had only two hospitals each. Cairo, with a much larger population, also had only two hospitals throughout the me-dieval period. Smaller cities and towns in Syria, Iraq, and especially Anatolia had just one hospital each. Many other towns had no hospitals at all.

In contrast Florence had about thirty hospitals at the beginning of the four-teenth century, and a century later there were ten more. Paris had sixty hospitals, and the smaller towns of Narbonne and Arles had fifteen and sixteen, respectively. According to Miri Rubin, "in England alone some 220 hospitals were founded in the twelfth century and some 310 in the thirteenth."[36] Such numbers can be produced for nearly all European cities and towns.

This striking discrepancy can be minimized by the fact that the medieval European hospital primarily comprised almshouses, hospices, and pilgrimage rest stops. These hospitals, according to Carole Rawcliffe, "offered little or nothing in the way of professional medical or surgical facilities."[37] In many cases, the truly ill were even turned away because their presence would have exhausted the limited resources of these hospitals and disturbed their ultimately spiritual purpose.

In contrast, Islamic hospitals, especially those built between the twelfth and fourteenth centuries and under the Ottomans, were intended for both medical treatment and charitable relief. But even here, it is often difficult to distinguish between the ideal conditions prescribed by their endowment deeds *(waqfiyyas)* and the day-to-day functioning of these hospitals. Waqfiyyas prescribe, but in the absence of account books or daily records for any pre-Ottoman hospital, there is no consistent way to find out whether or for how long their prescriptions were followed. Nevertheless, as a group, these endowments unanimously prescribe their related hospitals as places primarily for the treatment and convalescence of the poor—both men and women. For example the waqfiyya of al-Nuri, excerpted in Abu Shama, specifically limits overnight stay at the hospital to the poor and indigent, while restricting its use by all others to mere dispensation of drugs.[38] The waqfiyya for the bimaristan al-Nasiri in Cairo also specifies the needy *(dhawi al-haja)* as its primary users.[39] Possibly, the only exception is the waqfiyya of Qalawun's famous hospital in Cairo, which, despite emphasizing the poor and needy as its target beneficiaries, also includes "the strong and the weak, the wealthy and the poor, the commander and the commanded, the owner and the slave, and the famous and the unknown."[40] But this is probably just pious hyperbole because it is very unlikely that any persons of means would have sought long-term treatment outside of their own homes.[41] At most, such persons would only have used hospitals as pharmacies or infirmaries, which is perhaps the sense in which the all-inclusive statement of the waqfiyya of Qalawun should be understood.

In general, the continued functioning of a given medieval Islamic institution, including hospitals, was directly related to the size and prescriptive details of its endowment, and perhaps indirectly to the prevailing intellectual climate. For example, the extremely long waqfiyya of Qalawun's hospital and several early descriptions of this hospital give us a reasonably good idea of the appearance and functions of its various wards (figure 5.6). According to these descriptions, the building was divided into sections for various diseases or parts of the human body, each with a specialist in charge. There were sections for fevers, a section for ophthalmic medicine, and one for surgical cases. Bedridden patients *(murada')* were segregated from convalescent patients *(nuqaha')*: the former were in enclosed spaces, whereas the latter benefited from the water and air circulation of the partly

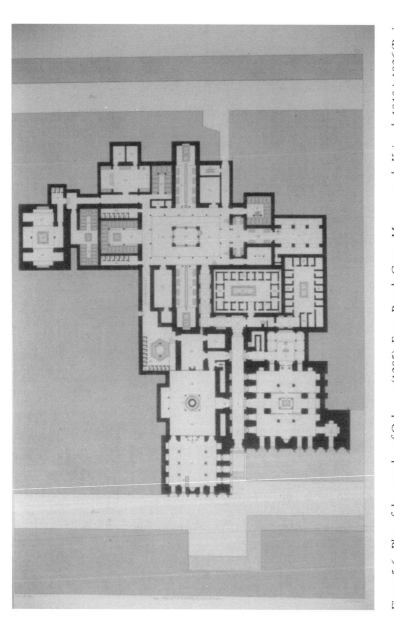

Figure 5.6. Plan of the complex of Qalawun (1285). From Pascale Coste, *Monuments du Kaire, de 1818 à 1826* (Paris: Typide Firmin Didot Frères, 1839), pl. xvii.

open iwans. Sexes were strictly separated, so that many of these wards were duplicated for women. Mental patients had their own wards, typically composed of an open courtyard surrounded by secure individual cells (figure 5.7). The hospital also had a large kitchen, storerooms, dispensaries, and several chambers with latrines. The chief physician had his own quarters in the hospital and gave lectures on medicine in a specific location. Finally, the hospital contained a mortuary—a constant reminder of the presence of death within the possibility of cure.[42]

The later continuity of these prescribed, normative functions must be checked against travelers' accounts, references in literary sources, and, where they exist, documents. Interestingly, the hospital of Qalawun seems to have continued its original function up to the seventeenth century, when it was glowingly described by the Ottoman traveler Evliya Çelebi:

> It has no equal in Anatolia or among the Arabs and Persians. . . . There is a magnificent pool in the middle of a great court, which is paved with polished marble. . . . A dome with an ornamented ceiling rests on twelve pillars over this splendid pool [actually, four columns and four piers]. At each of the four sides of this court is a great hall. . . . In them are the beds of those afflicted with illness. The sick wear bedclothes and have silk sheets. Some of those who are ill relax next to the flowing ornamental fountains when they are close to recovering their health. The servants look after them with great care. Some of our insane brothers are in gloomy cells while others are in open rooms . . . [others] are bound like lions with chains around their necks. During our time there were 306 ill and insane people in the Hospital of Qalawun.[43]

Curiously, European travelers who visited this hospital before and after Evliya Çelebi's visit generally depicted it in the most dismal terms. Already by the end of the sixteenth century, the Venetian physician Prospero Alpin, described a state of utter decline in Egyptian medicine, but without specifically referring to the hospital of Qalawun.[44] Two Frenchmen, Benoît de Maillet and Jean de Thévenot, who visited Cairo in the seventeenth century, commented on the dilapidated state of the hospital and the general lack of medical treatment in it.[45] Finally, a series of more scientific assessments of this hospital by French physicians and architects in the late eighteenth and early nineteenth centuries describe a building and an institution in utter decline, with only a handful of chained lunatics suffering from total neglect.[46] The conflicting descriptions of Muslim versus European travelers are all the more curious because this hospital seems to have been substantially stabilized and rebuilt by the Mamluk governor 'Abd al-Rahman Katkhuda in 1746.[47] Although it is quite likely that the hospital of Qalawun, much like the rest of Egypt, fell on very hard times in the second half of the eighteenth century,[48] we cannot altogether discount the difference of perspective that would have colored European travelers' perceptions of a hospital that differed so markedly from the ones in Europe.

Figure 5.7. View from one of the chambers of the insane at Bimaristan of Arghun al-Kamili (c. 1285), Aleppo. Photograph by Yasser Tabbaa.

However, even if we assume that the hospital of Qalawun in Cairo had declined beyond repair by the end of the eighteenth century, it had nonetheless fulfilled its intended function for nearly five hundred years—a feat directly attributable to its substantial endowment. Conversely, the hospital founded by al-Mu'ayyad Shaykh in Cairo in 821/1418 had to cease all its hospital functions immediately after the death of its founder in 1421 because its endowment did not specify enough funds to support its operation. By the following year, the patients had to be removed and the building was converted into a Friday mosque, having been furnished with a pulpit and provided with the appropriate personnel.[49]

Factors of Decline: Intellectual

With the exception of the poorly endowed and short-lived hospital of al-Mu'ayyad in Cairo (1418), very few hospitals were built in the later Mamluk or classical Ottoman period, outside of the three Ottoman capitals.[50] Even the earlier hospitals suffered greatly from the fifteenth century onward from embezzlement and general neglect. Although it is easier to attribute this decline to economic factors, I think it reflected an earlier and broader cultural reorientation that valorized the juridical and other Islamic sciences over all branches of the ancient sciences, including medicine. Doris Behrens-Abouseif, for example, notes that "specialized physician's biographies were no longer written after the thirteenth century," proposing that this was "an indication of a decline in the physician's image."[51] It also seems likely that the complete futility of Galenic medicine in the face of the bubonic plague, particularly the Black Death of the 1340s, would have greatly eroded the credibility of physicians, while enhancing belief in magical cures and Prophetic medicine.[52]

Although "spiritual" medicine seems to have gained over Galenic medicine in the later middle ages, evidence suggests that the two branches had coexisted since early times. The proliferation of hospitals and the unquestioned growth in scientific medicine does not necessarily mean that the majority of the population held rational views about medicine and sought treatment in hospitals. In fact, the literature is full of references to all kinds of shrines, sacred springs, rocks, trees, ancient columns, or marks left by passing saints to which *baraka* (blessing) and curative powers were attached. These sacred spots transcended specific religious affiliation, as we can see in al-Shabushti *(Kitab al-adyira)* and al-Harawi *(Kitab al-ziyarat)*, and seem to have been used by people of various creeds.[53] Even more important than these healing shrines was street or *dukkan* medicine, which seems to have been practiced with little or no control in medieval Islam.[54]

This cultural shift from Galenic to Prophetic medicine and faith healing negatively affected the quality and quantity of doctors in the Islamic world. Physicians dealt with these changes in various ways. They gradually substituted Dawla with Din-composed epithets (e.g., Fakhr al-Din, "pride of the [Islamic] religion," instead of Amin al-Dawla, "trustworthy one of the dynasty")—ones that were intended to soften their scientific image and highlight their pious demeanor. Some incorporated Prophetic medicine into their practices, insisting on the value of prayer and *dhikr* (the ritual Sufi "remembering" of God's name) and rarely mentioning wine as an appropriate medication. But most eventually abandoned the profession for more prestigious careers in jurisprudence or administration. This seems to have opened the way for Christian and Jewish physicians, who would presumably settle for jobs with lower status and the increasingly harsh treatment of their patrons.[55] By the sixteenth century some European physicians were even imported.

Factors of Decline: Economic

Economically, bimaristans, other than those founded by the Ottomans themselves, suffered in two main ways under Ottoman administration. First, it seems clear from biographical dictionaries and archival documents that the large staff required for their operation was greatly abbreviated and that it rarely included doctors. Thus, while there is plenty of evidence for continuity in the appointments of *nazirs* (supervisors) and *khadims* (custodians), there is little mention of physicians.[56] In other words, these hospitals (and madrasas as well) were being run at a much lowered capacity—a shrinkage that could be attributable to their dwindling endowments or to acts of usurpation. For example, a royal decree dated 1130/1718 stipulates that one nazir should be appointed for the two hospitals in Aleppo (al-Nuri and al-Kamili), his sole responsibility being to provide soup once a day for the inmates and bury them when they died.[57] The hospital had become a mortuary.

The decline of proper medical care in bimaristans also explains why most of those in Anatolia were given over in the Ottoman period to various Sufi fraternities who practiced some sort of faith healing within them. For example, the Kastamonu hospital, founded in 1272, had already been converted into a *tekke* (dervish lodge) by the seventeenth century, with the patients' rooms turned into a mosque and a tomb.[58] Likewise, the hospital at Çankırı, outside Ankara, built in 633/1235 by Farrukh al-Lalla during the reign of Alaeddin Kayqubad, became a place of spiritual medicine and snake charming.[59]

Second, it seems abundantly clear that late Mamluk and Ottoman administrators employed legal and illegal means to usurp the substantial endowments of medieval institutions, including hospitals, and redirect them to other ends. Usurpation of waqf properties through *istibdal* (replacement, substitution) and *khuluww* (vacating) has been noted recently by Behrens-Abouseif, who proposes that the

Ottomans had no alternative since most of Egypt had become waqf by the end of the Mamluk period.[60] Even though this policy, which was also practiced in Damascus and Aleppo, may have served the economic and political purposes of the Ottomans, it could only have been detrimental to the continuity of the few remaining hospitals in these cities.[61]

A case in point is the bimaristan al-Nuri in Damascus, founded in 1154, expanded in 1242, and restored in 1285 and 1410. By the end of the fifteenth century, its endowments had been so thoroughly pilfered that, according to the historian Yusuf al-Basrawi, it was "ruined beyond repair."[62] In the sixteenth century, we know of two seizures that effectively ended the financial viability of this institution. In the first, water rights coming from the Qanawat (quarter) and the *hammam* (public bath) al-Ghazzi, both waqfs of the bimaristan, were appropriated between 1529 and 1587 by a succession of officials and notables, who diverted the water and annexed parts of the hammam to their own residences.[63] But the final blow for the bimaristan may have been the usurpation of the village of Qtaife and its two *khans* (hostels), which were still "a *waqf* for the *bimaristan* in Damascus" as late as 1477.[64] Within a few decades, however, the khans were declared ruins requiring istibdal, making it legally feasible to rededicate the Qtaife waqf for a new complex, consisting of a mosque, *imaret* (soup kitchen), *ribat* (inn or hospice), hammam, and shops. But this complex and its redirected waqfs were intended for pilgrims on their way to Mecca, which was far more important for the Ottomans than the hospital of Nur al-Din.[65] Such occurrences can be multiplied and they stand at the root of the decline of hospitals and other pious institutions in the Arabic-speaking world under the Ottomans.

Conclusion

The medical and charitable role of Islamic hospitals has been overstated by some polemicists seeking further affirmation for Islamic achievements in science. It has also been generally understated by medical historians who have tended to view these hospitals anachronistically, as a phenomenon that reaches its peak of development just when Islamic medicine is thought to have begun its decline. I have attempted in this chapter to avoid these polarities by studying various aspects of Islamic hospitals—medical, charitable, economic, and architectural—over a long period to allow for emphasis, comparison, and change.

From its origins as an appendage of the 'Abbasid caliphate in Baghdad to its revival in Syria by Nur al-Din to its dispersion within the cities and towns of the central Islamic world, this chapter has shown that the hospital underwent considerable development in function, financial support, and architecture. Although we remain ill-informed about the earliest hospitals in Baghdad, with the exception of al-'Adudi, the short period of their functioning suggests that they may have especially suffered from inadequate funding. Medieval hospitals, on the other hand, were relatively large, well-built structures that were founded and maintained by means of the waqf, a charitable mechanism that was little used for public institutions before the twelfth century. Specifying funds for the doctors, personnel, patients, and the building itself, waqfs ensured the functional continuity and formal integrity of pious and charitable foundations long after the death of their founders.

Nevertheless, as I have noted, the conditions of these waqfs were occasionally transgressed because hospitals, which had been designated for the treatment of the poor, were used by persons of means or as prisons. More important, the waqfs of some hospitals were pilfered or confiscated in later periods, contributing to the decline of these hospitals and to the curtailment of most of their medical services. Although the abrogation of waqfs is attested in all periods and places, it seems to have become increasingly common in the late Mamluk and Ottoman periods.

Just as detrimental to the continued prosperity of Islamic hospitals in the later Middle Ages was the increasingly negative attitude among the ruling and learned classes toward the ancient sciences, including Galenic or humoral medicine. These traditionalist pressures led to the demotion of medicine as a desirable career among the Muslim learned classes, who generally turned their attention to more properly "Islamic" pursuits, such as jurisprudence and governmental service. The gap was gradually filled by Prophetic medicine and by other forms of faith healing that did not require a specialized institution for their practice.

But Islamic hospitals were not just passive recipients of external pressures and changing cultural modes. Their architectural presence, relative financial independence, and an increasingly professionalized class of physicians helped them negotiate an important place within this significant cultural shift and important epistemological divide. As long as the intellectual climate permitted, and provided their endowments remained intact, the bimaristans continued to treat the sick and the insane, provide drugs, and teach medicine. And even after external pressures finally forced them to abandon their intended medical and therapeutic functions, Islamic hospitals continued to provide food, shelter, and solace for the poor and the weak.

For several centuries during medieval Islam, the Islamic hospital occupied an increasingly restrictive cultural space, perpetuating and refining earlier medical practices but rarely going beyond them. Despite its auspiciously early start and its efflorescence during the twelfth and thirteenth centuries, the medieval Islamic hospital could not withstand cultural and epistemological forces that opposed, or at least challenged, its basic scientific outlook. Compromises with religious orthodoxy contributed to the continued toleration of the hospital and its medical practices long after the rejection of other rational sciences. But in the end, the hospital could only delay, not prevent, the ultimate decline of humoral medicine—a vibrant tradition that had flourished in Islam since the eighth century.

Notes

I would like to thank the following institutions for supporting my ongoing work on Islamic hospitals: Center for Advanced Study in the Visual Arts, National Gallery of Art, Washington, D.C. (1994–1995); Social Science Research Council (1996–1997); and Fondation Max van Berchem (1997).

1. Michael W. Dols, "The Leper in Medieval Islamic Society," *Speculum* 58 (1983): 901.

2. Ahmad 'Isa, *Tarikh al-bimaristanat fi l-Islam* (1939; reprint, Beirut: Dar al-Hayat, 1981); Gönül Cantay, *Anadolu Selçuklu ve Osmanı Darüşşifaları* (Ankara: Atatürk Kültür Merkezi Yayını, 1992); Françoise Cloarec, *Bimaristans, lieux de folie et de sagesse* (Paris: Editions l'Harmattan, 1998). To these books one must add the numerous articles on hospitals and medicine written by Arslan Terzioğlu over the past thirty years, which have now been collected in *Beiträge zur Geschichte der türkisch-islamischen Medizin, Wissenschaft und Technik*, 2 vols. (Istanbul: Isis Press, 1996).

3. The present volume (chapter 6) shows that scholarly attention to hospitals is increasing. I am referring here to the important work being done on Ottoman hospitals by Miri Shefer.

4. In this respect, the medieval Islamic hospital differed from its Western medieval counterpart, which was essentially an institution of charity. On this distinction see Jole Agrimi and Chiara Crisciani, "Charity and Aid in Medieval Christian Civilization," in *Western Medical Thought from Antiquity to the Middle Ages*, ed. Mirko D. Grmek (Cambridge: Harvard University Press, 1998), 182–187.

5. For the early history of hospitals in Byzantium, see Timothy S. Miller, *The Birth of the Hospital in the Byzantine Empire* (Baltimore: Johns Hopkins University Press, 1985).

6. Cited in Michael W. Dols, *Majnun: The Madman in Medieval Islamic Society* (Oxford: Clarendon Press, 1992), 113–114. See also idem., "The Origins of the Islamic Hospital: Myth and Reality," *Bulletin of the History of Medicine* 61 (1987): 367–390.

7. Concerning the myth and reality of Jundishapur, see Nabia Abbott, "Jundi Shapur: A Preliminary Historical Sketch," *Ars Orientalis* 7 (1968): 71–73; Dols, "The Origins of the Islamic Hospital," 369–370; Lawrence I. Conrad ("The Arab-Islamic Medical Tradition," in *The Western Medical Tradition, 800 BC to AD 1800*, ed. Lawrence I. Conrad et al. [Cambridge: Cambridge University Press, 1995], 101) argues against the existence of a hospital at Jundishapur, suggesting that it was a later myth intended to provide a precedent for the hospitals of Baghdad.

8. Bimaristan continues to be used in *waqfiyyas* (endowment deeds) and other legal documents throughout history. The shortened maristan, on the other hand, enters literary usage from early on and becomes the norm.

9. Another indication of the marginal status of Islamic hospitals is that they often went unnoticed by urban topographers and, therefore, were omitted from their lists of

princely or pious institutions. This is certainly the case in several medieval topographies of Damascus and Aleppo, including Ibn 'Asakir and Ibn Shaddad. Maqrizi, on the other hand, does list the hospitals of Cairo. See Gary Leiser and Michael Dols, "Evliya' Celebi's Description of Medicine in 17th c. Egypt," *Sudhoffs Archiv* 71 (1987) and 72 (1988).

10. See Lawrence Conrad, "Did the Caliph al-Walid Build a Hospital in Damascus?" *Aram* 6, no. 1–2 (1994): 2–22 where the author definitively demonstrates that the Umayyad caliph al-Walid did not build any hospitals.

11. The biographies and genealogies of the Bukhtishu' physicians are detailed in Ibn Abi Usaybi'a, *'Uyun al-anba' fi tabaqat al-atibba'* (Beirut: Dar al-Hayat, 1974), 183ff.

12. For a summary of this period, see Emilie Savage-Smith, "Tibb," *EI²* 10:452–453.

13. 'Isa, *Tarikh al-bimaristanat*, 187–197.

14. The evidence for the existence of Christian hospitals in Baghdad is limited to the text cited above concerning the hospital in Ctesiphon, which is a suburb of Baghdad. Franz Rosenthal, *The Classical Heritage of Islam*, trans. E. and J. Marmorstein (Berkeley: University of California Press, 1965), 183.

15. The well-known historian of Islamic medicine, Emilie Savage-Smith, has informed me that in her comprehensive reading of al-Razi's *Kitab al-hawi*, she did not come across a single case of a patient seeking treatment in a hospital. See also Conrad, "The Arabic-Islamic Medical Tradition," 131–133.

16. See, in particular, Ibn Abi Usaybi'a, *Tabaqat al-atibba'*, 188–284.

17. The only hospitals known to have been built outside of Baghdad before the twelfth century are the following: Ibn Tulun (872) and Kafur (957), both in Cairo; Wasit (south of Baghdad) (1022); Mayyafariqin (modern Silvan in southeastern Turkey) (1031); and Antioch (c. 1035). See the lists in 'Isa, *Tarikh al-bimaristanat*. The first two of these hospitals must be seen as direct transplants from Baghdad because Cairo, at the time, was subject to great 'Abbasid influence.

18. Max Meyerhof and Joseph Schacht, *The Medico-Philosophical Controversy between Ibn Butlan of Baghdad and Ibn Ridwan of Cairo* (Cairo: n.p., 1937), 16.

19. On the architectural patronage of Nur al-Din, see Nikita Elisséeff, "Les monuments de Nur al-Din: inventaire, notes archéologiques et bibliographiques," *Bulletin d'études orientales* 13 (1951): 5–49; and Yasser Tabbaa, "The Architectural Patronage of Nur al-Din, 1146–1174" (Ph.D. diss., New York University, 1983), esp. 225–232.

20. 'Isa, *Tarikh al-bimaristanat*, 71–82, 230–233.

21. The early source on eastern Christian monasteries—Abu'l-Hasan 'Ali al-Shabushti, *Kitab al-Adyira*, ed. Kurkis Awwad (Beirut: Dar al-Ra'id al-'Arabi, 1986)—contains several references to Christian shrines with places of healing, for example, pages 176, 284, 301, 311.

22. Sa'id al-Daywaji, *Tarikh al-Mawsil* (Mosul: Al-Majma' al-'Ilmi, 1982), 218.

23. J. B. Segal, *Edessa, the Blessed City*, trans. Yusuf I. Jabra (Oxford: Oxford University Press, 1970), esp. 87–100, which contain numerous instances of magical cure.

24. Nur al-Din's hospital in Aleppo is a huge field of ruins south of the Great Mosque. The only remains of his hospital in Hama are two inscriptions, located today in a restaurant.

25. For the foundation and description of the bimaristan of Nur al-Din, see the still useful study by Salahuddin al-Munajjid, *Bimaristan Nur al-Din* (Damascus: Al-Majma'

al-'Ilmi al-'Arabi, 1946); and Ernst Herzfeld, "Damascus: Studies in Architecture—I," *Ars Islamica* 9 (1947): 2–12.

26. An especially vivid description of this hospital is provided by the twelfth-century Andalusian traveler Ibn Jubayr in his *Rihlat Ibn Jubayr* (Beirut: Dar Sader, 1980), 255–256.

27. This part of the building was converted approximately twenty years ago into a display room.

28. This is true for all pre-Ottoman hospitals and for all Ottoman ones except the hospital complex of Beyazid II at Edirne (1421), which is located about two kilometers west of the city.

29. On the uses of the four-iwan plan for palaces and madrasas, see Yasser Tabbaa, *Constructions of Power and Piety in Medieval Aleppo* (University Park: Pennsylvania State University Press, 1997), 84–92, 129–134.

30. This design feature may have been introduced in consideration of the patients, whose fragile health would not have allowed them to climb stairs. Equally, questions of sunlight and air circulation may have been involved.

31. The lack of mosques is quite astonishing, particularly when we compare these hospitals with their medieval European counterparts. Small mosques were subsequently added at al-Nuri in Damascus and Arghun al-Kamili in Aleppo. In hospitals containing the mausoleum of the founder (see note 32), that space may have doubled as a mosque.

32. Several pre-Ottoman hospitals included mausoleums: al-Ghiyathiyya in Kayseri; Keyka'us I in Sivas; Turan Melik in Divriği (626/1228); the so-called TaşMescit in Çankırı (633/1235); al-Qaymari (654/1256) in Salihiyya, Damascus; and Qalawun in Cairo. Interestingly, most of these hospitals are in Anatolia, where the custom of including the founder's mausoleum continues in the Ottoman period.

33. Leiser and Dols, "Evliya' Celebi's Description."

34. Franz Rosenthal, "The Physician in Medieval Muslim Society," *Bulletin of the History of Medicine* 52 (1978): 490.

35. A somewhat more measured view of the role of the hospital in the Islamic world has been recently offered by Conrad in "The Arabic-Islamic Medical Tradition," 135–138.

36. Miri Rubin, *Charity and Community in Medieval Cambridge* (Cambridge: Cambridge University Press, 1987), 1.

37. Carole Rawcliffe, *Medicine for the Soul: The Life, Death, and Resurrection of an English Medieval Hospital, St. Giles's Norwich, c. 1249–1550* (Stroud, U.K.: A. Sutton, 1999), xiii.

38. Abu Shama, *Kitab al-rawdatayn fi akhbar al-dawlatayn al-nuriyya wa'l-salahiyya*, 2 vols., ed. Muhammad H. Ahmad (1956; reprint, Cairo: Matba'at Dar al-Kutub al-Misriyah, 1998), 1:21.

39. Waqfiyya 1/2, dated 29 Ramadan 613/1216.

40. Waqfiyya 2/15, dated 12 Safar 685/1285. Excerpted in 'Isa, *Tarikh al-bimaristanat*, 134–149; see esp. lines 301–304.

41. The main exception to this rule are the students and employees of some of the larger pious complexes, who could receive medical treatment in hospitals adjoining their place of study. I am aware of three such annexed hospitals: the madrasa al-Mustansiriyya in Baghdad (1233); the funerary madrasa of Sultan Hasan in Cairo (1356); and the so-called

Rabʿ-i Rashidi near Tabriz, founded by Rashid al-Din (d. 1318) as a mosque, tomb, *khanqa* (dervish lodge), hospital, and hospice.

42. This description is directly based on the waqfiyya of this hospital. See ʿIsa, *Tarikh al-bimaristanat*, 141–146, esp. lines 331–388.

43. Leiser and Dols, "Evliyaʾ Celebi's Description," 24–25.

44. Prospero Alpin, *La médecine des Égyptiens, 1582–1584*, 2 vols., trans. R. de Fenoyl (Cairo: IFAO, 1980): 1:12–15.

45. Both accounts are cited in Dols, *Majnun*, 131–132.

46. Also cited in Dols, *Majnun*, 121. The most important of these accounts are J. J. Marcel, "Précis historique et descriptif sur le Moristan ou le grand hôpital des fous au Kaire," in *Contes du Cheykh al-Mohdy* (Paris: IFAO, 1835), 2:151–156, which recounts the description of the French doctor-in-chief Desgenettes in 1798; and E. Jomard, "Description de la ville de Kaire," in *Description de l'Egypte: état moderne*, ed. M. Jomard et M. Jacotin (Paris: Imprimerie de C. L. F. Pankouche, 1822), 1:211.

47. *Wizarat al-Awqaf*, Cairo, no. 940. For the substantial endowments of ʿAbd al-Rahman Katkhuda, see Doris Behrens-Abouseif, "The ʿAbd al-Rahman Katkhuda Style in 18th Century Cairo," *Annales Islamologiques* 26 (1992): 117–126.

48. For the declining economic and political situation in the second half of the eighteenth century, see Afaf Lutfi al-Sayyid Marsot, *Egypt in the Reign of Muhammad Ali* (Cambridge: Cambridge University Press, 1984), 3–18.

49. Taqi al-Din Ahmad al-Maqrizi, *Al-Mawaʿiz wal-iʿtibar fi dhikr al-khitat wal-athar*, 3 vols. (Beirut: Dar al-ʿIrfan, 1959), 3:324.

50. Several hospitals were built in the different quarters of Istanbul and before that in Bursa and in Edirne. To these should be added an Ottoman hospital in Manisa and two hospitals in Mecca and Medina, brought to my attention by Miri Shefer.

51. Doris Behrens-Abouseif, "The Image of the Physician in Arab Biographies of the Post-Classical Age," *Der Islam* 66 (1989): 342–343.

52. To my knowledge, the effect of the Black Death on the medical profession has not been studied. Meanwhile, see Michael W. Dols, *The Black Death in the Middle East* (Princeton: Princeton University Press, 1979), 83–142, passim, in which he discusses the total inefficacy of the miasmic theory in dealing with the bubonic plague and the increasing reliance on magic. See also Behrens-Abouseif, "Image of the Physician," 343.

53. Al-Shabushti, *Kitab al-Adyira*; and Ali al-Harawi, *Kitab al-isharat ila maʿrifat al-ziyarat*, ed. Janine Sourdel-Thomine as *Guide des lieux de pélerinage* (Damascus: Institut Français de Damas, 1953).

54. Conrad, "The Arabic-Islamic Medical Tradition," 128–133.

55. Behrens-Abouseif, "Image of the Physician,"345–346; and Anne-Marie Eddé, "Les médecins dans la société syrienne du VIIe/XIIIe siecle," *Annales Islamologiques* 29 (1995): 91–109.

56. For example, the following documents in Dar al-Wathaʾiq al-Qawmiyya, Damascus: *Awamir Sultaniyya*, Aleppo, 5/182, 183, 184, 185, 186, 542 only mention appointments of officials, not doctors.

57. *Awamir Sultaniyya*, Aleppo, 5/186. A similar conclusion regarding the state of the two hospitals of Aleppo (al-Nuri and al-Kamili) around the end of the eighteenth century

was reached by M. Kamal Shihade in *"Al-Tibb wal-madaris al-tibbiyya"* (Ph.D. diss., University of Aleppo, 1995), 209–210. I was able to read this first-rate dissertation at the library of the Institute for the History of Arabic Science at the University of Aleppo.

58. Arslan Terzioğlu, *Mittelaterliche islamische Krankenhäuser* (Berlin: Technical University, 1968), 131–135.

59. Ibid., 126.

60. Doris Behrens-Abouseif, *Egypt's Adjustment to Ottoman Rule: Institutions, Waqf, and Architecture in Cairo (15th and 17th Centuries)* (Leiden: E. J. Brill, 1994), 154–157.

61. Abraham Marcus in *The Middle East on the Eve of Modernity: Aleppo in the Eighteenth Century* (New York: Columbia University Press, 1989), for example, notes that "no new hospitals were built, and none of the hundreds of recorded charitable endowments of the period donated property for the support of the existing ones" (266).

62. 'Ala' al-Din b. Yusuf al-Basrawi, *Tarikh al-Basrawi: safahat majhula min tarikh Dimashq fi 'asr al-mamalik*, ed. Akram al-'Ulabi (Damascus: Dar al-Ma'mun,1988), 217, 241.

63. Jean-Paul Pascual, *Damas à la fin du XVIe siècle d'après trois actes de waqf ottomanes*, tome 1 (Damascus: Institut Français de Damas, 1983), 74n. 1.

64. M. M. al-Arna'ut, *Mu'tayat 'an Dimashq wa-Bilad al-Sham al-junubiyya fi nihayat al-qarn al-sadis 'ashr* (Damascus: Wizarat al-Thaqafa, 1993), 53–54.

65. On the Ottomans' overriding interest in the pilgrimage to Mecca, see M. Adnan Bakhit, *The Ottoman Province of Damascus in the Sixteenth Century* (Beirut: Librairie du Liban, 1982), 107 ff.; Karl K. Barbir, *Ottoman Rule in Damascus, 1708–1758* (Princeton: Princeton University Press, 1980), 108ff. Although the Takiyya al-Sulaymaniyya, founded by Süleyman I in 962/1554–1555, did not include a hospital as such, it did comprise a large soup kitchen and several residential units, all intended for pilgrims.

CHAPTER SIX

Charity and Hospitality

*Hospitals in the Ottoman Empire in the
Early Modern Period*

MIRI SHEFER

Members of the Ottoman elite commissioned the foundation of several hospitals in major cities. The first hospital to be established in the Ottoman Empire by a member of the Ottoman dynasty was built in Bursa by Beyazit I (r. 1389–1402). The second one was established in Istanbul, then a new capital, by Mehmet II (r. 1444–1446, 1451–1481). His son Beyazit II (r. 1481–1512) had one erected in Edirne. In the sixteenth century three hospitals were erected in Istanbul. Both Süleyman I (r. 1520–1566) and his favorite concubine *(haseki)* and later wife Hürrem Sultan and Nurbanu Sultan, mother of Murat III (r. 1574–1585) included hospitals in their complexes in the capital. So did Sultan Ahmet I (r. 1603–1617) in his Istanbul complex.

Hospitals were built in the provinces as well. One example is the hospital in Manisa added to a complex initiated by Hafsa Sultan, mother of Süleyman I, while she accompanied her son, then a governor of the province. Other examples are the hospitals built in Tunis in 1662 by Hamudah Basha al-Muradi, the Ottoman governor of the province, and in Mecca—by the famous grand vizier Sokullu Mehmet Paşa at the end of the sixteenth century, and one hundred years after him, that of Gülnûş Sultan, the haseki of Sultan Mehmet IV (r. 1648–1687) and later the mother of two sultans: Mustafa II (r. 1698–1703) and Ahmet II (r. 1703–1730).

This chapter, however, focuses on the three cities that served in turn as the official capital of the Ottoman Empire: Bursa, Edirne, and Istanbul. It considers the roles of hospitals as charitable institutions. Hospitals were founded in the premodern Ottoman Empire for different reasons, varying with the specific times and places of their foundation and the different people involved in the initiative. However, there was also a common denominator among their diverse aims: Hospitals were founded to provide medical help to those deemed needy and to enhance the image of the founders as benefactors of those in need.

In this chapter I consider one of the motivations for the founding of hospitals. The general context of hospital foundation was medical charity. In Islamic societies medical aid was a recognized and accepted form of benevolent action. Institutionalized medical treatment in hospitals was only one among a number of forms of medical care in the Ottoman Empire. The hospitals in Bursa, Edirne, and Istanbul were considered by contemporaries to be prime examples of benevolence. Yet how and why did people view the founding, the maintenance, and the functioning of hospitals in these cities as philanthropic actions? Three points in this regard are noteworthy:

1. Hospitals were founded as institutions of *vakıf*, the legal format creating an administrative and financial mechanism for charitable institutions in premodern Islamic societies.
2. The act of hospital foundation was regarded as benevolent. It seems that hospital foundation was the privilege (and duty) of a small circle within the Ottoman elite.
3. Contemporaries regarded the audience that hospitals were meant to serve as needy. Therefore, by analyzing the social, economic, and religious characteristics of this audience we can learn something about who was deemed needy, that is to say, worthy of support, in sixteenth- and seventeenth-century Ottoman society.

Despite what has been said, it seems that hospitals could not provide for all those in need of their services. Istanbul of the sixteenth century—one of the largest cities in the world at the time, with an estimated population of several hundred thousand people[1]—held only five hospitals with a total of a few hundred beds altogether. In Cairo and Aleppo, the two next largest cities in the Ottoman Empire, the situation was the same.

This begs the question to what extent hospitals really were hospitable: Were they open to all? Who got in? Why and what were the services offered there? These issues can all be explored by examining foundation deeds (singular: *vakfiye*), as well as decrees of the sultan (singular: *ferman*), biographical dictionaries, and budget reports.

The Foundation of Hospitals as a Charitable Act

The foundation of hospitals was regarded in the Ottoman society as an expression of charity. This principle was accepted to such an extent that contemporaries did not find it necessary to articulate what was in their minds that made such an endeavor a benevolent one. They found it sufficient to express their position in saying that hospitals were aimed at the benefit of the society at large. This is much to the chagrin of modern scholars trying to decipher the multifaceted intents of the founders and the ways in which their acts were received in society. Scholars need, therefore, to look for clues elsewhere.

Some clues to what was considered charitable in medical aid can be found in the canonic collections of *hadith*s (sayings) of al-Bukhari (d. 870). This collection was compiled toward the end of the ninth century, hundreds of years before the Ottomans, yet it was regarded as authoritative in the early modern period as well.

Al-Bukhari organized his hadith compilation by subjects. Prophetic sayings concerning medicine were collected in "The Book of the Sick" *(Kitab al-marda)* and "The Book of Medicine" *(Kitab al-tibb)*. The sayings contained in these two chapters and other similar collections form the basis for the Islamic–Arabic popular medicine known as "Prophetic Medicine" *(al-tibb al-nabawi)*, that is, popular Arabic medical lore that was legitimized by sayings of the Prophet, thus receiving an Islamic flavor.

An important theme in "The Book of the Sick" is the religious duty to assist the sick. In section four of this book, al-Bukhari quotes two sayings. In the first, Muhammad bade the believers feed the hungry, visit the sick and set those who suffer free. In the second, Muhammad forbade seven acts (among them wearing gold rings, wearing silk clothes, and betting) and ordered seven other actions. Among these are attending funerals, visiting the sick, and spreading peace (i.e., Islam).[2]

One important aspect in al-Bukhari's discussion deals with the question to whom such charity should be extended. It seems that many regarded visiting the sick as a kindness that should be offered only to other members of the *umma* (the Islamic community). This can be deduced from section eleven in "The Book of the Sick," which deals with the question of a Muslim who visits a non-Muslim *(mushrik)*. Some Muslim scholars claimed that visiting a non-Muslim is an important duty as, in addition to helping a sick person, it may turn out to be beneficial to Islam—what the Quran terms "reconciliation of hearts."[3] Also discussed were the obligations to visit any sick person regardless of sex and the type of illness. Al-Bukhari includes in his collection hadiths maintaining that women are allowed—indeed obliged—to visit sick men. As for types of disease, apparently the duty to visit the sick includes those invalids who are unconscious as well, even though they cannot be aware of their visitors. Visiting the sick is intended not only for the benefit of the sick but also to alleviate the distress felt by the family of the sick person.[4]

These and many other similar hadiths may be part of the "spirit of medical charity," the phrase coined by a Scottish medical doctor by the name of C. Bryce, who visited Istanbul in the 1830s and described the medical scene he encountered. Bryce was impressed with the Ottoman–Muslim tradition of founding hospitals as charitable institutions.[5]

Indeed, imperial hospitals—hospitals founded by members of the Ottoman dynasty—were established as vakıf institutions.[6] In this respect hospitals in the Ottoman Empire were not different from similar institutions in other Muslim societies. The vakıf regulated the financial base of hospitals. Treatment was distributed free of charge, and as a result hospitals needed other sources of funds and could easily find themselves short of cash. In two versions of Mehmet II's vakfiye, physicians are warned not to give food, drinks, or medications to people other than those lying in the hospital. However, the earlier version includes an exception: If some particular medication was not available elsewhere, the hospital doctor was indeed allowed to give it.[7] This suggests that it proved too costly and, as a result, was later revoked. A remark added to one budget report of the Süleymaniye complex in the sixteenth century confirms the assumption about the financial hardships experienced by the managers of Mehmet II's hospital. The clerk wrote that the daily budget of Mehmet II's hospital, amounting to 200 *akçe*, was not sufficient. It was therefore decided to raise it to 300 akçe—the amount spent daily at the hospital in the Süleymaniye.[8]

Hospitals also existed in the imperial palaces. They were exceptions to the rule that hospitals in a premodern Muslim society (here Ottoman) were established as vakıf institutions. In Topkapı, for instance, there was a hospital for the pages in the outer court *(Bimarhane-i Hassa)*, and one in the harem compound for the female slaves. There were also hospitals in the palaces in Galatasaray (Pera) and in Edirne. These hospitals were integral organs of their respective palaces, not "extraterritorial" independent vakıf institutions that happened to be within the palace.

The funds for these hospitals came from the palace budget and their staffs were all on the palace payroll. For this reason, there was no need to come up with another means to finance them. The hospital for pages in Topkapı, for example, was run by a eunuch from the palace service.[9]

Two Sides of the Charity Equation:
Those Who Give and Those Who Receive

According to one school of thought in the history of philanthropy, charity is a simple reaction to a situation of need and demand for help. This school stresses the roles of the recipients. This reasoning suggests that hospitals were not widely founded in Ottoman times because the population had little need for such institutions. However, diseases, injuries, and their severity did not especially diminish in the Ottoman Empire from the fifteenth to the seventeenth centuries.[10] On the other hand, the circumstances that prompted the inclusion of a hospital in the Süleymaniye complex, shortly after Hürrem commissioned her own medical institution in a nearby area in Istanbul, are unclear. The sources do not claim that there was a particular need in this period for hospital services, yet they provide no clear motivation.[11]

Another school of thought focuses on the roles of the givers. Miriam Hoexter's contribution to this volume (chapter 7) is an example of this view. Studies on early modern Europe have shown that hospitals were designed to serve the interests of their founders rather than to fulfill patients' needs. They stressed the fact that there are two parties to philanthropy: those who distribute it and those who receive it, each acting for their own ends.[12] In the Ottoman case, one should ask why hospital founders chose this vehicle for their beneficence, and also why so few Ottoman philanthropists chose it.

The Hospital Founders and Their Motives

One historian of European medicine in the early modern period concluded that whatever the founders of hospitals' respective merits were, they expected a "return," a recompense, a reciprocity: be it in the form of gratitude, of legitimization, of honoraria, or in the other world, with an open door to Heaven.[13] This conclusion applies also to the Ottoman Empire. Their patrons supported hospitals for several reasons, among them social, political, and economic considerations. At the same time, religious beliefs and practices shaped the founders' actions.

The act of founding a hospital and laying down its future functions was expressed in terms taken from the language of religious charity. Endowment deeds explain that this act is a *qurba*, that is, a means through which one is getting nearer to God. The descriptions of the donors who founded hospitals included also religious and moral expressions.[14]

Nevertheless, the fact that hospitals in the imperial palaces were not part of the vakıf system does not mean they were not considered an expression of philanthropy. Vakıf was only one means of action in the arena of benevolence. Palace hospitals, much like others, expressed the commitment on the part of the sultan to the members of his household and therefore were considered charity. One piece of evidence for this is the description of the sultan's visits to the hospital in the outer court in Topkapı. In this palace, thousands of people, in addition to the imperial family, worked, studied, and served; the hospital took care of the pages among them. When the French merchant and traveler Jean Baptiste Tavernier visited Istanbul in 1688, he described the pages' hospital within the palace compound as a well-organized and efficiently administered institution, thanks—among other things—to frequent visits by the sultan to check on the patients' condition. The sultan would interview them and inquire whether they were being treated well by the physicians and staff.[15]

However, hospitals were but one agent of medical aid in the imperial palaces; the palace physicians constituted another. Not all the physicians in the palace were necessarily connected with the hospital there. Physicians were also employed in palaces where formal hospitals did not exist, such as that of the Grand Vizier İbrahim Paşa. Such palace physicians were regular members of the staff and were paid out of the palace budget like other servants and artisans.[16] Yet these two forms of medical aid—institutionalized care given by a staff that included physicians, and treatment offered by an individual physician—were not unique to the palaces. Both options were open in theory to all in Ottoman society. (Whether someone could afford treatment at all was another question.)

In contrast, only select members of the elite were allowed to take part in the founding of hospitals in the Ottoman Empire. Among these were first and foremost the sultans. Female members of the Ottoman dynasty also participated: the sultans' mothers and wives or concubines. The act of founding a hospital demanded substantial funds. This fact surely restricted the number of possible donors. Nevertheless, it is clear that those who could have afforded such an undertaking were more numerous than those who chose to do it. Why was this particular form of benevolence restricted to so few within the sultanic household? Leslie Peirce suggests that active philanthropy on the part of an Ottoman prince could have created for him an image that clashed with that of the reigning sultan himself. The activities of female members of the household, on the other hand, did not contain a similar threat.[17]

Therefore, the sultan was the only male figure to found hospitals in the Ottoman urban centers, where female members of the imperial household were notably active in medical charity as well. Other male members of the Ottoman elite did found hospitals, yet these were situated outside the political centers. Examples of these are the hospital of Sokullu Mehmet Paşa in Mecca and the seventeenth-century hospital founded in Tunis by the Ottoman governor; both were also noticeably smaller than those in the imperial cities. Medical charity, therefore, can be said to be a marker of internal stratification within the Ottoman elite and the sultanic household.

Hospitals Were Designed for the Weaker Elements in Society

An imperial Ottoman vakıf complex included several institutions. These differed among other aspects, in their separate, if overlapping, audiences. Only the mosque, for example, served the whole community. Other institutions were targeted at specific groups deemed worthy of public support. *Medrese*s (colleges) served the learned, some of them working toward a career as scholars, the next generation of *ülema* (scholars). In contrast, other institutions are described as supporting socially and economically marginal groups who were nonetheless worthy or in need of support. Some primary schools *(mektebs)* were specifically for poor boys, and soup kitchens *('imarets)* fed the poor *(faqir)*, the miserable *(miskin)*, the needy and the weak, in addition to the 'imaret employees and others.

The poor, the miserable, the needy, and the weak, the categories named in the documents, are fluid and therefore problematic because it is hard to pinpoint whom exactly they included. The modern use of the word *poor*, which refers primarily to those who have little money and as a result are not able to obtain the necessities of life, is only one of several possible meanings. The categories of the entitled were many and varied, whether such entitlement was based on religious or social standing or vocational activity. They may not have been the richest people in town, but they were not in real need of free service. Rather, they were perceived as deserving such help and sympathy. However, it is interesting to note that being entitled to such support was expressed in terms referring to economic, social, and physical hardships.

The mission of Ottoman hospitals was to help the sick, the injured, and those suffering from mutilations and pain, or so the endowment deeds claim. In this sense, hospitals were part of a group of institutions to which soup kitchens and inns for the wayfarers in towns and along commercial routes also belonged. They were all intended to serve people who for a number of reasons could not take care of themselves: They might have lacked financial means, health and strength (physical and mental), and supportive family (through accident or distance).

Medical treatment and care were usually distributed within the family; hospitalization, then, signaled the absence or the dysfunction of a family. The function of the hospital institution together with or in addition to the family exemplifies the balance between different supportive agents: family, the neighborhood, and the community at large.[18] The story of a sick person who is cared for by his loving family and close friends is a literary topos popular in the genre of biographical dictionaries. Hospitals as a place of care are mentioned rarely in such works.

Within the group of institutions that offered physical services to the community we should differentiate between hospitals and institutions, like inns *(tabhane, han, caravansaray)* and soup kitchens ('imaret). All distributed physical help, but the hospital was unique in that it offered professional medical care to the physically and mentally ill, not only shelter, food, and rest for the physically weak.

In this context it is interesting to note the great detail in which Jean Thevenot, a French traveler of the seventeenth century, described the hospital of Sultan Süleyman (*morestan* as he called it) in Damascus. He was impressed greatly by the hospital's domed roof and extensive gardens. The building also included small domed rooms, each equipped with a chimney and two windows. On the right there was a soup kitchen and across from the hospital a mosque distinguished by another large dome with beautiful minarets of lead. There were stables nearby for the horses of the visitors. When Thevenot toured the site it was a very busy place, full of pilgrims on their way to Mecca who gathered in Damascus, the starting point of the northern *hajj* (pilgrimage) caravan. What Thevenot described was actually a travelers' inn (a caravansaray, not a hospital), part of the complex commissioned by Süleyman I. The complex is still known locally as Takiyya Sulaymaniyya.[19] The mistaken identification of a lodge and kitchen with a hospital reveals how similar these institutions may have been physically or in the minds of contemporaries. However, it is unclear whether this mistake was Thevenot's or a local misdirection.

The Sick and the Patients

> We have histories of diseases but not of health, biographies of doctors but not of the sick.[20]

In this section I am concerned not to add to the genre of "famous illnesses of famous people," but rather to analyze who the patients in premodern Ottoman hospitals were. First, we should note that these hospitals were established as charitable institutions: Their patrons intended them for people who were worthy of support, and therefore the act of founding them gained the patrons much respect. Whom did these donors consider worthy of support? Second, why did some people seek help in hospitals, that is, who were the patients in reality and why were certain sick people treated privately by their families while others were admitted to hospitals? From this set of questions stems another: To what extent were hospitals indeed hospitable to the population they were supposed to serve? I will attempt to answer these questions through a discussion of five subjects: economic and social standing of hospital patients, their religious affiliations, sex, age, and types of illnesses that were treated in Ottoman hospitals.

Social and Economic Standing

The renowned Ottoman traveler Evliya Çelebi (c. 1611–1685) included in his book on his extensive accounts of the Ottoman Empire in the mid-seventeenth century the biography of his relative and patron Melek Ahmet Paşa, a senior Ottoman official. In the winter of 1656, Melek Ahmed's neck swelled up and he fell sick. A pustule developed and after five to ten days his neck became red and as thick as a loaf of bread. Many physicians, surgeons, and phlebotomists were brought in, and although each of them prescribed a different treatment, the paşa's condition deteriorated: he lost his voice and could only hum like a bee. Many in his household, believing his end was near, left to look for a new (and living) patron. However, Evliya Çelebi, the faithful companion, dreamt a dream whose interpretation gave the paşa new hope. Once again a surgeon was summoned who opened the paşa's collar, drained the pus, and removed the rotten flesh. Within two months he had fully recovered.[21]

From these and other pieces of evidence, one could deduce that poor people were admitted into hospitals where medical care was distributed free, whereas the well-to-do engaged private doctors and were treated in the privacy of their own homes. But a simplistic explanation based solely on the social and economic standing of hospital patients versus people treated at home does not reflect the Ottoman reality of the time.

Muhammad Amin b. Fadlallah al-Muhibbi (d. 1700) included in his biographical dictionary the biography of a family member of an earlier generation, one Ahmad b. Muhammad from Damascus, known by his nickname Ibn al-Munqar (d. 1623). Ahmad b. Muhammad became famous as a poet before he was twenty years old, renowned for his expertise in both science and the Arabic language. After his father's death in Istanbul, Ahmad traveled to the Ottoman capital, where his father had held a position as a judge, to claim his inheritance. His fame spread in the capital as well and the Head Müfti of the empire made him his assistant. But soon Ahmad succumbed to melancholy, lost his reason, and his speech became slurred. He was put in a hospital but later was sent back to his hometown accompanied by some other Damascene notables returning from Istanbul. In Damascus, he was put in a house where he was under constant care and supervision. He was allowed to leave the house only accompanied by a guard and for limited periods of time. He never regained his reason and after thirty years died still a madman.[22]

The fate of Ahmad b. Muhammad reveals that under certain circumstances even a member of a famous and well-off family could be a patient in a hospital. Sultan Süleyman indeed expected that people carrying with them money and goods would be admitted into his Istanbul hospital. He instructed what should be done in such cases: The clerk *(katip)* in the hospital was to record in detail the belongings that patients brought with them when admitted; special attention was to be given to recording money and other valuables. The clerk's duty was to return to the patients leaving the institution whatever they had brought with them according to his records. A special area in the hospital was reserved for the treasury *(bayt-ül-mal* or *hazine),* into which no one was allowed to enter except the head physician. The hospital funds and the patients' valuables were kept here.[23]

Who, then, were the patients in hospitals in the Ottoman capitals? Certainly, some were poor, but wealthy people were also patients in hospitals. The Istanbul qadi court records reveal that some of the people who died in the hospitals in town left behind estates. It was the qadi's duty to dispense these estates between the legal heirs. The estates in question were rather modest, but they clearly show that the deceased were people of some means. They left behind houses and flats, slaves and concubines, cash, riding beasts, and so forth.[24]

Other hospital patients were strangers in a faraway place with no family close by to support them. "If travelers and wayfarers are sick, they come to the hospital of Sultan Mehmet the Conqueror and they treat them."[25] This was Evliya's description of the patient population in the hospital. The English traveler George Sandys visited the Ottoman Empire at the beginning of the seventeenth century. According to him, the hospitals in Istanbul were a place where the ill were cured and foreigners were hosted and entertained.[26] Foreigners, among them merchants, immigrants from the provinces, scholars, and adventurers, came to the Ottoman capital for many different reasons.

Even the healthiest and strongest of travelers were foreigners in town, and when they fell sick some of them had to seek help at the local hospitals. They did not know the physicians there and could not rely on supportive friends and relatives. Thus, hospital patients in these cities might be rich people who would have contracted a private physician in their hometown—they certainly could have afforded one—but on their travels to foreign lands used hospital services, which were given free of charge.[27]

Other urban centers were magnets as well. The Ottoman capitals are the principal focus of this chapter; however, we should not forget the holy cities of Mecca and Medina to which thousands of Muslims from all corners of the world flocked both to fulfill the duty of the hajj and to study. The long road and its hardships proved too difficult for many and they fell sick or died along the way, or else arrived sick and died there. In Ottoman Mecca and Medina there existed hospitals founded in pre-Ottoman times. To these were added Ottoman institutions, like the hospitals of Sokullu Mehmet Paşa and Gülnüş Sultan mentioned previously.[28]

Viewing the foreign traveler as someone who might especially need medical aid was not new in Ottoman society; medieval Muslim–Arabic society was also well acquainted with this problem, as we can learn from Franz Rosenthal's article on the stranger in medieval Islam. By analyzing the literary conventions used by several authors to describe strangers and strangeness, Rosenthal was able to point to wretchedness as a constantly threatening companion of strangers. Two possible sources of wretchedness are poverty and ill health. These conditions are always hard, but they are especially difficult to bear when one is in a foreign place.[29]

A different group of patients in hospitals were the pages in Topkapı Palace who were treated in the hospital there which served only members of the palace service. In contrast to strangers who were alone in their illness, the palace pages could rely on the friends and colleagues with whom they lived and worked. The palace hospital was situated in the first and outer court, to the right of the Imperial Gate, a mere few hundred meters from their private rooms in the inner third court. Yet even though the physical distance was rather short, there was a major difference in lifestyles between the two courts: The severe rules of conduct of the third court, befitting those close to the sultan, were not enforced as heavily in the first court. This was one of the reasons why the hospital was attractive to patients.[30]

Finally, and in keeping with this same division, the members of the Ottoman family living in Topkapı were not treated in either of these hospitals; rather, they were treated privately by the palace doctors.[31]

Religious Affiliations

In Ottoman society hospitals did not serve members of different religious communities. The evidence for this comes from various sources. In the imperial hospitals, for example, the patients were Muslims. The foundation deeds specify the aims of the endowment and usually refer to the benefit provided to Muslims when emphasizing the advantages of hospitals. Thus, for example, the vakfiye of Mehmet II, repeats that Muslims (and mentioned only them) can avail themselves of this hospital.[32] And the vakfiye of Beyazit II states that the hospital is intended for the religious (i.e., religious Muslim) poor.[33]

Hospitals offered religious services of various sorts to their Muslim patients. On the hospital staff there were imams, muezzins, and *ghassals* (launderers) who brought the dead for Muslim burial; a special space within the hospital building was reserved for a mosque. Non-Muslims were cared for separately: Ottoman Jews had autonomous hospitals run by the community.[34] Near the hospital of Mehmet II in Istanbul there was an institution especially for *dhimmi*s (non-Muslims), according to Evliya.[35] It is not clear what Evliya was referring to here, as other sources do not mention an institution connected with the hospital of Mehmet II specializing in the treatment of non-Muslim patients.

The separation between Muslims and non-Muslims in Ottoman hospitals should not come as a surprise. In the past—as also today—medical practice can contradict religious beliefs on various levels: Medical theories, therapeutic procedures, and even seeking the help of medicine and doctors rather than that of religion and religious scholars could (and still can) contradict religious beliefs. The Cairo Geniza includes numerous references to Jewish physicians practicing their craft in hospitals; however, there is not a single reference to Jews being patients there. Apparently, Jews did not wish to be hospitalized because of fear of the food in the institution: Medical exigencies were not sufficient to transgress dietary regulations.[36] In sixteenth-century Jerusalem there were hospitals that served the Jewish community (or subcommunities within it) exclusively.[37] But it is difficult to know whether the intra-community medical system was a substitute for quasi-state hospitals that were closed to Jews. Possibly, too, an ideology of communal autonomy was the reason for ethnic and religious separation in hospital admissions policies.

Gender

Mamluk vakfiyes stress that there should not be any kind of discrimination—for example, based on sex—among those who wish to be admitted into the hospital, whereas the Ottoman foundation deeds under study here do not comment at all on this issue. However, the evidence suggests that patients in Ottoman hospitals were usually male. Among the evidence is a miniature included in an album prepared for Sultan Ahmet I. This miniature depicts a scene in a hospital for the insane. The patients are all bearded men.[38]

The moral code in traditional Ottoman society—in Muslim and non-Muslim communities alike—prescribed segregation of the sexes. The aim of this segregation was to defend the modesty and honor of both sexes, although the importance of these issues to women was especially emphasized. Modesty and honor were achieved by concealing private parts of the body *('awra)*. To look at these parts, even if someone was of the same gender, was regarded as transgressing the boundaries of decency. Therefore, Muslim deontologists were bound to discuss the question of male physicians treating female patients and vice versa. However, the very nature of medical examination demands physical contact between patient and physician in seclusion *(khalwa)* and therefore allows for rumors about sexual misconduct. Based on this realization, deontologists discouraged patients from being treated by doctors of the opposite sex, especially in cases of female patients and male doctors.[39]

One way around this restriction is described by Bobovi, a Pole who served as a page in Topkapı for nineteen years in the middle of the seventeenth century. Bobovi claimed that the male patients in the palace hospital in the first court in Topkapı were taken care of by old female servants called *anne* (mother) who acted as the laundry women in the institution.[40] Old, that is, "post-sexual," women in Ottoman society were freed from many of the legal and cultural restrictions of female seclusion enforced on younger women.[41] Thus, older women who did not present a sexual challenge anymore could be employed as "nurses" to young men in an all-male hospital.

That means that male and female patients could not have been treated together in the same space. Indeed, in the rare cases in which there is a direct reference in the sources to female patients in a hospital, it is specifically stated that there was a special space for the treatment of women within the all-male hospital, or even a building solely for their use. Evliya Çelebi claimed that in a corner near the hospital of Mehmet II in Istanbul there was another hospital that was dedicated to women.[42] Again, it is not clear what Evliya was referring to here, as other sources do not mention an institution—or a wing in the all-male hospital—specializing in the treatment of female patients. Evliya is probably referring to the same institution referred to earlier for dhimmis. It is interesting that according to Evliya this second hospital served both women and non-Muslims, not necessarily female dhimmis.

Evliya Çelebi reported that in Cairo, too, there existed a hospital dedicated only to female patients. This institution was situated near the Qala'unid hospital for men: "On one side of this *darüşşifa* [hospital] is a *bimarhane* [hospital] for women. It is also a magnificent, sumptuous building. Moreover, all the servants [in it] are also women, but the [male] physicians are allowed inside. [The physicians] enter [the building] fearlessly and without scruple and give medication according to the different illnesses."[43]

Here we encounter another issue raised by the segregation of the sexes: Should women be treated by male staff? The physicians in the Qala'unid hospital for women were described as *mahram*, a legal term denoting people in close biological family relations that forbid them to marry each other.[44] By this legal stratagem the problem of privacy between male doctors and female patients was avoided. The male physician was given the status of a close relative to sanction his proximity while treating a female patient; hence, this encounter was not considered to be crossing forbidden boundaries. In other cases it was mentioned specifically that the staff also included female attendants.[45]

Female patients in the Ottoman palace were a special case. Hand in hand with the prerogatives came restrictions as well: Female members of the elite, especially the women in the imperial Ottoman harem, had to be more committed to gender separation and their isolation in the harem than did women in general. This social–moral code had a direct bearing on the medical care given to palace women. Male physicians were called on when necessary, but they were allowed to treat their female patients in the harem only under close supervision of the harem eunuchs. The female servants and other non-ranking women in the harem were not taken to the first court of the palace. The sick among them were treated in a separate hospital situated under the harem living quarters, thus maintaining the segregation of the sexes in the palace (and keeping the women "within their family" inside the larger households).[46]

Age

Ottoman foundation deeds do not include a direct reference to the ages of patients or a possible connection between their ages and hospital admission policy, but several pieces of evidence indicate that patients were not young but mature men. For example, the roles of the *hamam* (bath) attendants in the hospital. In Süleyman's hospital they had to shave the patients—a task that would not have been required if the patients were children.[47] In fact, the endowment deeds do not refer to a situation in which the institution would have to adjust to the presence of young boys, for example, by supplying special food or clothes of smaller size.

Circumstantial evidence (and as such not too strong) corroborates this. Evliya writes that "old and young" populate the hospital in Edirne,[48] but he does not add anything concrete to explain his figure of speech. When talking of Cairo, Evliya takes the trouble to mention that in the hospital for women adjacent to the central Qala'unid institution some female patients had given birth. He tells the story of a boy born in the hospital who was named "health" *(şifa)*—a play on words of the name of the institution: the literal meaning of the term *hospital* is "the house of health." From Evliya's description, it is clear that giving birth in a hospital was a rare occurrence.[49] Apparently, what Evliya had heard of was a boy born to a female patient and not a child patient in his own right.

Types of Illnesses Treated in Ottoman Hospitals

Hospitals resembled hans, caravansarays, and tabhanes in that all four institutions offered temporary lodgings. But hospitals were different in that the lodgers were sick, not healthy people. The various hostels for merchants and other way-farers perhaps hosted exhausted people, people who needed bed and board to recover their strength or their health. Yet such people did not make use of pro-fessional healers because this kind of service was officially offered only by hospitals.

The evidence for Ottoman society indicates that the patients in hospitals were indeed sick. The vakfiye of Ahmet I said: "the sick, the wounded and those who suffer injuries and aches."[50] In this respect, Ottoman hospitals resembled similar institutions in other premodern Muslim societies and were different from Euro-pean hospitals of the time. In the Middle Ages and the early modern period in Europe, the institution called "hospital" was not necessarily associated with sick-ness and medical care. The clear identification of hospitals with sick people who are being treated medically within the institution of a hospital is a relatively re-cent phenomenon in the Western world. In many cases the medical treatment of the time prescribed no more than rest in a clean and warm place with a nourishing and balanced diet, without medication; even for "real" patients, hospitals offered not much more than the promise of these.

Ottoman hospitals were expected to admit all patients regardless of their med-ical problem. In contrast, even where they existed to serve sick patients, some European hospitals—as, for example, Florentine hospitals in the sixteenth cen-tury—were selective in their admissions policies. For budgetary reasons, the managers preferred to concentrate their limited resources on the acutely rather than the chronically sick because it could be expected that they would either recover quickly or succumb to their illnesses; either way, the bed would soon become avail-able for another patient.[51]

The Ottoman inclusive policy may be deduced from the composition of the medical staff, which included various specialists such as "internists," oculists, and surgeons. According to Bobovi, the Polish page, the most common illnesses in the Ottoman palaces were caused "either by the fear and misery of liver disease or from eating spoiled foods; sicknesses such as hepatitis, consumption, bowel obstructions and dropsy, are rampant . . . and the plague is ever present."[52]

Yet many Ottoman sources mention only the madmen among the patients, to a great extent totally disregarding other types of patients. The foundation deeds refer to the possibility of lunatics among the patient population, and travelers de-scribed the antics of the mad in the hospitals.[53] The fascination of the sources with this group of patients should not come as a total surprise: Lunatics are, after all, more picturesque than people who suffer, for example, from dysentery.

Lunatics could be found in "regular" hospitals throughout the empire. The Zangid hospital founded in Damascus, the Ayyubid hospital in Jerusalem founded by Saladin and the female section in the Qala'unid hospital in Cairo included many madmen among their patients.[54] For Thevenot, the French traveler, the patients in the Qala'unid hospital were first and foremost lunatics; almost as an afterthought he adds that there were also sick, poor people in the institution.[55]

The hospitalization of lunatics in "regular" hospitals is not unique to the Ottoman institutions. Treating the madmen alongside the physically ill suited the medical theory of the time, according to which both physiological ailments and mental illnesses were caused by problems in the body and the soul. Michael Dols claimed that the devotion of separate space to the mentally ill in the "regular" hospital was the most notable characteristic of hospitals in Muslim societies.[56]

Were Hospitals Indeed Hospitable?

The previous section dealt with the questions of who were ideally worthy of medical help in the eyes of benevolent patrons and the identity of actual patients in their hospitals. From these two queries stems a third: To what extent were hospitals indeed hospitable to the population they were supposed to serve?

One conclusion that may be drawn from the preceding discussion is that the patient population in hospitals was rather heterogeneous. Yet the patients constituted a more homogeneous group than is implied in the foundation deeds—which described an institution open almost to all—or in Evliya's account. It is possible that both the authors of the endowment deeds and Evliya Çelebi aimed to give the impression of an ideal situation—or perhaps they wished to set a high standard for Ottoman philanthropists. In reality, however, only certain groups in society were represented among hospital patients.

The tendency toward homogeneity in the patient population was due to a double selectivity. On the one hand, reality—the social and cultural codes accepted as norms in Ottoman society—restricted the variety of people approaching hospitals and the circumstances in which they did so. Although the sources do mention well-to-do people as patients in hospitals, it seems that they were the exceptions. On the other hand, we should take into account the limited number of beds in Ottoman hospitals. In sixteenth-century Istanbul, the number of beds is estimated at no more than four hundred.[57] The population of the city at the time was a few hundred thousand. At the same time, some hospital administrators directed their limited resources toward the more deserving (at least in their eyes) among their patients.[58] The planners of modern hospitals aim to bring the best medical facilities and treatment to the most people, naturally at the lowest cost.[59] In contrast, the managers of Ottoman hospitals restricted their efforts deliberately to a specific and small audience.

However, the tendency toward homogeneity in the patient population does not mean that only a small number of people or limited types of patients could benefit from hospitals. Rather, hospitals offered different types of services to different individuals and groups within the community they served. Ottoman hospitals provided a variety of services: a "package deal" in which medical treatment was only one component among many, not all necessarily medicine-related.[60] Even in Ottoman hospitals, which aimed to treat sick patients who needed medical care, these patients were only one of the groups that used the institutions' services. There were several concentric circles of services focused around the hospitals.

The first circle of service contained those patients admitted to the hospitals who had to spend time there. What did the patients in hospitals receive? First and foremost, they received treatment, including warm and clean beds, food, and physical and mental therapy. And, as I have already mentioned, when the treatment proved ineffective and the patient passed away, the dead were looked after as well: The institution had the bodies ritually cleansed and buried in shrouds.

In addition to the treatment time, patients were allowed to stay in the hospital for unlimited periods. This hospital policy was in marked contrast to that in tabhanes, hans, and caravansarays. These hospices and inns enforced the maximum three-day-stay rule, after which the visitors could no longer enjoy free food, lodging, and other services offered there.[61] We should not underestimate the possibility of an unlimited stay in a hospital. For foreigners who fell sick far away from home, the hospital was also a hotel, and thus they were spared the need of looking for suitable lodging.[62]

The second of the service circles comprised the outpatients, that is, persons who visited the hospital during the day for treatment but returned to their homes for the night. Generally, the endowment deeds warned hospital administrators against financing the medical needs of people outside the hospital. At the same time, they clarified the circumstances in which administrators could depart from this rule: If some particular medication was not available outside, the doctor was indeed allowed to give it. Even this exception was short-lived, however; it was revoked at the hospital of Mehmet II within seventy years or so, perhaps because it was too costly.[63] In Hürrem Sultan's Istanbul hospital, the two physicians were instructed to hold "open days" twice a week, on Mondays and Thursdays. Those in need could come and ask for their help. But the donor stressed that in these cases, too, medication was to be given only to the truly needy (and deserving), not to just anybody.[64]

Those who received treatment and medication at home constituted a third circle of patients around the hospital, as is suggested by the provision of Mehmet II that a herbalist was to make special medications and take them to the "assigned places." Once a week the administrator, the head physicians, and the clerk should convene in the hospital to discuss medical cases of people sick at home who were not strong enough to visit a doctor or who had no money to pay for a private physician and the medication which he prescribed. To these people a doctor was to be sent with medications from the hospital's supply depot.[65]

Hospitals also catered to the non-sick, that is, the healthy members of the community; these defined the fourth circle. The most obvious way in which they did so was by being employees. People with different training and skills—medical and other—earned their living in the hospital. But we can find other services for the healthy offered both metaphorically and practically by hospitals. Many medical treatises were to be found in the hospital of Mehmet II in Istanbul,[66] probably for the doctors in the institution and perhaps also to be lent to other physicians. Ottoman hospitals thus functioned as teaching institutions and libraries to some extent. In the hospital in Manisa, the head physician in the sixteenth century used to prepare a medicinal paste *(ma'cun)* based on a secret recipe. This paste was very famous in the area and it was believed to have magic therapeutic properties. It was distributed during public ceremonies on special occasions like the *Nevruz* celebration for the Persian New Year's Day. Because it was in great demand, the sultan issued an order in July 1664 to the judge in town: The paste would be first served to the patients in the hospital, then to the poor, and finally to healthy locals[67]—thereby defining a clear hierarchy of entitlement of services from the hospital.

The founders were another healthy group served by the hospitals, or, rather, the founders used this institution for their own ends: namely, social control. Patronage of hospitals was an important tool in enhancing the image of donors and earning them support and legitimacy. Health, like food, was a means by which to create (and nurture) ties of loyalty and dependence in Ottoman society.[68]

The variety of services offered by hospitals to the community at large, not only to the small number of patients within the institutions themselves, is a characteristic that Ottoman hospitals share with others, such as those in Florence and England. All the various functions hospitals fulfilled for the community were considered as so many aspects of charity and the brotherhood of humanity. The distinctions between hospitals in different societies lie not in the variety of their services but rather in the particular services offered, which changed according to the managers' understandings of what their communities required and expected from their institution. Historically, they show the extent to which hospitals adjusted themselves to the requirements of the population in whose midst they functioned.[69]

At this point I would like to draw the reader's attention to the fact that Ottoman imperial hospitals were established not for the benefit of the community at large but for the individual. The vakfiyes speak of the hardships of individuals, not of possible problems that sick people might pose for their community. We cannot help but notice the very small number of hospitals in comparison with the size of the population. As might be expected, the number of beds in these very few hospitals could not possibly fulfill all the needs of Ottoman society.[70] However, the patrons and the managers of hospitals did not pretend to care for all the sick in the community, nor did they wish to do so.

Additional evidence for the central place of the individual is the attitude demonstrated by hospitals toward the inherent danger posed to the community by contagious diseases. Hospitals in the Ottoman Empire were not intended to remove those suffering from contagious illness from the streets, thus preventing the spread of disease. The medical explanation for this non-role of hospitals was that contagion theory was peripheral to the belief in miasma, or vapors, as a cause of illness within the medical system at the time. The social and cultural explanation was that hospitals were not intended to function as defense mechanisms, as a form of quarantine, keeping diseases at bay, away from society and those who were medically healthy. Rather, hospitals in the Ottoman Empire were supposed to help certain individual people who were deemed worthy of support and to enhance the image of their patrons as benevolent Muslims.

Notes

This chapter is based on parts from my Ph.D. dissertation submitted to Tel Aviv University and supervised by Dr. Amy Singer. I am glad to acknowledge my debt to her.

1. H. Inalcik, "Istanbul," *EP*, 4:238–244.

2. Muhammad b. Isma'il al-Bukhari, *"Kitab al-marda," Sahih* (Leiden: Brill, 1908), 4:4.

3. A reference to Quran, *sura* 9:60, which specifies the categories of recipients of the *zakat* (alms). Among these are "those whose hearts must be reconciled," referring to Muhammad allowing the booty from his campaigns to be given to new converts to Islam, thus convincing them to maintain their allegiance to the new religion and to Muhammad.

4. Al-Bukhari, *"Kitab al-Marda,"* 4–5, 8–11; Ibn Hajar al-'Asqalani, *Fath al-Bari bisharh al-Bukhari* (Misr: Mustafa al-Babi, 1378/1959), 12:217. The text and commentary do not elaborate whether men should also visit sick women.

5. C. Bryce, "Sketch of the State and Practice of Medicine at Constantinople," *Edinburgh Medical and Surgical Journal* 35 (1931): 2.

6. Vakıflar Genel Müdürlüğü Arşivi (The Archives of the General Directorate of Pious Foundation, hereafter VGM), D. 608/22, 79–82 and D. 990, 167–170 for Beyazit I. For Mehmet II's hospital, see VGM, D. 575, 82–106; D. 613, 27–50; n.a., *Fatih Mehmet II Vakfiyeleri* (Istanbul: Cumhuriyet Matbaasi, 1938); A. Süheyl Ünver, "Fatih Külliyesinin İlk Vakfiyesine Göre Fatih Darüşşifası," *Türk Tıb Tarihi Arkivi*, 1940, 5/17:13–17. VGM, D. 613, 65–70 for Beyazit II's hospital; n.a., *Süleymaniye Vakfiyesi* (Ankara: Resimli Posta Matbaası, 1962) for Süleyman's. Hürrem's endowment deed is archived at VGM, D. 608/23, 222–235. Nurbanu's at VGM, closet *(dolap)* 1550, 51–94. Ahmet I's hospital is described in VGM, D. 574, 80–86. Hafsa Sultan's complex in Manisa is dealt with in VGM, box *(kasa)* 58; İbrahim Hakki Konyalı, "Kanunî Sultan Süleyman'ın Annesi Hafsa Sultan'ın Vakfiyesi ve Manisa'daki Hayir Eserleri," *Vakıflar Dergisi* 8 (1969): 47–56; Topkapı Sarayı Müzesi Arşivi (Topkapı Palace Museum Archives, hereafter TSMA), D. 7017/1. For the hos-

pitals in Mecca, see VGM, dolap 1550, 207–232 (Sokollu Mehmet Paşa's hospital) and VGM, D. 2138, 1–7 for Gülnuş Sultan.

7. *Fatih Mehmet II Vakfiyeleri*, 275; Ünver, "Fatih Külliyesinan İlk Vakfiyesine Göre Fatih Daruşşifası," 16.

8. TSMA, D. 1116, f. 11b.

9. On the identity of the caregiver, see a miniature in Loqman's *Hünername*, 1:15r as cited in Gülru Necipoğlu, *Architecture, Ceremonial, and Power: The Topkapı Palace in the Fifteenth and Sixteenth Centuries* (Cambridge: MIT Press, 1991), 43; Barnette Miller, *Beyond the Sublime Port* (New Haven: Yale University Press, 1931), 167.

10. See, for example, Michael W. Dols, "The Second Pandemic and Its Recurrences in the Middle East: 1347–1894," *Journal of Economic and Social History of the Orient* 22 (1979): 162–189.

11. J. M. Rogers, "Sinan as Planner: Some Documentary Evidence," *Enviromental Design* 5, nos. 5–6 (1987): 182.

12. For the Italian case, see Sandra Cavallo, *Charity and Power in Early Modern Italy: Benefactors and Their Motives in Turin, 1541–1789* (Cambridge: Cambridge University Press, 1995); "Charity, Power, and Patronage in an Eighteenth Century Italian Hospital: The Case of Turin," in *The Hospital in History*, ed. Lindsay Granshaw and Roy Porter (London: Routledge, 1989), 93–118; "The Motivations of Benefactors: An Overview of Approaches to the Study of Charity," in *Medicine and Charity before the Welfare State*, ed. Jonathan Barry and Colin Jones (London: Routledge, 1991), 46–62. On England, see Margaret Pelling, "Healing the Sick Poor: Social Policy and Disability in Norwich 1550–1640," *Medical History* 29 (1985): 115–137. See also a special issue of *Continuity and Change* 3, no. 2 (1988), dedicated to this subject.

13. J. P. Goubert, "Twenty Years On: Problems of Historical Methodology in the History of Health," in *Problems and Methods in the History of Medicine*, ed. Roy Porter and Andrew Wear (London: Croom Helm, 1987), 43.

14. See, for example, the endowment deed of a hospital in Tunis in the seventeenth century in Nancy E. Gallagher, *Medicine and Power in Tunisia, 1780–1900* (Cambridge: Cambridge University Press, 1983), 102. In medieval European cities, east and west, the use of terminology taken from the realm of religious charity to describe the establishment of hospitals was common, too. For Cambridge, see Miri Rubin, "Development and Change in English Hospitals, 1100–1500," in *The Hospital in History*, ed. Lindsay Granshaw and Roy Porter (London: Routledge, 1989), 50. For the Spanish case, see James William Brodman, *Charity and Welfare: Hospitals and the Poor in Medieval Catalonia* (Philadelphia: University of Pennsylvania Press, 1998), 54ff. For the Byzantine situation, see Timothy S. Miller, *The Birth of the Hospital in the Byzantine Empire*, rev. ed. (Baltimore: Johns Hopkins University Press, 1997), 50; idem., "Byzantine Hospitals," *Symposium on Byzantine Medicine. Dumbarton Oaks Papers* 38 (1984): 54.

15. Jean Baptiste Tavernier, *A New Relation of the Inner-Part of the Grand Seignior's Seraglio* (London: R. L. and Moses Pitt, 1677), 22–23.

16. See Ömer Lûtfi Barkan, "İstanbul Saraylarına ait Muhasebe Defterleri," *Belgeler* 9, no. 13 (1979): 1–380; Rifki M. Meriç, "Osmanlı Tababeti Tarihine ait Vesikalar," *Tarih Vesikaları*, 1 no. 16 (1955): 37–113 and 2, no. 17 (1958): 267–293.

17. Leslie S. Peirce, *The Imperial Harem* (New York: Oxford University Press, 1993), 199.

18. Peregrine Horden, "A Discipline of Relevance: The Historiography of the Later Medieval Hospital," *Social History of Medicine* 1 (1988): 373n. 47.

19. Jean Thevenot, *The Travells of Monsieur de Thevenot into the Levant* . . . (London: H. Clark, 1687), 20; Evliya Çelebi, *Seyahatname* (Istanbul: Devlet Matbaası, 1935), 9:540–541; N. Elisseeff, "Dimashk," *EI²*, 2:288; Aptullah Kuran, *Sinan: The Grand Old Master of Ottoman Architecture* (Washington, D.C.: Institute of Turkish Studies, 1985), 75–76.

20. Roy Porter, ed., "Introduction," *Patients and Practitioners: Lay Perceptions of Medicine in Pre-Industrial Society* (Cambridge: Cambridge University Press, 1985), 1.

21. Evliya Çelebi, *The Intimate Life of an Ottoman Statesman: Melek Ahmed Paşa (1588–1662)*, trans. and ed. R. Dankoff (Albany: State University of New York Press, 1991), 207–214. Evliya also related stories about other cases of illness and other sick people, treated at home by private physicians, not in hospitals. See, for example, 99–104, 108–110, 231, 263–264.

22. Muhammad Amin b. Fadl Allah al-Muhibbi, *Tarikh khulasat al-athar* (Misr: al-Matbaʻa al-Wahbiyya, 1284 A.H.), 1:296–297.

23. *Süleymaniye Vakfiyesi,* 1:145–146, 151.

24. Said Öztürk, *Askeri Kassama ait Onyedinci Asır İstanbul Tereke Defterleri (Sosyo-Ekonomik Tahlil)* (Istanbul: Osmanlı Araştırmaları Vakfı [OSAV], 1995), 135–137, 301, 310–311, 327, 330, 360, 369, 377, 442, 462, 466.

25. Evliya Çelebi, *Seyahatname* (Istanbul: Akelam Matbaası, 1314 A.H.), 1:321.

26. George Sandys, *A Relation of a Journey Begun an Dom 1610 Containing a Description of the Turkish Empire*, 6th ed. (London: Robert Clavel, 1670), 45.

27. On wealthy pilgrims who were among those who died in the Meccan hospital, see Prime Ministry Ottoman Archive (Başbakanlık Osmanlı Arşivi, İstanbul; hereafter BOA), *Mühimme* 7, 365/item 1057 (14 Ramazan 975 [13 March 1568]), 402/item 1154 (28 Ramazan 975 [27 March 1568]).

28. BOA, *Mühimme* 73, 242/item 564 (20 Ramazan 1003 [29 May 1595]); Öztürk, *Askeri Kassama ait Onyedinci Asır İstanbul Tereke Defterleri*, 133. The hospital founded by ʻImad al-Din Zangi (d. 1174) continued to function as a hospital in the sixteenth century as well, despite financial hardships as the vakıf supporting it shrank; see Suraiya Faroqhi, *Pilgrims and Sultans* (London: I. B. Tauris, 1990), 122.

29. Franz Rosenthal, "The Stranger in Medieval Islam," *Arabica* 44 (1997): 43.

30. Tavernier, *A New Relation*, 22–23.

31. Compare this with an imperial Byzantine hospital founded by Constantine IX in the middle of the eleventh century in Constantinople, which aimed specifically to serve members of the top social and political echelon of Byzantine society, including royalty; see *The Birth of a Hospital*, Miller, 149.

32. VGM, D. 575, 43–44.

33. M. Tayyib Gökbilgin, *XV.–XVI. Asırlarda Edirne ve Paşa Livası* (Istanbul: Üçler Basımevi, 1952), 150–151, 168–171. For a late-nineteenth-century policy of admitting non-Muslims into hospitals in Istanbul, see Nuran Yıldırım, "Meclis-i Vükelâ'nın, Akıl Hastası Musevi bir Kadın için Aldığı karar," *Yeni Tıp Tarihi Araştırmaları*, 2–3 (1996–1997): 258–259.

34. For Jerusalem, see Amnon Cohen and Elisheva Simon-Pikali, *Jews in the Moslem Religious Court—Society, Economy, and Commercial Organization in the XVIth Century: Documents from Ottoman Jerusalem* (Jerusalem: Yad Izhak Ben-Zvi, 1993), 321 (doc. 366), 339 (doc. 382) [in Hebrew]; Amonon Cohen, *A World Within: Jewish Life as Reflected in Muslim Court Documents from the* Sijill *of Jerusalem (XVIth Century)* (Philadelphia: Center for Judaic Studies, University of Pennsylvania, 1984), 163 [F/297], 165 [F/299]; Amnon Cohen, Elisheva Simon-Pikali, and Ovadia Salama, *Jews in the Moslem Religious Court—Society, Economy, and Commercial Organization in the XVIIIth Century: Documents from Ottoman Jerusalem* (Jerusalem: Yad Izhak Ben-Zvi, 1996), 172 (doc. 138), 176 (doc. 142n. 3), 319 (doc. 278) [in Hebrew].

35. Evliya Çelebi, *Seyahatname*, 1:321.

36. S. D. Goitein, *A Mediterranean Society: The Jewish Communities of the Arab World as Portrayed in the Documents of the Cairo Geniza*, 5 vols. (Berkeley: University of California Press, 1971), 2:251.

37. Cohen, *A World Within*, 163, 165.

38. Topkapı Sarayı Müzesi Kütüphanesi (Topkapı Palace Museum Library), B. 408. During my work in the library, access to this manuscript was restricted. The miniature was published and discussed by Ahmet Süheyl Ünver in his "L'album d'Ahmed Ier," *Annali dell'Istituto Universitario Orientale di Napoli* 13 (1963): 137–138, 161–162. More recently it was analyzed by Michael W. Dols in *Majnun: The Madman in Medieval Islamic Society* (Oxford: Clarendon Press, 1992), 130–131.

39. See, for example, al-Bukhari, *"Kitab al-Tibb,"* 4:2; al-'Asqalani, *Fath al-Bari*, 12:241ff. The debate on this issue continues into modern times. See Vardit Rispler Chaim, "Doctor–Patient Relations," in his *Islamic Medical Ethics in the Twentieth Century* (Leiden: Brill, 1993), 62–71.

40. C. G. Fisher and A. Fisher, "Topkapı Sarayı in the Mid-Seventeenth Century: Bobovi's Description," *Archivum Ottomanicum* 10 (1985 [1987]): 76; Miller, *Beyond the Sublime Port*, 166.

41. The changes in the legal and cultural status of Ottoman elite women in the different stages of their lives is one of the themes in Peirce, *The Imperial Harem*.

42. Evliya Çelebi, *Seyahatname*, 1:321.

43. Evliya Çelebi, *Seyahatname* (Istanbul: Devlet Matbaası, 1938), 10:264; Gary Leiser and Michael Dols, "Evliyā Chelebi's Description of Medicine in Seventeenth-Century Egypt, Part II: Text," *Sudhoff's Archiv* 72 (1988): 55. For a similar case in twelfth-century Ayyubid Cairo, see Neil D. MacKenzie, *Ayyubid Cairo: A Topographical Study* (Cairo: The American University in Cairo Press, 1992), 143–144.

44. Joseph Schacht, *An Introduction to Islamic Law* (Oxford: Clarendon Press, 1964; reprint, 1991), 162 and throughout the book.

45. This was, for instance, the situation at the Argunid hospital in Aleppo during the first years of Ottoman rule. BOA, Ali Emiri, Selim I /15, p. 1.

46. Otaviano Bon, *The Sultan's Seraglio: An Intimate Portrait of Life at the Ottoman Court* (London: Saqi Books, 1996), 89–90, 146n. 14. And see also Tavernier, *A New Relation*, 22–23; n.a., *A Collection of Curious Travels and Voyages . . .* (London: S. Smith and B. Walford, 1693), 2:60; Göl A. Russell, "Physicians at the Ottoman Court," *Medical History* 34 (1990): 263.

47. *Süleymaniye Vakfiyesi*, 1:150.

48. Evliya Çelebi, *Seyahatname*, 3:469.

49. Ibid., 10:264; Leiser and Dols, "Evliyā Chelebi's Description," 55.

50. VGM, D. 574, 83.

51. Katherine Park, "Healing the Poor: Hospital and Medical Assistance in Renaissance Florence," in *Medicine and Charity before the Welfare State*, ed. Jonathan Barry and Colin Jones (London: Routledge, 1991), 34–36; Katherine Park and John Henderson, "'The First Hospital among Christians': The Ospedale di Santa Maria Nuova in Early Sixteenth-Century Florence," *Medical History* 35 (1991): 174.

52. Fisher and Fisher, "Topkapı Sarayı in the Mid-Seventeenth Century," 35.

53. *Süleymaniye Vakfiyesi*, 148–49. Many travelers included anecdotes on the Ottoman lunatics they saw. Evliya Çelebi's description of the mad are especially famous; see *Seyahatname*, 1:530–531 (the description of the guilds' procession in Istanbul that included a section on the keepers from the hospitals for the mad), *Seyahatname*, 3:468–470 (the description of the hospital of Sultan Beyazit II in Edirne). European travelers as well were not indifferent to the Ottoman madmen. See, for example, Thevenot, *The Travells of Monsieur de Thevenot*, 143, on the lunatics of Cairo.

54. Evliya Çelebi, *Seyahatname*, 9:542; Kamil Jamil al-'Asali, *Muqaddama fi tarikh al-tibb fi l-Quds* (Amman: Imadat al-Bahth al-Ilmi, 1994), 166; Evliya Çelebi, *Seyahatname*, 10:264; Leiser and Dols, "Evliyā Chelebi's Description," 55.

55. Thevenot, *The Travells of Monsieur de Thevenot*, 143.

56. In addition to Dols' book on madmen in medieval Islam *(Majnun)*, other works should be mentioned as well: Michael W. Dols, "Insanity in Byzantine and Islamic Medicine," *Symposium on Byzantine Medicine, Dumbarton Oaks Papers* 38 (1984): 136–148; idem, "Insanity and Its Treatment in Islamic Society," *Medical History* 31 (1987): 1–14.

57. Maurice Cerasi, "The Many Masters and Artisans of the Ottoman Town's Form and Culture: Chaos Out of Order, Syncretism Out of Separation—The Eighteenth and Nineteenth Centuries" (unpublished paper), from the international workshop *Order in Anarchy: The Management of Urban Space and Society in the Islamic World* (Be'er Sheva, 1997), 6; Nil Sarı, "Osmanlı Darüşşifalarına Tayin Edilecek Görevlilerde Aranan Nitelikler," *Yeni Tıp Tarihi Araştırmaları* 1 (1995): 11; Inalcik, "Istanbul," 238–244; Robert Mantran, *XVI ve XVII Yüzyılda İstanbul'da Gündelik Hayat* (Istanbul: Eren, 1991), 45–48.

58. This was the explicit policy in the Qala'unid hospital in Ottoman Cairo. See Evliya Çelebi, *Seyahatname*, 10:263; Leiser and Dols, "Evliyā Chelebi's Description," 53.

59. Ray H. Elling, "The Hospital-Support Game in Urban Center" in *The Hospital in Modern Society*, ed. Eliot Freidson (London: Free Press of Glencoe, 1963), 73.

60. A similar phenomenon existed in other societies as well; see Martha Carlin, "Medieval English Hospitals," in *The Hospital in History*, ed. Lindsay Granshaw and Roy Porter (London: Routledge, 1989), 21–25; *Oxford English Dictionary*, s.v. "hospital"; Park, "Healing the Poor," 26, 33–34; Park and Henderson, "'The First Hospital among Christians,'" 171.

61. See, for example, Nicolas de Nicolay, *The Navigations, Peregrinations, and Voyages Made into Turkie . . .* (London: n.p., 1585), 57b; Ahmet Süheyl Ünver's article "Anadolu ve İstanbulda İmaretlerin Aşhane, Tabhane ve Misafirhanelerine ve Müessislerinin Ruhî

Kemâllerine dair," *İstanbul Üniversitesi Tıb Fakültesi Mecmuası* 4, no. 18 (1941): 2390–2410. Hospitals in fifteenth-century Fez may also have had a three-day limit; see Leo Africanus, *The History and Description of Africa and the Notable Things Therein Contained*, 3 vols. (New York: B. Franklin, 1960), 2:245.

62. For an anecdote on the hospitality of hospitals included by Khalil b. Shahin al-Zahiri, an Egyptian traveler in Damascus in the year 831 [1427–1428] in his treatise on the Mamluk sultanate, see Ahmad al-Ibash and D. Qutayba al-Shihabi, *Dimashq al-Sham fi nusus al-rahhalin wal-jughrafiyyin wal-buldaniyyin al-'arab wal-muslimin* (Damascus: Manshurat Wizarat al-thaqafa, 1998), 2: 617–619; Sh. Inayatullah, "Contribution to the Historical Study of Hospitals in Medieval Islam," *Islamic Culture* 18 (1944): 9.

63. VGM, D. 575, 106; Ünver, "Fatih Külliyesinin İlk Vakfiyesine Göre Fatih Darüşşifası," 16; *Fatih Mehmet II Vakfiyeleri*, 275.

64. VGM, D. 608/23, 231.

65. *Fatih Mehmet Vakfiyeleri*, 281–182.

66. Ünver, "Fatih Külliyesinin İlk Vakfiyesine Göre Fatih Darüşşifası," 17.

67. Nihad Nuri Yürükoğlu, *Manisa Bimarhanesi* (Istanbul: n.p., 1948), 25, 51, 57–58.

68. Halil Inalcik, "Matbakh," *EI²*, 6:809.

69. Park, "Healing the Poor," 33; Rubin, "Development and Change in English Hospitals," 48.

70. Horden, "A Discipline of Relevance," 367.

CHAPTER SEVEN

Charity, the Poor, and Distribution of Alms in Ottoman Algiers

M I R I A M H O E X T E R

The importance of extending alms to the poor in society as well as the merit promised to the charitable believer in the world beyond is repeated in the Quran as one of the important injunctions of the Prophet on all believers.[1] Of the various modes of extending charity in Islam—*zakat, sadaqa, waqf*—only the waqf became a fully developed legal institution. Zakat, which took the form of a tax incumbent on all believers and was collected by the political authorities, quickly fell into desuetude. Originally, voluntary charity of all sorts came under the general heading of sadaqa. With the elaboration of the law in the eighth and ninth century, a differentiation was introduced between various forms of charity, for example, a simple gift inter vivos *(hiba)*; a gift post mortem, that is, from that part of an inheritance that could be freely disposed of; and endowments—waqf or *habs*.[2] Sadaqa remained a generic term for a charitable gift and in fact for voluntary charity of all sorts. It often appears in connection with endowments. However, it also refers to occasional, unregulated charity of all kinds.

In contrast to sadaqa, endowments were institutionalized and closely regulated. The waqf soon became the most popular form of extending charity in Islam. Its popularity and regulation enable us to study the concept of 'charity' as embodied in the institution, the way it worked, its distinctive forms compared with charitable or philanthropic organizations in other cultures, and the way its specific characteristics reflected basic values of the particular culture in which it functioned. I will focus here on one of these subjects—the conception of charity as embodied in the endowment institution—which I believe is important for the understanding of the connection between charity and the poor.

In an unpublished article comparing the waqf with similar institutions in other cultures, the late Gabriel Baer found that the Islamic endowment institution was the only one that combined both public and private beneficiaries, both general and personal purposes within one framework, governed by the same laws.[3] This special characteristic of the waqf ensued from its basic ideology. With the institutionalization of the waqf it was necessary to define what should be considered a legitimate beneficiary of an endowment. The definition that appears in virtually every treatise on the waqf is that of a continuous or eternal charity for the sake of God and his religion: *al-waqf sadaqa jariya fi sabil Allah ta'ala*.[4] A valid purpose for the benefit of which one could endow the produce of one's property was defined as *qurba*, that is, anything likely to bring the founder nearer to God.[5] Obviously, this is a very broad definition: it allowed for the inclusion as beneficiaries of family members, freed slaves, other individual Muslims, a group of people, the poor in general, or the poor belonging to a specific social group, even a group of animals, side by side with a large variety of public services such as the religious cult, education and learning, welfare and health services, and also political and economic purposes such as colonization, urbanization, economic infrastructure, and municipal services.

Endowments soon became by far the most popular form of voluntary charity in Islam. They were made by all strata of the population: rulers, high officials, men and women, rich people, and people of modest means. Endowed assets covered considerable proportions of the properties in every Muslim town, as well as vast agricultural areas. They included large as well as very modest properties and, eventually, also large sums of money, as cash waqfs. The scope of voluntary charity in Islam, the purposes it served, and its importance in the public sphere thus reached proportions beyond what was common in other civilizations.

Moreover, the broad definition inherent in the idea of qurba allowed for endowments by *ahl al-dhimma* (non-Muslims) and in their favor. The rules governing such endowments followed the logic of qurba—that is, the purpose of the endowment by a non-Muslim had to be such as would be considered qurba according to both Islam and the founder's religion. An endowment by a non-Muslim in favor of his offspring, of the poor of his religious community, of his church or synagogue, of the poor of his neighborhood, or of the poor in general qualified as valid under these rules. However, endowments by a non-Muslim to benefit a mosque or in favor of a synagogue, a church, priests, or monks were invalid because the designated beneficiaries did not constitute qurba either according to the founder's religion (the mosques) or according to Islam (all the others). If the ultimate beneficiaries of such endowments were the poor, then only the first part of the endowment would be considered null and void, and any income from the endowment would be spent for the poor only.[6]

Like the waqf, many of the early endowment systems in other civilizations—the Jewish *heqdesh*, the Greek and Roman foundations, and Christian Church foundations, as well as those of the Indian subcontinent—were originally connected to religion. However, many of these systems eventually lost their specifically religious nature, were subjected to secular law, or lost their exclusivity when modern foundations were created that had no religious basis whatsoever. Baer's cross-cultural investigation showed that the waqf was the only endowment institution that maintained its religious nature and remained the exclusive institution of its kind in its civilization until modern times.[7]

Indeed, across the centuries, the endowment institution had retained its basic characteristic as an Islamic institution whose rules were an integral part of the *shari'a* (the sacred law). Application of waqf laws, and difficulties and conflicts arising from endowments, were thus handled by the *'ulama'* (the shari'a specialists) who alone were qualified to interpret the laws.

In terms of its ideology and the purposes it served, the Islamic endowment institution thus goes beyond the common definition of philanthropy as a "voluntary action for the public good"[8] or as "giving and sharing beyond the family."[9] Its scope and dimensions were certainly much broader than those characteristic of philanthropy in other civilizations. Although the origins of the institution and some of its rules may have been borrowed from other civilizations,[10] the raison d'être of the institution and its development through the centuries were rooted in the culture in which it was functioning. Indeed, both the broad conception of charity and the continuous religious nature of the endowment institution derived from some basic tenets of Islam, which, from its inception, never conceived of itself as a religion regulating only the sphere of worship but as a political community guided by and devoted to Allah in all spheres of human activity.[11] The central importance accorded in Islamic political discourse to the *umma* (the community of believers), to all aspects of its well-being and the protection and the advancement of its interests, followed from this basic conception. The notion of qurba thus did not differentiate between private and public well-being; both had equal value and importance in furthering the interests of the community of believers. Moreover, contributions toward practically every aspect of the umma's life were considered apt to bring the contributor closer to God. One can hardly imagine such an institution functioning outside the confines of the shari'a. The inclusion of the endowment institution as an integral part of the shari'a established it as part and parcel of the values and norms of social behavior and at the same time gave it lasting legitimacy. Both aspects were essential for the functioning of the waqf and its survival across the centuries in all parts of the Islamic cultural area.[12] Thus, rather than an institution concerned with philanthropy, M. G. S. Hodgson's description of the waqf as the vehicle for financing Islam as a society seems to reflect much better the significance and function of the endowment institution.[13]

Care for the poor in society was certainly included in the broad definition of *charity*. The rest of this discussion will address the role of the poor in endowments and the development of the understanding of who was included in the category of "poor." An in-depth study of two groups of poor entitled to shares in the proceeds of endowments made in Ottoman Algiers will serve to illustrate these points.

The Poor

The poor *(fuqara', masakin)* have always been considered among the worthiest and most meritorious beneficiaries of all kinds of charity.[14] They have certainly been regarded as the charitable purpose par excellence of an endowment.[15] Thus, al-Khassaf (d. 261/874–875), the author of one of the earliest treatises on the waqf, stated that if someone made an eternal endowment *(sadaqa mawqufa)* in favor of God's cause and did not mention a beneficiary, the income from the endowment would go to the poor (masakin).[16] Because of the idealization of the poor,[17] making an endowment in their favor was perhaps the best way to bring the founder closer to God. Such an endowment, therefore, fulfilled the ideological requirement of the waqf to the highest degree.

Interestingly enough, the idealization of charity for the poor cut across the otherwise thick dividing line separating Muslims and non-Muslims. An endowment by a non-Muslim for the poor of his religion was considered valid, that is, a qurba according to both the founder's and the Islamic religion: A Muslim could endow for the poor belonging to non-Muslim communities, or a non-Muslim could endow for poor Muslims. Finally, when the poor were mentioned in an endowment deed without further specification, the income could be divided among the poor of all religions.[18]

Inclusion of the poor as beneficiaries of endowments fulfilled yet another purpose. Basically, endowments fell into two categories: Those whose immediate beneficiary was a charitable or public establishment (*khayri* endowments in modern terminology), and those whose immediate beneficiaries were private people, usually members of the founder's family, his freed slaves, or the like (*ahli* endowments in modern terminology). However, in the latter case, the founder was required to designate an ultimate beneficiary, which would ensure the eternal nature of the endowment if and when the chain of primary and intermediate beneficiaries died out. An endowment that did not include the element of perpetuity was considered null and void.[19] The existence of poor people in the community was conceived of as a permanent fact. Their inclusion as the ultimate beneficiaries of a waqf therefore ensured that the endowment would never lack beneficiaries and the founder would eternally receive his reward for the good deed he had done. The poor were thus both the ideal purpose of charity and the ultimate beneficiary par excellence of endowments.

With the proliferation of endowments, the understanding of who came under the category of "poor" developed in two main directions: First, diversification of the definition of poor people, that is, allotment of the proceeds of an endowment to specific groups of poor or needy people; and second, broadening of the definition of *poor* to include as beneficiaries people who were not necessarily poor insofar as their material situation was concerned.

Endowments for specific solidarity groups, rather than for the poor in general, became very common in the course of time. Elsewhere I have shown how the endowment institution served as a vehicle for the crystallization of various autonomous groups in the public sphere. Indeed, on many occasions founders selected as beneficiaries of their waqfs not a general Islamic purpose but a more limited one to which they felt personally attached, such as a specific school of law, a Sufi order, a neighborhood *zawiya* (dervish lodge), a professional guild, the inhabitants of a particular neighborhood, the *ashraf* (descendants of the Prophet), groups of common geographic origin, and so forth. The income from these endowments catered first and foremost to the poor and needy of these groups, distributed charity among them, and helped them with payment of their taxes.[20]

The same combination of a desire to contribute to the welfare of the poor with the inclination to do so within the framework of one's solidarity group was found in the case of endowments by non-Muslims. An interesting example is that of an endowment made by a Greek Orthodox priest in Jaffa in 1889. The endowment was intended basically to profit the monks of the Greek Orthodox monastery of Jerusalem and its dependencies. If they became extinct, the founder next designated as beneficiaries several groups of poor in the following order: the Greek Orthodox poor of Ramla and Ludd (the founder was born in Ludd); those of the Jerusalem Patriarchate in general; those of the Patriarchate of Damascus, then of Aleppo; any poor of the Jerusalem *liwa'* (administrative district); and, finally, the poor in general wherever they resided, giving priority to those residing closest to the Jerusalem Patriarchate.[21] The first three groups of poor belonged to the founder's religion and were listed in order of their geographic proximity to his place of birth and probably of residence; the same rule of geographic proximity was followed concerning the last two groups that include the poor in general, with no specific religious denomination. It is certainly a good example of the existence of a sense of local solidarity (some would go further and say territorial identity[22]) among the inhabitants of Ottoman Palestine.

In the second development, the category of poor expanded to include people fulfilling various religious functions: readers of Quran portions, religious personnel attached to mosques and *madrasas* (colleges), Sufis and *fuqaha'* (experts on the shari'a) in general. As Claude Cahen showed, endowments to benefit mosques, *khans* (caravansarays), *ribat*s (Sufi lodges), and so on were originally designed to take care of the maintenance of the building and were not meant to provide salaries for the personnel of these institutions. Cahen based his argument on al-Khassaf, who explicitly prohibited an endowment in favor of traditionalists, lecturers, and so forth, who could not be considered poor as such.[23]

The problem raised by endowments in favor of fuqaha' as well as of other groups of people—such as the blind, poets, the people of Baghdad—was that these groups of beneficiaries were designated without further specification and therefore could include rich and poor people.[24] It reflects the original attitude of the 'ulama' according to which only the poor and needy were legitimate beneficiaries of public endowments. Eventually, however, jurists found a way to allow such endowments. The justification they offered in the case of the fuqaha' was that need or poverty *(haja)* was inherent in this group, since the occupation with *'ilm* (religious knowledge) prevented them from earning, and poverty was the norm among them. Another solution was that if no further specification was included in the endowment deed, only the poor among the fuqaha' would receive a share in the proceeds of the endowments.[25] As far as I can tell, the second solution was never really put into practice. I have not come across any case attesting to an examination of the economic situation of these men of religion.

Rather, it seems that the inclusion of 'ulama' in the category of "poor" has become a cultural norm. Endowments in favor of 'ulama' of various kinds became very popular all over the Islamic cultural area, at least from the tenth century onward.[26] Indeed, men of religion became the predominant group of beneficiaries of public endowments. It soon became the normal procedure for people who built a mosque to lay down meticulously in their endowment deeds the number and nature of the servants of the mosque and determine the functions they were to fulfill as well as their remuneration. In these cases, their shares in the endowment were no more and no less than salaries.[27] There can hardly be a question that many of the recipients were not really poor or needy or that their financial situation served as a criterion for the allotment of shares in the endowment's proceeds.

Moreover, 'ulama' serving in religious institutions, Quran readers, and people with some kind of religious status became the most frequent ultimate beneficiaries of endowments.[28] They were also frequently included in the category of "poor" designated as the ultimate beneficiaries of endowments. Eyal Ginio has pointed out that in the administrative discourse of eighteenth-century Salonica the term *poor*, particularly in its plural form, *fuqara'*, acquired an extended meaning. Besides its original meaning, describing an economic condition, the term came to denote modesty, humility, devotion, and piety and was in many cases attached to 'ulama' and particularly to Sufis.[29]

A good example of this extended meaning of the term *poor*, and particularly of the development of a common understanding or norm according to which 'ulama' were included in the category of "poor," is that of the Hasseki Sultan endowment in Jerusalem. In the endowment deed, dated 1552, the beneficiaries of the *imaret* (soup kitchen) were described as "the poor and the humble, the weak and the needy . . . the true believers and the righteous who live near the holy places . . . who hold on to the *shari'a* and strictly observe the commandments of the *sunna*

[sayings and doings of the Prophet]." Yet in a legal document of 1773, the beneficiaries were described as "the people and residents of Jerusalem including the
ulama, the *sadat* [direct descendants of the Prophet], the poor and the pilgrims
who remain in Jerusalem."[30] Indeed, as O. Peri shows, many of the richest notables of Jerusalem benefited from the endowment; the legal basis for their inclusion
as beneficiaries was that they belonged to the 'ulama'.[31]

The extension of the meaning of *poor* to include men of religion seems to have
been applied in non-Muslim communities as well. In his discussion of Christian
and Jewish endowments in Palestine in the late Ottoman period, R. Shaham found
that "in some *awqaf* in Jaffa the *qadis* permitted exclusive endowments for the benefit of the monks." He remarks that by approving such an endowment the qadis
actually disregarded the explicit rule prohibiting an endowment of a non-Muslim,
which was considered qurba by his religion but not by Islam.[32] Moreover, as I have
shown earlier, endowments in favor of monks were explicitly considered invalid according to this rule.[33] I would suggest that rather than disregarding an explicit rule,
the qadis in fact drew a parallel between the monks and the various kinds of
'ulama', who, as we have seen, came to be considered as poor by definition. Moreover, at least in some of the cases, the founders made a point of describing as
beneficiaries of their endowments not the monks in general but the poor monks
(fuqara' ruhban).[34] Their designation as a specific group of poor people probably
provided the legal justification for their approval by the qadi as valid beneficiaries
of the endowments.

Distribution of Charity in Ottoman Algiers

Only rarely does archival material provide us with information on the people who
actually benefited from charity or on the way the distribution of alms from the endowments' proceeds was carried out. The following is an analysis of some rare
examples where information on these subjects was found. They refer to Ottoman
Algiers mainly in the eighteenth century, up until the French conquest of the town
in 1830, and deal with two groups of poor entitled to shares in the proceeds of endowments made in Algiers: the poor of Mecca and Medina and those of the town
of Algiers. The composition of these two groups reflects how far the extended
meaning of the term *poor* applied in Ottoman Algiers and how large a share the
needy received from the proceeds of endowments.

The largest and most important endowment institution of Ottoman Algiers
was the waqf in favor of the poor of Mecca and Medina. Its patrimony was composed of a large number of small endowments, established by individuals from all
strata of the Muslim population of Algiers, who usually named the poor of the
two holy cities of Islam as the ultimate beneficiaries. All these endowments were

administered by the institution known as "the Haramayn," short for Waqf al-Haramayn.[35] Between 1667–1668 and 1830 the Algerian Haramayn sent to the two holy cities a charitable allocation amounting to between 1,100 and 1,500 gold dinars whenever a pilgrimage caravan set off from Algiers to the Hijaz. Two-thirds of this sum were to be distributed among the inhabitants of Medina, while those of Mecca received the remaining one-third. The gold pieces were divided among ten soldiers of the Algerian *ocak* (Janissary corps)departing on the pilgrimage. They were handed a list of beneficiaries and instructions as to the distribution of gold pieces among them. I examined two of these documents. One is an original document in Arabic and pertains to the allocation for 1116/1704–1705.[36] The other, reproduced in translation by A. Devoulx, pertains to the Algerian allocation for 1192/1778–1779.[37]

The list of beneficiaries was prepared in Algiers and was based on individual requests by people in Mecca and Medina, addressed to the ruler of Algiers, to have their names entered on the list of the poor entitled to a share in the Algerian charity. It comprised the names of all beneficiaries and the exact sum, in figures as well as fully written out, that each of them was to receive.

The instructions handed to the soldiers made them responsible for the distribution of the money among the beneficiaries. Upon arrival in Medina, they were instructed to hand over personally to each beneficiary the sum indicated on the list. Shares of beneficiaries who had passed away or were missing were to be distributed to other poor people, and the letter *ta'*[38] written over the deceased's name so that he would be dropped from the list in the future and his share allotted to someone else. The instructions emphasized quite unequivocally that the money was to support only the poor of the two holy cities; the rich were to have no share whatsoever in the charitable allocation. All instructions were to be followed to the letter, and any modifications, iniquitous acts, or breaches of faith were subject to punishment by both God and man.[39]

Examination of the lists of beneficiaries, particularly the one attached to the earlier document, revealed that the technical instructions at least were carried out to the letter. A ditto mark or the word *paid* was entered next to each beneficiary's name to indicate actual payment. The letter *ta'* with the ditto mark drawn across it apparently indicated that the beneficiary named in the list had passed away or had not been found and that his share had been granted to some other poor person. Only in a very small number of cases was there no ditto mark across the letter *ta'*. This probably meant that the original beneficiary had died and his share was not given to someone else. On the other hand, in two cases a sum was added to the list, probably in Medina, without the recipient being named.

The shares designated on the earlier list had totaled 1,023 dinars, whereas the sum distributed seems to have amounted to only 992 dinars.[40] Of the 250 Medinese beneficiaries on the original list 86 or 88 were not found. It seems that suitable replacements were found for seventy-four or seventy-six of them. Unfortunately, no description of how the distribution actually took place has been found. The more prominent people on the list presumably had their grants delivered in person, as a mark of respect for their status; the rest of the beneficiaries probably clustered around the Algerian delegation to receive their shares. As for the replacements for beneficiaries who had passed away or disappeared, we have only the marks on the list to attest to the fact that the money was handed out and no further information on how this was handled. The lists, including all the indications, were ultimately returned to Algiers to be deposited in the Haramayn's offices for use in the future.

A look at some of the letters sent by inhabitants of Medina to the ruler of Algiers and particularly at the lists of beneficiaries may give us a good idea of what kind of people were considered worthy of inclusion in the category of "the poor of Mecca and Medina."

Devoulx published translations of two of the numerous letters sent by people from Medina to the ruler of Algiers.[41] One letter was signed by thirteen people belonging to three families. The head of the first family was a *farrash* (responsible for spreading the carpets in a mosque and taking care of them), and the members of the family included his wife, two of his sons, his wife's daughter, and his mother. The second family was somehow involved with caring for the poor in Medina because its head was called *"serviteur des pauvres"* (servant of the poor). His son, his daughter, his slave, and a person who was presumably a servant attached to the household [42] also signed the letter. The third family included a father and son, but no details were given concerning their occupation. In the letter the signatories declared that they were weak and needy and therefore supplicated the ruler of Algiers to include them in the list of beneficiaries of the Algerian allocation. The letter does not reveal much about the financial situation of the first and third families. However, the second family, comprising a slave and a servant, could hardly have been destitute. Both the first and the second families obviously were employed in the religious–charitable institutions of Medina.

The second letter included six signatories and all but one bore the title of *shaykh* or *shaykha*. The signatories included two shaykhs of the same family, a shaykha who was a disciple of one of the two shaykhs, that same man's wife, and his granddaughter. His son was the only one not bearing the title of shaykh, yet since his son's daughter was described as shaykha, the possibility cannot be ruled out that her father's title was omitted by mistake. Although this title has more than one meaning, I would opt in this case for a Sufi family or a family of scholars. Remarkably, the family did not refer to itself as poor or needy, but simply asked for inclusion in the list of the Algerian allocation.

The lists of beneficiaries of the Algerian allocation sent with the pilgrimage convoy provide more information. Of the two lists I consulted, that pertaining to the allocation for 1116/1704–1705 included the full list of 250 beneficiaries of the allocation destined for the poor of Medina.[43] The one pertaining to the Algerian allocation for 1192/1778–1779 included both the Meccan and Medinese beneficiaries and totaled 360 people. However, in his translation, Devoulx reproduced details of the first twelve beneficiaries only.

Both lists opened with a number of officeholders. Most of them appeared on both lists and were allotted identical shares in both allocations. These were the shaykh of the *haram*, the holy enclosure of Medina (37 dinars); the amir of Medina (50 dinars); the qadi of Medina (6 dinars); the *agas* guarding the holy enclosure (37 dinars); some groups of people attending to various needs of the haram—its farrashin (16 dinars), imams, *mu'adhdhins* (announcers of the time of prayer), and so on, who together were allotted 8 dinars; and the secretaries *(kuttab)* of the haram, who together received 7 dinars.[44] None of the names of these people was mentioned in the lists, so obviously they received their shares ex officio.

The remaining beneficiaries were private individuals all mentioned by name. Among them were men, many women, families, and other groups of people. In most cases the list included only the names of the people, although sometimes additional details were provided, such as the occupation of the beneficiary, his or her place of origin or personal status. They were a mixture of people: some freed female slaves, shaykhs, ashraf, servants and former servants of the holy enclosure and some other mosques, scions of distinguished families, and people who had their origins in Algeria or other countries of the Maghrib.[45]

The allocations received by the beneficiaries varied between 2 and 12 dinars each.[46] Most received either three or four gold coins; larger amounts were usually allotted to a group of people—for example, a family, a group of servants of a mosque, and so on—and on some occasions also to some individuals who apparently enjoyed higher status, such as three of the teachers at the haram (one received 5 dinars, another 10, and yet another 12). Some of the beneficiaries evidently originated in Algeria or other North African regions. Most of these received the usual 3 or 4 dinars; however, the shaykh of the North Africans in Medina—*shaykh al-Maghariba*—was allotted 7 dinars and his secretary—*katib al-Maghariba*—5 dinars.

Although the instructions given by the Algerian authorities unequivocally excluded the rich from receiving a share of the allocation and emphasized that money must be distributed to the poor only, both the lists and the letters addressed to the ruler of Algiers indicate that indigence was not the only criterion for inclusion in the lists of beneficiaries. Those who received ex officio shares belonged to the administrative, military, and religious leadership of Medina. They most probably owed their inclusion in the list to a cultural norm or a kind of informal protocol that expected Muslim rulers, whose subjects flocked to the Hijaz on the occasion of the annual pilgrimage, to honor the guardians and servants of the holy places of Islam with a token of respect and gratitude. Former inhabitants of the Maghrib seemingly owed their shares in the Algerian allocation to what was conceived of as an extension of the idea that charity begins at home, which in modern terminology would be characterized as territorial solidarity. The bulk of the remaining beneficiaries belonged to the category of "poor." Among them the 'ulama' and various servants of mosques constituted a sizable proportion. The cultural norm that conceived of people with some religious status as an integral part of the group of fuqara' was thus applied in the case of the Algerian allocation to the poor of Mecca and Medina as well.

The Waqf al-Haramayn and the allocation sent under the auspices of the Algerian ruler to the Hijaz served many purposes besides the distribution of charity to the poor. Ideologically, endowments for this purpose expressed the attachment of Muslims in faraway regions to the two holy cities of Islam and their concern for the well-being of their guardians and inhabitants. An allocation to be distributed among the people of Mecca and Medina obviously was considered a contribution to the general interests of the community of believers. The significance of the Algerian allocation thus fell within the broader concept of charity in Islam.

Endowments in favor of the poor of Algiers were handled quite differently. Although endowments for other ultimate purposes, such as the Jerusalem mosques or the poor of Mecca and Medina, were all lumped together and run jointly by a special administration such as the Waqf al-Haramayn, this was not the case when endowments for the poor in general were concerned. In fact, I have not come across even one centralized organization, anywhere in the Islamic world, whose task it was to collect all the endowed assets in favor of the poor, administer them jointly, and distribute their income among the poor. The absence of such an institution is perhaps the main obstacle in the way of historians who seek to evaluate the extent of charity based on endowments in favor of the poor and needy in Islamic societies. Yet, the story of how the distribution of alms to these groups was handled in Ottoman Algiers may throw some light on the subject.

From the last part of the seventeenth century and particularly in the course of the eighteenth, the Waqf al-Haramayn in Algiers assumed the character of a multipurpose endowment institution, joining under the same administration the management of various endowments other than those designed to serve the poor of the two holy cities of Islam. In the course of this process, four mosque endowments came under the Haramayn's purview, as did, from 1158/1745–1746 onward, a category of endowments described in the institution's registers as *awqaf fuqara' al-Jaza'ir wa'l-usara' wa'l-talaba*—that is, endowments for the poor of Algiers, the captives, and a category of people who carried out a variety of religious services.[47] What we have here is, in fact, a collection of individual endowments, some for general charitable or religious purposes, others of a more private religious nature.

This entire category of endowments was relatively small and included only 25 assets out of the 1,748 gathered under the Haramayn's administration by 1830. As with all waqfs, the Haramayn's administrators were charged with the task of spending the income from the endowed assets for the purposes designated by the founders. Obviously, the proceeds of the assets endowed in favor of the poor of the town of Algiers were to be employed to alleviate their lot, in one way or another. The Haramayn did not fail this mission.

Support for the poor of Algiers was provided by the Haramayn in the form of alms distribution, which was carried out in a rather informal manner, graphically described in one of the French reports:

> Deux fois par semaine 40 boudjoux [*bucus*][48] (144 francs) sortent de la caisse de la Mecque pour figurer au chapitre des dépenses, sous le titre de distribution d'aumônes. Aucune formalité n'entoure ces distributions. L'oukil [*wakil*-administrator], accompagné de son chaoun [*shawush*-guard] portant des sacs remplis de sous, se rend à une boutique où les sacs sont vidés dans un vase; le chaoun y puise à pleines mains et va dans les rues distribuer un, deux ou trois sous à chaque pauvre sauf dix d'entre eux qui reçoivent trois ou cinq boudjoux par semaine. La boutique se referme et l'oukil est libéré de 80 boudjoux (2880 sous)![49]

Beneficiaries of the charity were men and women from the indigenous population as well as Christian captives.[50] They were not registered and did not have to sign any receipts. However, those who were disabled and could not leave their homes were listed and had the alms delivered to them.[51] It seems hardly questionable that what we have here is a case of "pure charity," that is, a distribution of alms on a regular basis to poor people. Although the financial situation of the recipients was not verified in any way, one can hardly imagine that anybody but the really destitute clustered around the Haramayn's offices in the manner described previously, or that the rich would dare ask for alms in a public place where everybody would see them.

French reports, based on information gathered from local officials who had been involved in the distribution of alms under the Ottomans, cited 1,300 poor people as recipients of this charity and evaluated the Haramayn's expenses for this purpose at between 15,000 and 18,000, even 20,000, francs per year.[52] It is likely that both the number of poor and the amount spent on this charity were somewhat exaggerated to impress the conquerors. However, even if we deduct a few thousand francs from this amount, it would still represent a sizable sum, one that probably exceeded the annual allocation sent by the Haramayn to Mecca and Medina which, toward the end of Ottoman rule, reached 10,800 francs. Moreover, the number of assets endowed for the benefit of the poor of Algiers was rather small and could never have provided anywhere near the above-mentioned sum.[53] This means that the Haramayn must have added quite considerable sums out of the funds collected from the endowments in favor of the poor of Mecca and Medina to finance the distribution of alms in Algiers itself.

As we have seen, poor relief was only one of many purposes of public endowments. Because the waqf remained a voluntary institution, the choice of beneficiaries of each endowment rested with the individual founder, whether it was a simple member of the community or the ruler himself. Studying poor relief in eighteenth-century Aleppo and Salonica, A. Marcus and Ginio reached the conclusion that support of the poor from endowments was minimal or marginal and that the poor were mainly dependant on charity provided within the family, within the various solidarity groups as well as on occasional almsgiving by individuals.[54] True, in Algiers, as in Aleppo and Salonica, the number of endowments for the local poor was negligible. However, as demonstrated, their actual share in the proceeds of endowments was much larger than what is suggested by the number of endowments in their favor. The fact that the distribution of alms to the poor of Algiers by the Haramayn was handled in such an informal manner and that the Haramayn actually diverted sums designated for other purposes to provide for the poor of the town, suggest that similar patterns of alms distribution may have been practiced by endowment institutions in other parts of the Islamic world as well and that the share of the poor in the proceeds of endowments may have been more important than what we have heretofore understood.

However, the general picture one gets from the ever-growing body of waqf studies[55] is that founders preferred as beneficiaries of their endowments establishments that served to advance their solidarity group and even more frequently those which catered to the general community of believers. One of the reasons for the relatively marginal share of the poor in endowments may have been the cultural norm that made the family responsible for its weaker members and the widespread custom of extending alms to the poor in general on various occasions. When making endowments, the general idea seems to have been that, rather than singling out the poor as beneficiaries, they should benefit from institutions set up and financed by endowments and serving the entire community.

Conclusion

Awareness of the broad definition of *charity* and the extension of the understanding of who was included in the category of "poor" may further our understanding of the connection between charity and the poor. The broad definition of legitimate beneficiaries of endowments turned the waqf into the principal vehicle for financing Islam as a society. Although the poor retained their special role as the ideal beneficiaries of charity, in general, and of endowments, in particular, poor relief thus became only one of many more popular purposes of endowments. Moreover, the category of "poor" was extended to include people, mainly 'ulama', who were not necessarily poor insofar as their material situation was concerned. What ensued was a very flexible understanding of the meaning of "the poor" and their normative share in charity. The composition of the two groups of poor that received charity from endowments made in Ottoman Algiers demonstrates how this flexible interpretation of charity to the poor worked in practice.

Although the recipients of charity in both cases—that of the Algerian allocation for Mecca and Medina and that distributed in the town of Algiers—were defined as poor, there was a marked difference in the composition of the two groups. The recipients of alms in Algiers were most probably needy people only; the lists of beneficiaries in Mecca and Medina, however, comprised an array of people who owed their inclusion in the lists to a more complex set of criteria. Thus, there was obviously more than one understanding of who the poor were. The distribution of alms to the needy of Algiers was an expression of the early Islamic idealization of the poor and the idea that they were the most meritorious beneficiaries of charity. The diversity in the group of recipients of the Algerian allocation to the poor of Mecca and Medina, on the other hand, exemplified the broader conception of charity as expressed in the definition of legitimate beneficiaries of endowments and of the development of the understanding of the term *poor*. Both the ideal and the broader designation of the poor were represented in Ottoman Algiers.

What both groups of recipients had in common was the absence of specific rules defining the criteria for inclusion in the group and of any administrative mechanism to verify the deserving character of recipients. Basically, I believe, this was determined by cultural and social norms shared by all. In the case of the poor of the two holy cities, these norms were interpreted by the ruler of Algiers and his advisors. In the case of the poor of Algiers, it was left to individuals to decide whether their need was such as to justify their inclusion in the distribution of alms. The fact that the distribution took place in a public place, that is, under the watchful eyes of the community, seems to have constituted a social control mechanism sufficient to guarantee against gross misuse of this generosity.

Notes

1. T. H. Weir-[A. Zysow], "Sadaka," *EI²*, 8:708–716.

2. C. Cahen, "Réflexions sur le *waqf* ancien," *Studia Islamica* 14 (1961): esp. 45. For the various kinds of gifts, see D. Powers, "The Islamic Inheritance System: A Socio-historical Approach," in *Islamic Family Law*, ed. C. Mallat and J. Connors (London: Graham and Trotman, 1990), 11–29.

3. G. Baer, "The Muslim *Waqf* and Similar Institutions in Other Civilizations," paper presented at the Workshop on Economic and Social Aspects of the Muslim *Waqf*, Jerusalem,

February 1–20, 1981. The paper compares the waqf with the following institutions: the Jewish *heqdesh* (endowment); Greek and Roman charities and foundations; the Christian *piae causae* (pious work); the property of the Catholic and Orthodox churches; European secular regulations of inheritance, such as the *fideikommiss* (feoffment in trust)and entail; charitable trusts; private trusts; modern foundations; Brahman and Buddhist endowments; Hindu religious and charitable trusts; and the Nepalese *guthi* (land set aside for socioreligious purposes).

4. For example, Abu Bakr b. Mas'ud al-Kasani (d. 587/1189), *Kitab bada'i' al-sana'i' fi tartib al-shara'i'* (Cairo: Matba'at al-Jamaliyya, 1910), 4:221. The idea of perpetual charity, the terms *sadaqa jariya* (perpetual charity), and *sadaqa mawqufa* (endowed charity), appear in virtually every treatise on the waqf. See, for example, Abu Bakr Ahmad b. 'Amr al-Shaybani (al-Khassaf) (d. 261/874–875), *Kitab ahkam al*-waqf (Cairo: Bulaq, 1904), passim.

5. On the notion of qurba, see J. N. D. Anderson, "The Religious Element in Waqf Endowments," *Journal of the Royal Central Asian Society* 38 (1951): 292–299.

6. See al-Shaybani (al-Khassaf), *Kitab ahkam al-waqf*, 335–339; Zayn al-Din Ibn Nujaym (d. 970/1563), *al-Bahr al-ra'iq sharh kanz al-daqa'iq*, including Muhammad Amin Ibn 'Abidin's (d. 1252/1836), *Minhat al-khaliq 'ala al-bahr al-ra'iq* (Cairo: al-Matba'a al-'Ilmiyya, n.d.), 5:204; Muhammad Qadri Pasha, *Kitab qanun al-'adl wa'l-insaf lil-qada' 'ala mushkilat al-awqaf*, 3rd ed. (Cairo: Bulaq, al-Matba'a al-Kubra al-Amiriyya,1902), arts. 87–94.

7. Baer, "The Muslim Waqf."

8. R. L. Payton, *Philanthropy: Four Views* (New Brunswick, N.J.: Transaction Publishers, 1988), 1.

9. W. F. Ilchman, S. N. Katz, and E. L. Queen II, "Introduction," in *Philanthropy in the World's Traditions*, ed. W. F. Ilchman, S. N. Katz, and E. L. Queen II (Bloomington: Indiana University Press, 1998), ix.

10. For literature on the origins of the waqf see M. Hoexter, "*Waqf* Studies in the Twentieth Century: The State of the Art," *Journal of the Economic and Social History of the Orient* 41 (1998): 484 n. 32.

11. See G. E. Pruett, "Islam and Orientalism," in *Orientalism, Islam, and Islamists*, ed. A. Hussain, R. W. Olson, and J. Qureshi (Brattleboro, Vt.: Amana Books, 1984), 43–87. The article revolves around the idea that "for the Muslim, Islam is the command to submit to Allah in every aspect of his life," and a critique of the Orientalist who "has dismissed this fundamental consideration from his reading of Islam. That is to say, he fails to see the transcendent truth and good in the Muslim tradition and thinks of it as a cultural artifact only" (44).

12. For more details on these subjects, see M. Hoexter, "The *Waqf* and the Public Sphere," in *The Public Sphere in Muslim Societies*, ed. M. Hoexter, S. N. Eisenstadt, and N. Levtzion (Albany: State University of New York Press, 2002), 119–138.

13. M. G. S. Hodgson, *The Venture of Islam* (Chicago: University of Chicago Press, 1974), 2:124.

14. See Weir-[Zysow], "Sadaka." For early definitions of poverty, see M. Bonner, "Definitions of Poverty and the Rise of the Muslim Urban Poor," *Journal of the Royal Asiatic Society*, 3rd ser., 6 (1996): 335–344.

15. As for Abu Hanifa's rejection of an endowment inter vivos in favor of the poor, which was based on the impossibility of securing the actual transfer of the endowed property

from the endower to a specific person, see J. Schacht, "Early Doctrines on Waqf," in *Mélanges Fuad Köprülü* (Istanbul: Osman Yalçin Matbaasi, 1953), 451–452. See also Muhammad Amin Ibn 'Abidin (d. 1252/1836), *Radd al-muhtar 'ala al-durr al-mukhtar* (Cairo: Matba'at Mustafa al-Babi al-Halabi, 1966), 4:338–339. As in many other cases, it was not his view but that of his disciple Abu Yusuf, who allowed such endowments, that prevailed.

16. Al-Shaybani (al-Khassaf), *Kitab ahkam al-waqf*, 20. This remained the Hanafi opinion in such a case. As to other schools of law, see Anderson, "The Religious Element in Waqf Endowments," 293–294.

17. See L. Kinberg, "Compromise of Commerce," *Der Islam* 66 (1989): 193–212.

18. See, for example, Qadri, art. 5.

19. For the basic rules of the waqf, see, for example, R. Peters, "Wakf," *EI²*, 11:59–99.

20. Hoexter, "The Waqf and the Public Sphere." For examples and literature, see G. Baer, "The *Waqf* as a Prop for the Social System (Sixteenth–Twentieth Centuries)," *Islamic Law and Society* 4 (1997): 279–285, 288, 291–297; Hoexter "*Waqf* Studies in the Twentieth Century," 481n. 22; E. Ginio, "Marginal People in the Ottoman City: The Case of Salonica during the 18th Century" (Ph.D. diss., The Hebrew University of Jerusalem, 1998) (in Hebrew).

21. The terms used in the document were *al-diyar al-Qudsiyya, al-Shamiyya*, and *al-Halabiyya*. In these cases I believe *al-diyar* should be understood as the area under the patriarch's authority. (*Waqfiyya* [endowment deed] of al-Khuri Ibrahim b. al-Khawaja Nikula b. al-Khawaja Hana al-Buri, Sijill of the Jaffa Shari'a court.) For additional examples, see R. Shaham, "Christian and Jewish *Waqf* in Palestine during the late Ottoman Period," *Bulletin of the School of Oriental and African Studies* 104 (1991): 463. For examples of endowments for various local purposes, see Baer, "The Waqf as a Prop," 280–282.

22. For this interpretation, see H. Gerber, "Palestine" and Other Territorial Concepts in the Seventeenth Century," *International Journal of Middle East Studies* 30 (1998): 563–572.

23. Cahen, "Réflexions sur le *waqf* ancien," 47–48.

24. Al-Shaybani (al-Khassaf), *Kitab ahkam al-waqf*, 33, 125, 276.

25. This is a combination of the wording of the same idea by Kamal al-Din Muhammad 'Abd al-Wahid Ibn al-Humam (d. 861/1457), *Sharh fath al-qadir* (Cairo: Bulaq, 1316/1898–1899), 5:71–72 and Ibn 'Abidin, *Radd al-muhtar 'ala al-durr al-mukhtar*, 4:366.

26. S. A. Arjomand, "The Law, Agency, and Policy in Medieval Islamic Society: Development of the Institutions of Learning from the Tenth to the Fifteenth Century," *Comparative Studies in Society and History* 41 (1999): 263–293.

27. On the development of remuneration for performance of rites, see B. Johansen, "The Servants of the Mosques," *Maghreb Review* 7 (1982): 23–31.

28. A random sample of registered endowments within the walls of Istanbul by 953/1546 gave the following results for ultimate beneficiaries: recipients of charity amounted to 6.8 percent, servants of religious institutions 9.2 percent and Quran readers and other 'ulama' 78.5 percent; see G. Baer, "Women and Waqf: An Analysis of the Istanbul Tahrir of 1546," *Studies in the Social History of the Middle East in Memory of Professor Gabriel Baer. Asian and African Studies* 17 (1983): 21.

29. See chapter 8 of this volume.

30. O. Peri, "Waqf and Ottoman Welfare Policy: The Poor Kitchen of Hasseki Sultan in Eighteenth-Century Jerusalem," *Journal of the Economic and Social History of the Orient* 35 (1992): 172

31. Ibid., 173 and n. 17 there. See also 173–174 for the inclusion as beneficiaries of some high officials.

32. Shaham, "Christian and Jewish *Waqf* in Palestine," 462. On the rules, see p. 146 above.

33. See note 6 above.

34. This was the wording in the waqfiyya mentioned in note 21 above, as well as in at least one of the endowment deeds examined by Shaham; see Shaham, "Christian and Jewish *Waqf* in Palestine," 463.

35. See M. Hoexter, *Endowments, Rulers, and Community: Waqf al-Haramayn in Ottoman Algiers* (Leiden: Brill, 1998), chap. 1. The description that follows is based on chapter 6 (144–156), with some additions.

36. Archives d'Outre-Mer, Aix-en-Provence (hereafter Aix) /1 Mi 52, Z-116.

37. A. Devoulx, *Notice sur les corporations religieuses d'Alger*, extrait de la *Revue Africaine* (Algiers: Impr. de Bastide, 1862), 10–14.

38. Probably short for *tuwuffiya*, "passed away."

39. These details were practically identical in both documents.

40. This is the sum I obtained by subtracting from the total the twelve cases in which the letter *ta'* was not crossed and adding the two sums added in Medina. Because the marks drawn on the list were not always clear, some minor mistakes may have occurred in my calculation.

41. Devoulx, *Notice sur les corporations religieuses d'Alger*, 18–20. Both letters are undated.

42. Devoulx rendered him as *"suivant"* (attendant) of the head of the family. His name was Bilal, a common name of dark-skinned people, probably Africans.

43. Because the depositaries received 1,500 dinars and Medina as a rule received two-thirds of the Algerian allocation, it is clear that this list included the beneficiaries residing in Medina only. Instructions as to the distribution of the remaining one-third, designated for the poor of Mecca, must have been included in another document that did not come to my attention, to which was presumably appended a list of the poor of that city entitled to shares in the allocation.

44. The latter appeared in the earlier allocation only.

45. M. le Baron Pichon's impression that beneficiaries were either poor and distinguished families or elderly 'ulama' of the two cities conveyed the general picture; see his *Alger sous la domination française: son état présent et son avenir* (Paris: T. Barröis, 1833), 214–215. For some details on the beneficiaries of Moroccan endowments for Mecca and Medina, who constituted very similar groups of people, see 'Abd al-Hadi al-Tazi, "Tawzif al-waqf li-khidmat al-siyasa al-kharijiyya fi'l-Maghrib," in *Le waqf dans l'espace islamique: outil de pouvoir socio-politique*, ed. R. Deguilhem (Damascus: IFEAD, 1995), Arabic sec., 78–81.

46. According to the list attached to the earlier document. For the later allocation, Devoulx cited 1 to 10 dinars.

47. For more details, see M. Hoexter *Endowments, Rulers, and Community*, chap. 2. The following is based in the main on chapter 6.

48. This obviously is a mistake and should read "80 boudjoux." *Bucu* is a Turkish word usually rendered boudjou in French. Its rate of exchange in the first years of French rule in Algeria was 1.80 to 1.86 francs for one boudjou.

49. Archives Nationales (hereafter AN)/F 80 1082 (the F 80 series is now located in Aix-en-Provence), Extrait du Rapport de l'Inspecteur Chef du Service des Domaines et Contributions Diverses sur la situation et l'organisation définitive de cette administration, n.d. [beginning of 1834]. For similar descriptions see Pichon, *Alger sous la domination française*, 213–224; Venture de Paradis, *Alger au XVIIIe siècle*, ed. E. Fagnan (Algiers: A. Jourdan, 1898), 164.

50. Concerning the bequest for the Christian captives, see T. Campbell, *Letters from the South* (London: n.p., 1837), 2:100 That Christians were indeed among those who received regular alms from the Haramayn is corroborated by the statement to the French by the administrator of the institution; see P. Genty de Bussy, *De l'établissement des Français dans la Régence d'Alger et des moyens d'en assurer la prospérité*, pièce justificative no. 7 (Paris: Didot Frères, 1835), 2:32.

51. Ibid.; AN/F 80 1082 Extrait du Rapport.

52. Pichon, *Alger sous la domination française*, 213–214; AN/F 80 1082 Extrait du Rapport; Vérificateur des Domaines à l'Intendant Civil, Rapport sur l'administration des Corporations religieuses, 1837; F 80 1747, Draft of a letter to Paravey, Chef du Bureau d'Alger, April 25, 1837; F 80 1632, Contrôleur des Domaines au Directeur des Finances, August 6, 1836.

53. In fact, this sum was way above the annual income of the entire group of endowments for the poor of Algiers, the captives, and the *talaba*.

54. A. Marcus, "Poverty and Poor Relief in Eighteenth-Century Aleppo," *Revue du Monde Musulman et de la Méditerranée* 55–56 (1990): 171–179; Ginio, "Marginal People in the Ottoman City," 131–155.

55. See Hoexter, "*Waqf* Studies in the Twentieth Century."

Part III

The State as Benefactor

Chapter Eight

Living on the Margins of Charity

Coping with Poverty in an Ottoman Provincial City

Eyal Ginio

King Süleyman (Solomon), the gifted prophet king, founded Salonica while touring the world. He arrived there, accompanied by his beloved Bilkis (Queen of Sheba), on a magic throne *(taht)* that was lifted into the air by jinns and *divs* (demons). The remains of the king's stunning castle were still visible when the seventeenth-century Ottoman traveler Evliya Çelebi (1611–1682) visited the city. He later recorded this legend in his travelogue.[1] Unfortunately, being bereft of any other religious or imperial relics, Salonica had to share the prestige of being established by the highly endowed king with many other localities, as similar legends existed in various cities that boasted pre-Islamic remains.[2]

The lack of any religious or imperial prestige meant that Ottoman Salonica was not furnished with any sultanic endowments. Although the economic and administrative importance of the city made it one of the most vital cities in the Ottoman Balkans,[3] the Ottoman sultans did not regard Salonica, or indeed its fifty-thousand-odd inhabitants,[4] as primary targets for their generosity and philanthropy. When they designated assets in Salonica and its surroundings in favor of an endowment, the beneficiaries were situated faraway—overwhelmingly in Istanbul.[5] This point bears much significance with regard to the scope of institutional charity in this port city. Sultanic endowments were the principal mode of large-scale charities initiated and maintained by the state. By founding endowments, the sultans supported hospitals, public poor kitchens, water systems, bridges, and religious and educational establishments.[6] These endeavors reflected the sultans' concern for the common good of their subjects—an acknowledgement of their responsibility as patrimonial sovereigns.[7] Bringing relief to poor people was acknowledged and heralded as one of the sultan's major responsibilities and concerns. A formula repeated at the beginning of various edicts illustrates this commitment: "[M]y sultanic wish lies in attaining aspects that bestow ease upon the poor among my subjects and inhabitants of the state and in allotting [them] defense and protection against all occurrences of oppression and aggression."[8]

However, the sultanic endowments were not part of an all-embracing policy toward the poor, but rather constituted private altruism undertaken by different sultans to bolster their legitimacy. Their charity aimed only at preferred poor in select Ottoman cities. The main targets were found primarily in the prominent urban centers—the ones that displayed religious, historical or imperial prestige. Because many of the provincial Balkan cities, such as Salonica, lacked such prominence, they did not benefit from sultanic benevolent foundations. Evliya Çelebi's observation illustrates Salonica's inferior position. He reported that the Salonican sick were hospitalized in two small rooms adjacent to two neighborhood mosques, unlike their counterparts in Edirne, Bursa, and Istanbul who benefited from the services of magnificent hospitals.[9]

Local society and local officials determined who among the poor would be marginalized, ignored, or accepted in Salonica. Society either used its mechanisms to marginalize the poor by exploitation or abuse or it assisted them by dispensing charity. This chapter deals with the way local society distinguished between the deserving poor and the undeserving poor and the strategies adopted by paupers in a provincial Ottoman city to ensure rudimentary survival.

Poverty and Poor in the Şeriat Court Records

This chapter relies to a large extent on the documents of the Salonican Şeriat court, known as *sicil*.[10] Consequently, some methodological remarks must be made at the outset. The sicil records reflect the diversity of the *kadi*'s (judge) responsibilities in the Ottoman city: Notarial deeds, litigations, correspondence with local and central authorities, and reports about public and urban matters are found among the variety of files. However, the sicil records are not detailed protocols; rather, they are stylized summaries written in a rigid and standardized language that reflects the authorities' narrative. As such, they correspond to the stereotypes and notions formed by the elite with regard to the poor. The latter have to be glimpsed through the prism of administration records and initiatives.[11] Although uncovering the "social control" strategies of the administrative elite by examining these official records is feasible, retrieving informal charity or the paupers' strategies are rather elusive tasks.[12]

However, this generalization has its own exceptions. The sicil are records written and formed by the elite, but the poor themselves were not merely passive bystanders who watched their destiny being shaped and determined by others. In some instances they had recourse to the court to obtain justice, in other cases they pleaded with the central authorities to redress their grievances. Both types must be regarded as initiatives set forth by the poor themselves. In these documents, though the words of the poor may be obscured and blurred by the official language of the authorities, one can still gain insights into their strategies and experiences.

'Poverty' and 'poor' are not universally rigid concepts. Their usage and meaning differ across time, context, and place. Indeed, language, as Robert Jütte demonstrates in his book on poverty in early modern Europe, can serve as a guide to social reality and attitudes toward the poor.[13] In the parlance of the Salonican sicil, the term *poor (fakir)* alluded to diverse notions such as modesty, pious asceticism, vulnerability, and economic dearth.[14] The term *poor* could symbolize humility, a designation used, for example, by the kadi to manifest his humbleness to the authorities;[15] it could mean the emphasizing of the subjects' vulnerability when tormented by corrupt officials, thus demonstrating that abuse of the poor was regarded as obnoxious;[16] it could signify a turning away from material life to dedicate one's life to pious activity in dervish lodges;[17] and it could mean absolute scarcity—an ambiguous term in itself. This chapter deals with the last category: the impoverished people. Here again, one must remember that the definition of *absolute poverty* is vague because "a poverty line is necessarily defined in relation to social conventions and contemporary living standards of a particular society."[18]

In eighteenth-century Salonica, the court's scribes defined poverty as a total lack of resources. This definition must not be understood as the underlying historical reality but rather as the formalized language of the court. The scribes used the terms "from a poor condition" *(fakirülhal)* or "the poor of the Muslims" *(fukara-i müslimin)* when describing the absolute poor. A general definition of poverty was given when the court handled requests of bankrupt persons to be declared insolvent. In these cases, poverty was considered an economic phenomenon that resulted in an utter dearth of economic resources: "I am poor, indebted, bankrupt and utterly a pauper; I do not possess anything except for the clothes that I am wearing now. As I do not have any property whatsoever, I cannot pay my aforementioned debt."[19]

Thus, the poor were characterized as unable to survive by their own means. How did Salonican society understand and cope with the problem?

The Limited Scope of Institutional Charity for the Poor

Islam obliges the faithful to distribute alms to those who are in need. In consequence, the philanthropic faithful can hope for recompense in the hereafter. The foundation of an endowment *(vakıf)* is regarded as a favorite mode of approaching and attaining nearness to God *(kurbet)* and, consequently, enhancing one's reward. Indeed, endowment deeds—as well as gifts, wills, and manumissions—are all, to some degree, the benevolent outcome of proprietors' fears and hopes regarding the hereafter. These documents thus disclose the Salonicans' view of charity in the crucial moment of their lives when they contemplated their own death and the menacing afterlife.[20]

Constructing a pious endowment became the legal foundation of philanthropy in Islam. The definition of beneficiaries was broad enough to include a great variety of public beneficiaries. The poor, who were designated in the Quran as the main beneficiaries of alms *(sadaka, zekat)*, later became only one target of charity. Their position with regard to other beneficiaries was determined according to the various founders' perceptions and wishes.[21]

Whereas local governors and high-ranking army officers who were posted to Salonica established pious endowments in the fifteenth and sixteenth centuries, most eighteenth-century endowments were the result of local initiative.[22] Beneficiaries of these endowments might receive a fixed allowance or benefice in kind or in money, the right to dwell in an endowed house or to be appointed to serve as the endowment's administrator in return for a fixed salary.

Who were considered deserving recipients of charity in Ottoman Salonica? Two types of records help to determine the answer: sixty-two new endowment deeds *(vakfiye)* that articulate the founders' stipulation of beneficiaries to their charity, and the financial records *(iradat ve ihracat-i vakıf)* of ninety-seven existing endowments that reflect the actual financial administration of existing endowments. In addition, these records specify the proportional entitlement of the different beneficiaries.[23] The Salonican sicil for the years 1694–1768 shows the registered public beneficiaries of new endowments (in some endowments more than one public beneficiary was designated) as follows:

Neighborhood Mosques	30
Sufi Lodges	28
The Poor of Salonica	19
Guilds	8
The Poor of the Holy Cities	4

The types of beneficiaries mentioned in the reports submitted by the administrators of the different endowments are as follows:

Vakıf Officials	97
Religious Functionaries	76
Founders' Descendents	10
Water Supply	10
The Poor	7
Guilds	5
Neighborhood	5

Before assessing these numbers, one must remember a major distinction among the beneficiaries mentioned here: While Sufi lodges, neighborhood mosques, and guilds were designated as the immediate beneficiaries following the endowment's establishment or the death of its founder, the poor were designated as beneficiaries mainly of family endowments. They were the remote and ultimate beneficiaries who would be entitled to receive their share in the endowment only following the total extinction of all the founder's descendants.[24]

These lists clearly indicate the proprietors' attitudes toward charity and its recipients. First, the broad population of poor people was not regarded as the primary target of altruism. Most benevolent Salonicans preferred to make their bequests to the various local religious establishments and their residents and officials. The worthy poor were clearly identified with the pious poor who held a position in the neighborhood mosque or lived in the Sufi lodge. Providing these poor with allowances in return for reciting from the Quran and praying for the donor's soul was a frequent charitable exchange. In such cases, financial aid was bestowed in return for spiritual aid.

Next came the poor who benefited from belonging to a solidarity network: guild or neighborhood. Such networks could assist their members who fell on hard times. Their spheres of charity reflected their domains of activity: Guild endowments mainly occupied themselves with offering loans on favorable terms to their members and assistance in paying taxes. Others sought to boost the guild members' solidarity by financing banquets for the entire guild.[25] Neighborhood endowments distributed relief in the private domain by supplying the neighborhood poor with food, clothing, or shrouds when the time came.[26] Orphans, widows, and bankrupted members were singled out as particular objects of charity by guild or neighborhood endowments. The deserving destitute person was one who had reached his humble position by a sudden misfortune, such as the death of the family's male breadwinner or by a bankruptcy. His attachment to social and professional networks could ensure him some degree of assistance should he be in desperate need.

The broader population of poor people was somehow the lowest of the donors' priorities, serving to fill up the rubric of the eternal beneficiary mentioned at the end of the formal entitlement deeds. Although the founders put some effort into explaining and specifying the exact division of their endowment revenues among all the beneficiaries, when they reached the poor as the last beneficiary they were satisfied with a general stipulation. Furthermore, two recorded cases demonstrate that administrators were rather reluctant to allocate the due entitlement to the poor: In these two cases the administrators were admonished by the kadi for failing to allot the poor their share. It is worth noting that these were the only cases in which such a rebuke was mentioned.[27]

Some paupers in Salonica were outsiders who lacked any access to social networks in the city. Their numbers cannot be assessed, but their presence is evident in the sicil: They were rural migrants who searched for work in this bustling port town, fugitive slaves, unskilled workers who roamed the streets looking for random employment, itinerant peddlers, beggars, dismissed domestic servants, and solitary women. For them, institutional charity did not provide regular assistance or a promising refuge. They lived on the margins of Salonican society and consequently found themselves in the margins of charity as well. This distinction had crucial results with regard to access to formal charity. The distinction fits, to some extent, John Illife's dichotomy of structural poverty versus conjunctural poverty. Illife demonstrates—following Jean-Pierre Guttons' discussion of poverty in early modern Lyon—that structural poverty is the long-term poverty of individuals caused by their personal or social circumstances, while conjunctural poverty is the temporary poverty into which ordinarily self-sufficient people may be precipitated by sudden crisis.[28]

The absolute poor were marginal in the minds of the Salonican benefactors. The poor kitchen seems to be the only institution that was designated to serve them. As I have mentioned, Salonica was not provided with a poor kitchen set up and financed by sultanic endowments. Notwithstanding this, during the Ottoman period Salonica became a favorite place to confine pensioned grand viziers, political exiles, and ousted dignitaries—Sultan Abdülhamid the Second (1876–1909) being the last and most prominent example. Some of these voluntary or forced guests bestowed relatively small charitable establishments on the city. İshak Paşa (grand vizier from 1468 to 1471), resided in Salonica as a pensioned statesman and established a poor kitchen adjacent to a mosque. Machiel Kiel describes this poor kitchen as "an imaret of a middle-size."[29] The endowment deed stated that the poor kitchen was designated for the poor, the paupers, and for the wayfarers among the Muslims—those who inhabited Salonica and those who arrived there.[30] However, published data about Jerusalem's poor kitchen in the eighteenth century suggest that religious men and other dignitaries formed the bulk of the beneficiaries who enjoyed hot meals in this kind of charity establishment.[31] A similar phenomenon may also have occurred in Salonica, although, oddly enough, no activity of this poor kitchen appeared in the sicil files. It was rarely mentioned in these records—a possible testimony to this institution's relative insignificance as a city landmark during the eighteenth century.[32]

Indeed, Evliya's brief description is a rare allusion to the network of poor kitchens and their clientele in Salonica. According to him, the seven poor kitchens provided their clients with a daily bowl of hot soup and a loaf of bread. Meals were served in the mornings and in the evenings. The poor kitchens' diverse clientele dovetailed with the Salonican understanding of charity: rich and poor *(cemi-i bay u geda)* dervishes, Gypsies, and itinerant beggars huddled there in the quest for hot meals.[33]

In an attempt to provide general aspects of a comparative history of the poor, Iliffe argues that both European and African poor had to rely chiefly on their own efforts to ensure their survival: Hawking or begging in the street or turning to crime would be regarded as possible strategies.[34] As we shall see, similar strategies had to be adopted by Salonican paupers because institutional charity was not available to them.

Improvised and Short-Term Charity

Some of the Salonican poor were excluded from institutional and formal charity. C. Dyer, who depicts the scope of charity offered by pious institutions in medieval England, remarks that given the restricted scope of charity distributed by the well-off to the poor, the "survival of the medieval poor still remains something of a mystery. Given the inadequacy of charitable institutions, the networks of relatives and neighbors must be assumed to have worked with some effect."[35] Abraham Marcus got a similar impression from the sicil files of eighteenth-century Aleppo where funds for poor relief were also limited.[36] Thus, the question arises with regard to the outsider Salonican poor: How did they cope with their plight?

Spontaneous and haphazard encounters between benevolent donors and paupers must have been a prevalent option. However, from the historian's point of view, retracing such encounters is almost impossible. The nature of this charity—isolated cases with nothing preceding and nothing following—resulted in its almost total absence from court records. However, a few documents shed light on single instances; I will turn to these at some length because they reveal possible strategies for survival.

In these cases, paupers had to rely on random, if less discriminating, charity given in the street or in the field. One example mentions groups of beggars who traveled from place to place. They were all blacks *(kara arap)*, possibly manumitted or fugitive slaves, gathered in small groups and roving the vast area around Salonica. Their leader petitioned the authorities and complained about their mistreatment by local officials. Being destitute and possessing nothing, as he described their plight, they were in constant search of casual charity. Sometimes they were well received, at other times they were abused by officials who extorted from them their humble alms.[37]

This petition describes a group whose members can be defined as "structural" poor. We can assume that most of them were former slaves who apparently lacked any supportive connections with their former masters. They were outsiders with no kinship, social, or professional ties in the local communities. To compensate, they tried to organize themselves into cohesive groups—much like their counterparts in early modern Europe, who were insightfully described by Bronislaw

Geremek.[38] Their organization apparently had the benefit of some degree of administrative recognition as is evident from the scribes' terminology: They are referred to by the collective *taifa* or *cemaat* (tribe, group).

The authorities' attitude toward these "idle" poor was rather different from that in early modern Western Europe, where loitering and vagrancy were regarded as a threat to public morality, health, and security.[39] The Ottoman authorities were content, in this case, to admonish the abusive officials, but they ordered no action against the itinerant beggars. Although we have evidence for the Ottoman authorities'—including the Salonican authorities'—suspicion and even persecution of the idle poor, it seems that such measures were most likely applied against the urban poor in agitated times. Furthermore, the state resented migration from rural areas because this could consequently threaten its revenues. However, in the case previously mentioned, the local authorities demonstrated their indifference to and toleration of the begging poor who roamed the countryside and whose origin was not among the rural population.

Another example deals with a widow and her daughter. As the case alludes to a widespread custom, based on the şeriat, it usefully demonstrates another accepted form of charity. The litigation involved a claim submitted by the brothers of a widow, named Fatıma. The plaintiffs contended that the widow was stabbed to death in a field. The defendant, who was the field's owner, claimed to be innocent. According to him, the widow and her daughter were impoverished, without means or provisions. To support themselves, they used to follow the harvesters and glean the wheat that fell on the ground and the ears of grain *(sünbüle)* that were scattered during the harvest. The field's owner argued that Fatıma had died following the terrible heat that prevailed that day. As a final grace he performed her funeral in the field.[40] I cannot deduce whether this counterclaim was true; however, the field owner's reply demonstrates that gleaning *(lukta)* was customary, based on the principle of şeriat that allows the poor to pick up the leftover sheaves from the ground.[41]

Festive days were regarded as suitable occasions for distributing informal charity. Thus, for example, Hadice Hatun stipulated in her endowment deed that the poor of her neighborhood, Timurtaş, be fed on the Prophet's birthday.[42] Funerals of affluent persons were another occasion when charity could be offered. Wills, mainly of childless people and foreigners, provide us with information on funeral customs in Salonica. These documents demonstrate that the poor could expect to receive at least a cup of coffee while attending a funeral. At more generous funerals, they could expect a decent meal or might even be fed for two successive days following the funeral.[43]

All the strategies previously mentioned were limited, short-term palliatives. They obliged the poor to improvise encounters with potential donors each and every day in order to survive. However, other modes of self-reliance had to be adopted to obtain a reliable source of regular income.

Self-Reliance Strategies for the Long Term

The sicil sheds light on various examples of long-term options that were adopted by the poor in eighteenth-century Salonica. One was the migration of mainly men, individually or in groups, to the urban center in search of work. Albanians migrated extensively from the barren, mountainous hinterland to find seasonal or regular work in the port city of Salonica and its rural vicinity. The city docks, for example, offered unskilled migrants casual labor as porters. The Albanians were occasionally organized into groups to compete with local unskilled laborers for the limited work available in the port. Some Albanians served as apprentices and subsequently moved into the ranks of artisans. Others opted for criminality by taking part in rural banditry. Because the authorities regarded rural migration to the cities and banditry as threats to the public order and the state's revenues, the migrants had to adopt various strategies to secure their position.[44]

Religious conversion to Islam could be seen as another strategy adopted by a few individuals. My only evidence suggesting a correlation between poverty and conversion is the relatively high percentage of young migrants among the converts.[45]

In one type of claim, the actual explanations and arguments of the poor come forth, though voiced in the rigid parlance of the scribes. A dozen cases in the sicil are claims against employers reluctant to pay overdue wages. In most cases, the claimants were female servants who submitted such claims against former employers. These claims reflect one possible strategy adopted by desperate parents: giving away their children—mostly daughters—to serve in non-kinsmen's houses, virtually to become slaves.[46] Domestic service was one of the few genuine labor opportunities open to poor girls and women in Ottoman society. A discussion of this form of labor reveals the attitude of Salonican society toward an important segment of the poor: the female pauper.

Employing domestic servants was much less expensive than acquiring slaves in eighteenth-century Salonica. Purchasing a slave—a lucrative imported commodity—required a fortune of at least two hundred guruş, whereas a servant's wages could cost as little as a few guruş annually. Domestic servants not only took the place of slaves, but they also shared many legal and social features with them. Their similar position demonstrates the blurred boundaries between free persons and slaves in Ottoman society—a boundary that was ostensibly rigid and evident. Given the documentation at hand, I cannot quantify the number of servants who resided in Salonica or assess the spread of domestic service among the poor. However, the records clearly demonstrate that this phenomenon included different groups of destitute people: Muslims as well as Christians,[47] poor city dwellers alongside impoverished villagers.

A similar pattern appears in the claims or declarations given by domestic servants: despairing parents handed over their children at a very young age (six or seven) to bring some relief to their precarious condition. In return, the children had to serve their benefactor–employers for an unspecified length of time.[48] These children had no formal contract with their employers—a practice at odds with the şeriat, which requires the proposal and acceptance of a fair wage *(ecir-i misil)* in any work contract.[49] In the case of child labor, these legal requirements were set aside. No hiring period or wage was stipulated. Employment was based on an oral agreement, according to which the employers pledged to supply the child with his or her basic needs—shelter, food, and clothing—while the child, in turn, had to perform household chores. The court referred to these minor servants as "those who were employed without any salary contract" *(ücret kavlınsız makulesinden)*. The court displayed no objections to this kind of employment, thus showing its implicit acceptance of such an agreement.

For example, the parents of Maruda bint Yorgaki delivered her as a child to a Christian couple to be raised; in return she was expected to serve in their house. Her parents entrusted some old household objects to the fostering couple for their daughter to use after reaching puberty.[50] The father of Osman Beşe handed over his daughter while she was still a minor to serve at Ümmetullah's house. In return, he assumed that his daughter would receive food and clothes in lieu of a fair wage.[51]

The employers' arguments for avoiding the payment due relied on the assumption that taking custody of the children was no less than a charity, a benevolent act that did not result in an employer–employee relationship.[52] They depicted themselves as a foster family providing the pauper child with his or her basic necessities. Furthermore, based on the assumption that theirs was an act of charity rather than employment, some employers gave their servants only perquisites, such as old clothes, used items, a pair of tattered boots, or a small and insignificant amount of money when they decided to dismiss them after long years of domestic service. Such a dismissal would occur following a servant's marriage, or, if the employers were Christians, as a consequence of the servant's conversion to Islam. Yet, in other cases, servants worked in their employers' house until their death, being transferred within the family almost as part of the inheritance.

When the employers were confronted with the demand to pay their servants a fair wage, they reacted with what seems to be sheer astonishment. By way of illustration, Bakiye bint Mustafa argued that Rabi'a's claim of payment due must be rejected as she, Bakiye, had taken Rabi'a into her house when the latter was only seven years old. She provided the young girl with all her needs while the plaintiff was too young to perform any work. After four years, during which the plaintiff dwelled in the defendant's house where all her needs were furnished, it was obvious that she should take upon herself some of the household tasks.[53]

Any payment was portrayed as generosity stemming from the employer's goodwill and not from any commitment. Thus, for example, Daniel bin Marta, a "beardless youngster" *(şab-i emred)* acquitted his employers of any future claim. He told the court that his father had handed him over eight years previously, when he was still a boy, so that his employers would raise him. He declared that they had allocated him a fair wage, even though he was one of those who were not entitled to a salary.[54] Fatıma bint Abdullah declared that all the household objects she had received from her former employer were far more than what should have been regarded as her fair wage for six years of working as a servant.[55]

Today, we cannot determine whether these declarations were freely given. In some cases, real generosity probably motivated the fostering of pauper children. Relatives who decided to take in orphans, to grant them a share in endowment entitlements or to give them presents, even though the children were not their legal heirs, exemplify charity bestowed within the extended family.[56] In other cases, servants genuinely became a part of the household. A demand made by the custodian of an affluent orphan to receive an allowance for sustaining the servants that the minor had "inherited" from his deceased parents illustrates how servants could be regarded as heritable objects; yet it also illustrates the fact that servants, like slaves, were regarded as an integral part of the household.[57] Adding the funeral costs of a male servant to the debts that had to be refunded from his dead employer's estate is another example.[58]

However, Hadice bint Hüseyin's claim describes another experience. She asked the court to force her former employer to pay her a fair wage for the ten years she had served in his house. She admitted to declaring previously in court that she had exonerated him from any responsibility to her, but she now argued that she had done so because of his threats and against her will.[59] Hadice's claim demonstrates how poor female servants were marginalized by local society. Their helplessness, dependence, and vulnerability are evident in the documents. Some of them contended that they were required to perform, without pay, supplementary tasks such as burying their employer's spouse. In this case the clerk registered the employer's presumably commanding language: "bury the Christian!" *(zimmiyi defn et)*.[60] Other servants were beaten and forced to relinquish their rights.[61] Still others were exposed to sexual abuse, made possible by their total subservience to and dependence on their employers. In one case a female servant, Rabi'a bint Musa sued her employer, Ahmet Beşe, for raping her. Her claim describes a case of illicit sexual relations between a master and a female servant and an attempt by the servant to negotiate recompense from her employer. Therefore, it is interesting to observe how her claim was handled in court.[62]

The servant's claim to receive a certain type of compensation *(ukr)* clearly signals the socially inferior position of servants in general: She requested—presumably following some advice that she had received—compensation that was due only in cases in which the rapist could reasonably assume that his sexual intercourse with his victim was legally acceptable.[63] Islamic law sanctions sexual intercourse only in cases of marriage or ownership of a female slave. All other cases of sexual intercourse are unlawful and are defined as fornication *(zina)*. Adulterers are punished with the Quranic penalty of stoning or lashes. However, these penalties are not applicable in case of a legal doubt *(şüphe)*. Such doubt exists only if the man mistakenly, but still reasonably, assumes that the woman is bound to him in marriage or owned by him as a slave. For example, the Quranic penalty is not applicable in cases of sexual intercourse between husband and wife when the husband was not aware of their marriage's invalidity, or between a freeman and a female slave when the man could have assumed that she was legally permitted to him (for example, if he had sold her to another but had not yet delivered her, or if she was his wife's slave). Returning to the above-mentioned case, the servant's demand to receive ukr demonstrates that sexual intercourse with a female servant could raise a similar legal doubt. It shows that the employer could plausibly consider intercourse with his female servant as lawful, as if she were his slave. In this case, the legal dispute was resolved with a compromise between the servant and her employer.[64]

The vulnerability of female servants is demonstrated likewise in their application to the court for unpaid wages. In all cases, the claims were submitted only after the servants' dismissal. Sometimes it took them years to sue their employers. Claims for nonpayment are actually a rare example of claims rejected by the court on the grounds that the statute of limitations had expired.[65] Other claims were submitted by the heirs only following the servants' deaths.[66]

Finally, the servants' vulnerable position is clear from their failure to receive favorable verdicts. In reality, all of their claims were settled through compromise *(sulh)*.[67] Their vulnerable position derived from the basic assumption of their employers that the servants' employment was recompense for a charitable deed; the former servants relinquished their claims to receive a fair wage in return for an insignificant sum of money, normally five or six guruş. The compromise agreement underlines the prevalence and acceptance of unpaid child labor in eighteenth-century Salonica. Where former servants resisted and turned to the court, their actions were in vain; the kadi did not feel obliged to interfere on behalf of these servants and did not hesitate to legitimize the compromise just mentioned by issuing a court deed.

The employment of child servants, overwhelmingly girls, in Ottoman Salonica reveals the blurred line between charity and abuse. In these cases, the benefactor expected the beneficiary to recompense him for his charity. Indeed, fostering a pauper girl could turn out to be a profitable charity in which a servant's employment could be secured at little or no expense. As the benefactor enjoyed a much higher social and economic position, the servant was totally dependent on his employer's goodwill and was forced to accept his so-called benefactor's conditions. In many cases, this unequal relationship resulted in the marginalization of pauper girls to such an extent that they became veritable slaves. The authorities, for their part, tacitly approved of this mode of employment.

Conclusions

Charity in the Ottoman state was a private deed performed by the individual. Even sultanic charity, ostensibly the Ottoman counterpart of welfare policy, must be regarded in this light as the beneficent deed of an individual directed toward select groups of poor. One does not find any attempt at constructing a centralized, secular, and rigid policy toward the poor such as developed gradually in most parts of Europe starting from the sixteenth century.[68]

Inhabitants of provincial cities were not targets for sultanic endowments. In these cities local residents and officials were the main benefactors in the charity market. Ottoman Salonica can serve as an example: Being a large port town, it attracted rural migration and had to cope with the presence of riffraff from all over the western Balkans. However, its economic importance did not accord it a place among the beneficiaries of sultanic endowments. The Salonican paupers had to depend on local initiatives in the charity market or be self-reliant. The sicil provides insights into the priorities of the Salonican people of means with regard to charity. Benevolent Salonicans used the pious endowment as a tool to improve their fortunes in the hereafter, as well as to enhance their reputations in local society. Accordingly, they cherished the pious poor who worked or lived in a religious institution. These pious poor were chosen and designated as the main beneficiaries of endowments. Belonging to a solidarity network—such as a neighborhood or guild—could augment one's access to assistance and charity when in need. Here again, specific targets were considered as worthy beneficiaries: widows, orphans, and bankrupt members of the network.

Such institutional charity could not answer the needs of all the Salonican poor. For some of them, who lacked any solidarity network, pious endowments did not provide a solution to their problems. Like the poor of pre-Industrial Western Europe, they had to opt for alternative strategies and to improvise their own "economy of makeshifts."[69] They had to rely on their own talents and initiative to receive charity or to earn a living by other means. This struggle for survival was channeled into a continuous search for casual alms; it was also manifested in a variety of activities adopted and initiated by the poor: Peddling, migration, conversion, crime, prostitution, and the placing of children to serve in the houses of others are the main strategies mentioned in the sicil.

The poor, however, were not one homogeneous group that shared the same features and possibilities: Although poor men could use various means to earn their living, women and children were much more limited in their choice of work options in Ottoman Salonica. For poor women, the urban labor market offered employment only in domestic service or prostitution. As unskilled workers, they were offered unskilled and low-wage jobs. This want of alternatives placed poor women and children in a position inferior to poor men. As a result, they were the weakest among the poor, being much more dependent on charity. The state and local society unambiguously acknowledged their vulnerability and singled them out as the most deserving poor, the intrinsic recipients of charity who particularly merited society's protection and benevolence.

Affiliation with a social network such as a neighborhood or a guild (through a male relative) made the distinction between the deserving poor woman and the "invisible" poor woman. When denied access to formal charity or simply ignored, women and children were much more easily exploited and abused. Their experiences demonstrate the thin boundary between charity and exploitation. The position of servants in Salonican society clearly demonstrates the plight of marginalized poor girls and women. Being detached from their family at a young age, these girls had to struggle alone in precarious conditions and in clearly unequal power relationships. Some of them were relegated to the position of genuine slaves. In the employers' narratives these girls were given shelter and provided with their basic needs in return for which they were expected to share the household chores. From the servants' perspective they were abused and exploited—free people demoted to the rank of slaves.

This chapter emphasized the secondary role played by institutional charity—the vakıf—in giving relief to most of the absolute poor. In the absence of the state, with no access to solidarity networks and marginalized by local society, most of these people lived on the margins of charity as well as on the fringes of society. For them—the invisible poor—self-reliance and their own improvisations were the only recourse. Some of them discovered that assistance had to be repaid by long years of service, and that charity could bring with it exploitation and abuse.

Notes

This chapter is based on a chapter of my Ph.D dissertation supervised by Professor Haim Gerber, to whom I am deeply indebted. I am also grateful to Dr. Ruth Roded for her valuable comments and to the Skilliter Centre for Ottoman Studies, Newnham College, Cambridge, for its grant in support of this research.

1. Evliya Çelebi, *Evliya Çelebi Seyahatnamesi* (Istanbul: Orhaniyya Matbaasi, 1928), 8:142. On the importance of his travel account as a source for local legends and beliefs, see Suraiya Faroqhi, *Approaching Ottoman History: An Introduction to the Sources* (Cambridge: Cambridge University Press, 1999), 160–161.

2. Istanbul, Kabul, Tadmor, and Persepolis are some of the cities that boast identical legends; see Priscilla P. Soucek, "Solomon's Throne/Solomon's Bath: Model or Metaphor?" *Ars Orientalis* 23 (1993): 109–134; Serpil Bağcı, "A New Theme of the Shirazi Frontispiece Miniatures. The Dîvân of Solomon," *Muqarnas* 12 (1995): 101–111.

3. The most comprehensive research regarding Ottoman Salonica is that of Vassilis Demitriades; see his *Topographia tes Thessalonikes kata ten epokhe tes Tourkokratias* (Thessa-

loniki: Etaireia Makedonikon Epoudon, 1983). See also S. Faroqhi, "Selânîk," *EI²*, 9:123–126.

4. For different European estimations of the eighteenth-century Salonica population, see N. K. Moutsopoulos, *Thessaloniki 1900–1917* (Thessaloniki: Molho, 1980), 54–55.

5. See, for example, the list of revenues of various villages that belonged to the *kaza* (judicial district) of Salonica. All revenues supported the endowment of a mosque and *medrese*s (colleges) situated in Eyüp. See sicil [Thessaloniki] TH/IER (hereafter *sicil*) 7/97, 19 Şaban 1111/8 February 1700.

6. See the following examples for sultanic endowments and their support for the local poor: Haim Gerber, "The Waqf Institution in Early Ottoman Edirne," *Asian and African Studies* 17 (1983): 43–45; Oded Peri, "Waqf and Ottoman Welfare Policy: The Poor Kitchen of Hasseki Sultan in Eighteenth-Century Jerusalem," *Journal of the Economic and Social History of the Orient* 35 (1992): 167–186; Çiğdem Kafescioğlu, 'The Image of Rūm': Ottoman Architectural Patronage in Sixteenth-Century Aleppo and Damascus," *Muqarnas* 16 (1999): 70–96.

7. On the development of one aspect of public charity—the educational–charitable complex—and its relationship to the early Muslim patrimonial states, see Said Amir Arjomand, "The Law, Agency, and Policy in Medieval Islamic Society: Development of the Institutions of Learning from the Tenth to the Fifteenth Century," *Comparative Studies in Society and History* 41(1999): 263–293. On the Ottoman state as a patrimonial state, see Şerif Mardin, "Power, Civil Society, and Culture in the Ottoman Empire," *Comparative Studies in Society and History* 11 (1969): 259–264.

8. *Memalik-i mahrusemde olan fukara-i reaya ve ahali-i memleketin husul-i esbab-i rahatleri veariza-i mezalim vetaaddiyattan emniyet ve selametleri matlup-i hümayunun olmaktan naşi*; see *sicil* 87/69, *evail-i* Receb 1168/13–22 April 1755.

9. Evliya Çelebi, *Evliya Çelebi Seyahatnamesi*, 8:164.

10. The sicil of Salonica is preserved today in the Historical Archives of Thessaloniki. I am indebted to the staff for their invaluable help and patience.

11. For a general examination of the sicil as a historical source, see Dror Zeevi, "The Use of Ottoman Sharī'a Court Records as a Source for Middle Eastern Social History: A Reappraisal," *Islamic Law and Society* 5 (1998): 35–56.

12. Tim Hitchcock, Peter King, and Pamela Sharpe, "Introduction: Chronicling Poverty—The Voices and Strategies of the English Poor, 1640–1840," in *Chronicling Poverty—The Voices and Strategies of the English Poor, 1640–1840*, ed. Tim Hitchcock, Peter King, and Pamela Sharpe (London: Macmillan, 1997), 1–18. For using the sicil to retrieve the role of charity institutions in an Ottoman city, see Abraham Marcus, "Poverty and Poor Relief in Eighteenth-Century Aleppo," *Revue du Monde Musulman et de la Méditerranée* 55–56 (1990): 171–179. See also his book *The Middle East on the Eve of Modernity: Aleppo in the Eighteenth Century* (New York: Columbia University Press, 1989), 212–218.

13. Robert Jütte, *Poverty and Deviance in Early Modern Europe* (Cambridge: Cambridge University Press, 1994), 8–20.

14. For a general survey on the meaning of poverty in Islamic treatises, see Leah Kinberg, "Compromise of Commerce: A Study of Early Traditions Concerning Poverty and Wealth," *Der Islam* 66 (1989): 193–212.

15. See, for example, *sicil* 109/14, 7 Cemazi el-evvel 1179/22 October 1765.

16. See, for example, a petition pleading with the authorities to hand back articles taken from the poor of Salonica *(fukara-i selanikten ahiz)*. These items had been put into the provisional residence of the governor of Hania and included lavish cushions, pillows, stools upholstered with French textiles, and other luxuries that one doubts had existed in the houses of impoverished people. *Sicil* 59/68, 3 Muharrem 1154/20 March 1741.

17. In the sicil of Salonica the Sufi lodge dwellers were labeled as "the poor among those who follow the right way" *(fukara-i salihin)*. See, for example, a declaration given in court by Mehmet Efendi, the *shaykh* (head) of the Salonica branch of the *Mevlana* order, one of the wealthiest lodges in Salonica. He argued that the lodge revenues from their allowances were not sufficient to cover all the expenses of the poor who dwelled in the lodge. He mentioned their due revenues collected from the imperial salt mines and the mill endowed in favor of the lodge. Consequently, he decided—with the consent of all the poor who lived in the lodge—to borrow money. The correlated use of the terms *derviş* and *fakir* in his declaration further emphasizes the use of these terms as synonyms. See *sicil* 25/30, 20 Cemazi el-ahır 1127/22 June 1715. On the term *fakir* and its designation of sufis, see Carl W. Ernst, *The Shambhala Guide to Sufism* (Boston: Shambhala, 1997), 3–4.

18. See D. A. Baugh, "Poverty, Protestantism, and Political Economy: English Attitudes toward the Poor, 1660–1800," in *England's Rise to Greatness, 1660–1763*, ed. S. B. Baxter (Berkeley: University of California Press, 1983), 75.

19. *Ben fakir, vemedyun, ve müflis, ve mu'sir olup işbu labis olduğum libasimdan gayri isim-i mal ıtlak olunur bir nesneye malik olmadığımdan din-i mezkuru olan bir vechla edaya iktidarım olmayıp.* See, for example *sicil* 36/21, 26 Ramazan 1127/25 September 1715.

20. See Eyal Ginio, "'Every Soul Shall Taste Death': Dealing with Death and the Afterlife in Eighteenth-Century Salonica," *Studia Islamica* 93 (2001): 113–132.

21. See Said Amir Arjomand, "Philanthropy, the Law, and Public Policy in the Islamic World before the Modern Era," in *Philanthropy in the World's Traditions*, ed. Warren F. Ilchman, Stanley N. Katz, and Edward L. Queen II (Bloomington: Indiana University Press, 1998), 109–132.

22. See Vassilis Demetriades, "*Vakıfs* Along the Via Egnatia," in *The Via Egnatia under Ottoman Rule (1380–1699)*, ed. Elizabeth Zachariadou (Rethymnon: Crete University Press, 1996), 85–95.

23. The reports include the various incomes and expenses of each endowment and consequently demonstrate the charity that was distributed to the poor through these diverse endowments. The reports were fully recorded in volume 13 of the sicil. They are all dated 1 Muharrem 1114/28 May 1702, or 1 Muharrem of the following year, 1115/17 May 1703. For using endowment deeds to gauge the social significance of the founders' determination of beneficiaries in eighteenth-century Anatolia, see Bahaeddin Yediyıldız, *Institution du vaqf au XVIIIe siècle en Turquie: étude socio-historique* (Ankara: Société d'Histoire Turque, 1985).

24. On the development and distinction between family endowment and public endowment, see Arjomand, "Philanthropy," 111.

25. See, as examples, *sicil* 13/5, 1 Muharrem 1115/17 May 1703; 29/208, 2 Receb 1132/9 May 1720; 29/209, 2 Receb 1132/9 May 1720; 60/61, 1 Safer 1154/17 April 1741.

26. See, as examples, *sicil* 13/60, 1 Muharrem 1114/ 28 May 1702; 13/62, 1 Muharrem 1114/28 May 1702; 13/77, 1 Muharrem 1117/17 May 1703; 13/144, 1 Muharrem 1116/5 May 1704.

27. See *sicil* 13/5, 1 Muharrem 1115/17 May 1703; 13/64, 1 Muharrem 1115/17 May 1703.

28. See John Iliffe, *The African Poor: A History* (Cambridge: Cambridge University Press, 1987), 4; Jean-Pierre Gutton, *La société et les pauvres: l'example de la généralité de Lyon 1534–1789* (Paris: Press Universitaires de France, 1971), 51–53; see also Jütte, *Poverty and Deviance*, 21–44.

29. See Machiel Kiel, "Notes on the History of Some Turkish Monuments in Thessaloniki and their Founders," *Balkan Studies* 11 (1970): 138–139. A. S. Ünver, who made a general survey of Islamic institutions that existed in Salonica before 1912, mentions three poor kitchens in his "Selânik'te Yüz Eserimiz Hakkında," *Güney-Doğu Avrupa Araştırmaları* 1 (1972): 257–260.

30. In 1958, Vehbi Tamer published, along with a modern Turkish translation, a photocopy of the original Arabic endowment deed that is kept in Istanbul; see "Fatih Devri Ricalinden İshak Paşanın Vakifyeleri ve vakıfları," *Vakıflar Dergisi* 4 (1958): 107–124.

31. Peri, "Waqf and Ottoman Welfare Policy," 172–175.

32. In addition, a petition, registered in the sicil, referred to a poor kitchen built by Ya'kub Paşa, another former fifteenth-century grand vizier who was pensioned with the governorship of Salonica. The petition mentions that the poor received food in this poor kitchen in accordance with the founder's stipulation. However, the petitioner does not provide us with further information regarding the beneficiaries or the internal functioning of the institution. In this case we know that his endowment was under the jurisdiction of the *Şeyhülislâm* (chief religious authority of the Ottoman Empire)—a possible explanation for its absence from the kadi's files. See *sicil* 107/17, 26 Şaban 1178/17 February 1765; 107/38, 16 Zilhicce 1178/5 June 1765; 109/6, 8 Safer 1199 [1179]/26 July 1765. On Ya'kub Paşa, see Kiel, "Notes on the History of Some Turkish Monuments," 144–145.

33. For a discussion of the various beneficiaries—pious men, pilgrims, the Prophet's descendents and the poor—to the poor kitchen of Jerusalem, see Peri, "Waqf and Ottoman Welfare Policy," 171–178.

34. Iliffe, *The African Poor*, 1–8.

35. C. Dyer, *Standards of Living in the Later Middle Ages* (Cambridge: Cambridge University Press, 1989), 257.

36. Marcus, *The Middle East*, 212.

37. *Fakirülhal olduklarından sadakat-i nas geçinip*; see *sicil* 41/82, 19 Muharrem 1141/25 August 1728. On the gathering of blacks, former slaves, in groups, see Suraiya Faroqhi, "Black Slaves and Freedmen Celebrating (Aydın, 1576)," *Turcica* 20–23 (1991): 205–211; Ronald C. Jennings, "Black Slaves and Free Slaves in Ottoman Cyprus, 1590–1640," *Journal of the Economic and Social History of the Orient* 30 (1987): 286–302.

38. Bronislaw Geremek, "Criminalité, vagabondage, paupérisme: la marginalité à l'aube des temps modernes," *Revue d'histoire moderne et contemporaine* 21 (1974): 337–375.

39. On "idleness" in early modern England, see Paul Slack, *Poverty and Policy in Tudor and Stuart England* (London: Longman, 1988), 22–27.

40. *Sicil* 71/12, 25 Şevval 1160/29 October 1747.

41. The legal authorization to glean without the prior approval from the field's owner relies on the assumption that leaving the strewn ears behind constitutes consent to gleaning. See the legal discussion of the Hanafi jurist al-Halabi: *Al-Sanabil ba'da al-hisad yuntafa'u biha bi-dun ta'rif li-anna ilqa'aha ibaha lil-akhdh dalalatan.* See al-Halabi, *Majma' al-anhur bi-sharh multaqa al-abhur* (Istanbul: Matba'a-i Osmaniyya, 1327/1909–1910), 1:716. For an interesting comparison between the Islamic *luqta* (gleanings) and the Jewish *leqet* (gleanings), see Hava Lazarus-Yafeh, "Some Halakhic Differences between Judaism and Islam," *Tarbiz* 51, no. 2 (1982): 210 [in Hebrew with English summary].

42. *Sicil* 108/36, 20 Safer 1180/27 July 1766.

43. Thus, for example, Rukayye bint Mahmut Ağa stipulated that food and coffee would be distributed for two days following her funeral. See *sicil* 90/19, 12 Rebiülevvel 1170/4 December 1756. See the following examples for testators who stipulated money in their wills for feeding the poor: *sicil* 89/68, 18 Cemaziel-evvel 1169/19 February 1756; 95/50, 7 Receb 1172/6 March 1759.

44. For a discussion of the migrant workers in Salonica, see Eyal Ginio, "Migrants and Unskilled Local Workers in an Ottoman Port-City: Ottoman Salonica in the Eighteenth Century," in *Outside In: On the Margins of the Modern Middle East*, ed. Eugene Rogan (London: I. B. Tauris, 2002), 126–148.

45. See Eyal Ginio, "Childhood, Mental Capacity, and Conversion to Islam in the Ottoman State," *Byzantine and Modern Greek Studies* 25 (2001): 110–119.

46. Evidence for children handed over by their parents to others as servants and then relegated to a status not far above slaves is found with regard to other Ottoman cities. See, for example, Suraiya Faroqhi, *Towns and Townsmen of Ottoman Anatolia* (Cambridge: Cambridge University Press, 1984), 278–280; Marcus, *The Middle East*, 157–158, 162. On the "ambiguous at best" status and the vulnerability of female servants in Egypt, see Judith E. Tucker, *Women in Nineteenth-Century Egypt* (Cambridge: Cambridge University Press, 1985), 91–93.

47. The absence of Jews—at least one-third of the total population—does not attest to their disapproval of such a regulation, but rather testifies to their reluctance at having recourse to the kadi court.

48. Another type of unpaid child labor in Salonica was that of apprenticeship in a master's workshop. In this case, boys were given to masters to learn a craft. The sicil shows that the children did not receive wages, as their work in their master's shop was regarded as a part of their apprenticeship. See, for example: *sicil* 36/8, 20 Şaban 1137/3 May 1725. See also Faroqhi, *Towns and Townsmen*, 280.

49. According to Islamic law, any act of hiring—of the use of a thing or labor—must be accompanied by an offer of payment by the employer and the consent of the employee. See 'Ali ibn Abi Bakr, *The Hedaya or Guide: A Commentary on the Musulman Laws*, trans. Charles Hamilton (Lahore: New Book Company, 1957), 489–490; Joseph Schacht, *An Introduction to Islamic Law* (Oxford: Oxford University Press, 1964), 154–155. For the legal status of women's wage labor as understood by Islamic law, see Maya Shatzmiller, "Women

and Wage Labour in the Medieval Islamic West: Legal Issues in an Economic Context," *Journal of the Economic and Social History of the Orient* 40 (1997): 174–206.

50. *Sicil* 18/243, 5 Muharrem 1122/6 March 1710.

51. *Sicil* 71/32, 6 Muharrem 1161/7 January 1748.

52. Because Islamic law does not recognize legal adoption, fostering is the only legal option for taking in a pauper child. On the forbidding of formal adoption in Islamic law, see Amira Al-Azhary Sonbol, "Adoption in Islamic Society: A Historical Survey," in *Children in the Muslim Middle East*, ed. Elizabeth Warnock Fernea (Austin: University of Texas Press, 1995), 45–67.

53. *Sicil* 36/12, 22 Şaban 1137/5 May 1725.

54. *Ben ücret ile hizmet eder makulesinden değil iken bana ecir-i misil ta'yin.* See *sicil* 25/90, 17 Rebiülevvel 1128/11 March 1716.

55. *Sicil* 86/36, 6 Rebiülahir 1168/19 January 1754.

56. See, for example, the request of Emine bint Ahmet to receive a regular allowance from her defunct brother's estate. The allowance was required to finance the needs of all her orphan nieces; see *sicil* 100/10, 17 Rebiülevvel 1175/16 October 1761.

57. *Sagir-i mezburun ve hadim ve hadimesinin nafaka ve kisvete eşed-i ihtiyacı olmakla.* See *sicil* 68/81, 5 Zilkade 1157/10 December 1744.

58. *Sicil* 60/135, 26 Rebiülahir 1154/10 July 1741.

59. *Sicil* 74/4, 20 Ramazan 1162/3 September 1749.

60. *Sicil* 63/18, 28 Receb 1120/13 October 1708.

61. *Sicil* 74/4, 20 Ramazan 1162/3 September 1749.

62. On sexual relations between employers and employees in early modern England, see Tim Meldrum, "London Domestic Servants from Depositional Evidence, 1660–1750: Servant–Employer Sexuality in the Patriarchal Household" in *Chronicling Poverty: The Voices and Strategies of the English Poor, 1640–1840*, ed. Tim Hitchcock, Peter King, and Pamela Sharpe (London: Macmillan, 1997), 47–69.

63. On ukr, see Schacht, *An Introduction*, 178; David Powers, "*Kadijustiz* or *Qadi-Justice*? A Paternity Dispute from Fourteenth-Century Morocco," *Islamic Law and Society* 1 (1994): 339.

64. *Sicil* 58/22, 29 Rebiülevvel 1153/24 July 1740. On sexual crimes in the sicil, see Leslie P. Peirce, "Le dilemme de Fatma: crime sexuel et culture juridique dans une cour ottomane au début des temps modernes," *Annales* 53 (1998): 291–319.

65. See *sicil* 36/5, 12 Şaban 1137/25 April 1725; 36/12, 22 Şaban 1137/5 May 1725. The legal basis for the statute of limitations is an order issued in 1550 by the Ottoman Sultan Süleyman Kanuni. He instructed kadis not to hear claims for which valid grounds had not been brought for more than fifteen years. This introduced a statute of limitations that became typical in Islamic law as applied in the Ottoman state. See Schacht, *An Introduction*, 90–91; Haim Gerber, *State, Society, and Law in Islam: Ottoman Law in Comparative Perspective* (Albany: State University of New York Press, 1994), 91.

66. See, for example, *sicil* 78/25, 9 Safer 1164/7 January 1751.

67. On sulh in Ottoman law, see Schacht, *An Introduction*, 181. On its application in Ottoman Salonica, see Ginio, "The Administration of Criminal Justice in Ottoman Selanik (Salonica) during the Eighteenth Century" 30 (1998): 204–208.

68. Jütte, *Poverty and Deviance*, 105–142.
69. For a survey of the economy of makeshift measures adopted by the poor in pre-Industrial Western Europe, see the introduction of Marco H. D. van Leeuwen, *The Logic of Charity: Amsterdam, 1800–1850* (London: Macmillan, 2000), 16–20.

CHAPTER NINE

The Charity of the Khedive

MINE ENER

On a Tuesday morning in October 1847, Maryam bint (the daughter of) Ibrahim, a Coptic woman, spotted an infant boy who had been left on a mosque's steps. She brought the boy home and waited nearly four days to see if anyone would claim the child. Realizing that the infant's parents and relatives were nowhere to be found, Maryam brought the infant to the Dabtiyya (the central police department) of Cairo to have him admitted into the Madrasat al-Wilada, a midwifery training school located in the Civilian Hospital of Azbakiyya, which contained a foundling home and orphanage.[1]

We know of Maryam's request to have this foundling admitted into the Madrasat al-Wilada for she, like many other Cairenes who had either come upon abandoned children or who were seeking care for their own children, presented their requests to the Dabtiyya of Cairo. Officials of the Dabtiyya recorded particulars of each case, noting the name of the person bringing in a child, and in instances of children found in the streets, alleys, and markets of Cairo—or on the steps of mosques—the officials were sure to note where exactly the child had been found.

Parents abandoned their children, noted Edward Lane, a British resident of Egypt in the early nineteenth century, due to financial straits, frequently leaving them on the steps of mosques in the hopes that a wealthier coreligionist might take the child home and raise it as their own. In many cases foundlings were taken care of by a neighbor.[2] Even though Lane implied that these neighbors were a child's coreligionists, we know from the case of Maryam that even she, as a Copt, took a child identified as a Muslim (leaving him on the steps of a mosque was the means by which the person who abandoned him designated his religion) into her care.[3]

Simultaneous to Maryam's case illustrating how neighbors took in abandoned children, we see from her interaction with the Dabtiyya, as well as a multitude of other similar episodes captured in the records of this office, that new institutions were being established in nineteenth-century Cairo to provide for abandoned children as well as others in need, and that the populace of Cairo and beyond availed themselves of these state-initiated forms of assistance. Utilizing records of this office and documents pertaining to the provisioning of a variety of social services, this chapter discusses the Egyptian government's involvement in poor relief and other forms of care for the needy during the nineteenth century and the times when the poor sought the state's charity. Although the state's provisioning of care was built on an Islamic ethos of assistance to the poor, its interventions reflected new mechanisms of care and emerged within the context of other social, economic, and political transformations underway in Egypt during this era.

The Centralization of Poor Relief

The creation of the Dabtiyya of Cairo (alongside the establishment of police departments in other major cities and provinces of Egypt) was one of the modernizing reforms introduced in early nineteenth-century Egypt.[4] Its formation was nearly coterminous with other government-initiated public health and poor relief efforts, oversight of insane asylums and prisons, and the establishment of state-sponsored poorhouses. The Dabtiyya also, arguably, carried out repressive functions: This office fulfilled procedures of criminal justice such as apprehending and processing individuals accused of crimes; and the physical structure of the building included facilities for the confinement of criminals and suspects.[5]

In terms of assistance for the populace of Cairo and beyond who sought care, the Dabtiyya served as a place of recourse for those in need. It received and acted on requests for the care of abandoned infants and applied government directives to the care of other persons in need, namely, people seeking admittance to state-run shelters and/or medical care. The Dabtiyya also processed the cases of individuals who had not directly sought the state's assistance. With the implementation of prohibitions on begging in the first half of the nineteenth century, the Dabtiyya apprehended individuals engaged in this act.

In enacting policies toward the indigent and through its interactions with the poor seeking assistance, the Dabtiyya's activities illustrate the centralization of poor relief efforts and the bureaucratization of forms of relief initiated in early-nineteenth-century Egypt. In many ways, the Dabtiyya's obligations in poor relief were similar to actions of the police during the reign of Peter the Great in Russia. There, the police assumed responsibility for poor relief and the eradication of begging with the goal of instilling public order.[6] However, in the case of Egypt, even though the Dabtiyya's actions draw our attention to new administrative practices and resemble the responsibilities of the police in European locales such as Imperial Russia, the policies the Dabtiyya applied also reflected tradition and religious continuity. The various institutions of Cairo that served the poor of that city fulfilled the ruler's religious obligations to the poor. The facilities established in early-nineteenth-century Egypt—hospitals for civilians, the Madrasat al-Wilada, and poor shelters—represented direct state involvement in poor relief. Throughout the Middle East, as other chapters in this volume illustrate, private citizens' and rulers' commitments to the poor and needy have been manifested through the establishment of religious endowments and other means of charity (individual almsgiving, distribution of food and clothing on religious occasions, financial support for one's less well-off neighbors or family). However, alongside these varied means of assistance, Egypt's government in this era introduced its own state-funded and state-administered institutions. Similar to religious endowments established in other areas of the Islamic world, these structures were intended to ensure at least a bare modicum of care for the poor. Like the institutions founded and supported by rulers and statesmen that served pious purposes in other areas of the Islamic world, the functions of state-initiated forms of relief were in great part intended to fulfill Egypt's rulers' obligations to the destitute and needy within Egyptian society.

The charitable institutions established in early-nineteenth-century Egypt and the Dabtiyya's role as a conduit for the provisioning of care, however, also differed from charitable works of other areas of the Ottoman Empire and earlier eras of Islamic history. Many features of Islamic forms of poor relief are very personal in nature, ensuring face-to-face interactions between charity providers and their recipients. Better-off neighbors have a regular clientele of needy persons to whom they, at designated times, provided charity.[7] In the Ottoman Empire, sultans came into direct contact with the poor when they distributed alms and handed out meat on religious holidays.[8] During the month of Ramadan and in the celebrations that follow, Muslim families—through to the present—distribute meat and food to the poor living in their neighborhoods. In contrast to the personal and less centralized forms of relief in many other regions of the Middle East under Ottoman rule, as the poor of Cairo sought the assistance of the state, they came into contact with a welfare bureaucracy (albeit a small one, when compared to today's provisioning of social services). Those in need presented their petitions to numerous offices of the state (the Dabtiyya, the Civilian Hospital, and, later, municipal agencies which determined the eligibility of a petitioner for care or assistance), hence giving the ruler who was identified as the source of beneficence and care—in reality—little or no contact with those upon whom his government's charity was bestowed. At this juncture, the very strategies and tactics of poor relief were also centralized and secularized: A range of government-appointed personnel, including police officers, neighborhood *shaykhs* (heads), night watchmen, employees of poor shelters, and health officials enacted the government's new policies toward the poor.[9]

The depersonalization of poor relief must have been daunting at times for those who needed assistance. The poor requesting care were faced with scribes (who set down in writing their particular cases) and medical examiners (who ascertained their physical health). They also experienced numerous exchanges with poorhouse officials and the police as they sought to prove their dependent status or, in the case of friends and relatives who endeavored to procure the release of a loved one from state shelters or insane asylums, attempted to demonstrate their financial abilities and willingness to support a destitute family member. Yet the presence of such a range of individuals (from throughout Egypt and from other areas of the Ottoman Empire as well) seeking the assistance of state agencies also proved the existence of people who had astute abilities to negotiate their way through various offices and institutions in their pursuit of different forms of assistance.

For the benefit of the historian, the poor's interchanges with government agencies also left archival records of their experiences with the state and evidence of the procurement of state assistance heretofore unavailable in other sources. Dabtiyya records reveal (1) how the poor considered the state's assistance a viable option for care, (2) how the Egyptian government introduced criteria of deservedness intended to distinguish between the deserving and the less worthy of care, and (3) how the poor presented themselves and their poverty to prove their eligibility for state assistance. Unlike the case of records from institutions funded and maintained through religious endowments that only outline information on the ideals of charity, the centralization of poor relief practices and the records of these offices allow previously unavailable insights into the very functioning of poor relief services.

Although social services available in nineteenth-century Egypt were bureaucratized and centralized, their use remained firmly set within an Islamic rubric of charity. Accounts of care for a variety of individuals, whether from the poor who petitioned for admittance to state-run shelters or from the sick who requested to be cared for in the Civilian Hospital located in Azbakiyya Square or the Qasr al-'Ayni Hospital situated on the banks of the Nile (which served civilian and military patients after mid-century), and records pertaining to the admittance of abandoned children to the Madrasat al-Wilada emphasize in the account of each petition that the person seeking assistance was being provided for *ihsanan min al-khidiwi* (out of the charity of the khedive) or *min ihsanat wali al-ni'am* (out of the charity of the Supreme Benefactor).[10] While calling attention to the ruler's religious obligations to the needy among his subjects, such appellations also served to personify the government as the ruler and embodied the state's charity in his very person. This discourse of charity as well as its practice served a number of purposes. Statements affixed to the end of records describing the provisions made for a needy person exemplified how the governor of Egypt saw his role as that of pious benefactor, while they simultaneously illustrated how the ruler/government hoped to be perceived (i.e., as a provider of good works—a legitimating factor domestically at a period in Egypt's history when the governorship was becoming a hereditary form of rule[11]). Overseas, advertisements of Egypt's rulers' charitable works—particularly those of Muhammad 'Ali who was vilified in British diplomatic circles—might have also served public relations purposes.[12] On yet another front, these statements, as well as the intent behind them, represented the government's consciousness of the importance of the populace's health and productive potential.

The medical care and poor relief services provided to the Cairene populace (and individuals who came from areas outside of Cairo as well) fit within the ruler's obligations to his subjects but simultaneously reflected the Egyptian government's interest in the health and productivity of its populace. Government investments in hospitals and other types of care represented the commencement of a new focus on its population, with population—in the meaning ascribed to it by Michel Foucault—as the ultimate end of government.[13] This newly initiated concern for the Egyptian population and its health was first made manifest in the military, with the Egyptian government introducing various means to secure the health of its soldiers, but it soon extended to the broader population.[14]

As the most immediate medical concerns of Muhammad 'Ali were in regards to the health of his army, the first hospitals he had established (in the late 1820s) were intended for his troops: the Abu Za'bal Hospital in northern Cairo and the Mahmudiyya Hospital in Alexandria. To train indigenous health practitioners, the Abu Za'bal Hospital also included a medical school. Civilians in need of medical attention were cared for in this hospital (it also included facilities for midwifery before their transfer to Azbakiyya) and in the Maristan of Qalawun, a hospital established in the thirteenth century which, in the early nineteenth century, also served as an insane asylum and poor shelter. Given the insalubrious conditions in the Maristan, and on the urging of Muhammad 'Ali's French medical advisor, Clot Bey, Ibrahim Pasha (Muhammad 'Ali's son) established another hospital for civilians in the suburb of Azbakiyya in 1837. This hospital, known as al-Isbataliyya al-Mulkiyya (or, the Civilian Hospital) comprised sections for the care of men and women as well as a vaccination clinic, the Madrasat al-Wilada, and an asylum for the insane.[15] The indigent were treated free of charge.

In sum, this vast array of medical services and welfare projects was part of the public health programs initiated during this era to ensure the health of Muhammad 'Ali's military as well as the public at large. The goals of these services and projects were pragmatic, in that a healthy population provided the military manpower necessary for Egypt's armies and ensured that the population would be less susceptible to disease and more productive. However, the enactment of these programs also reflected continuity with the provisioning of social services in other times and locales. Egypt's khedives emulated Islamic rulers who bestowed their beneficence on their populaces through the construction of hospitals and soup kitchens, and Egypt's population sought the charity that the khedives (read, the state) provided.

Policing Public Spaces

The state's new involvement in charity must also be understood within the broader context of new social policing efforts. One example of these actions was the Cairo authorities' attention to public spaces and efforts to clear the streets of the itinerant poor. These new interventions in the lives of the poor, like care for infants and foundlings, were couched within a religious ethos of charity, but they also served pragmatic purposes. Prohibitions on begging issued in 1835 in Cairo were made during the height of a plague outbreak, thus indicating authorities' concerns about contagion and the spread of disease.[16] At this juncture, apprehended beggars were sent to the Maristan Qalawun. However, those among the poor who were deemed fit to work were to be put to work in government projects such as workshops.[17]

Nearly a decade later in 1844, the application of government directives regarding prohibitions on begging were framed in language displaying charitable purposes, but simultaneously, the ends served were pragmatic. Accounts of the arrest of beggars made note that those who were deemed deserving of assistance were to be admitted into the government-run shelter of the Maristan (renamed Mahall al-Fuqara') out of the charity of the khedive. Those deemed "deserving" *(mustahiqq)* of care included the invalid, elderly, single women, and mothers with small children. Individuals identified as able to work who were residents of areas outside of Cairo were subject to different policies: They were expelled from Cairo back to their home villages. Such policies of deporting the able-bodied poor represented the Egyptian government's ongoing attempts to control flight from the countryside. This flight was a direct result of conscription policies (in that male peasants sought to evade government recruitment drives), taxation (in which peasants, unable to pay their taxes, fled from their debts), and the desire to gain a better livelihood in the city.[18]

While Cairo authorities had one set of policies for the sturdy poor, they had greater sympathy for individuals they identified as meriting assistance. Islamic injunctions of care for the poor mandated that the government treat with kindness those who were unable to provide for themselves. Officers of the Dabtiyya (including a medical staff) examined beggars arrested in the streets and determined their eligibility for admittance to the state-run shelters. In these assessments, they decided whether these individuals could financially support themselves and the extent of assistance they required. Those individuals admitted to the shelters—including the invalid, elderly, and otherwise deemed "deserving" poor from the countryside as well as the city of Cairo—received a roof over their heads, daily food rations, and extra allotments of food, blankets, and clothing on religious holidays. However, upon their admittance to the state shelters, these individuals forfeited their freedom. Beggars admitted into these shelters were only released on the intercession of a friend or relative who could vouch for the beggars' good behavior (including, most explicitly, abstaining from begging).[19]

The centralization of government involvement in poor relief activities resulted in members of different religious denominations coming face to face with Cairo authorities. Historically, Christians and Jews in the Middle East provided for their own needy within their respective communities. As Mark Cohen's chapter (3) in this volume illustrates, the Jewish poor—even those who were new to Cairo and had no one to vouch for them—frequently sought assistance from members of their community.

In contrast to the relative autonomy each religious denomination had in caring for its own poor, the centralization of poor relief in nineteenth-century Egypt meant that Christians and Jews were sometimes recipients of state-sponsored charity. Police documents and other records affirm that care for non-Muslims was at times relegated to religious communities, although non-Muslims also were, on occasion, found among shelter inmates. The Armenian Ibrahim al-Fayan had once been a resident of Takiyyat Tulun, but on his release he was caught begging again. The Egyptian government called on the chief patriarch of the Armenian community to ensure that members of the community (like Ibrahim al-Fayan) would not beg. They issued a similar warning to the heads of the Levantine, Syrian, and Coptic communities.[20] Lists of shelter residents for the period 1859–1861 include at least one Coptic Christian—Girgis 'Abd al-Masih.[21] Members of the Jewish community also received hospital care. On many occasions foreign nationals arrested by government officials in Cairo for begging and vagrancy were sent on to their consuls who were responsible for their punishment.[22]

The Egyptian government's involvement in poor relief served both pragmatic and religious ends. Demands for labor in agriculture and government-initiated projects such as a nascent textile industry, the need for military recruits, and other efforts to control the mobility of the peasantry resulted in new levels of state intervention in the health and lives of the populace. But, at the same time, the establishment of state-run shelters such as the Maristan and Takiyyat Tulun fulfilled one aspect of the government's religious obligations to the poor. Those individuals admitted into these poorhouses received care "out of the charity" of Egypt's khedive. The poor also availed themselves of the state's charity. Although some of these shelters' residents included beggars apprehended in government sweeps of Cairo's public spaces, other individuals housed in this shelter had petitioned for admittance. Records of petitions for admittance to Takiyyat Tulun provide us with information on the circumstances that brought the poor into contact with the state.

Seeking the Charity of the Khedive

'Aisha arrived at the Dabtiyya in November 1853, her three children and mother beside her. With her husband in the army, as she related to the officials, she did not have the means to provide for herself and her family, and requested that she and her family be admitted to the shelter of Takiyyat Tulun, an institution that served at one and the same time as a refuge (for people like 'Aisha who petitioned for care) as well as a place of confinement (for individuals who had been arrested for begging).[23] 'Aisha's account of her own family's plight and difficult circumstances is echoed in other records of petitions found among the Dabtiyya's registers. Desperation brought many single women and women with small children to the Dabtiyya as they sought assistance. Without families to provide for them and lacking (or having exhausted) other networks of support, they turned to the charity of the state. Prior to petitioning they had perhaps gotten by on the charity of their neighbors and community. But by the time they reached the Dabtiyya's doors, state assistance may have remained their only viable option for care.

Although many accounts provide details as to the circumstances bringing women to seek the state's aid, most records of petitions are devoid of specific information on the reasons for women's desperate circumstances. When women arrived at the Dabtiyya, alone or accompanied by small children, the scribe often left only the notation that a particular woman had no one to care for her or that she was elderly or invalid. Remarks were also made as to the age of children accompanying single women. Frequently, these children were described as "still nursing" or of a young age, hence indicating that the mother's responsibilities for her youngsters denied her the ability to seek any form of employment.[24] Lacking other male family members to provide for them, these women turned to the Egyptian government for aid. In this capacity, the state was responsible for the care of women whose gender and circumstances denoted their dependent status.

Women and children made up the majority of Takiyyat Tulun's residents, but men also made this shelter their temporary or permanent home. The records of men's petitions to the Dabtiyya indicate that health officials of the Dabtiyya charged with assessing the eligibility of petitioners and people arrested for begging had confirmed that these men were "deserving" of admittance to the Dabtiyya, given that they were elderly or invalid. Like women's petitions, which mentioned that the person seeking assistance had no one to care for her, records of men's requests for assistance also highlight their desperate straits: They had "no one" to provide for them and they "owned nothing."[25] Al-Hajj Muhammad ibn 'Ali, doctors determined, though old, had good eyesight. Yet al-Hajj Muhammad proved his deserving status in another way: He noted that because he was *gharib* (a stranger), he had no one to take care of him. Like the foreign Jewish poor discussed by Mark Cohen, the poor of nineteenth-century Egypt drew attention to their "foreignness" and lack of networks to elicit the sympathy of charity providers.[26] Among the poor of Takiyyat Tulun were also entire families. Records of their petitions illustrate that the overriding reason for their need for assistance was the father's inability to work.[27]

The absence of familial networks of care and families' inability to provide for their own kin forced Egypt's most destitute and vulnerable to make state-run shelters such as Takiyyat Tulun their permanent residence. However, records of the release of residents illustrate how this shelter also served, at times, as a temporary home and indicate that the poor used it and the state's assistance as a short-term relief measure. In some cases the poor stayed in the shelter until their families learned of their whereabouts and/or could build up the means to provide for them again. Relatives living in Cairo, as well as in rural areas, appeared before the Dabtiyya to secure the release of a family member.[28] Until the arrival of relatives or better economic circumstances—involving the return of a conscript husband, the maturity of children, or an increase in family resources—a person or family living within the walls of the shelter received the bare necessities to survive. In such a manner, state-run shelters served as safety nets—temporary or more permanent means of care—for the most desperately needy from throughout Egypt.

Another initiative of Muhammad 'Ali's government—attention to the welfare of children—grew out of new concerns about the health of the Egyptian populace and resulted in the creation of foundling homes and orphanages. Efforts to ensure the health of children emerged because of concern for infant mortality, disease, and depopulation.[29] Infant mortality owing to smallpox prompted the government to begin vaccination programs for the first time in 1819.[30] In 1824, Muhammad 'Ali called for the procurement of French medical doctors to carry out these campaigns in various regions of Egypt, and shortly after the arrival of Clot Bey in Egypt, vaccination was introduced throughout the country in the 1830s. Resistance to these various initiatives was high because parents of children feared that the vaccinations were intended to "mark" their children for future military service.[31] Government officials enlisted the assistance of neighborhood shaykhs in Cairo to ensure that vaccination orders were carried out thoroughly.[32] The vaccination center located in the Civilian Hospital of Azbakiyya was just one aspect of these efforts.

The government's concern for the health of children was also reflected in its actions toward children who needed other forms of assistance, namely, wet-nursing and care for orphans, foundlings, and children with one or both parents still alive.[33] The extent to which parents and others sought assistance from the government in caring for their children or children found in the public spaces of Cairo illustrates their reliance on the state to provide aid. Initially, parents had feared that vaccination would result in the future conscription of their children. However, there is ample evidence that demonstrates that inhabitants of Cairo, both parents of children who needed wet-nursing and individuals who had found children abandoned in the streets and markets, trusted the government with the care of these children, bringing their own infants as well as foundlings to the Dabtiyya from where they were brought to the midwifery training school.[34] Just as in the case in which the state would supplement the role of the extended family in providing for society's weaker members (the sick and infirm), the Madrasat al-Wilada provided surrogate care for infants without mothers to nurse them or parents or other relatives to take care of them.

Analysis of care for abandoned children exemplifies the welfare role of the state both in terms of the populace's reliance on the state to provide this form of care and also in regards to the records kept by the state, which bear witness to its involvement in this charitable endeavor. Accounts of the Dabtiyya demonstrate the various circumstances befalling infants and children that resulted in individuals (relatives as well as strangers) seeking the help of the state in caring for these young wards. When a mother's breast milk was not sufficient for her infant (due perhaps to malnutrition) or when a mother had passed away or left, a father might seek to have his infant child wet-nursed in the Madrasat al-Wilada.[35] Mothers also brought their own children to the Dabtiyya to request that they be admitted to the Madrasat al-Wilada that served as not only a foundling home but also as an orphanage.[36] Takiyyat Tulun also took in orphaned children.[37] As illustrated at the outset of this chapter, residents of Cairo's various quarters also found abandoned infants and small children and brought these foundlings to the Dabtiyya.[38] Accounts of each interchange note how the person bringing in the child could not care for it. At the same time, they represent a symbolic "handing over" of a child from a private citizen to the state. The historian can only wonder, but never know with certainty, whether the person bringing in an "abandoned child" was the child's own mother or father.

Records of child abandonment and the admittance of infants to the Madrasat al-Wilada illustrate the government's role in providing care. But they also indicate new government attention to child abandonment in Cairo. To enumerate fully the children who were abandoned in this era of Egypt's history is impossible. In a period of eight years (between 1846 and 1854) when the most extensive discussion of their abandonment and admittance to the Madrasat al-Wilada is found in the Dabtiyya registers, the number generally ranged from one to three abandoned infants in one month (with some months not including any accounts of abandonment). Even though these numbers are quite far from, for example, those of child abandonment in major nineteenth-century European cities (and even though the registers do not provide the number of infants found abandoned who were directly taken in by families), they indicate that desperate straits forced many mothers to abandon their infants and that government agencies were beginning to enumerate the incidents of abandonment.[39]

Availing Themselves of the State's Charity

At the same time that the Civilian Hospital of Azbakiyya and later the Civilian and Military Hospital of Qasr al-'Ayni (after its closure) cared for orphans and foundlings, both of these institutions also provided free medical care to residents of Cairo and beyond and oversaw the care of insane persons brought in by government officials or by family members and relatives. Records of petitions illustrate how poor Egyptians sought admittance to the Civilian Hospital and Qasr al-'Ayni

Hospital and how they were granted care "out of the charity" of Egypt's ruler. Individuals in need of medical care included people from Cairo, Egypt's provinces, and other regions of the Middle East.[40]

Although direct government involvement in medical care was first initiated during Muhammad ʿAli's reign and intended, at the outset, to serve the medical needs of his military, medical assistance for the indigent lasted long after his reign. Men and women, as noted in registers of the Dabtiyya and the governorate of Cairo through at least the year 1870, requested and received free medical treatment.[41]

Although the Dabtiyya registers contain accounts of individuals only needing short-term medical attention (as well as longer treatments as in the case of the insane), some accounts of individuals seeking medical care recount how the person, having no one to take care of them or being unable to earn a living, was admitted to the government-run shelter of Takiyyat Tulun after being treated at the hospital.[42] Free care for the sick—as well as admittance to Takiyyat Tulun—was not in any way limited to inhabitants of Egypt alone, in many instances records pertaining to petitions made by sick people for care and shelter were presented by non-Egyptians. For example, al-Hajj Saʿd Hasan from Mecca, whose right eye needed medical attention, was sent to the hospital and then admitted into the Takiyya, thus illustrating, as in Miri Shefer's chapter (6) in this volume, that hospitals were also used in the nineteenth century by individuals who had no means of care close at hand.[43]

When a family was unable to care for an insane relative, the state stepped in. The quality and scope of government provisions of care are difficult to determine. European accounts of the conditions in Cairo's insane asylums report inadequate facilities, an absence of medical practitioners, and the use of mechanical constraints. Written at the juncture in medical history when England was experimenting with more humane treatments of the insane, these accounts must be read with an eye to the impact they were intended to have on their audience: the European medical community.[44] But despite the purported deficiencies in mental health facilities, relatives requested that their family members be provided for in such institutions. Egyptians considered government-run insane asylums to be an option for care.[45]

Simultaneous to requests for the admittance or release of family members or neighbors to the insane asylum, municipal officials (such as foot patrols and neighborhood guards [*nöbetçi*]) apprehended the wandering insane from urban public spaces.[46] The insane found in rural areas or cities such as Alexandria were also transported to Cairo for admittance to the insane asylum where they were to receive treatment. The Dabtiyya of Alexandria instructed the governorate of Alexandria to have an unnamed man, found wandering around in Alexandria and identified as insane, to be sent first to the Naval Hospital, but if he could not receive treatment there, he was to be sent on to the insane asylum of Cairo. The admittance of this

196 | *Mine Ener*

individual to the various hospitals for treatment, noted the Dabtiyya, was within his rights as an insane person.[47] A woman and man found wandering in Alexandria initially were put in the Dabtiyya prison there, but prison officials, determining that being in prison would only worsen their condition, had them transported to Cairo to be admitted to the insane asylum there.[48]

Individuals identified as deserving of care—by virtue of their status of poverty or through other means of proving their dependency—received assistance from the government. In the eyes of the state (and invoking concepts set forth in the early Islamic period, as detailed by the chapters in this volume of Michael Bonner [1] and Ingrid Mattson [2]), these individuals had a right *(haqq)* to assistance. Hence, for example, infants had rights to charity, an insane person was deemed deserving of admittance to government hospitals or the state-run insane asylum because she or he had the right of someone who is insane; and an indigent woman found dead in the streets of Cairo would deserve a free burial.[49]

Conclusion

Registers of the Dabtiyya provide us with rare insights into the avenues of assistance available to the poor, the extent to which the poor sought the state's charity, and the circumstances of the poor who came into contact with the state. An Islamic ethos of care for the poor pervaded the very language documenting the provisions made for the needy: The care Egypt's most desperately poor (and the poor of other regions of the Ottoman Empire) received was depicted as stemming from the ruler's benevolence. Simultaneous to this aid fulfilling religious obligations, records of the poor's interactions with the Egyptian government illustrate how the state's involvement was increasingly interventionist and more centralized. Beggars found in Cairo's streets and markets were arrested for engaging in this activity, individuals admitted to state-run shelters forfeited their freedom to come and go as they pleased, and Cairo authorities closely monitored the admittance and dismissal of the poor from the government's numerous institutions.

As this chapter has documented, the poor frequently sought the aid the state provided. They also acquired skills in navigating through the application procedures in terms of both requesting care and seeking the release of a loved one from the state's institutions. The existence of these multiple forms of care served to create what Peregrine Horden and Richard Smith have termed a "mixed economy" of relief. The poor of Cairo and Egypt and beyond sought assistance from a variety of sources including their families, neighbors, and the state.[50] State-run centralized institutions provided supplementary or primary forms of assistance for individuals whose families and communities could not care for their own members. This assistance might be partial or it might be long-term. Through records of interchanges between the poor and the Dabtiyya authorities, we find that on exhausting other avenues of care, the poor considered the state a viable option for assistance. They presented their cases in such a manner as to prove, in compliance with government criteria, that they deserved the khedive's charity.

Notes

1. Dar al-Watha'iq al-Qawmiyya (the Egyptian National Archives, hereafter DWQ), L 2/1/11/89/188 14 Dhu l-Qa'da 1263/24 October 1847.

2. Edward Lane, *Manners and Customs of the Modern Egyptians* (1836; reprint, The Hague: East West Publications, 1989), 197.

3. Infants were also left at the entryway of churches and taken in by missionary groups; see Victor Guerin, *La France Catholique en Egypte* (Tours: Alfred Mame et fils, 1894), 50.

4. For a discussion of economic, social, and political transformations underway over the course of the nineteenth century and their impact on the populace of Egypt, see Judith Tucker, *Women in Nineteenth-Century Egypt* (Cambridge: Cambridge University Press, 1985).

5. Khaled Fahmy shows that the Cairo populace also saw the Dabtiyya as a place where they could settle disputes and present charges against wrong doers; see his "The Police and the People in Nineteenth-Century Egypt," *Die Welt des Islams* 39 (1999): 340–377, esp. 374.

6. Adele Lindenmeyr, *Poverty Is Not a Vice: Charity, Society, and the State in Imperial Russia* (Princeton: Princeton University Press, 1996), 32.

7. Norman Stillman, "Charity and Social Services in Medieval Islam," *Societas* (1975): 105–115, esp. 114.

8. Halil Inalcik and Donald Quataert, eds., *An Economic and Social History of the Ottoman Empire* (Cambridge: Cambridge University Press, 1994), 47.

9. Among other forms of assistance, the government also oversaw the functioning of large-scale religious endowments, such as Al-Azhar mosque, and the distribution of food to the students and families affiliated with this institution.

10. The title *khedive (khidiwi)* meaning "prince" in Persian, was used unofficially by Muhammad 'Ali and his successors. It was only during the reign of Isma'il that the title was officially granted to the governor of Egypt; see Afaf Lutfi al-Sayyid Marsot, *A Short History of Egypt* (1985; reprint, Cambridge: Cambridge University Press, 1988), 68.

11. The Treaty of London (1841) granted Muhammad 'Ali's family the right to hereditary rule of Egypt.

12. In this regard, the writings of the Frenchman Clot Bey are most revealing. In describing the various medical projects underway in Egypt (which he was hired to supervise), Clot Bey describes these endeavors (and Muhammad 'Ali's commitment to them) as humanitarian; see, for example, A. B. Clot, *Aperçu Général sur l'Egypte*, 2 vols. (Paris: Fourtin, Masson et Cie, 1840), 2:420; Jacques Tagher, *Mémoires de A. B. Clot Bey* (Cairo: Imprimerie de L'Institut Francais d'Archéologie Orientale, 1949), 320.

198 | *Mine Ener*

13. Michel Foucault, "Governmentality," in *The Foucault Effect: Studies in Governmentality*, ed. Graham Burchell, Colin Gordon, and Peter Miller (London: Harvester/Wheatsheaf, 1991), 100. Also see Foucault's discussion of biopolitics in his *The History of Sexuality* (1976; reprint, New York: Vintage Books, 1990), 139–140.

14. Laverne Kuhnke, *Lives at Risk: Public Health in Nineteenth-Century Egypt* (Berkeley: University of California Press, 1990), 134.

15. I discuss the transformation of the Maristan into a shelter for the poor and the transfer of the insane to other institutions in "At the Crossroads of Empires: Poor Relief Policies in Early Nineteenth-Century Egypt," *Social Science History* 26 (2002), 393–426.

16. For government quarantine efforts during this juncture, see Kuhnke, *Lives at Risk*, 69–91.

17. DWQ, S 1/79/1/376, 28 Ramadan 1250/28 January 1835; S 2/32/1, 7 Muharram 1253/13 April 1837; Shura al-Mu'awana Register 274/1007/346, 25 Ramadan 1253/23 December 1837.

18. The most comprehensive study to date of peasant flight from the countryside is Zayn al-'Abidin Najm, "Tasahhub al-fallahin fi 'asr Muhammad 'Ali: Asbabuhu wa-nata'ijuhu" (The Absconding of Peasants in the Era of Muhammad 'Ali: Its Reasons and Effects), *Al-Majalla al-Tarikhiyya al-Misriyya* 36 (1989): 259–316.

19. See, for example, DWQ, L 2/1/4/102/127 16 Dhu l-Qa'da 1261/16 November 1845 and L 2/11/2/165/840, 19 Rajab 1275/22 February 1859. I discuss further examples of family members' efforts to procure the release of their loved ones from shelters in chapter 3 of *Managing Egypt's Poor* (Princeton: Princeton University Press, forthcoming).

20. See DWQ, L 2/1/41/82/494 3 Safar 1270/5 November 1853; L 2/1/41/117/ 562 10 Safar 1270/12 November 1853; L 2/1/41/117/563 10 Safar 1270/12 November 1853; L 2/1/41/117/564 10 Safar 1270/12 November 1853. Being a member of an ethnic minority, however, did not exempt someone deemed "fit to work" from being forced to work. L 2/1/41/ 117/ 567 10 Safar 1270/12 November 1853. Takiyyat Tulun was utilized as a shelter from the late 1840s until 1880. For a discussion of its use, see Mine Ener, "Getting into the Shelter of Takiyyat Tulun," in *Outside In: On the Margins of the Modern Middle East*, ed. Eugene Rogan (London: I. B. Tauris, 2002), 53–76.

21. DWQ, L 1/60/3.

22. For medical attention to a Jewish man, see, for example, DWQ, L 2/11/42/100/11 2 Rajab 1285/19 October 1868. The arrests of Europeans for vagrancy, prostitution, and other crimes can be found in PRO/FO 97/410.

23. DWQ L 2/1/41/82/495 3 Safar 1270/5 November 1853 and L 2/1/41/84/498 3 Safar 1270/5 November 1853.

24. Judith Tucker discusses how the courts of nineteenth-century Egypt might consider women who engaged in some types of trades to be unfit mothers in her *Women in Nineteenth-Century Egypt*, 82. For discussion of child custody cases following divorce or the death of a spouse, see Judith Tucker, *In the House of the Law: Gender and Islamic Law in Ottoman Syria and Palestine* (Berkeley: University of California Press, 1998), 113–147.

25. The following documents record the requests made by a number of men: L 2/1/41/38/427, 23 Muharram 1270/26 October 1853; L 2/1/41/153/643, 18 Safar 1270/20 November 1853; L 2/1/41/45/809, 5 Rabi' I 1270/6 December 1853;

L 2/1/120/51/2217, 10 Safar 1280/27 July 1863; L 2/1/121/6/2380, 14 Rabiʿ I 1280/29 August 1863.

26. L 2/1/124/56/38, 23 Rajab 1280/3 January 1864. For more on the precarious position in which "the stranger" found himself, see Franz Rosenthal, "The Stranger in Islam," *Arabica* 44 (1997) 33–75.

27. DWQ, L 2/11/51/53/1231 29 Dhu l-Hijja 1286/1 April 1870 and L 2/1/41/144/633 17 Safar 1270/19 November 1853.

28. See, for example, L 2/11/2/287/1142, 7 Ramadan 1275/10 April 1859 and L 1/60/4 and L 2/11/2/274/1111, 3 Ramadan 1275/6 April 1859 and L 1/60/3.

29. On concerns about depopulation, see R. R. Madden, *Travels in Turkey, Egypt, and Palestine*, 2 vols. (London: Henry Colburn, 1829), 1:298. For interventions in women's reproductive activities in this era, see Mervat Hatem, "The Professionalization of Health and the Control of Women's Bodies as Modern Governmentalities in Nineteenth-Century Egypt," in *Women in the Ottoman Empire: Middle Eastern Women in the Early Modern Era*, ed. Madeline Zilfi (Leiden: Brill, 1997), 66–80, esp. 70. Laws concerning abortions and child abandonment were decreed in 1857, DWQ, S 7/33/1/248 17 Shaʿban 1273/12 April 1857.

30. Khaled Fahmy, *All the Pasha's Men* (Cambridge: Cambridge University Press, 1997), 210.

31. Laverne Kuhnke, *Lives at Risk* (Berkeley: University of California Press, 1990), 116–119.

32. Examples of orders concerning vaccination of children and shaykhs' responsibilities for upholding these efforts can be found in L 2/1/16/579/1209 8 Shawwal 1265/27 August 1849; M 6/1 5 Dhu l-Qaʿda 1266 to 10 Dhu l-Qaʿda 1267/12 September 1850 to 6 September 1851; L 2/1/19/587/114 10 Rajab 1266/ 22 May 1850; S 1/19/3/18/4, 24 Shawwal 1281/22 March 1865.

33. Care for orphans is mandated in the Quran and the Hadith. Records pertaining to the provisioning of wet nurses and the acceptance of infants and young children into orphanages and other institutions included statements that the child was being admitted out of "the charity of the khedive." For discussion of assistance to orphans in other eras of Islamic history, see Amira al-Azhary Sonbol, "Adoption in Islamic Society: A Historical Survey," in *Children in the Muslim Middle East*, ed. Elizabeth Warnock Fernea (Austin: University of Texas Press, 1995), 45–67, esp. 54–57.

34. Distrust of vaccination decreased in subsequent decades. Lucie Duff Gordon describes vaccination efforts of Egypt in the 1860s to be more widespread (and accepted) than those in Europe at this time; see her *Letters from Egypt (1862–1869)* (1902; reprint, London: Routledge and Kegan Paul, 1969), 176.

35. DWQ, DWQ, L 2/1/6/591/931 4 Ramadan 1262/26 August 1846; L 2/1/10/616/1006 26 Shaʿban 1263/9 August 1847; L 2/1/12/337/640 16 Rabiʿ II 1264/22 March 1848; L 2/1/19/475/1053 27 Jumada I 1266/10 April 1850; L 2/1/42/160/1031 30 Rabiʿ I 1270/31 December 1853.

36. DWQ, L 2/1/12/309/606 1 Rabiʿ II 1264/7 March 1848.

37. Examples of orphans are found in DWQ, L 1/60/9; L 1/60/13; L 2/11/42/59/130.

38. For example, see DWQ, L 2/1/375/567 11 Rabi' II 1263/29 March 1847; DWQ, L 2/1/7/172/255 21 Dhu l-Hijja 1262/10 December 1846 and L 2/1/43/157/1421 11 Jumada I 1270/9 February 1854. Records of petitions for wet nurses continue through the 1870s; see, for example, L 1/6/35/159/44 29 Jumada I 1290/25 July 1873 and L 1/6/61/11/2 23 Safar 1295/26 February 1878. Naguib Mahfouz discusses how foundlings and orphans were among the only patients in the Qasr al-'Ayni Hospital in the late nineteenth century in his *The History of Medical Education in Egypt* (Cairo: Government Press, 1935), 46.

39. Having a child out of wedlock in a country such as Egypt incurred harsher social consequences than having an illegitimate child in England or France. A mother in nineteenth-century Egypt most surely would never leave an identifying item with the child she had abandoned (as was the case in England), nor were there facilities that catered to unwed mothers as there were in France. Once abandoned, mothers in Egypt (assumedly) never saw their children again. British health officials in the late nineteenth century accused mothers of abandoning their children and then coming to the hospital offering their services as wet nurses to receive a stipend. See DWQ, Majlis al-Wuzara' 2/alif, letter dated May 27, 1886.

40. DWQ, L 2/1/42/96/919 17 Rabi' I 1270/18 December 1853; L 2/1/44/31/1583 24 Jumada I 1270/22 February 1854; L 2/1/42/15/751/29 Safar 1270/1 December 1853; L 2/1/43/1/1078 7 Rabi' II 1270/7 January 1854. Records of the Egyptian military *(Jihadiyya)* for 1857 pertaining to the functioning of the Civilian Hospital in Azbakiyya and the Qasr al-'Ayni Hospital note that the Civilian Hospital was used more frequently by women, while men received treatment in the hospital of Qasr al-'Ayni; see S 3/122/6/48 19 Rajab 1273/15 March 1857.

41. For example, the woman Mahbuba bint Hajj 'Isa received medical assistance when she injured her leg (DWQ, L 2/1/43/180/1467 16 Jumada I 1270/14 February 1854; Ya'qub al-Yahudi, sent by the chief rabbi of Cairo to the Civilian Hospital, was treated free of charge because he was poor (L 2/11/42/100/11 2 Rajab 1285/19 October 1868); and numerous records of petitions from the 1860s and 1870s recount the poor's receipt of medical assistance.

42. DWQ, L 2/1/41/86/500 3 Safar 1270/5 November 1853 and L 2/1/124/136/468 9 Sha'ban 1280/19 January 1864.

43. DWQ, L 2/11/16/20/2 2 Rabi' I 1280/17 August 1863.

44. I discuss European critiques of Egypt's treatment of the insane in chapter 4 of *Managing Egypt's Poor*.

45. DWQ, L 2/1/44/98/1669, 5 Jumada II 1270/ 5 March 1854. Friends or family members also sought the release of their friends and relatives from the insane asylums of Cairo, providing a guarantee *(daman)* that they would be responsible for the conduct of the released inmate and ensure that person's care. In this manner, they proved that their care would sufficiently replace the (surrogate) care that the state had provided. See DWQ, L 2/11/2/213/972, 9 Sha'ban 1275/14 March 1859; L 2/11/3/237/1789 24 Muharram 1275/23 August 1859; L 2/11/14/31/48 3 Dhu l-Hijja 1275/22 May 1863; L 2/11/17/48/23 15 Rajab 1280/ 26 December 1863.

46. DWQ, L 2/1/43/30/1144 14 Rabi' II 1270/14 January 1854. The English doctors W. S. Tuke and A. R. Urquhart, visiting the insane asylum when it was located in Bulaq,

made note of how the police brought patients to this facility; see their "Two Visits to the Cairo Asylum, 1877 and 1878," *Journal of Mental Science* 25 (1880): 43–53. The asylum at Bulaq was in use from 1856 to 1880 when a building on the palace grounds of 'Abbasiyya was converted into an asylum; see F. M. Sandwith, "The Cairo Lunatic Asylum, 1888," *Journal of Medical Science* 34, no. 148 (January 1889): 473–490.

47. DWQ, L 4/1/3/58/88 10 Safar 1272/22 October 1855.

48. DWQ, L 4/1/3/76/113 19 Safar 1272/31 October 1855.

49. DWQ, L 2/1/43/157/1421 11 Jumada I 1270/9 February 1854; L 4/1/13/58/88 10 Safar 1272/22 October 1855; L 2/1/1/11/4 3 Ramadan 1260/16 September 1844. See also Tagher, *Mémoires de A. B. Clot Bey*, 316.

50. See, in particular, Peregrine Horden and Richard Smith, "Introduction" in *The Locus of Care: Families, Communities, Institutions and the Provision of Welfare since Antiquity*, ed. Peregrine Horden and Richard Smith (London: Routledge, 1999), 1–18.

CHAPTER TEN

Imperial Gifts and Sultanic Legitimation during the Late Ottoman Empire, 1876–1909

Nadir Özbek

> At the courtyard [of the sultan's hospital] the sons of both poor and rich fathers gather like members of a single family, as if they were the sons of one father, and as if they were beloved brothers of one another.
> —*Sabah* (n. 3429, June 7, 1899)

On August 15, 1908, just three weeks after the Young Turk Revolution, an imperial decree abolished the practice of distributing alms on a weekly basis to the poor and needy *(fukara ve muhtâcîn)* during Abdülhamid II's Friday Prayer ceremony at Hamidiye Mosque, near the Yıldız Palace.[1] Henceforth, this service of providing weekly alms on behalf of the sultan was transferred to the Municipal Administration *(Şehremanati)*. Thereafter, the Ministry of the Imperial Treasury *(Hazine-i Hassa Nezareti)* would provide the specified amount of money *(sadaka-i seniyye haftalığı)* to the Municipal Administration.[2] This single decree put an end to a sultanic practice that had been in place since at least the late eighteenth century—one that had gained special importance during the Hamidian period (1876–1909). The timing of this decree is particularly important: Abdülhamid II was still on the throne, but his power had been radically curtailed by the Young Turk Revolution of 1908. On August 4, 1908, in response to the pressures exerted by Young Turk circles, Abdülhamid II dismissed his first secretary, Tahsin Paşa, and replaced him with Cevad Bey, known for his revolutionary credentials.[3] As this chapter demonstrates, it was not accidental that, within a week after his appointment, Cevad Bey had the sultan issue the decree that eradicated Abdülhamid II's alms system.

Almost two years later, and after the deposition of Abdülhamid II, Fehim, son of Osman, a poor man who had migrated to Istanbul from Kosovo with his wife and children, presented a petition directly to the Prime Ministry *(Sadaret)*. In the petition, Fehim complained that for some time the weekly allowance of two mecidiye (an Ottoman coinage), the imperial alms that he had been granted, was no longer being paid. Because he and his family were in desperate need, Fehim asked that either this allowance be paid to him or proper employment be provided. A series of departmental correspondences followed between the Prime Ministry, the Ministry of the Interior, and the Municipal Administration of Istanbul. Finally, on June 16, 1910, the mayor sent a memorandum to the Ministry of the Interior explaining that he was not able to provide the specified alms to Fehim because the Ministry of the Imperial Treasury no longer distributed the weekly allowances of imperial alms.[4]

Fehim, obviously not alone, experienced hardship as a result of the Young Turk regime's attack on the deposed sultan's system of gift and alms distribution. His case clearly illustrates that the new regime did not hesitate in eliminating the Hamidian system of benevolence (*hayrat* and *meberrat*), which had played an important role in securing loyalty to the old regime. The constitutional regime initiated a wholesale attack against not only Abdülhamid II's gift system but also all of his charitable institutions and private coffers that had enabled the sultan to operate a huge system of benevolence. The constitutionalist revolution abruptly ended the system of gift distribution that Abdülhamid II had created so carefully.[5] The Young Turks' concern with Abdülhamid II's alms distribution indicates that during the Hamidian period imperial benevolence had emerged as a means through which a certain conception of power was manifested and legitimized.

Since Marcel Mauss's pathbreaking essay, *The Gift*, anthropological theories of gift exchange have been concerned mainly with reciprocity in such relations.[6] Mauss tried to establish a theory of gift exchange, which can be compared to that of commodity exchange. Well before Mauss, in the 1920s Bronislaw Malinowski argued that one gives because of the expectation of return and one returns because of the threat that one's partner may stop giving. Throughout the 1980s, anthropologists conceptualized the gift as something inalienable from the giver. The "inalienability principle" implies that the principle in a gift relation is "keeping-while-giving." According to this new approach, though the giver may lose possession of the gift for some time, it will return back to him eventually.[7]

This chapter benefits from the anthropological literature on gift relationships. Yet, in looking at imperial gifts, it situates the reciprocal gift relationship in a broader historical and political context. Imperial gifts were intended to deliver political messages to a wider public. That is, each gift-giving did not concern only the receiver of the gift; rather, the act of giving was aimed at a wider social and political spectrum. In other words, the imperial gift relationship was not simply a personal relationship between the sultan and the individual subject who received the gift, even though a personalized narrative of such giving was crucial to that relationship. In accord with the inalienability principle, which puts emphasis on donors and their intentions, I am concerned here mainly with the "supply side" of the reciprocal gift relationship.[8] In brief, this chapter focuses on the Hamidian conception of rule in which the gift relationship plays a crucial political role in its manifestation and its popular legitimation.

An important characteristic of the Hamidian political system is that the palace and the sultan sought to exert greater influence on politics than had been exercised in the reigns of sultans Abdülmecid (1839–1861) and Abdülaziz (1861–1876). During the Tanzimat period (1839–1876), the locus of power to a great extent lay within the grand vizier's office *(Bab-ı Ali)*. Due to the centralization, rationalization, and bureaucratization of state power in that era, the newly emerging ministries and ministerial bureaucracies gradually gained control of the governmental machinery. With the Hamidian period, however, the sultan gained greater control over political issues, and the Yıldız Palace became the major executive office of the Ottoman governmental system. The shift in the locus of power from the grand vizier's office to the Yıldız Palace was clearly reflected in the fact that while the constitutional opposition of the Young Ottomans of the 1860s was concerned with the high ranking ministers, and not exclusively with the sultan, the constitutional opposition of the Young Turks of the 1890s focused on the sultan's personality and his autocratic rule. This contestation illustrates that from the 1860s to the late nineteenth century the legitimation crisis of the monarchical/sultanic system of rule had deepened seriously. Parallel to this, the sacred or divine conception of the figure of the sultan eroded considerably. Accordingly, as the civil and military bureaucracy expanded and a corresponding new intellectual class emerged in the nineteenth century, the tension between a monarchical/sultanic rule and a liberal constitutional form of politics intensified. This tension deepened the legitimation crisis of the monarchical system of rule, forcing Abdülhamid II to reframe the symbolic and ceremonial representation of rulership.

Regarding the symbolism of power and legitimation concerns of the Hamidian regime, this chapter is influenced to a great extent by the recent work of Selim Deringil in which he argues that as Abdülhamid II, for security concerns, retreated further and further behind the high walls of Yıldız Palace he needed to establish more extensive communication with his people and the outside world through a world of symbols to remind the Ottoman populace of his power and omnipresence.[9] Although he emphasizes the domestic aspects of the legitimation crisis, Deringil is much more concerned with the rituals, ceremonials, and symbolism aimed at impressing the international realm. Deringil's study focuses on the competition between the European states through symbolic means, Abdülhamid II's effort to participate in this competition, and his attempt to present a modern appearance to the outside world. Here, I am concerned mainly with the domestic aspects of legitimation and the symbolic manifestation of Hamidian rulership, focusing most exclusively on the tension between state and society and between the sultan and the constitutionalist intelligentsia.

The political tension between a monarchical/sultanic rule and a liberal constitutional form of politics was the major dynamic that gave the symbolic representation of power through the gift system its particular color during the Hamidian period. Imperial philanthropy, in general, and imperial gift-giving, in particular, were one means, among many, employed by the Hamidian autocracy as legitimation themes to counteract the constitutionalist challenge. As such, one of the fundamental functions of the Hamidian benevolence was to present an image of a popular monarchy and establish an intimacy between the sultan and his poor subjects. The reciprocity of the gift relationship between the sultan and his poor subjects—that is, the sultan's concern for his subjects and the subjects' expected loyalty to and love for the sultan—are crucial here. The strategy, however, was based not only on the principle of reciprocity. In other words, the sultan was concerned with not only the poor subjects' immediate loyalty but, more important, the broadcasting of the reciprocal relationship to a wider Ottoman public. During the period under study, occasions of imperial gift-giving became ceremonial, and these occasions were publicized through modern means of communication, like the newspapers. The overall performance was intended to cultivate the necessary popular support from the subordinate classes, hence proving its strength and legitimacy.

Though it might seem anachronistic and paradoxical, the Hamidian strategy of power resulted in the "over-personalization" of rulership in the Ottoman Empire. During the Hamidian period great efforts were made to carry on the personal, paternalistic, and unbureaucratic aspect of the monarchy. It should be emphasized, however, that during the late nineteenth and early twentieth centuries the relatively greater weight that monarchical forms carried was not a peculiarity of the Ottoman Empire. As pointed out by various historians, it is hard to deny the persistence of monarchical values, if not political forms, not only in Russia and Germany but also in some other Western European countries, like in Britain, in Italy, and to some extent even in France.[10] In this context, for example, the Meiji reforms in Japan are far more interesting because, as eloquently examined by T. Fujitani, the monarchical forms turned out to be an integral part of modern state formation in late-nineteenth-century Japan.[11] The Hamidian political regime, however, was more similar to its Russian contemporary than it was to the Meiji regime. As Dominic Lieven has emphasized, "[T]he most basic difference between Japan, on the one hand, and Germany and Russia, on the other, was, however, that in the former the monarch reigned but never attempted personally to rule."[12] Similar to the nineteenth-century Russian tsars, especially to Nicholas II, Abdülhamid II tried to centralize the executive power in his own hands. The manifestation and legitimation of this over-personalized monarchical regime of the Hamidian period was to be achieved in part through the sultan's gift system. The gift system helped the sultan present an image of a popular monarchy and of a paternalistic sultan and establish an intimacy between himself and his poor subjects. Briefly, the imperial gift system had an important role in the Hamidian "scenarios of power."[13]

It should be pointed out that the practice of imperial gift-giving was not an invention of the Hamidian period. The practice of charity and gift-giving for political means can be seen in all periods of Islamic history. Michael Bonner, for example, has shown in his contribution to this volume (chapter 1) that in early Islamic history, gift-giving, as a form of charity, should be understood in relation to leadership and domination. He has located, for both pre-Islamic Arabia and the early Islamic period, episodes of competition over status involving feasting and gift-giving. In her study of Ottoman imperial endowment-making, Amy Singer examines in a broader historical perspective the endowment institution *(waqf)* as the established form of giving in the Islamic context. Among other functions, she shows various political uses of this form of giving.[14] Miriam Hoexter's study of the endowment institutions in Ottoman Algiers also demonstrates how important this formal way of giving was for constructing a political community through definitions of poor and needy and through inclusions and exclusions.[15]

For centuries Ottoman sultans and other members of the imperial family used gift distribution for political means. For instance, the distribution of coins to the crowd at public appearances of the sultans or queen mothers was an integral motif used to demonstrate the munificence of the dynasty during the early modern period. Leslie Peirce has demonstrated that as the sultans of the post-Süleymanic period became less visible, the female members of the dynasty filled the vacuum in the ceremonial realm.[16] However, from the late eighteenth century on, especially during Mahmud II's reign (1808–1839), this changed radically. Mahmud II, for example, was very generous in distributing coins to the poor during his journeys throughout the empire. Mahmud II, like Alexander II (1855–1889), was concerned with constructing and promoting the image of a "popular monarchy" or a "modern monarchy."[17] During his journeys throughout the Russian Empire, Alexander II carefully sought contact with the people and popular approval and tried to show how devoted he was to them.[18] In terms of broadcasting a popular image of the sultan and the symbolic presentation of power, the Hamidian period was radically different from the reigns of Mahmud II, Abdülmecid, and Abdülaziz. As Deringil writes, Abdülhamid II, "[u]nlike his immediate predecessors, but somewhat like his ancestors," strove to create "vibrations of power without being seen."[19] Because he had secluded himself within the walls of his palace office, he needed to put much emphasis on the person of the sultan in the symbolic presentation of state power.

The sultan and his palace bureaucracy invested enormous energies in the field of social welfare to portray personal, paternalistic, and unbureaucratic aspects of power. Indeed, the Hamidian strategy of power was based on an effort to person-ify the government as the intimate paternal sultan. Historians usually have been inclined to emphasize the trends toward bureaucratization and de-personalization of social welfare and relief efforts throughout the nineteenth century. In his study of nineteenth-century Egypt, Khaled Fahmy, for instance, portrays the Egyptian police as a bureaucratic intermediary between the poor and the state.[20] In his nar-rative, the Egyptians gradually became accustomed to presenting their petitions to local police bureaus, the agencies of a bureaucratic state, not to the khedive in per-son. As Mine Ener has shown in her contribution to this present volume (chapter 9), this bureaucratization, however, was accompanied by an attempt to personify the government through embodying the state's charity in the khedive's very person. Though she acknowledges the personalized manifestations of state power through a particular discourse of charity, Ener's major concern is bureaucratization and hence the de-personalization of poor relief efforts throughout the nineteenth cen-tury in Egypt.[21]

As for the late-nineteenth-century Ottoman Empire, I would argue that the bureaucratization model does not reflect the social and political transformation of the nineteenth century in all its dimensions. Until the aftermath of the Young Turk Revolution of 1908, for example, petitioning directly to the sultan during his Fri-day Prayer ceremony *(Cuma Selamlığı)* retained important symbolic functions. The Ottoman sultans of the nineteenth century had indeed established a palace bureau *(Marûzât-ı Rikâbiyye İdâresi)* to manage the increasing number of petitions sub-mitted to the sultan. Similarly, in mid-nineteenth-century Iran, installing sealed wooden boxes—"boxes of justice"—in public places in every major provincial cen-ter, enabling the local people to send their petitions directly to the shah, was indeed the expansion of the "unbureaucratic" and "personalized" nature of power.[22] Within the context of the Hamidian strategy of power, the personalization of rulership was staged through the monarchical welfare system and the performances of imperial benevolence.

The over-personalized representation of the Hamidian rulership stimulated a change in the disposition of the Ottoman imperial gift system *(atiyye-i seniyye* or *atiyye-i şahane),* which had gradually acquired a bureaucratic form before the reign of Abdülhamid II.[23] At least from the late eighteenth century on, there even ap-peared a budgetary allowance for the sultan's gifts. Those who presented petitions for monetary assistance were usually provided support from this particular al-lowance. Before the mid-nineteenth-century Tanzimat reforms, the imperial gifts were paid for out of the sultan's privy purse *(ceyb-i hümayun).* Later, expenses for imperial gifts were covered by the imperial allowance *(tahsisat-ı seniyye),* which the central treasury granted annually to the ruler.[24] Beginning in 1841, however, the allowance for imperial gifts *(atiyye-i seniyye tertibi)* appeared as a separate item in the central budget.[25] These changes in the gift system clearly illustrate the bureaucratization of state power; the imperial gifts were no longer the bounty of a personal ruler, but of the head of an impersonal institution: the bureaucratic state.

In accordance with the bureaucratized nature of the Ottoman gift system, the imperial gift allowance, before the Hamidian period, was mainly used as a bonus, an incentive, or a complementary payment to state officials. In the absence of a regularized and rationalized wage system for the state employees, occasional payments as imperial gifts continued to perform an important function. Throughout the mid-nineteenth century the imperial gifts allowance also was used for a variety of other purposes, such as occasional poor relief or disaster relief payments to the needy. However, the poor relief function of the imperial gift allowance was relatively limited during the reigns of Abdülmecid and Abdülaziz as compared to the Hamidian period.

Though the budgetary allowance for the imperial gifts was important in financing the Hamidian gift system, it would be misleading to assume that this was the only source funding the sultan's strategy of gift distribution. Abdülhamid II was able to carry out his system of benevolence thanks to the financial power that he had concentrated in his hands through the Ministry of the Imperial Treasury and the Ministry of Imperial Farms *(Emlak-ı Seniyye İdaresi)*.[26] The financial power that the sultan exerted in this period was significantly greater than in any previous period, thus enabling Abdülhamid II to present imperial benevolence as his personal generosity. In other words, during this period the person of the sultan was at the very center of the imperial act of giving. At the same time, the importance gained by the Ministry of the Imperial Treasury and the personalized nature of the Imperial Farms—that is, their being the personal property of Abdülhamid II himself and not that of the sultanate—are key to understanding the Hamidian system of benevolence.

Since the early seventeenth century, when the finance department gradually had become independent of the sultan's household, the sultan's private expenses became separated from the costs of government.[27] This separation was reflected in the creation of the privy purse, the predecessor of the imperial treasury. As the Ottoman Empire continued to evolve into a modern rational and bureaucratic state, the position of the privy purse within the administrative system changed considerably.[28] During the early nineteenth century, the government transferred most of the revenue sources of the privy purse to the central treasury as part of its financial rationalization and reorganization program. In 1840, the Ministry of Finance provided a specified annual imperial allowance to the sultan as compensation for this transfer. Later, in 1847, in accordance with this rationalization, the name of this branch was changed from privy purse to imperial treasury *(hazine-i hassa)*. Furthermore, in 1850, during the reign of Abdülmecid, the government reorganized the imperial treasury as the Ministry of the Imperial Treasury, which henceforth was responsible for administering all palace revenues.

These financial rearrangements reflect an ongoing intra-elite power struggle within the Ottoman polity. The ministerial bureaucracy of the time attempted to limit the power of the sultan. As the Ottoman state became more centralized and bureaucratized, the palace gradually lost its control over the decision-making process. Yet this course was not unilinear. The new administrative and bureaucratic elite could not resolve easily the possible internal conflicts among themselves, and this provided an opportunity for the sultan to regain control. As pointed out by Engin Akarlı, the final years of Abdülmecid's reign, especially from 1871 to 1876, constitute such a period, yet this sultan was unable to exploit that opportunity successfully.[29]

The shift within the intra-elite balance of power was directly reflected in financial affairs. In this period, the Ministry of the Imperial Treasury and especially the Ministry of Imperial Farms grew and expanded enormously. These two administrative bodies were located at the Yıldız Palace under the direct supervision of Abdülhamid II and were both central to the functioning of the sultan's Yıldız Palace–based gift distribution. To have access to funds, Abdülhamid II first seized the properties returned to the central treasury during the reign of Abdülmecid. The Ministries of the Imperial Treasury and the Imperial Farms carefully tried to expand their possessions in land and farms through all possible means. One means to achieve these goals was the seizure of so-called fallow lands *(mahlûl topraklar)*. The Ministry of Imperial Farms provided incentives to the peasants to increase the land cultivated within its jurisdiction, which meant diverting tax revenues from the coffers of the central treasury. While the extent of lands it possessed increased, the administration of these imperial lands required a bureaucratic organization with branches and sub-branches throughout the empire. Had the imperial farms belonged, in the final analysis, to the state, these arrangements could be considered as having had something to do with the administrative system. However, Abdülhamid II considered most of those imperial lands as his own personal possessions and registered them as his private property.

Establishing exact figures for the revenues controlled by the Ministry of the Imperial Treasury is challenging. For instance, in 1908, the revenue of some of the imperial farms, which were being returned to the Ministry of Finance at the time, equaled 404,347 Ottoman gold liras. The revenue of the other farms, which were to be kept under the control of the ministry, was 200,000 liras.[30] That same year, the finance department also transferred some 900,000 liras to the Ministry of the Imperial Treasury as an annual allowance. So the revenues controlled by the ministry must have amounted to at least 1,500,000 Ottoman liras annually, roughly 6 to 7 percent of the Ottoman budgetary expenditures at the time. This figure represents the minimum possible revenues because I left out the calculation of the revenues from the various concessions, businesses, and mines controlled by the ministry.

A comparison of the revenues controlled by the ministry during the final years of Abdülhamid II's reign with the total budgetary expenditures of the central government reveals that the revenue channeled into the sultan's institution accounted for approximately 6 to 10 percent of the total government expenditures. In addition to some other allowances by the central treasury—such as the imperial gift allowances, which were paid by the ministry until 1899 but then were shifted to the budget of the Ministry of the Interior—this huge amount of money was the basis for Abdülhamid II's operation of gift distribution and his other charitable endeavors. With these resources, Abdülhamid II financed his system of benevolence, that is, his favor to his subjects for various concerns, the gifts and bounties he granted *(atiyye, ihsan, lûtuf)*, and good actions and pious deeds that he performed *(hayrat* and *meberrat)*.

Having briefly examined the financial basis of Abdülhamid II's system of benevolence, I turn next to the functioning of his gift system. The imperial gift system of the Hamidian regime constituted a massive and complex structure with a repertoire of various forms of gifts, each aimed at different strata of the society and employed on different occasions.[31] In this chapter I do not aim to provide an extensive account of this complex gift system. Rather, I focus on three cases, or three forms of gifts, and try to analyze how these particular gifts reflected a certain conception of power and legitimized the Hamidian rule.

A few words on the sources I will be using are in order here. I mainly used newspaper reports as well as archival documents and government publications. It should be noted that the Ottoman press during the Hamidian period was totally under the control of the Yıldız Palace and monitored by a strict regime of censorship. Furthermore, without the sultan's cash grants, his gifts and favors, none of the newspapers would have been able to survive. This forced them to express their gratitude to the sultan in a very exaggerated manner, which was indeed the expectation of the sultan. As a result the Ottoman newspapers of the time turned into advertising agents of the sultan's achievements in all spheres of life, as well as his charity and benevolence. This obviously produced a distortion in their account of the events. Yet, since this study is concerned with the symbolic representation of the Hamidian rulership, the newspapers and governmental documents remain useful sources.[32]

Turning the sultan's gift-giving into a ceremonial occasion and presenting a dramatized version of the occasion to a wider public with the help of the modern mass media distinguished Hamidian gift-giving from its predecessors. The intended audience of the gifts was much wider than the immediate receivers. One good example of this was the distribution of alms on a weekly basis every Friday in one of the districts of the capital. This form complemented the alms distributed to poor subjects following the Friday Prayer ceremony at the Hamidiye Mosque. The occasion was orchestrated as a ceremonial visit of the sultan's palace aides to one of the districts of the city. One of Abdülhamid II's specially appointed aides coordinated the occasion on behalf of the sultan. Each week twenty-one animals were sacrificed and the meat was distributed to the residents of the dervish convents of the region, or to the students of religious schools *(medreses)*. The area's poor residents also benefited from this meat distribution. The major Istanbul newspapers regularly reported on similar visits and the food distribution under the title *"sadaka-i seniyye,"* or sultan's alms. On March 20, 1903, for example, the sultan's delegates arranged for a ceremonial distribution of meat at Atpazarı, a district of Üsküdar.[33] On another occasion, the same ceremony took place at Yeniçeşme, a quarter of Fatih, and meat was distributed to the students of Şeyhülislam Hayrullah Efendi Medresesi, the district's religious school.[34]

A newspaper account from 1899 provides more information on how these occasions were turned into ceremonials.[35] A commission, carrying Abdülhamid II's gift of 300 Ottoman liras, visited Kağıthane, then an outlying village of Istanbul, and distributed the money to the needy villagers as an imperial gift. On the same occasion, eighteen animals were sacrificed at the Daye Hatun tomb and the meat distributed to the poor residents of the village. Later, the same team went to Alibeyköy, another district near the village, and distributed to the poor residents 100 liras and meat as the sultan's gifts. After the noon prayer approximately two hundred villagers and one hundred students of the primary school of the district gathered in the courtyard of the tomb. Hafız İsmail Hakkı Efendi, the imam of the village and also instructor of the district school, delivered a speech emphasizing the generosity of the sultan and expressing the villagers' gratitude to their ruler. Following this speech the audience greeted their sultan by shouting three times "Long live my padişah [sultan]!" *(Padişahım Çok Yaşa!).* This was a slogan that turned into one of the key signifiers of the sultan's relation with his subjects, especially in those instances which called for the subjects to express their love and gratitude as well as their loyalty to him.

It should be pointed out that the form of this ceremonial occasion was entirely religious. Providing alms to the poor and needy, after all, was one of the duties of every wealthy Muslim. It was not accidental that the ceremony was carried out on Fridays, the day of public prayers. Sacrificing animals and distributing meat to the poor were also religious acts, and, again, every wealthy Muslim was expected to perform these acts once a year during the religious festivals. Furthermore, the ceremony was staged in a religious establishment, such as a religious school, a dervish convent, or a tomb of a saintly figure. The specificities of this particular gift relation illustrate that Abdülhamid II intended to appeal to the religious sentiments of the common Muslim people.

Though the form of giving ceremonials appears to have been exclusively religious, what is important here is the staging of the scenario itself, in which the receivers of the gifts were expected to play an active role. Thus, they participated in the ceremony, prayed for the sultan at the Friday Prayer, and, more important, greeted the sultan by shouting the anticipated "Long live my padişah!" These ceremonies sought to achieve two goals simultaneously: to secure popular approval for the sultan and to demonstrate that the approval the sultan's regime enjoyed was already widespread.

Newspaper accounts of the crèche (in this instance meaning foundling hospital) and an orphanage established at a poorhouse (Darülaceze) in 1903 provide insights into the particular conception of power embedded within the imperial gift relationship. The daily *Sabah* recorded a striking story to illustrate the personal, patriarchal, and non-bureaucratic aspects of the sultan's rule. A young mother, in deep poverty and desperate need and unable to feed her newborn child, eventually decided to hand the child over to the poorhouse. Months later, having found employment as a domestic servant, she returned to the poorhouse to retrieve her child. Yet, when she saw how well her child was being cared for she decided to leave the child there, contrary to what her strong maternal instincts demanded. The author of the article claimed that "the compassion of the sultan was even stronger than maternal instinct."[36]

This example illustrates how Abdülhamid II's gifts and philanthropic acts were aimed at projecting an image of imperial paternalism, of a concerned monarchical father. Family metaphorically represents the desired relationship between the sultan and his subjects. In this metaphor, family unity symbolizes the bond between the sultan and his subjects. It is no mere coincidence that in this paternalistic representation the sultan's care and protection for his subjects was portrayed as being deep, as that of a father's commitment to the welfare of his children. The subjects were expected to nurture feelings of loyalty, respect, and love for their sultan, much like a child does for its father. Such a paternalistic dramatization of the family metaphor aimed to demonstrate the existence of the deep attachment subjects felt for their ruler, as well as the sultan's fatherly love for them.

Abdülhamid II also invested a great deal of energy in circumcision ceremonies to foster an image of imperial paternalism. In a Muslim context, circumcision has a prominent symbolic meaning for both the male child and his father. For the child, it symbolizes the passage from childhood to adulthood, whereas it is the responsibility of the father to organize the event. The Hamidian autocracy appropriated the paternalistic/symbolic meaning of circumcision into its own strategy of power. Circumcision ceremonies for the imperial princes constituted an integral part of the Ottoman ceremonial system for centuries. Until the nineteenth century, circumcision ceremonies, and also wedding ceremonies of princes and princesses, were used as a means of displaying royal power. For example, as elegantly examined by Tülay Artan, in the early eighteenth century these ceremonies served as occasions to display power for competing political parties.[37]

In addition, the Hamidian autocracy embedded in the circumcision ceremonial scientific and progressivist themes. Science *(ilm)* and progress *(terakki)* had entered the vocabulary of the Ottoman elite as catchwords since at least the mid-nineteenth century, and thereafter positivist and progressivist themes conditioned the worldview of the Ottoman elite. The Hamidian regime presented its achievements in the fields of education, welfare, and medicine as reflections of the sultan's dedication to progress and modernity. Medicine and the medical sciences were the basic measures of modernity in the late nineteenth century, and the sultan made significant investment in these fields.

During Abdülhamid II's time, public circumcisions were performed by qualified medical professionals in modern hospitals, meeting modern standards of hygiene. An article published in the *Yearbook of the Imperial Hospital for Children* describes in detail how the methods used in the sultan's hospitals revolutionized circumcision techniques while sparing boys pain and their families concern.[38] On this occasion, the sultan was pictured as a fatherly figure caring for even the minor pains a child has to suffer during the circumcision procedure. Medicine was now put to use in the service of a sultan who sought popular approval for his political regime.

Another aspect of the Hamidian circumcision ceremonies was their mass scale and the routinized nature of the operation. Public circumcisions were staged not only during the circumcision of princes, they also became one of the major events in the annual celebrations of the sultan's accession to power *(cülus-ı hümayun)*. On such occasions thousands of boys were circumcised.[39]

One of the biggest performances surrounded the circumcision of the prince Abdurrahim Efendi in 1899.[40] The huge celebration lasted more than a week. At six different venues, including the Hospital for Children and other major hospitals of the capital, thousands of boys were circumcised; the total number exceeding twelve thousand.[41] Abdülhamid II paid particular attention to this and other circumcision ceremonies; in fact, he had a team of his immediate associates (officials from the Ministry of the Imperial Treasury, the Ministry of Imperial Farms, and other palace departments) organize the events.

During the 1899 princely circumcision, newspapers provided very detailed descriptions of the arrangements and celebrations at each venue and underlined the sultan's generosity toward his people. The dailies *Sabah*, *İkdam*, and *Tercüman-ı Hakikat* each allocated almost half a page each day to the ceremonies. The organizational team brilliantly decorated all of the hospitals and other sites for the ceremonies, paying particular attention to the comfort of the children and their parents, and organizing various activities to entertain both the children and their families. Abdülhamid II presented the circumcised boys with presents of clothes and shoes and imperial gifts in the form of cash allowances. The newspapers emphasized that the sultan covered all the expenses out of his own pocket, that is, from the coffers of the Ministry of the Imperial Treasury.

The staging of such a ceremonial was intended to foster a sense of intimacy and loyalty toward the sultan. As an article in the *Yearbook* explicitly stated, the circumcision of thousands of children would guarantee the loyalty to the state and the sultan of tens of thousands of people.[42] The Hamidian regime used these ceremonials to cement the familial bond between the ruler and his subjects. It is not accidental that the newspapers were full of highly dramatized descriptions of the public enthusiasm generated by Abdülhamid II's generosity. Both the dramatization of the public circumcision and its broadcast to the public were critical to the workings of the Hamidian gift system.

Consider, for example, the following occasion. A group of approximately one hundred people from the villages of Üsküdar paraded with their sons sitting in decorated ox-driven carts all the way to the Haydarpaşa Hospital to have them circumcised. While en route they stopped at every neighborhood, and the imam, leading the villagers, prayed for the sultan. At the end of the prayer, the people who in the meantime had gathered around the parading villagers exclaimed, "Long live my padişah!" three times to express their gratitude to their ruler.[43] The newspaper *Sabah* used this example to demonstrate that the people were celebrating the occasion with great joy as if it were a festival.

Sabah also dramatized the circumcision ceremonies at Darüşşafaka, the high school for orphans. Hundreds of families met in the area in front of the school. Some of them were bringing their sons to the school in carts, while others, whose children had been circumcised the day before, were returning to their homes. The school was decorated with flags and banners proclaiming "Long live my padişah!" Every so often, the crowd expressed its gratitude to the sultan by shouting the expected formula. According to the newspaper accounts, everybody celebrated the circumcision in the school courtyard as if it were a festival. As the daily *Sabah* tellingly put it, staging such dramas was intended to project an image of imperial paternalism, an image of a concerned monarchical father, and a picture of the sultan and his subjects united by familial bonds. On such occasions, the *Sabah* report went on, "The sons of both poor and rich fathers gather like members of a single family, as if they were the sons of one father, and as if they were beloved brothers of one another."[44]

The circumcision ceremonies and the way these occasions were covered in Ottoman newspapers prove that imperial philanthropy during the Hamidian period served as a means of disseminating a certain conception of power. The Hamidian circumcision ceremonies were not simply a reciprocal gift relationship, even though the reciprocal return—that is, the immediate receivers' loyalty to the sultan—was one of the expectations. More important in the sultanic gift-giving enterprise was the construction of a familial picture, depicting the sultan as a fatherly figure and his subjects as loyal and respectful sons and daughters. In this sense, the symbolic presentation of the bond between the giver and the receiver is much more important. Through ritualized, ceremonial acts of sultanic benevolence, Abdülhamid II appealed to a wider Ottoman public that might fall prey to the constitutionalist propaganda of the sultan's Young Turk opponents.

In the ceremonials of gift-giving, the recipients were expected to participate actively. Expressed in the contemporary codified language, the subjects' display of loyalty to the sultan was a crucial, and expected, element in the whole scenario. However, this imperial gift system sent out broader political messages than the one implicit in the "reciprocity principle." In these gift relations, the sultan embedded a paternalistic conception of power framed around the family metaphor, which demonstrated a virtual bond between the sultan and the people. The intended audience of such dramatizations was obviously the wider Ottoman public and particularly those who were potentially under the influence of constitutionalist propaganda of the Young Turks. These dramatizations were also used to broadcast the image that the regime was cultivating popular support among poor Ottomans. The constitutional regime's immediate attack on the constituent parts of the Hamidian gift system after the Young Turk Revolution proves that the Young Turks were well aware of the intended effects of the imperial gift system.

The cases examined in this chapter illustrate a clear shift in the form of rulership: from a distant to a personal and intimate sultan. To create this intimacy effect, the Hamidian autocracy employed imperial philanthropy and benevolence as a key strategy. Though colored with Islamic religious motives, the Hamidian scenario was designed to promote a popular monarchical/sultanic conception of power. In reality, there was little or no contact between the recipients of the imperial gifts and the sultan. However, the scenario was designed to make the sultan intimate and visible to his subjects through personalized forms of imperial giving. A similar process took place in nineteenth-century Egypt, as described in chapter 9 of this volume: In Egypt, too, despite the bureaucratization of poor relief practices, a personalized language of charity—the charity of the khedive—was persistent. In this chapter I have argued that in the Hamidian period the expansion of personalized and unbureaucratic forms of rule, or a strategy of power based on monarchical forms of politics, should be understood as the very framework of Ottoman modernity.

Notes

While writing this chapter I benefited from invaluable comments offered by numerous people. I am particularly indebted to Jean Quataert, who read an earlier version and offered extensive guidance, and to Rifaat A. Abou-El-Haj and Donald Quataert, who read the drafts various times. Leslie Peirce, as the commentator at the conference, funded by the National Endowment for the Humanities, offered extensive and very useful comments. I benefited greatly from the conference discussions and owe special thanks to all the participants. Their suggestions were invaluable, and all errors and misjudgments remaining are my responsibility.

    1. For a brief discussion on the Friday Prayer ceremony, see Mehmet İpşrli, "Osmanlılarda Cuma Selamlığı (Halk-Hükümdar Münasebetleri Açısından Önemi)," in *Prof.*

Dr. Bekir Kütükoğlu'na Armağan (Istanbul: İstanbul Üniversitesi Edebiyat Fakültesi Tarih Araştırma Merkezi, 1991), 459–471.

2. Başbakanlık Osmanlı Aşivi (hereafter BOA), İrade Hususi (hereafter İ.Hususi), 16/B.1326, 17 Receb 1326 (15 August 1908). The Ministry of the Imperial Treasury was a palace administrative body and it was separate from the Ministry of Finance *(Maliye Nezareti)*.

3. For Tahsin Paşa's deposition and Cevad Bey's appointment as the first secretary to the sultan, see Aykut Kansu, *The Revolution of 1908 in Turkey* (Leiden: E. J. Brill, 1997), 125. See also Faik Reşit Unat, ed., *İkinci Meşrutiyetin İlânı ve Otuzbir Mart Hâdisesi: II. Abdülhamid'in Son Mabeyn Başkâtibi Ali Cevat Bey'in Fezlekesi* (Ankara: Türk Tarih Kurumu, 1991).

4. BOA, Dahiliye Nezareti-Muhaberat-ı Umumiye İdaresi (hereafter DH.MUİ), 101/46, 1328.C.9 (18 June 1910).

5. During the constitutional period, in contrast to Abdülhamid II's charitable activities and relief institutions focusing on the sultan's personality, the emphasis shifted to "public assistance." For a study of this shift, see Nadir Özbek, "The Politics of Poor Relief in the Late Ottoman Empire, 1876–1914," *New Perspectives on Turkey* 21 (Fall 1999): 1–33.

6. Marcel Mauss, *The Gift: The Form and Reason for Exchange in Archaic Societies,* trans. W. D. Halls, foreword Mary Douglas (New York: Norton, 1990).

7. For a brief summary of anthropological approaches to the gift relation, see Yunxiang Yan, *The Flow of Gifts, Reciprocity, and Social Networks in a Chinese Village* (Stanford: Stanford University Press, 1996). See also Roy Porter, "The Gift Relation: Philanthropy and Provincial Hospitals in Eighteenth-Century England", in *The Hospital in History*, ed. Lindsay Granshaw and Roy Porter (London: Routledge, 1989), 149–178.

8. My usage of "supply" approach is mainly inspired by Sandra Cavallo's work on early modern Italy. As she points out, the supply approach emphasizes that "policy toward the poor was not determined solely by the statistical extent of poverty"; see her *Charity and Power in Early Modern Italy, Benefactors and Their Motives in Turin, 1541–1789* (Cambridge: Cambridge University Press, 1995).

9. Selim Deringil, *The Well-Protected Domains, Ideology, and the Legitimation of Power in the Ottoman Empire, 1876–1909* (New York: I. B. Tauris, 1998).

10. See Arno J. Mayer, ed., *The Persistence of the Old Regime: Europe to the Great War* (New York: Pantheon Books, 1981); David E. Barchlay, "Ritual, Ceremonial, and the 'Invention' of a Monarchical Tradition in Nineteenth-Century Prussia," in *European Monarchy: Its Evolution and Practice from Roman Antiquity to Modern Times,* ed. Heinz Duchhardt, Richard A. Jackson, and David Sturdy (Stuttgart: Franz Steiner Verlag, 1992), 207–220.

11. T. Fujitani, *Splendid Monarchy, Power, and Pageantry in Modern Japan* (Berkeley: University of California Press, 1998), 44–45.

12. Dominic Lieven, *Nicholas II, Twilight of the Empire* (New York: St. Martin's Press, 1993), 126. I am grateful to Adele Lindenmeyr for pointing out Lieven's monograph on Nicholas II, which provides a useful comparative basis with the Hamidian period.

13. I borrowed this concept from Richard Wortman; see Richard S. Wortman, *Scenarios of Power: Myth and Ceremony in the Russian Monarchy, From Peter the Great to the Death of Nicholas I*, vol. 1 (Princeton: Princeton University Press, 1995).

14. See Amy Singer's contribution to this volume (chapter 15).

15. See Miriam Hoexter's contribution to this volume (chapter 7).

16. Leslie Peirce examined in detail the role played by the female members of the imperial family, especially the *valide sultan*s (mothers of sultans) and *haseki sultan*s (sultans' favorites) in the symbolic and expression of power, especially during the sixteenth and seventeenth centuries; see Leslie P. Peirce, *The Imperial Harem, Women and Sovereignty in the Ottoman Empire* (New York: Oxford University Press, 1993).

17. For the concepts of 'popular monarchy' and 'modern monarchy,' see Barchlay, "Ritual, Ceremonial, and the 'Invention' of a Monarchical Tradition."

18. For Mahmud II's journeys through the Ottoman Empire, see Abdülkadir Özcan, "II. Mahmud'un Memleket Gezileri," in *Prof. Dr. Bekir Kütükoğlu'na Armağan* (İstanbul: Istanbul Üniversitesi Edebiyat Fakültesi Tarih Araştırma Merkezi, 1991), 361–379. For Alexander II's trips, see Richard Wortman, "Rule by Sentiment: Alexander II's Journeys through the Russian Empire," *American Historical Review* 95 (June 1990): 745–771.

19. Deringil, *The Well-Protecetd Domains*, 18.

20. Khaled Fahmy, "The Police and the People in Nineteenth-Century Egypt," *Die Welt Des Islams* (1999): 340–377.

21. See Mine Ener's contribution in this volume (chapter 9).

22. Nader Sohrabi, "Revolution and State Culture: The Circle of Justice and Constitutionalism in 1906 Iran," in *State/Culture, State-Formation after the Cultural Turn*, ed. George Steinmetz (Ithaca: Cornell University Press, 1999), 253–288.

23. *Atiyye*, an Arabic word, literally means "gift." Mehmet Zeki Pakalın defines *atiyye-i seniyye* as sultan's gifts, or sultan's favor, to those who were in the service of the state. Pakalın's definition depicts the concept in a very narrow sense; see his *Osmanlı Tarih Deyimleri ve Terimleri Sözlüğü* (İstanbul: Milli Eğitim Bakanlığı, 1992), 1:110–111.

24. Yavuz Cezar, *Osmanlı Maliyesinde Bunalım ve Değişim Dönemi, XVII. Yüzyıldan Tanzimat'a Mali Tarih* (İstanbul: Alan Yayıncılık, 1986), 289.

25. Tevfik Güran, *Tanzimat Döneminde Osmanlı Maliyesi: Bütçeler ve Hazine Hesapları (1841–1861)* (Ankara: Türk Tarih Kurumu Basımevi, 1989).

26. The term *imperial farms* used here has a specific meaning during the Hamidian period and it should not be confused with "crown lands," or *hass*. During the reign of Abdülhamid II, *emlak-ı seniyye*, literally meant the sultan's own lands, estates, or farms. The administration of these lands or farms was the responsibility of the Ministry of Imperial Farms.

27. See Linda T. Darling, *Revenue-Raising and Legitimacy, Tax Collection and Finance Administration in the Ottoman Empire, 1500–1660* (Leiden: E. J. Brill, 1996), 79, and/or fn. 54.

28. For Hazine-i Hassa Nezareti and Abdülhamid II's property, see Vasfi Şensözen, *Osmanoğullarının Varlıkları ve II. Abdülhamid'in Emlaki* (Ankara: Türk Tarih Kurumu Basımevi, 1982); Arzu Terzi-Tozduman, "Hazine-i Hassa," in *İslam Ansiklopedisi* (İstanbul: Türkiye Diyanet Vakfı Yayınları, 1998), 17:137–141.

29. Engin Deniz Akarlı, "The Problems of External Pressures, Power Struggles, and Budgetary Deficits in Ottoman Politics under Abdülhamid II (1876–1909): Origins and Solutions" (Ph.D. diss., Princeton University, 1976), 94–98.

30. Şensözen, *Osmanoğullarının Varlıkları*, 66–69.

31. For further analysis and documentation on Abdülhamid II's gift system, see my unpublished dissertation: Nadir Özbek, "The Politics of Welfare: Philanthropy, Voluntarism, and Legitimacy in the Ottoman Empire, 1876–1914" (Binghamton University, 2001).

32. It is almost impossible to find a negative mention of the Hamidian gift system in the Ottoman newspapers of the time. However, this does not mean that the outcome of staging of ceremonials, for instance, was always as expected. For instance, Cemil Paşa, a famous surgeon during the Hamidian period, noted that the mass circumcisions of the period frequently turned into disasters. According to him the physicians did not pay much attention to hygienic conditions, and post-operational complications were the rule of the time. Yet, we should also remember that the memoirs of Cemil Paşa and other memoirs written after the deposition of Abdülhamid II have their own biases and distortions. See, for example, Cemil Paşa's article on circumcision: Cemil Topuzlu, "Sünnet Lüzumlu mudur?" *Tıp Dünyası* 8, (no. 5/85) (15 Mayıs 1935): 2909–2910. I am grateful to Adele Lindenmeyr for pointing out to me the possible negative consequences, contrary to the intentions of the ruler, of the staged scenarios.

33. *Sabah*, n. 4811, 21 March 1903.

34. *Sabah*, n. 6043, 4 August 1906.

35. *Sabah*, n. 3315, 13 February 1899.

36. *Sabah*, n. 4785, 23 February 1903.

37. Tülay Artan, "18. Yüzyıl Başlarında Yönetici Elitin Saltanatın Meşruiyet Arayışına Katılımı," *Toplum ve Bilim* 83 (Kış 1999/2000), 292–322. For the prominent role played by women in the 1582 celebrations of the circumcision of Murad's son Mehmed, see Peirce, *The Imperial Harem*, 192. Peirce points out that in the decades following the reign of Süleyman, the prince's circumcisions were the greatest events held in the capital.

38. *Etfal Hastahane-i Alisinin İstatistik Mecmua-i Tıbbiyesi* (Yearbook of the Imperial Hospital for Children; hereafter *Yearbook*), 1907, 8:10–25.

39. The Hamidian bureaucracy orchestrated circumcision ceremonies not only in the Imperial Hospital for Children but in most other medical centers of the capital. From 1899 to 1906, 7,813 children were provided hygienic and modern circumcision in the Hospital for Children alone; see *Yearbook*, 7:217–218.

40. Ayşe Osmanoğlu, *Babam Sultan Abdülhamid (Hatıralarım)* (Ankara: Selçuk Yayınları, 1986), 72. Another huge celebration was held at the circumcision of the princes Abdülkadir, Ahmed, and Burhaneddin in 1891. See BOA, Y.MTV, 50/65, 22/10/1308 (31 May 1891).

41. *Türcüman-ı Hakikat*, n. 6503, 14 June 1899. During the circumcision celebrations of 1891, 2,830 boys were circumcised in two days. See BOA, Y.MTV, 50/65.

42. *Yearbook*, 8:10–25.

43. *Sabah*, n. 3434, 12 June 1899. Circumcision was provided not only to Istanbul residents; for example, residents of Kartal, İzmit, and some other closer districts of the empire also brought their children to the Haydarpaşa Hospital for circumcision. See *Sabah*, n. 3433, 11 June 1899. Another celebration was also conducted in İzmir, at the Hamidiye Vocational School *(Hamidiye Sanayi Mektebi)*, where approximately ninety-six

orphans were circumcised. See *Sabah*, n. 3423, 1 June 1899 and *Sabah*, n. 3429, 7 June 1899. The latter example also illustrates the fact that, contrary to the previous centuries, Hamidian benevolence aimed to reach the localities; and the sultan was indeed successful in this.

44. *Sabah*, n. 3429, 7 June 1899.

Part IV

Changing Worlds

CHAPTER ELEVEN

Al-Tahtawi on Poverty and Welfare

JUAN R. I. COLE

Rifa'ah Rafi' al-Tahtawi (1801–1873), a major figure of the Arab Renaissance of the mid-nineteenth century, was born in the small town of Tahta in Upper Egypt. In his major work on political economy written in the 1860s, al-Tahtawi is concerned mainly with the sources of wealth and poverty and with the position and ideal treatment of the poor. He is concerned with two groups among the poor: the idle poor and the working poor. The idle poor include the disabled (the blind, handicapped, and old), the indolent, and those idled (al-'atala) by poor economic conditions. The working poor are mainly peasants but also include urban craftsmen, who are inadequately compensated for their labor in al-Tahtawi's view. Al-Tahtawi rose to become one of Egypt's great landlords and a pillar of the establishment in Ottoman Egypt under the khedives. One might have expected him to disdain the poor and workers, as, in fact, many among the Egyptian notables did. Without at all wishing to deny a strong element of paternalism in his views, I can say that he is remarkably sympathetic to the poor. What were the ethical and theoretical sources for his views of poverty and the indigent? What explains his relatively progressive stance toward the working classes? What solutions does he put forward to the increasing problems he sees in the late 1860s?

Upon his father's death, al-Tahtawi was sent to study at al-Azhar seminary in 1817, following in the footsteps of many of his uncles. In 1822 he began teaching at al-Azhar, and in 1824 his mentor Hasan al-'Attar nominated him as the preacher for one of Muhammad 'Ali Pasha's newly formed military units. Again on al-'Attar's initiative, in 1826 he was appointed one of four prayer leaders for an educational mission to Paris. The likelihood is that al-'Attar and al-Tahtawi both saw this appointment as an opportunity for someone from al-Azhar to gain intimate knowledge of European sciences, to which al-'Attar had been introduced by the savants who had accompanied Napoléon Bonaparte. Muhammad 'Ali's preference for Ottoman-Egyptians as students had thus far excluded Arabophone Egyptians from these educational missions. Al-Tahtawi intended to be far more than a simple prayer leader and began studying French as soon as he boarded the ship at Alexandria. While in France, he completed a rigorous course of university studies. On his return in 1831 Ibrahim Pasha granted him thirty-one feddans of land as a reward for his accomplishments, and he became a French teacher at the medical school.

Throughout the 1830s and 1840s al-Tahtawi busied himself as a translator and promoter of language learning, and by 1846 was promoted to the civil rank of miralay and given a substantial grant of land. In 1850–1854 he was exiled to Khartoum in the Sudan by 'Abbas I but was allowed to come back to Cairo by Sa'id Pasha, working again as a translator, and then as a superintendent of the military academy in the Citadel until it was closed in 1860. By 1863 the government's financial woes had been assuaged by the Cotton Boom, and Isma'il Pasha had come to the throne, appointing al-Tahtawi head of a new Translation Bureau charged with rendering into Arabic the Napoleonic Code. In 1868 his history of ancient Egypt, *The Glorious Lights of Divine Confirmation (Anwar tawfiq al-jalil)* was published, and in 1869 he brought out a long and very important book on political economy: *Paths for Egyptian Minds to the Delights of Modern Culture (Manahij al-albab al-misriyya fi mabahij al-adab al-'asriyya).*

It is al-Tahtawi's treatment of issues regarding poverty and the poor in the latter work that forms the focus of this chapter. The heady atmosphere of the Cotton Boom years (1862–1866), as well as the class stratification, dislocations, high indebtedness, growing taxes, and spiraling population growth of the mid- to the late 1860s are apparent in this book, which was apparently intended as a textbook on political economy for Isma'il's new civil school system. Throughout this chapter, I reference in parentheses the *Paths* from the five-volume collected works of al-Tahtawi edited by Muhammad 'Imarah, of which the *Manahij* was the first volume.[1]

Issues in wealth and poverty were posed very powerfully in the decade of the 1860s. During this time millions of pounds flowed into the country from the cotton windfall produced by the Northern blockade of Southern exports during the U.S. Civil War. Because the South had supplied some 80 percent of Great Britain's raw cotton needs, this blockade produced a cotton famine in the textile industry, and British importers immediately looked abroad to Egypt, India, and elsewhere for other sources of cotton. Egypt's indigenous long-staple cotton was liked in Manchester, even though Egyptian strains were often considered too yellow or the bales insufficiently clean. Although the state and great landlords captured the lion's share of this new wealth, it percolated down even to village peasants, causing inflation and other dislocations.[2] In 1866 there was even a famine that appears to have been exacerbated by the large-scale switch to cash cropping for the world market. After 1850 Egypt's population growth rate also increased, so that the number of Egyptians rose from about 5 million in 1848 to about 8 million in 1882, a very substantial increase that put pressure on the land and contributed to the fragmentation of peasant estates. The number of landless laborers appears to have grown in this period. In the urban areas, the guilds faced challenges from new technologies, inflation, and extremely high taxes.[3]

The Poor Who Do Not Labor

According to al-Tahtawi, among the causes of poverty is natural indolence. He quotes a medieval Islamic "book of administration" to the effect that the lowest class of people is idle, and these are the greatest wrongdoers, since they eat of God's nourishment but do not improve the world (1:335–336). In another passage, he asserts, "Human beings by their original nature have fixed in their character a strong dislike of being obligated to labor, and try to get away from it as much as they can, even though they need to work in order to preserve themselves and their species" (1:312). The problem, he says, is that civilizational advance and economic progress depend on labor, and if the people are indolent (as they can afford to be in warm climes like the Sudan), then stagnation will set in.

Al-Tahtawi feels that this problem of natural indolence is resolved naturally, insofar as human beings' instinct to avoid work is counterbalanced by an instinct to procreate. This latter instinct leads to population growth that ultimately forces people to work to support their families. Moreover, as population pressure on the land grows, it at some point becomes a commodity that can be bought and sold, acquiring a value apart from the simple labor of subsistence farmers. This emergence of a market in private landed property in turn forces virtually the entire population to try to own and work land to improve it and to add value to it. Population growth and competition for land thus greatly reduce leisure time and greatly increase labor productivity (1:311–316). Elsewhere, he wrote,

> Even though the common people by nature incline toward indolence and lassitude, the conditions of the present time might force upon them the activity of labor until it becomes natural. The consequences of this development would be the advancement of societies via the proficiency of labor, which will benefit all communities and states. This prospect is especially bright for those states that formerly possessed an ample share therein, such as Egypt, which preceded all peoples in its wondrous monuments, and such as the rest of the Muslim states, wherein the varieties of human knowledge, social benefits, and civilizational progress formerly flourished. (1:338)

The problem of indolence, he thus suggests, would be solved naturally. It is noteworthy that al-Tahtawi's example in this discussion was the Dinka pastoralists of the Sudan (where he had lived for a time during the reign of 'Abbas I). Although his theory of population growth and land hunger as driving people to labor more intensively may have had roots in French thinking on political economy, it was also influenced by a sort of colonial anthropology of high Egyptian state officials concerned with the Sudan and its productive potential.

So far we have considered al-Tahtawi's views on the able-bodied people who decline to work. He has an entirely different attitude toward those who are poor because of a disability. For the disabled poor, al-Tahtawi is a strong advocate of both state welfare measures and private philanthropy. He begins his consideration of welfare policy on the part of the state by finding a double genealogy for it, in the practices of civilized (Western) nations, and in Egyptian-Islamic history.

> Philanthropy in civilized countries is expended on the needy, including the poor, the disabled, the retired, widows and the needy, whether they be natives or immigrants. It is well-known that the Islamic religion, which was revealed for the happiness of the community, is the greatest means to civilization. When first God conquered Egypt, in the reign of the Commander of the Believers, our lord 'Umar b. al-Khattab, the latter was the first to disburse and set aside such monies as were necessary from the Muslim treasury for philanthropy, for the 'ulama' [scholars] and the fighters in the holy war, as well as for their children and dependents, and for the needy. These legislated donations have continued in all states throughout the ages. The caliphs and sultans who succeeded the Commander of the Believers increased these donations and took measures for the enforcement of their legal claims (1:278–279).

Al-Tahtawi thus locates the tradition of and necessity for state assistance to the poor in normative Islam itself, especially the policies of the Caliph 'Umar, which he says were implemented in Egypt from the beginnings of the Muslim period there. The impetus to "return" wealth from the rich to the poor in early Islam through *zakat* (alms) and other means is discussed elsewhere in this volume by Michael Bonner (chapter 1) and Ingrid Mattson (chapter 2).

Al-Tahtawi finds a further genealogy for welfare practices in Mamluk and Ottoman Egypt before the eighteenth century, depicting a constant struggle between righteous and conscientious *'ulama'* (and often sultans, as well) on the one hand, and greedy and rapacious courtiers and high bureaucrats (and often sultans, as well) on the other hand. He especially praises Nur al-Din Zangi (d. 1174) for the stipends, free food, and pious endowments from the treasury that he is said to have bestowed on mosques and hospitals to ensure that the deserving got their portion (presumably in Syria, but thereby setting a precedent for the Ayyubids in Egypt). Al-Tahtawi tells an anecdote of how the sultan resisted suggestions from his courtiers that this money should be taken away from the poor and spent on holy war. He tells a similar story about the Ayyubid al-Malik al-Kamil (d. 1238). He then says that when the Mamluk Sultan Barquq (1382–1399) came to power he was determined to reduce the state's expenditure on philanthropy but ran into determined opposition from the great 'ulama' of the day. These stories have the stock form of a trope and may not be rooted in information in the medieval chronicles. Certainly, the account of Sultan Barquq by Ibn Taghribirdi makes no mention of any attempt by him to reduce charities; on the contrary it provides many instances of his liberality, though he admits the ruler had a reputation for stinginess.[4] However, as Adam Sabra makes clear in chapter 4 of this volume, the Mamluks and their clerics were deeply concerned with issues in the moral economy, which is al-Tahtawi's larger point.

Turning to the Ottomans, al-Tahtawi praises the Ottoman sultan Selim for maintaining philanthropic and welfare expenditures at the same level when he conquered Egypt, refusing suggestions from his generals that they were too high. He then reports a controversy that he says broke out during the reign of Süleyman the Magnificent. He says that some in the Ottoman court argued that the various expenditures in Egypt on the needy were not in accordance with Islamic law, and Süleyman determined to abolish them. Then, as he tells the story, the Egyptian 'ulama' insisted that these welfare expenditures derived their legitimacy from having been apportioned by previous representatives of absolute authority *(nuwwab al-saltana)*, and from their concord with the requirements of the public good *(al-masalih al-shar'iyya)*. The argument for public welfare *(maslaha)* as a source of Islamic law (an argument known as *istislah*) was accepted by a number of medieval Sunni jurisprudents from varying schools, including the Maliki and Shafi'i and was revived by nineteenth-century reformers such as al-Tahtawi (though he is less often given credit than his younger contemporary Muhammad 'Abduh).[5] The other argument, for the decrees of the Ottoman sultans as a set of binding precedents, derives from the Ottoman theory of the *qanun-name*, or what we would call the executive decree, as a form of legislation. (This idea of the legislating sultan, so different from Islamic ideas about law, is rooted in Mongol conceptions of the chieftain as lawgiver taken over by post-Mongol successor states such as the Mughals, Safavids, and Ottomans.) Here, both ideas, of the overriding importance of public welfare and the unalterable precedent of imperial decrees, are marshaled to support the continued expenditure of substantial welfare by the state on the poor, the needy, the disabled, and the religious classes. The Ottoman state's interest in providing for the poor is illustrated in the chapters in this volume by Mine Ener (9), Miriam Hoexter (7), and Amy Singer (15), among others.

Despite the implication that in Egypt the government has always cared for the poor and needy, al-Tahtawi does admit an eighteenth-century lapse of this practice. He writes:

> This nourishment continued to flow copiously to those who deserved it, and the eyes of the disabled, the widows, the learned, and the Quran specialists continued to be solaced by it. Then vicissitudes, civil strife, and the capricious tests of fate came to pass, and the French occupied Egypt after the injustice and oppression of the Mamluk state and their misrule of their subjects. Then the

difficulties of this trial were removed, and the late Muhammad 'Ali's conquest of Joseph's kingdom ordered the premises of the syllogism so as to produce the correct conclusion. (1:280–81)

Thus, the internecine battles and greediness of the late Ottoman slave–soldier beys and of the French colonialists under Bonaparte are blamed for an interruption of this practice of good government, rooted both in Islam and in the practices of civilization. He maintains that it was, however, restored under Muhammad 'Ali Pasha. He is silent about the vast appropriation of pious endowments and immiseration of the Muslim clergy decreed by the latter early in the nineteenth century, and one suspects that his high praise of this dynasty's philanthropy is more in the way of encouraging Isma'il than a statement of historical fact as al-Tahtawi knew it.

Clearly, al-Tahtawi is concerned not only to defend welfare as a key aspect of legitimate government but also to use the practice to bestow praise and blame. Thus, the early caliphs, the two medieval Mamluk regimes, and the Ottomans are commended for their attention to the poor, whereas the eighteenth-century slave–soldiers and Bonaparte are condemned for neglecting them. He employs the issue to draw the boundaries of his moral universe as an Ottoman subject and a Muslim under the viceroys of Egypt. He sees the Muhammad 'Ali dynasty of Ottoman vassals in Egypt as restoring traditional state welfare measures for the poor (or perhaps he is arguing that they should do so). The precise contours of the actual khedivial management of the poor have been detailed for us by Mine Ener, but here I am concerned not with what was but with what al-Tahtawi thought should be.[6]

He does not, however, put the entire onus for philanthropic activities on the state. He says:

> Among the things that are necessary is that the ruler be helped to multiply charitable institutions by the heads of associations of the wealthy and affluent, so that righteousness and piety might be increased. Thus, there should be more hospitals endowed for the sick and chronically ill who cannot be treated in their homes, and more hospitals should be set up and endowed for children who are picked up off the streets, for orphans, for the elderly who are advanced in age, for the blind, for idiots, for the insane, and for the handicapped who are disabled. Such charitable institutions [should include] interest-free loan companies, which concentrate on buying and selling on interest-free credit. They facilitate give and take, extirpate usury and bring relief to the distressed victims of highly usurious loans, as well as succoring impoverished and bankrupt merchants idled because of the occurrence of acts of fate that produce commercial stagnation and poor [market] conditions. All in all, the endowment of convents, schools, hospices, and such companies as are permitted by Islamic law, as well as everything else wherein public good lies, consists of philanthropic projects that the state or any one individual is unable to undertake alone. The hand of God is with the group, and the establishment of these philanthropies for the public good requires

that an association of the wealthy endow them, and make charitable donations which are inalienable and subject to exploitation in perpetuity. These are lasting charities. In respect to cooperative companies their profits will be shared, as will the thanks accruing from them. Associations for joint philanthropy are few in our country, in contrast to individual charitable donations and family endowments, which are usually endowed by a single individual. (1:281–282)

Al-Tahtawi goes on to mention and praise a number of endowments set up by the Ottoman-Egyptian elite, such as Ratib Pasha's endowment of a Hanafi dormitory at al-Azhar seminary, or Khalil Agha's school for orphans at al-Husayn square. (For the Ottoman tradition of making endowments for the poor, see chapter 7 and chapter 15 in this volume.) Still, these were the generous acts of individuals, and al-Tahtawi wished to promote new group philanthropies as an aspect of civil society; that is, he fully supports state welfare for the deserving poor and appreciates the endowments and donations of wealthy individuals. But he is convinced that neither of these is sufficient and that there are both civilizational and religious benefits to be gained from the formation of philanthropic *societies* that would work as a group to promote education (including of girls) and to ameliorate the lives of the disabled. Timothy Mitchell has noted that al-Tahtawi was among the first to speak in Arabic of organized associations, introducing the concept to his readers.[7]

The Working Poor

The very forces (private property in land and population growth) that resolve the initial problem of the indolent poor, such as (in al-Tahtawi's formulation) the nomadic Dinka in the Sudan, can create new crises if they are allowed to become unbalanced. The sources of potential imbalance are primarily, in al-Tahtawi's view, a societal disregard for the value of landed labor and the greed of the large landowners.

Much of his argument has to do with raising the status of those who he feels are the principal agents of prosperity, the practitioners of the modern arts and industries. In discussing the material aspect of civilization, al-Tahtawi writes:

The second [root of civilization] is material civilization, which is advancement in the social benefits, such as agriculture, commerce, and industry. Various countries are stronger or weaker therein, and it hinges upon the practice of labor and handicrafts. It is necessary for the progress of societal prosperity *('umran)*. But even though it is necessary, the specialists in ethics and manners fear the onslaught of the advancement of the practitioners of the arts and crafts, and dread the exaltation of the rank of the latter through the power of their earnings from the benefits. The philosophers and specialists in precious philosophical sciences believe that the crafts are among the mean professions and affairs. (1:251)

Here al-Tahtawi identifies two groups as being disdainful of labor and technology. The specialists in morals are undoubtedly the religious 'ulama' or clergy. But al-Tahtawi seems to be saying that even the group of Egyptians (the specialists in philosophical sciences) that has had training in the new Western sciences has little respect for the practical application of technology. This attitude was common. In medieval Islam, ethicists such as al-Mawardi (who otherwise deeply influenced al-Tahtawi's thinking) valued most highly those crafts that had the highest degree of input from reason. He called unskilled manual laborers the worst people in the society.[8] Al-Tahtawi here wishes to criticize the emphasis on the theoretical at the expense of the practical and empirical that had prevailed in his intellectual tradition.

If al-Tahtawi's positive attitude toward the material and toward activities such as farming, commerce, and crafts has some echoes in al-Mawardi and other medieval Muslim ethicists, it is nevertheless true that he has much more respect for manual labor and handicrafts than they do. The reformer's own poverty in his youth might have given him an ability to identify with the lower classes, and this might partially explain his positive attitude toward them. His thinking on the status of workers had both Islamic and European roots. One of these influences was the Sufi mystic Sayyidi 'Ali al-Khawass, a teacher of the influential Egyptian mystic 'Abd al-Wahhab al-Sha'rani (1491–1565).

Al-Tahtawi makes one extended reference to al-Khawass in the *Paths for Egyptian Hearts*, arguing that the 'ulama' should work for their living rather than subsisting on the charitable donations of the people (1:286). Al-Sha'rani recorded some of his conversations with al-Khawass, who was illiterate and left no writings. The spirit of respect for work and for the common people that led al-Khawass to make the statement, which al-Tahtawi then quoted, permeated all of his conversations with his disciple. Al-Khawass described the common people as humble, self-effacing, beloved of God, and deserving of the highest paradise. When al-Sha'rani interrogated his master as to the station of those spiritually intoxicated by their nearness to God, he replied, "Rather, I say that the common people and the practitioners of professions and crafts are of greater benefit than the spiritually intoxicated, insofar as they undertake means of livelihood that are beneficial to others, and because they fear God."[9] When asked if it is better for a Sufi to make his own living or not, al-Khawass replied that whoever does no labor should receive no wage. Labor and earning, he remarked, are praised by all the world and result in praiseworthy wealth. Al-Khawass warned that a Sufi should not visit someone if he thought his visit would keep the other from God, or from the practice of his profession *(hirfah)* that God has ordered him to perform. Moreover, al-Khawass attacked withdrawal from the world as selfish and asserted that those who live in the world and endure life's trials are more perfect because they are of greater benefit to the people.[10] There were, then, intellectual currents in al-Tahtawi's Egyptian milieu that put emphasis on the nobility and benefits of the crafts and of the kinds of manual labor performed by the common people. These currents would have been reinforced and would have taken on a special meaning from the time of Muhammad 'Ali, which witnessed social changes based on that practical industry and manual labor so despised by certain Muslim intellectuals.

Al-Tahtawi's emphasis on labor and technology is not merely a sentiment, rather, it is a conviction growing out of his theories of political economy. This conviction stems directly from a labor definition of value. The passage in which he defines his stance on this issue is worth quoting in full:

> Matters concerned with the means of living obviously have two aspects, an aspect of agency and an aspect of patiency—that is, of being a substrate. The first is the [various] tasks and the second is agricultural land. There is a difference [of opinion] over whether the source of riches and fortune, and the basis of wealth and nourishment is the earth, labor being merely an instrument and an intermediary, which has no value save for its application to husbandry; or whether labor is the basis of wealth and prosperity and the source of acquired riches, as well as the first principle for the people and the community. [The second position would] mean that people acquire their prosperity through the extraction of that which they need for their benefit or a comfortable way of life from the earth, the merit belonging to labor and the merit of the land being secondary and subsidiary. This is what people involved in husbandry assert, and they infer it from the fact that it is not possible to make land fertile save by perpetual labor and continuous work. Otherwise, it would remain barren, being severed from labor. Labor, then, gives value to all things that do not give themselves value without it. (1: 310)

Here, labor is seen to be more important because it is an agent, whereas the earth is only the patient. The use of this Aristotelian vocabulary suggests that al-Tahtawi is here drawing not just on modern European political economy but also on ideas already present in Greco-Islamic thought on economics. The earth is a substrate or locus wherein the activity of labor inheres. Al-Tahtawi does not restrict his theory of value to a statement that all value proceeds from labor; he also allows the input of capital in the form of fertile land and in the form of technology. But labor and technology are the most important factors (technology, again, being produced by labor), and fertile land is secondary. Thus, while no amount of labor and technology can make totally barren ground give forth a harvest, the difference between Europe and Africa, which contain many lands of equal fertility, is due, according to al-Tahtawi, to Europe's superior employment of labor and technology (1:311–313). His labor theory of value was probably rooted equally in his reading of Muslim thinkers such as Ibn Khaldun (the latter's *Prolegomenon* was published at the Bulaq Press in 1857) and in Europeans such as Ricardo and his school, as well as the Saint-Simonians. Although the Ricardian labor theory of value as an ideology bestowed no benefits on workers, that of the early-nineteenth-century French thinker Henri de Saint-Simon did, insofar as

Saint-Simonianism evolved into a form of utopian socialism. It is the latter that appears most influential for al-Tahtawi.

Saint-Simon divided society into producers, workers, and consumers. He asserted that the productive class was the only useful one, and that it would eventually become the only one. This category included cultivators, tradesmen and artisans, manufacturers, entrepreneurs, scientists in the positive sciences, artists, lawyers, industrial workers, and those priests who encourage people to work. The consumer class was made up of nobles, landowners, clergymen, judges, and the military. The goal of society, Saint-Simon argued, was to produce useful things, and therefore it is more important to respect the producers than the proprietors.[11] Saint-Simon's successor, Prosper Enfantin, led a group of Saint-Simonians to Egypt in 1833 with the goal of accomplishing the digging of the Suez Canal to hasten the development of world unity. By 1834, Ferdinand de Lesseps had arranged for Enfantin and his chief lieutenant to meet with Muhammad 'Ali and discuss the canal project with him. The pasha proved uninterested in pursuing the canal project but was pleased to have a group of idealistic European engineers and technicians in his realm. He gave them employment as teachers and as engineers on a barrage project. The outbreak of plague decimated their ranks, however, and Enfantin left for France in 1836. A few stayed on, and it seems certain from a number of passages in *Paths for Egyptian Minds* that al-Tahtawi was deeply influenced by Saint-Simonian ideas.[12]

Al-Tahtawi accepts Saint-Simon's division of society into productive and unproductive classes. He says that "in the technical language of industry," provincial governors, military officers, and troops "are not termed wealth-producing in themselves." He is careful to underline that he thinks these groups are essential to society but insists that their labor "does not produce a profit" and that they are "on the side of expenses rather than that of profits." Other such occupations include "judicial and religious posts," including endowment supervisors. "None of these jobs has a financial value or produces earnings or profits like the sort of work that does produce these things, since they do not make anything that can be sold and from which the labor expenses of the succeeding year can be obtained or such as will yield a profit" (1:326–327). He also includes musicians, authors, and entertainers in the unproductive category, though he does admit that their work can result in salable commodities. He accepts the Saint-Simonian argument that only laborers produce wealth, and all other social classes are to some extent dependent on them for prosperity. However, unlike Saint-Simon, al-Tahtawi does not perceive the division between productive and unproductive as a source of class conflict; rather, he had been seduced by Isma'il Pasha's dreams of a great civilization in an Egyptian empire and saw civil administration and the military as key sources of social order without which laborers could not produce wealth. The nobility and the military, which are in Saint-Simon's system the ultimate villains, are in al-Tahtawi's thought the raison d'être of the workers' labors. Despite this somewhat organicist approach to the social order, al-Tahtawi, nevertheless, does remain a supporter of better wages and working conditions for the peasants, and even appears to support a fifty–fifty split of profits between them and the great landlords, which would have been a social revolution of immense proportions in khedivial Egypt.

Al-Tahtawi's labor theory of value thus has important consequences for his conception of social justice. It leads him to champion the rights of the laborers and craftsmen. His defense of these classes is spirited and gives a great deal of insight into his way of thinking. His theory of political economy leads him to a key contradiction, which is the existence of large numbers of working poor, especially peasants. Population growth and the private ownership of land have driven the population to intensive agricultural labor, in contrast to pastoralist societies such as the Sudan (in al-Tahtawi's characterization). This labor infuses farm land with value in the form of crops. Yet ownership of the land gives landlords likewise ownership of the agricultural profits, such that laborers are essentially robbed of the surplus value that they instill into the land by their labor. He complains,

> The ones who pick the fruits of these agricultural improvements and reap the benefits of this betterment of farming—which is for the most part produced by labor and the use of tools—and monopolize the profitable yields are the owners alone. They, and not those who practice the profession of agriculture, enjoy the greatest advantages. The land and farm owners are the ones who seize the general proceeds, and who obtain their benefits, until everyone else hardly receives anything from these yields. (1:316)

He insists that the wages these owners pay their peasants are an "insignificant sum," which "does not requite the labor." As with Karl Marx, al-Tahtawi's labor theory of value drove him to believe that workers have an absolute right to the profits generated by their addition of value to commodities. A mere small wage is insufficient compensation. Unlike Marx, of course, al-Tahtawi did not mean to expropriate the landlords, only to adjust the ratio of shared profits between owner and worker.

Moreover, al-Tahtawi holds, peasants not only perform labor but frequently one among them has "improved agriculture through his work, and invented productive techniques for it, making great discoveries in causing agriculture to thrive and creating more work." He does not see technological improvement as the sole province of the engineers and technocrats but, rather, is willing to admit that workers themselves often hit on important improvements to tools. Nevertheless, he complains, they are not compensated for such advances because "the right of ownership and possession of the farms has permitted the owners to conduct the affairs of their property with complete freedom, and to give the workers whatever they think is appropriate for them." The owners, in this telling, decidedly did not have a labor theory of value; rather, they saw their farmhands as deserving of nothing more than a modest recompense for service rendered.

The existence of the working poor is, then, explained in part by a distortion, by a disjuncture between the realities of wealth creation by workers and the way in which the Egyptian elites devalued their contribution and were supported in doing so by land tenure laws and by social custom. The very population growth that drove peasants to greater agricultural productivity, moreover, can increase to the point at which it also devalues their labor by the law of supply and demand. A very great many more laborers means that the supply of labor can exceed demand for it. Al-Tahtawi laments,

> Everyone who wants to make his living from employment, which is labor, is compelled to work for whatever amount it is possible to get from the owners, depending upon the latter's pleasure, even though this amount be extremely small and incommensurate with the labor. This is particularly so in areas where there are a great many workers who then accept diminished wages and compete with one another in this to the benefit of the landowners.

This creation of a class of working poor occurs, he says, despite the fact that agricultural yields are only improved by the very labor of the workers who are now being paid less. Nor is it only the peasants who suffer in this way. Al-Tahtawi complains that the great landlords likewise do not reimburse sufficiently the iron smiths, carpenters, and other craftsmen who supply the needs of the farmworkers for tools and other goods.

In the political economy of Isma'il's Egypt, then, the only way the farmer could be freed from the manacles of working poverty is if the fates "aid someone to become the possessor of a plot of land." Otherwise, he is at the mercy of the landlord, who might be generous, but could be miserly. Al-Tahtawi knows that the sanctity of private property and the privilege of the landlords have much support in Egyptian customary law and also in Islamic law, and he takes care to argue against conservative interpretations of the *shariah* (sacred law). He recognizes the force of the customary saying, "He who sows shall reap," and a similar saying attributed to the Prophet Muhammad. These maxims had been interpreted to mean that the profits belonged to the owner of the land. Al-Tahtawi objects that, rather, "the meaning here is that the seed and its fruit belong to whoever sows it, though he has to pay a rent for the land"; that is, the actual sower was meant and not the metaphorical one (the owner). He told the story of how Muhammad treated, with his then vassals, the people of Khaybar by taking half their fruit and crops and leaving them the other half, implying that according to this *hadith* (tradition) fully 50 percent of the profits should go to the workers. He also argues that there were two arrangements under which landless peasants labored on landlords' estates, sharecropping *(al-musaqat)* and contracting *(al-mukhabara, al-musharata)*. In sharecropping, the landowner provides the seed, whereas in contracting, the peasant does. He says that contracting was not considered permissible in classical

Islamic jurisprudence, but that it had become more prevalent in the Egypt of the 1860s than the more Islamically licit sharecropping.[13] That is, in a majority of cases peasants were supplying the seed. But quite apart from this point, he insists, the saying of the Prophet about the crop belonging to the sower "does not at all indicate that the owner is allowed to usurp the yields without compensating the worker." He continues, quite vehemently:

> Nor can swindling the hired laborer be supported by the fact that the owner has paid his capital for the costs of farming and taken upon himself its expenses, and thus is the one who most deserves to usurp the enormous yields, and most deserves to profit from his vast wealth, since he is the basis of profit-making whereas the activity of the farmworkers is only secondary and is produced and improved by capital [investment]. Such analyses are pure fallacies, however, since [our] discussion of the worker has already determined that he is the cause of productive labor, without whom the land would not have yielded these great profits. For the landowner to shortchange the worker by decreasing his wages is pure injustice against him. His owning the land and making expenditures from his capital upon agriculture does not necessitate that he grab up the major portion of the yield and injure the wage laborer, in view of the numerousness of farmworkers, their [willingness to take] diminished wages, and their mutual haggling in bidding for reductions. This does not produce love for the owner on the part of the hired labor; and "Grapes are not reaped of thistles." In this lies mutual harm, which is revelationally forbidden. (1:317)

He then quoted a saying of the Prophet via Abu Hurayra that one Muslim ought not to profit at the expense of another since they were all siblings. Al-Tahtawi's obvious sympathy with the peasants and concern for social justice had many roots, but one suspects that the *gemeinschaftlich*, the organic relationship of owners and peasants in the Tahta of his youth, remained a model for him even in the 1860s, a period of large-scale agricultural capitalism under the Cotton Boom and the rise of extensive profit-oriented haciendas tied to the world market. Even though he himself held extensive lands and was part of the bureaucratic elite, he was clearly pained at the plight of the peasants under the new regime (and it may well be that these passages were written during the famine of 1866 when overconcentration on cash crops and the cattle murrain had combined to produce extensive peasant hunger).

Conclusion

Al-Tahtawi approaches the problem of poverty in different ways depending on whether he sees its roots as natural indolence, disabilities, or the usurpation from workers by owners of a fair proportion of the increased value with which their labor endows commodities, including agricultural crops. He begins with the premise that indolence is a natural inclination among all human beings, from which those in tropical climes with sparse populations are likely to suffer even more severely because of the ease with which they can feed themselves without steady labor or private property. He is convinced, however, that a Malthusian dynamic upsets this primitive state over time, as the drive to procreate multiplies the population and creates competition for scarce resources, resulting in the enclosure of land, the rise of private property, and the need to labor to secure a livelihood. Thus, natural indolence is overcome eventually by natural increase.

He firmly believes that the state has both an Islamic and a civil duty to care for those impoverished by disabilities, such as the blind, the lame, widows, and so on. He includes among the deserving poor seminary students. He locates this obligation to a welfare state for these classes of the poor centrally in Islamic sacred history, instancing early Muslim Egypt under the Caliph 'Umar, as well as subsequent Muslim rulers. In his telling, pious sultans insisted repeatedly on such welfare measures in the face of objections by pragmatic or greedy courtiers, and the sultans were reinforced or sometimes convinced by the Muslim 'ulama', carriers of the community's ethical norms. Only the late-eighteenth-century slave–soldiers and the French, he argues, departed from this practice. He thus ranges 'Umar, the Ayyubids, the Mamluks, the Ottomans, and the Muhammadi dynasty of Ottoman vassals in Egypt on the side of Islamic piety and beneficence, against the one great modern rupture in such ethical norms, the internecine eighteenth-century slave–soldier battles and the Bonaparte invasion. In addition to focusing on government welfare programs, however, he also urges the founding of collective philanthropic organizations that would go far beyond the individual acts of generosity exhibited by some Ottoman-Egyptian nobles when they established endowments for the poor. "The hand of God," he quoted the proverb, "is with the group." He explicitly modeled these philanthropic organizations on ones he had seen in France, and they clearly formed part of his vision for what we would now call a civil society in Egypt. Thus, it is not only the state that has a responsibility toward the poor, nor only wealthy individuals, but rather the collectivity of the well-off have a duty to band together to ameliorate the condition of the indigent.

Al-Tahtawi's labor theory of value and his appreciation for Malthusian demographic forces led him to sympathize with the underpaid peasants and craftsmen during the Cotton Boom, who, he insisted, were being exploited by the great landlords. Because their sheer numbers had led to a buyer's market in labor and because of landlords' lack of Islamic solidarity and misunderstanding of oral reports from the Prophet Muhammad, the workers were left in penury despite the great wealth their labor was creating as Egypt moved toward agricultural capitalism. He even went so far as to suggest that workers deserved fully half of profits generated. Although he formulated his ideas on this subject eclectically, referencing the medieval Sufi master 'Ali al-Khawass, as well as drawing arguments from utopian socialist political economy in France, one cannot escape the impression that the real impetus for this stance came from al-Tahtawi's own private moral universe, in which the Muslims as an organic community had a duty to share with one another and to avoid the loss of any brethren. Because he was himself a great landlord, it would be interesting to know if he remunerated his peasants differently than did most of his peers in the Ottoman-Egyptian elite. Yet for someone with his social status to make these arguments at all is remarkable in Isma'il's Egypt: a time of greed and rapacity that would end in state bankruptcy and, ultimately, revolution.

Notes

1. Rifa'ah Rafi' al-Tahtawi, *al-A'mal al-kamila*, ed. Muhammad al-'Imarah, 5 vols. (Beirut: Arab Foundation for Study and Publications, 1973–1981). Volume 1 is *Manahij al-albab al-misriyyah fi mabahij al-adab al-'asriyyah*, 1973. The bibliography on al-Tahtawi is vast but see, in English, the relevant pages in Albert Hourani, *Arabic Thought in the Liberal Age* (Oxford: Oxford University Press, 1962); Ibrahim Abu Lughod, *The Arab Rediscovery of Europe* (Princeton: Princeton University Press, 1963); Khaldun S. Husry, *Three Reformers* (Beirut: Khayats, 1966); Peter Gran, *Islamic Roots of Capitalism: Egypt, 1760–1840* (Austin: University of Texas Press, 1979); Juan Cole, "Rifa'a al-Tahtawi and the Revival of Practical Philosophy," *The Muslim World* 70 (1980): 29–46; John W. Livingston, "Western Science and Educational Reform in the Thought of Shaykh Rifaa al-Tahtawi," *International Journal of Middle East Studies* 28 (1996): 543–564; Mohammed Sawaie, "Rifa'a Rafi' al-Tahtawi and His Contribution to the Lexical Development of Modern Literary Arabic," *International Journal of Middle East Studies* 32 (2000): 395–410.

2. See Roger Owen, *Cotton and the Egyptian Economy, 1820–1914* (Oxford: Clarendon Press, 1969).

3. For the social history of this period see Juan R. I. Cole, *Colonialism and Revolution in the Middle East: Social and Cultural Origins of Egypt's 'Urabi Movement* (Princeton: Princeton University Press, 1993); Gabriel Baer, *Studies in the Social History of Modern Egypt* (Chicago: Chicago University Press, 1969).

4. Abu al-Hasan Ibn Taghri Birdi, *History of Egypt 1382–1469 A.D., Part I, 1382–1399 A.D.*, trans. William Popper (Berkeley: University of California Press, 1954), 1–45, 112–177.

5. Majid Khadduri, "Maslaha," *EI²*, 6:738–740.

6. Mine An Ener, "Managing the Poor in Nineteenth- and Early Twentieth-Century Egypt" (Ph.D. diss., University of Michigan, 1996). See also chapter 9 in this book.

7. Timothy Mitchell, *Colonising Egypt* (Berkeley: University of California Press, 1991), 119–120.

8. 'Ali b. al-Hasan al-Mawardi, *Adab ad-dunya wal-din*, ed. Mustafa al-Saqqa' (Cairo: Mustafa al-Babi al-Halabi and Sons, 1973), 209–212.

9. 'Abd al-Wahhab al-Sha'rani, *Durar al-ghawass 'ala fatawa Sayyid 'Ali al-Khawass,* printed on the margins of Ahmad al-Sijilmasi, *Kitab al-ibriz* (Cairo: n.p., 1927), 9. For al-Sha'rani see Michael Winter, *Society and Religion in Early Ottoman Egypt: Studies in the Writings of 'Abd al-Wahhab al-Sharani* (New Brunswick, N.J.: Transaction Books, 1982).

10. Al-Sha'rani, *Durar al-ghawass,* 31, 55, 57.

11 Henri de Saint-Simon, *Oeuvres,* 6 vols. (Paris: Editions Anthropos, 1966), 2:74, 186, 200–205.

12. For the Saint-Simonians in Egypt, see Tal'at 'Isa, *San Simun* (Cairo: Dar al-Ma'arif, 1959), 101ff.; Sami A. Hanna, "The Saint-Simonians and their Application of State Socialism in Egypt," in *Medieval and Middle Eastern Studies in Honor of A. S. Atiya,* ed. S. A. Hanna (Leiden: E. J. Brill, 1972); Magali Morsy, ed., *Les Saint-Simoniens et l'Orient: vers la modernité* (Aix-en-Provence: Edisud, 1989).

13. For the history of land tenure in nineteenth-century Egypt, see Kenneth M. Cuno, *The Pasha's Peasants* (Cambridge: Cambridge University Press, 1992).

Chapter Twelve

Islam, Philanthropy, and Political Culture in Interwar Egypt

The Activism of Labiba Ahmad

Beth Baron

Scholarship on women and philanthropy has generated heated debates. Recent works have focused on how philanthropy has empowered women and transformed political culture. Through the gift of time, one argument goes, women volunteers subsidized local and national governments, providing much-needed services to disadvantaged groups, particularly women, children, and the poor. Their associations worked to foster civil society, to strengthen the foundations of democratic institutions, and to lay the groundwork for welfare programs and states. At the same time, there have been critiques of the asymmetry of power between giver and recipient and efforts to explore the political, cultural, and social agendas of providers to see what they gained by giving.[1]

Forms of female giving in Egypt shifted in the late nineteenth century from private initiatives to collective enterprises. The emergence of benevolent associations, in Egypt as elsewhere, was intimately connected to the rise of nationalism and the spread of capitalism. Elite Egyptians sought to fill the gap left by a state under British occupation that offered inadequate health, education, vocational training, and other services to the poor and to counter the activities of missionaries, diplomatic wives, and other foreign providers, whose services came at a cultural price. Elites also competed with one another, and laymen and laywomen with religious hierarchies, for leadership.

Within these associations, in the new women's press, and elsewhere, literate Egyptians debated the contours of Egyptian society and culture. They argued that the upper classes needed to "save" impoverished and ignorant groups—the poor and women—so they could become more productive members of the nation. Elite Egyptian women saw their charitable work as a contribution to the national cause and used nationalism as a legitimation for their expanding roles. They came to play a prominent role in founding and administering philanthropic associations, especially as they were squeezed out of party and parliamentary politics in the interwar years. During this time, little progress was made in social and economic reform, and minimal welfare legislation existed. Meanwhile, urbanization and industrialization increased the ranks of the poor. Poverty was gendered: The bulk of the poor were women and children with few resources. Women's charitable associations generally targeted women and girls.[2]

This chapter focuses on the life and work of one interwar philanthropist, Labiba Ahmad (1870s–1951), whose volunteerism came in tandem with her Islamic politics. Building on projects already underway, as discussed in this volume by Mine Ener (chapter 9) and Juan Cole (chapter 11), Labiba Ahmad founded the Society of Egyptian Ladies' Awakening (Jam'iyyat Nahdat al-Sayyidat al-Misriyyat) a year or so after the 1919 Egyptian Revolution. Her group aimed to provide welfare services to the poor and to propagate a blend of Islamic nationalism.[3] Shortly after founding the association, she started the Arabic monthly *al-Nahda al-Nisa'iyya* (Women's Awakening) to disseminate the views of the society. Looking at her life gives us insight into the religious motivations and expectations of a "living *waqf*-maker." Yet those who founded associations differed from those who founded *waqf*s (endowments) in their direct involvement and their attempt to generate more profound social change than simply feeding or clothing the poor would have done. These associations were precursors to later development agencies.

Labiba Ahmad argued that the path to women's and national progress was through a return to Islam, not through copying Western ways. In this, she presents a distinct contrast to secular feminists in Egypt, who came from similar elite backgrounds but were oriented toward Europe. Labiba had a wide following among professional classes and struck a deep chord among those Egyptians yearning for the re-Islamicization of society. These Islamic, or proto-Islamist, currents have been ignored in the conventional historiography of Egypt. Yet Islamic nationalism did not suddenly appear from nowhere in the 1930s. It was part of Egyptian political culture from the late nineteenth century and was strengthened by activists such as Labiba Ahmad.

A Pioneer's Philanthropic Work

Labiba Ahmad was born in Cairo in the 1870s. Her father, Ahmad 'Abd al-Nabi Bey, was a physician, and her two brothers followed in his footsteps. Her son and a daughter later chose the medical profession as well.[4] Labiba had an excellent command of Arabic and a good knowledge of Islamic subjects; she also learned to play the piano.[5] Her husband, 'Uthman Pasha Murtada (d. 1935), rose through the judiciary to the post of judge in the Mixed Court of Appeals in Alexandria and for a short time became master of ceremonies for Khedive 'Abbas Hilmi II (r. 1892–1914), to whom he was closely tied.[6]

In the period before the First World War, Labiba had participated in women's associations, given speeches, and written in newspapers and journals.[7] A strong nationalist, she supported Mustafa Kamil's Watani (Nationalist) Party, founded in 1907 to work for the liberation of Egypt from de facto British control.[8] In 1919 she marched in the "ladies' demonstrations" and affixed her signature to the petitions submitted to foreign legations protesting British actions.[9] In the next few years, she worked to mobilize women and girls from working-class neighborhoods against the British occupation.[10] She presided over memorial services for Mustafa Kamil and spoke at the funeral of his brother 'Ali Fahmi Kamil, also a Watani leader. At the same time, she had close ties to Safiyya Zaghlul (Mother of the Egyptians) and Sa'd Zaghlul, head of the Wafd (Delegation) founded in 1918 to negotiate with the British for Egypt's independence.[11]

Labiba consciously chose not to join other female notables who, after the 1919 Revolution, formed the Women's Wafd Central Committee, an auxiliary of the Wafd Party.[12] Instead, she committed herself to philanthropy and education through the Society of Egyptian Ladies' Awakening. Organizations with similar names had been established in previous decades, and members had often spoken of their work as a contribution to the national cause. After the war, the two best-known philanthropies run by women—Mabarrat Muhammad 'Ali (Muhammad 'Ali Charity) and Jam'iyyat al-Mar'a al-Jadida (New Woman's Society)—focused on health care and training for the poor.[13] Societies were a way to disseminate founders' ideologies and win adherents to their political positions while reinforcing their social positions and the social hierarchy.

Labiba Ahmad framed her motivation for benevolent acts in both religious and nationalist terms. She wrote that in founding her society she had been "inspired by God" and motivated by the "desire to help the nation." Her philanthropic work and Islamic nationalist impulse were clearly linked. The goal of the society was "to raise girls and to teach them the commandments of their religion." She had a broad mission of inculcating young girls with Islamic values and a specific project for the society: She gathered together 170 girls who had been orphaned or abandoned by their parents and vowed to raise, protect, and provide for them.[14] When parents (or fathers) of orphans were unknown, they were presumed to be the offspring of illegitimate encounters and thus carried the stigma of the crime. Labiba not only wanted to "save" the girls but to shape them, inculcating Islamic values, nationalist ideals, and proper notions of social and gender relations, thereby enhancing her own prestige. Similar programs targeted orphan girls in Turkey during this period.[15]

Labiba presided over the society; other officers included a deputy, a secretary, and a secretary's assistant. Little is known about the officers or about the composition or size of the group or about the girls.[16] Labiba headed delegations that visited schools, hosted graduation celebrations, and called on ministers. She was the driving force: administering the society's affairs, raising funds, and taking responsibility for the girls in her care. Just as young girls in foster care provided domestic service in eighteenth-century Salonika, as Eyal Ginio discusses in this volume (chapter 8), these orphans were called on to march in nationalist demonstrations and to labor in the society's workshop. "The [Society of] Egyptian Ladies' Awakening saw that uplifting nations is by uplifting the mothers in it," Labiba wrote when announcing the founding of a workshop in July 1921 in which poor girls would be taught sewing and other skills so that they might later support themselves. This sort of vocational training was common elsewhere in the region.[17] Ahmad emphasized that the large workshop was in a healthy, well-lit, and airy space. The doors were opened to other girls to come to learn household management, embroidery, and handiwork, and the society set a sliding fee scale.[18] Labiba appealed for donations of clothes and money for the girls she had promised to raise, twenty of whom were shown in a photograph appearing in the journal. The office of the workshop stood ready, she wrote, to accept volunteers willing to render "holy national service" by lecturing on morality and teaching the principles of housekeeping and handiwork. Support came in different forms: Physicians (among them Labiba's son) examined poor women and children connected to the society free of charge, continuing a charitable practice of providing health care to the needy; and an administrator at a nearby girls' school offered to waive tuition for orphans from the society.[19]

In 1923 in the wake of a scandal in which authorities discovered a ring of Egyptians who apparently "debauched" young native girls—kidnapping, raping, and locking them in brothels in Cairo—Labiba resolved to broaden her educational program. "We all felt sorrow in our souls, a wound in our hearts, and pain in our core from that distressing affair," wrote Labiba. "It made an impression on me as it made an impression on many others. I resolved to dedicate what remained of my life in service to Egypt, and to sacrifice every valuable and dear thing for the sake of rescuing the Egyptian girl from the hands of those devils who abuse her." Although some authorities claimed that the girls in question were of age and volunteers, Labiba decided to open a public institute and workshop together to train girls so they could make an "honorable living" and would not be forced into prostitution.[20]

After searching for an appropriate site for the institute, Labiba reported that "God gave us success." The society rented the palace of the late 'Abd al-Qadir Pasha Hilmi in the working-class neighborhood of Sayyida Zaynab and had it outfitted with the necessary equipment. Labiba prepared to receive up to one hundred girls from the age of nine. A picture taken on opening day in late 1923 shows approximately forty-two students gathered around the bench where Labiba, the director of the institute, sits among three other veiled women. The bareheaded girls appear a bit ragged, clustered together so the faces of some do not even show. A photo taken a few months later in the same setting shows the girls arranged in straight rows, dressed in white uniforms, and now wearing white head scarves. (White head scarves would become a symbol of the Islamist movement.) A new sign was painted for the occasion: The Institute and Workshop of the Women's Awakening.[21] The poor were to be prepared to become productive workers for the nation and devout Muslims.

Labiba's actions won the praise of observers. "She does not limit herself to literary activity alone," noted Rose Haddad, a fellow journalist, announcing the opening of the institute, "but she also endeavors to promote social welfare in the country."[22] Labiba thanked the readers of *al-Nahda al-Nisa'iyya* profusely for supporting her effort to educate young girls. Earlier she had made an emotional appeal to "the sons of my country" to support the school in whatever way possible. To raise funds for the workshop, she offered a book for sale—a collection of pieces of wisdom, religious exhortation, and extracts from history as well as practical advice on health, housekeeping, and sport—which school inspectors helped her to distribute. Other students visited her school, a poet wrote a new song for the girls, and owners of businesses gave generously. In addition, the new Wafdist interior minister announced that his ministry would donate the proceeds of a special lottery to the education of the girls of the institute and the workshop.[23]

The Society of Ladies' Awakening not only established its own private education ventures, it also pressed for reforms in state education and sought to make a social difference. Labiba headed a delegation that met with the minister of education to demand that religious education be made compulsory and that fees for girls be equivalent to those for boys. It reiterated its call after the 1924 elections, pressuring the new Wafdist minister to comply. The latter decided to place the new primary school proposed by the governing body of the Institute and Workshop of the Women's Awakening under the supervision of his ministry. Labiba pressed for greater attention to religious education in state schools, emphasizing memorization of the Quran and the teaching of morality.[24] Her social welfare work inspired other Islamist initiatives, which proved to be important vehicles for winning adherents.

Disseminating the Message

Philanthropy not only served purposes of immediate need, but also was a blueprint for society as a whole. The Society of Egyptian Ladies' Awakening operated an orphanage, workshop, and institute on one track: one of philanthropic enterprises dedicated to poor women and children. On a second track, the society sought to encourage Islamic revival in other layers of society. In the fall of 1921, Labiba approached the administrators of Cairo University for permission to hold meetings on their campus. They turned her down, but officials at the American University in Cairo offered her space. A large assembly of women gathered in the main hall for the first session in late November 1921. Readings from religious texts opened the meeting, followed by remarks by the founder–president, piano playing, poetry, and a lecture by Dr. 'Abd al-'Aziz Bey Nizami, author of books on family health.[25] Members of the society planned to convene weekly to hear lectures on scientific and religious topics.

The society continued to meet throughout the interwar years to spread its message about morality. Labiba held that the state should take the lead in curbing vices such as drinking, narcotics, and dancing. When the head of the Cairo City Police issued regulations limiting dancing and preventing dancers from sitting with the crowds in large halls, the group sent him a letter of commendation.[26] The society issued a call for members in the mid-1930s with a promise of new guidelines "propagating moral virtue." As they prepared for "a war against innovation, immorality, and corruption," they asked other women to embark with them in this bold step "in service of religion and humanity."[27]

The society won accolades from observers, even those who condemned other women's groups in Egypt for pursuing Egyptian women's interests abroad rather than at home, which was a lightly veiled attack on Huda Sha'rawi and her Egyptian Feminist Union (EFU).[28] The EFU was founded some two years after the Society of Egyptian Ladies' Awakening with a secular orientation. Although Labiba, an honorary member of the union, occasionally praised Huda, the goals of her society and that of the EFU clearly diverged.[29] The society's oath emphasized its moral values: "I swear that modesty will be my crown, and virtue my light, and I will live purely: a useful and devout wife, whose hand in childraising is superior. I will fulfill my rightful and correct duty, toward God, the homeland, the family."[30] According to the society, every Egyptian girl and woman had to follow a special code of behavior: (1) to strive for the happiness of her household; (2) to maintain proper modesty in the street; (3) to wear traditional Egyptian dress and to cover her face, hands, and other body parts stipulated by Islamic law; (4) to avoid theaters and comedy houses; and (5) to leave behind corrupt ancient customs.[31]

This cluster of suggestions was hardly new: The Society for Woman's Progress, which had been founded in 1908, and contributors to the conservative press had made similar calls in the first two decades of the century.[32] These calls constituted an integral part of the program of Islamic reformers (Salafis), who sought a return to the ways of the early Muslims. The reformers opposed folk customs that deviated from Islamic injunctions as well as the infiltration of Western practices into Egyptian society. But Labiba Ahmad injected a new element into this battle: She balanced words with actions, organizing and spreading the message to wider circles of Egyptians through the activities of her association and through her journal. Despite the conservative language and the evocation of the past, her message was modern in that it advocated progress based on science and rationalism. It was also modern in terms of the means utilized to convey information.

Labiba published the first issue of *al-Nahda al-Nisa'iyya* in July 1921. A monthly founded to publicize the society's positions, it ran for nearly two decades—the first journal founded by an Egyptian Muslim woman to enjoy such longevity. This record alone presents strong evidence of its positive reception. For the title, Labiba chose the phrase "the Women's Awakening," which had come to stand for the sense of dramatic transformation in Egyptian women's lives.[33] The mottos that appeared on the front page summarized her political philosophy that women's awakening and national revival went hand in hand: "A people will not die so long as both sexes work together energetically toward a goal." And on the top and sides, in smaller type, the sayings, "Awaken your women, your nations will thrive," and "Men make nations; mothers make men." On the cover she placed a photo of Mahmud Mukhtar's award-winning sculpture *Egypt's Awakening*.[34]

No subject received more attention in Labiba's opening essays than the need for reforming education. As higher education for Egyptian women expanded during the interwar years, Labiba argued that women should enter fields such as medicine and teaching rather than law or literature. She valued the role of teachers highly, commending some by name, and called for a women's equivalent of Dar al-'Ulum (a male-teacher-training college). In general, she rallied for more religious education: greater study of the Quran, strengthening Arabic instruction, and boycotting foreign schools. She also appealed for more schools for the poor. Yet she critiqued a curriculum that trained boys and girls identically, preparing them for the same exams, when she saw them destined for different roles in life. "When will the people understand that the duty of a girl is to be a mother?"[35] Women lacked preparation for child raising, their true vocation, and needed greater religious instruction to guide the family. She referred to the "influence of the virtuous in shaping the nation—and what is the nation if not a collection of families?"[36] Labiba was troubled by easy divorce, the preoccupation with money in selecting spouses, and marriage to foreign women. That the domestic roles laid out for women in Labiba's Islamic ideology upheld the ideals of a modern bourgeois family rather than some "traditional" or "authentic" Islamic ideal is further proof of the very modernity of her enterprise.[37]

Labiba's essays also often attacked the presence of "un-Islamic" practices and Western influences in Egypt. She vehemently opposed legalized prostitution, alcoholic consumption, narcotics use, theatergoing, and gambling in Egypt. That the British occupation made it difficult or impossible to eliminate some of these practices only strengthened her nationalist convictions. She also condemned recreational activities such as mixed bathing at the beach and called on "morals police" to enforce separate swimming hours for men and women. In opposition to the building of a sports complex for girls, she asked, "Isn't the woman capable of exercising while she is at home. . . . [I]n prayer and its movements are the greatest exercise."[38]

Labiba opened the pages of the journal to male and female authors, providing an outlet for others to express their views on Islamic revival at a time when few such forums existed. *Al-Nahda al-Nisaʾiyya* enjoyed regular contributions from such figures as Muhammad Farid Wajdi, a prominent Salafi writer whose wife had founded the Society of Woman's Progress and who later edited al-Azhar's journal *Nur al-Islam* (Light of Islam, 1930). ʿAʾisha ʿAbd al-Rahman, who under the penname Bint al-Shatiʾ (Daughter of the Shore) later became famous for her biographies of the early women of Islam and her Quranic exegesis, also contributed.[39] The names of a few of those whose articles were published in Labiba's journal, particularly in its first decade, later appeared in the publications of the Society of the Muslim Brothers.

In a development that virtually guaranteed the financial security of the journal, Labiba received the backing of various Arab governments. The Egyptian and Sudanese Ministries of Education and Awqaf (Endowments) as well as the Egyptian Provincial Councils officially authorized the distribution of *al-Nahda al-Nisaʾiyya* in their schools; the Iraqi Ministry of Education assigned the journal as a text; the Syrian government purchased block subscriptions; and the Saudis subscribed to a "large number" at the instructions of King ʿAbd al-ʿAziz Ibn Saʿud.[40] Additionally, the journal received support from royal and wealthy donors, among them the kings of Egypt, Saudi Arabia, and Iraq.[41] Such support was unprecedented for an Egyptian women's journal and, indeed, rare for any periodical. It showed that Labiba had the backing of powerful personalities and politicians in high places. Yet it also indicated that they did not find her message threatening to the social and gender order they upheld. To the contrary, her influential supporters may have seen this Islamic journal as a good antidote to the secular feminist literature and socialist stirrings of the day. The journal had a circle of loyal readers who sent in letters of support.

Labiba Ahmad's activism took a new form when in the summer of 1933 she took to the airwaves. Once a week she went to the recording studio to deliver a regularly scheduled address on Royal Egyptian Radio. Readers, "who loved her and showered her with their affection and their encouragement," could tune in to listen. Labiba would not at that time have delivered a speech to a live male Egyptian audience, but as she was heard and not seen—a disembodied voice—she could speak on the radio. Radios were new to Egypt and probably existed mostly in the homes of the urban well-to-do and in coffee shops. They became a popular form of entertainment and instruction as they increasingly spread into towns and villages. Labiba's talks resembled her monthly column, treating moral, religious, and social themes.[42] Her access to the airwaves and a national radio audience suggests that the Sidqi government, which had dissolved parliament and abrogated the 1923 Constitution, thought her message might be of service. Labiba thus joined those conservative Muslim forces mobilized by Sidqi and his allies in the palace to counterbalance the secularism of the Wafd and help suppress it. She, on the other hand, may have used the opportunity to her own advantage to advance her own moral and cultural agenda. 'A'isha 'Abd al-Rahman described Labiba during this period: "She barely stops or rests! She is all movement and activity and sanctifies work, dedicating her life to it. She does not understand the meaning of living if it is not for the sake of work. These long years that have passed with sorrow and suffering [a reference to a daughter's death] were unable to harm her love for work or to cause in her any amount of despair or resignation."[43]

Holy Cities and Islamist Circles

Through her social welfare work and writings, Labiba disseminated a brand of Islamic nationalism that countered secular reform movements. But the combination of directing a complex of philanthropic operations and running a journal exhausted Labiba, who fell ill in the fall of 1924. She suspended publication of *al-Nahda al-Nisa'iyya* after the October 1924 issue and did not resume production until March 1926.[44] After her recovery, she resolved to go on *hajj*, making her sixth pilgrimage to Mecca. Two years later, Labiba traveled to the Hijaz on a seventh hajj and thereafter went almost every year. By 1938, she had made sixteen pilgrimages, equaling the number of years she had published her journal.[45] These trips reinforced her Islamic identity and enhanced her international reputation.

A journey incumbent upon Muslims once in their lifetime became an annual ritual for Labiba, who was drawn repeatedly to Arabia, she wrote, in an "attempt to satisfy the spirit."[46] Combining official business with her spiritual quest, her pilgrimages took on a familiar pattern over the years as her supporters vicariously undertook the journey with her. Prior to her departure, she announced her intention to travel and called on others to share the experience. Friends bade her farewell at home or at the train station, and *al-Nahda al-Nisa'iyya* published her photograph in celebration of her journey. She traveled with her daughter Malak or with other family members and friends.[47] After completing her duties in Mecca, she proceeded to Medina to visit the tomb of the Prophet Muhammad and then took the opportunity to enjoy a summer or two in the mountain resort of Ta'if.[48] The Egyptian press reported her successful completion of the hajj upon her return, and Labiba received telegrams and letters congratulating her from numerous friends in Egypt, Syria, the Hijaz, Iraq, and as far away as Singapore. She thanked those who had assisted her during her travels: consuls, doctors, boat captains, engineers, and especially King Ibn Sa'ud, who had consolidated his rule over Arabia in the 1920s and safeguarded the route.[49]

Labiba's pilgrimages gave her an opportunity to expand her circle of contacts. She nurtured ties with the Saudi king, who extended his hospitality to her and gave her journal a generous subvention. She met with *shaykhs* (leaders), government officials, professionals, and other pilgrims in a search for religious knowledge and political information. Others sought her out, giving receptions in her honor. She mingled with Muslims from different countries as she solicited essays and advertisers for her journal. She accomplished this despite the fact that Egypt had no official state relations with Saudi Arabia until 1936, when they concluded a much-celebrated agreement after the signing of the Anglo–Egyptian Treaty.[50]

Labiba's annual hajj enhanced her prestige as Egyptians praised "al-Hajja" in poems and letters. But at the same time, they urged her, as one wrote, to return "to your homeland to shine your light on the Nile Valley, which awaits your guiding hand, and to your children, who await your sympathy and affection."[51] While abroad or after returning, she wrote essays about the trip, sent her new acquaintances copies of the journal, and received letters and essays in return. She had a wide circle of correspondents that spread to India and East Asia.

Labiba also made a visitation to the third sacred city of Islam—Jerusalem—in the fall of 1930 in the company of another *hajja* (pilgrim) and her sons. A camera captured the group at al-Aqsa Mosque. Labiba also met such religious dignitaries as al-Sayyid Muhammad Amin al-Ansari, custodian of the mosques of 'Umar and al-Aqsa and the director of the Khalidiyya Library. After her return, the journal printed a picture on its cover of al-Sayyid Amin al-Husayni, the mufti of Jerusalem and president of the Supreme Muslim Council, who had recently visited Cairo.[52] Throughout the 1930s, and in particular in the midst of the Arab Revolt of 1936, the journal supported the cause of the Arabs of Palestine.

During her travels and at home, Labiba forged personal contacts with the other leading Islamic personalities of the day. Labiba had reached that stage in her life when she could hold discussions with unrelated men. She had particularly close ties to the leadership of the Young Men's Muslim Association, an organization founded in 1927. That Salafi group strove to teach Islamic morality, to disseminate knowledge adapted to modernity, to unify Muslims; and to adopt the best of Eastern and Western cultures.[53] Many members were "alumni" of the Watani Party, to which Labiba was linked. These included Dr. 'Abd al-Hamid Bey Sa'id (first president), Shaykh 'Abd al-'Aziz Shawish (vice president), and the Syrian émigré Muhibb al-Din al-Khatib (secretary–general), whom Labiba called "my son" and who later edited *al-Nahda al-Nisa'iyya* and periodicals of the Muslim Brothers. Labiba reported on speeches given at the club, sometimes to female audiences, and the journal covered a congress on education held in their hall in 1936 that was attended by more than four thousand participants. When Labiba was invited to speak, she picked a male delegate to deliver her address. She also published the communiqué drafted by the assembled Islamic groups calling on the government to institute various reforms.[54]

In the 1930s, Islamic organizations, such as Fatima Amin's Society for Memorizing the Noble Quran, flourished. At the opening of a charity bazaar to raise funds for their school for orphans and the poor, Fatima thanked journalists, especially "al-Hajja Labiba Ahmad," for supporting religious associations.[55] Labiba claimed a direct role in the blossoming of Islamic organizations in the late 1920s and 1930s and saw the rise of these societies—Islamic Guidance, Noble Islamic Characteristics, and Memorizing the Noble Quran, as well as the YMMA—as the "results of our cries on the pages (of *al-Nahda*)."[56]

Labiba forged links with Hasan al-Banna' (1906–1949), the founder of the Society of Muslim Brothers, whose speeches in Cairo in the early 1930s were covered in her journal.[57] Her role in the Muslim Sisters, which was composed mostly of female relatives of the Muslim Brothers, remains unclear. When the first branches were founded in the 1930s, she was probably a woman in her late fifties or early sixties. Her apparent presidency of the Cairo branch may have been an honorary position in acknowledgment of her pioneering work throughout the years, her commitment to the Islamic cause, and her seniority.[58] When the Muslim Sisters became more active in the 1940s, she would have been in her seventies. By then, the keeper of the flame, who had stoked the fire in a period when it had grown faint, had passed the torch to a new generation. This new generation of Islamists, who could have been her children or grandchildren, pushed the movement in a more militant direction. They spoke increasingly not only of an Islamic society but of an Islamic state.

When Labiba returned from the hajj in 1937, she went through her papers and began to prepare her memoirs. "Life is made of memory and hope: memory of the past and hope for the future," she wrote in the introduction. "It was among my greatest hopes to serve my homeland *(watani)*, my community *(ummati)*, and the daughters of my sex by producing the journal *al-Nahda al-Nisa'iyya*, which I founded sixteen years ago and persisted in publishing all this time without interruption, praise God." As a result of working on the journal, she explained, she had corresponded with kings, ministers, politicians, and clerics; and she arranged this correspondence chronologically and by region in her memoirs. The earliest letters had come from King Ibn Sa'ud, and with these she placed other correspondence from the Hijaz. Next followed a letter from Mustafa Kemal Ataturk, Turkey's nationalist hero and first president; notes and telegrams from the staff of the Egyptian royal family; and letters from Sa'd Zaghlul and other Egyptian politicians. Finally, she ended with letters from "the dear ones and people of virtue," religious scholars and thinkers. With her typical modesty, she presented the collection as a testimony of the sympathy of those mentioned for her "small service." She placed and dated the memoirs "Cairo 1356" and identified herself as she had throughout the years, as the founder of the Society for Ladies' Awakening. In this way, she created a testament to more than two decades of activism.[59]

The last issue of *al-Nahda al-Nisa'iyya* appeared in 1939.[60] Two other long-running Arabic women's journals—*al-Mar'a al-Misriyya* and *Fatat al-Sharq*—also folded on the eve of the Second World War, signaling the end of an era in the Egyptian women's press. By then Labiba, who had recently undergone surgery, was ready to retire.[61] In her final years she withdrew into ritual and prayer. Labiba died in 1951 at the age of about eighty. She left behind four children, six grandchildren, and numerous nieces and nephews. The obituary notices in the daily press specified that there would be no public mourning for women or a place for them in the funeral procession, a mixing in public that Labiba would probably have condemned.[62]

Conclusion

Labiba Ahmad started her interwar activism by building an orphanage and workshop for girls in the working-class Cairene quarters. The early photographic documentation of Labiba's philanthropic enterprises shows, as Natalie Davis suggests in her conclusion to this volume, the performance of charity. For elite women like Labiba, charity was a religious and nationalist duty that was fully legitimized. At a time when women lacked the right to vote, her philanthropic endeavors and journalistic activity gave her a political outlet and autonomy. In short, philanthropy clearly empowered Labiba and similarly engaged elite women of her generation, providing a motive for volunteerism. These institutions were part of a larger network of philanthropies founded and run by Islamic-minded and secularly minded women who influenced later Egyptian welfare legislation. The link between women's advocacy for the poor with legal debates over social reform needs further exploration. Collectively these associations strengthened civil society—the cushion between the state and the population—but civil society itself was not sufficiently strong to withstand the aftershocks of the 1952 revolution. In the wake of the revolution, most of the private clinics, workshops, and schools run by female activists were taken over by the state.

The ideology of Labiba Ahmad and her Islamist colleagues had helped to shore up the bourgeoisie. Unlike socialists, who looked for radical solutions to Egypt's poverty and recognized class conflict, interwar Islamists sought social harmony. They respected private property and capitalist relations, and saw charity as one of the main vehicles to combat poverty. Redistribution of wealth was in part a tool with which to ease their own class anxieties. At the same time, in supplying the poor with health care, child care, and other services, Islamists won adherents and broadened their base of support.

Labiba Ahmad used her benevolent institutions to disseminate an Islamic nationalist message. She played a critical role in nurturing the younger generation that made the transformation from Islamic reform (Salafiyya) to Islamic radicalism (Islamism). In helping to invigorate Islamic discourse and inject it into political debates, she contributed to a transformation of Egyptian political culture that out-lasted the revolution. Of course, the irony here is that although her philanthropic and other endeavors may have empowered her, and she supported interpretations of Islam that favored women, she could not control the direction of the Islamist movement. Future Islamists, more doctrinaire than her contemporaries, would push for limiting the power and opportunities of Egyptian women.

Notes

1. See, for example, Kathleen D. McCarthy, "Women and Philanthropy," *Voluntas* 7 (1996): 331–35; idem, ed., *Lady Bountiful Revisited: Women, Philanthropy, and Power* (New Brunswick, N.J.: Rutgers University Press, 1990); Seth Koven and Sonya Michel, eds., *Mothers of a New World: Maternalist Politics and the Origins of Welfare States* (New York: Routledge, 1993); Katherine Kish Sklar, "The Historical Foundations of Women's Power in the Creation of the American Welfare State, 1830–1930," in *Mothers of a New World* (see above); Lori D. Ginzberg, *Women in Antebellum Reform* (Wheeling, Ill: Harlan Davidson, 2000).

2. On the earliest women's charities, see Beth Baron, *The Women's Awakening in Egypt: Culture, Society, and the Press* (New Haven: Yale University Press, 1994), chap. 8; Margot Badran, *Feminists, Islam, and Nation: Gender and the Making of Modern Egypt* (Princeton: Princeton University Press, 1995), chap. 6; Clarissa Lee Pollard, "Nurturing the Nation: The Family Politics of the 1919 Egyptian Revolution" (Ph.D. diss., University of California, Berkeley, 1997); Mine Ener, *Managing Egypt's Poor and the Politics of Benevolence, 1800–1952* (Princeton: Princeton University Press, forthcoming); Hilmi Ahmad Shalabi, *Harakat al-Islah al-Ijtim'iyya fi Misr* (Cairo: n.p., 1988).

3. On Egyptian Islamic nationalism, see Israel Gershoni and James P. Jankowski, *Redefining the Egyptian Nation, 1930–1945* (Cambridge: Cambridge University Press, 1995), 79–96. Labiba Ahmad propagated an Islamic nationalism earlier than many of the nationalists discussed there.

4. Khayr al-Din al-Zirikli, *Al-A'lam: Qamus Tarajim*, 7th ed., 8 vols. (Beirut: Dar al-'Ilm lil-Malayin, 1986), 5:240; *al-Ahram*, 31 January 1951, p. 7.

5. *Al-Nahda al-Nisa'iyya* (hereafter *NN*) 1, no. 6 (January 1922): 159.

6. Maged M. Farag, *1952, The Last Protocol (Royal Albums of Egypt)* (Cairo: Max Group, 1996), 39; Muhammad Farid, *The Memoirs and Diaries of Muhammad Farid, An Egyptian Nationalist Leader (1868–1919)*, trans. Arthur Goldschmidt Jr. (San Francisco: Mellon University Research Press, 1992), 120.

7. *NN* 3, no. 11 (June 1924): 386.

8. For background on the party, see Arthur Goldschmidt Jr. "The Egyptian Nationalist Party: 1892–1919," in *Political and Social Change in Modern Egypt*, ed. P. M. Holt (Oxford: Oxford University Press, 1968), 308–333.

9. U.S. National Archives, State Department (hereafter SD) 883.00/135, Ladies of Egypt to the Diplomatic Agent and Consul-General of the United States, Cairo, 20 March 1919.

10. Ijlal Khalifa, *al-Haraka al-Nisa'iyya al-Haditha* (Cairo, 1974), 60. Khalifa interviewed Labiba Ahmad's daughter Zaynab 'Abduh as well as some Cairene housewives and students from that period.

11. *Al-Lata'if al-Musawwara* (1 March 1920): 5; SD 883.00/431, enclosure: "Cairo's Goodbye to Madame Zaghlul: A Monster Demonstration," Egyptian Mail (9 October 1922); *NN* 2, no. 4 (November 1922): 109; *NN* 4, no. 48 (November 1926): 419.

12. On female notables as political actors, see Beth Baron, "The Politics of Female Notables in Postwar Egypt," in *Borderlines: Genders and Identities in War and Peace, 1870–1930*, ed. Billie Melman (London: Routledge, 1998), 329–350.

13. Baron, *Women's Awakening*, 169–75; see also Margot Badran, *Feminists, Islam, and Nation: Gender and the Making of Modern Egypt* (Princeton: Princeton University Press, 1995), chap. 6; Afaf Lutfi al-Sayyid Marsot, "The Revolutionary Gentlewomen in Egypt," in *Women in the Muslim World*, ed. Lois Beck and Nikki Keddie (Cambridge: Harvard University Press, 1978), 261–276.

14. *NN* 1, no. 1 (July 1921): 3; *NN* 1, no. 12 (July 1922): 378. For background on orphanages, see Andrea B. Rugh, "Orphanages in Egypt: Contradiction or Affirmation in a Family-Oriented Society," in *Children in the Muslim Middle East*, ed. Elizabeth Warnock Fernea (Austin: University of Texas Press, 1995), 124–141.

15. See contribution by Kathryn Libal in this volume (chapter 13).

16. *NN* 1, no. 5 (December 1921): 129.

17. See contribution by Nadir Özbek in this volume (chapter 10).

18. *NN* 1, no. 1 (July 1921): 28.

19. *NN* 1, no. 1 (July 1921): 17; *NN* 1, no. 2 (September 1921): 32, 56; *NN* 1, no. 3 (October 1921): facing p. 68; *NN* 1, no. 5 (December 1921): 129; *NN* 5, no. 50 (February 1927): 67.

20. *NN* 3, no. 6 (January 1924): 209. See also Great Britain, Public Records, Foreign Office 141/466/1415–26, Eastern Department to Chancery, London, 31 January 1924; Hughes to Baker, Cairo, 3 March 1924.

21. *NN* 3, no. 5 (December 1923); *NN* 3, no. 7 (February 1924): 252; *NN* 3, no. 9 (April 1924): 316.

22. *Majallat al-Sayyidat wal-Rijal* 5, no. 1 (15 November 1923): 306.

23. *NN* 3, no. 11 (June 1924): 387; *NN* 3, no. 10 (May 1924): 343; *NN* 3, no. 12 (July 1924): 427; *NN* 3, no. 12 (July 1924): 419.

24. *NN* 3, no. 5 (December 1923): 156; *NN* 3, no. 11 (June 1924): 395; *NN* 4, no. 39 (October 1924): 103; *NN* 2, no. 10 (May 1923): 253–254.

25. *NN* 1, no. 2 (September 1921): 55; *NN* 1, no. 5 (December 1921): 135; *NN* 1, n. 6 (January 1922): 159.

26. *NN* 11, no. 12 (December 1933): 386.

27. *NN* 12, no. 2 (February 1934): back page; no. 4 (April 1934): back page.

28. See, for example, *NN* 4, no. 48 (November 1926): 399–401.

29. Badran, *Feminists*, 96.

30. *NN* 1, no. 1 (July 1921): 3.

31. *NN* 1, no. 2 (September 1921): 35.

32. Baron, *Women's Awakening*, 28–29, 32–34, 176–179.

33. See ibid.

34. See Beth Baron, "Nationalist Iconography: Egypt as a Woman," in *Rethinking Nationalism in the Arab World*, ed. James Jankowski and Israel Gershoni (New York: Columbia University Press, 1997), 105–124.

35. *NN* 12, no. 10 (October 1934): 326.

36. *NN* 1, no. 10 (May 1922): 260.

37. On this paradox, see Lila Abu-Lughod, "The Marriage of Feminism and Islamism in Egypt: Selective Repudiation as a Dynamic of Postcolonial Cultural Politics," in *Remaking Women: Feminism and Modernity in the Middle East*, ed. Lila Abu-Lughod (Princeton: Princeton University Press, 1998), 243–269.

38. *NN* 9, no. 77 (August 1931): 255.

39. *NN* 6, no. 10 (October 1928): 347; *NN* 11, no. 3 (March 1933): 95; Joseph T. Zeidan, *Arab Women Novelists: The Formative Years and Beyond* (Albany: State University of New York Press, 1995), 79–80; Issa J. Boullata, "Modern Qur'an Exegesis: A Study of Bint al-Shati''s Method," *Muslim World* 64 (1974): 103–113.

40. *NN* 2, no. 5 (December 1922): 136; *NN* 3, no. 2 (September 1923): back page; *NN* 8, no. 92 (August 1930): back page; *NN* 11, no. 8–9 (August 1933): 277; *NN* 12, no. 5 (May 1934): back page.

41. *NN* 6, no. 10 (October 1928): 346; *NN* 8, no. 86 (February 1930): 62; *NN* 8, no. 86 (February 1930): 63; *NN* 12, no. 3 (March 1934): 101; *NN* 16, no. 1 (January 1938): 2.

42. *NN* 11, no. 8–9 (August 1933): 310.

43. *NN* 11, no. 3 (March 1933): 95.

44. *NN* 4, no. 40 (March 1926): 136.

45. *NN* 4, no. 43 (June 1926): 227; *NN* 6, no. 6 (June 1928): 202; *NN* 8, no. 89 (May 1930): cover; *NN* 10, no. 85 (April 1932): 127; *NN* 11, no. 3 (March 1933): cover; *NN* 12, no. 2 (February 1934): back page; *NN* 12, no. 5 (May 1934): back page; *NN* 14, no. 3 (March 1936): 86.

46. *NN* 16, no. 2 (February 1938): 65.

47. *NN* 8, no. 89 (May 1930): 146.

48. *NN* 12, no. 5 (May 1934): back page; *NN* 12, no. 7 (July 1934): 237; *NN* 14, no. 5 (May 1936): 175.

49. *NN* 6, no. 5 (May 1928): 176; *NN* 6, no. 8 (August 1928): 278; *NN* 6, no. 9 (September 1928): 315; *NN* 6, no. 10 (October 1928): 357; *NN* 8, no. 88 (April 1930): 142; *NN* 8, no. 91 (July 1930): cover; *NN* 8, no. 92 (August 1930): 283–284; *NN* 10, no. 84 (March 1932): 102; *NN* 10, no. 84 (March 1932): 107; *NN* 10, no. 12 (December 1932): 429; *NN* 14, no. 4 (April 1936): 135.

50. *NN* 4, no. 45 (August 1926): 287–290; *NN* 8, no. 91 (July 1930): 15; *NN* 8, no. 92 (August 1930): 259; *NN* 9, no. 75 (June 1931): 206; *NN* 10, no. 11 (November 1932): 365–367; *NN* 14, no. 12 (December 1936): 397–398.

51. *NN* 8, no. 92 (August 1930): 283–284.

52. *NN* 8, no. 94 (October 1930): 353; *NN* 8, no. 95 (November 1930): cover, 361–362, photo, 372, 386.

53. J. Heyworth-Dunne, *Religious and Political Trends in Modern Egypt* (Washington, D.C.: n.p., 1950), 11.

54. Ibid., 11–14; correspondence from Arthur Goldschmidt Jr., 23 May 1997; *NN* 9, no. 72 (March 1931): 86; *NN* 14, no. 8 (August 1936): 253–255, 262–263, 269–272; *NN* 14, no. 9 (September 1936): 390.

55. *NN* 11, nos. 8, 9 (August 1933): 302; *NN* 14, no. 7 (July 1936): 250; *NN* 16, no. 9 (September 1938): 291.

56. *NN* 10, no. 12 (December 1932): 398.

57. Heyworth-Dunne, *Religious and Political Trends*, 11–14; *NN* 9, no. 72 (March 1931): 86; *NN* 9, no. 74 (May 1931): 148.

58. Amal al-Subki, *al-Haraka al-nisaʾiyya fi Misr, 1919–1952* (Cairo: al-Hayʾah al-Misriyah al-ʿAmmah lil-Kitab, 1986), 118. Al-Subki's notes seem to have been misnumbered. She may have found evidence that Labiba Ahmad headed the Cairo branch in the legal files compiled to try the assassins of Mahmud al-Nuqrashi dated 28 December 1948, which are stored at the High Court (p. 135, n. 36). Ghada Hashem Talhami draws on al-Subki for her account of Labiba Ahmad's activities in her *The Mobilization of Muslim Women in Egypt* (Gainsville: University of Florida Press, 1996), 46–49.

59. *NN* 16, no. 2 (February 1938): 65. The memoirs, which I have not seen, are described as a collection of correspondence rather than an autobiography.

60. I have not seen issues of *NN* from that year. In 1938 the Department of Education instructed school supervisors that it would no longer purchase blocks of subscriptions and that they should subscribe themselves. This hurt the circulation of journals that had been used in schools. (*NN* 16, no. 1 [January 1938]: notice in front of issue).

61. *NN* 16, no. 11 (November 1938): 361–362.

62. Khayr al-Din al-Zirikli, *Al-Aʿlam: Qamus Tarajim*, 7th ed., 8 vols. (Beirut: Dar al-ʿIlm lil-Malayin, 1986), 5:240; al-Ahram (31 January 1951): 7; al-Misri (31 January 1951): 7.

CHAPTER THIRTEEN

"The Child Question"

The Politics of Child Welfare in Early Republican Turkey

KATHRYN LIBAL

The government regards the child as the root of the country, as that which gives the nation its numbers, and as the foundation of the military. The child is in training to be a member of the country's governing body . . . and is the extension of today's power into the future. The child is the consumer of the country's products and the producer of agriculture and merchandise. The child is the greatest asset and resource of the country. The child is the nation itself.

—Dr. Salim Ahmed

Introduction

During the first Turkish republican Children's Week *(Çocuk Haftası)* held in April 1929, Dr. Salim Ahmed extolled the child from the perspective of parents, teachers, and the government.[1] To a mother the child provided an opportunity to realize her potential as a nurturer, as one who provided life to the child. For the father, the child was a product of his power *(kudret)* and required his protection. The teacher extended this role of nurturance and protection; yet his or her most important tasks were to educate, control, discipline, and teach respect to the child—in short, to raise a citizen. To those governing the new republic, the child was regarded as a future citizen, as the very building block upon which military strength and economic productivity and consumption were to be based. In the epigraph, the child was objectified as future producer and consumer, as soldier, and finally, as the nation itself. Ahmed's interpretation of the centrality of "the child" to the state points to a key preoccupation within the context of the early nation–state building efforts of Turkish modernizing elites.

Yet, Dr. Ahmed's invocation of the child as a symbol of national renewal and development reveals only part of the story of childhood and children's welfare during the early Turkish republic. Alongside an emerging discourse that celebrated the role of children in creating a new future for Turkey existed another discourse that focused on the "child question." Preoccupation with child welfare intensified in public discourse in the 1920s, particularly as supporters of the new, secular state began to embark on significant social and political reforms. The child question came to encompass a web of issues related to poverty. Most notable were how best to curb high infant and child mortality rates; improve overall child health; care for large numbers of orphaned, abandoned, or homeless children, many of whom congregated or were sent to Istanbul from other parts of the republic; and prevent begging and the most exploitative forms of child labor. In total, these "child problems" were debated as a part of the child question—a pressing social concern that was raised by the highest political officials and middle- or upper-class urbanites alike. The child question operated as shorthand for naming the obstacles faced by the government and citizens of the new nation–state and as a leverage point for both supporters and opponents of the new republican administration and its approach to nation–state building. In the 1930s, the child question persisted in public discourse: The visibility of poor children troubled professionals even as the issue of child welfare became increasingly politicized.

Debates on the child question were more than simply rhetoric on population and reconstruction. An emerging professional sector sought to ameliorate the conditions of poverty, homelessness, and high rates of illness among children living in urban areas in particular. Although health professionals and educators, for example, were concerned about health, hygiene, and education in rural areas, initial efforts focused on urban areas such as Istanbul. During the early republic, small steps were made to address the "village child's" health and educational concerns, though financial and personnel constraints (in both private and state-supported initiatives and institutions) were barriers to implementing projects in urban centers, let alone more rural areas.[2] By and large this growing cadre of professionals worked for humanistic reasons that were often refracted through a modernist and nationalist lens: In succoring the nation–state's weak children, in saving the lives of even just a few, such professionals and their institutions portrayed themselves as supporting Turkish nation–state building efforts.

Other professional and nonprofessional elites supported alleviating extreme conditions of deprivation and chronic child poverty, yet with a focus on local forms of giving rather than state intervention. This approach was one that promoted neighborhood-based "traditional charity"; it called into question the efforts of more radicalized social reformers who sought systemic institutionalization of child welfare as a part of the formal state bureaucracy. Between these two positions rested the work of semi-voluntary organizations such as the Children's Protection Society (*Himaye-i Etfal Cemiyeti/Çocuk Esirgeme Kurumu*, hereafter referred to as CPS) and the Red Crescent Society (*Türkiye Hilal-i Ahmer Cemiyeti*, hereafter referred to as TRCS). The CPS and TRCS both depended on the local-level giving that those calling for a revival of "traditional charity" drew on and lobbied for more state support of their growing efforts in child protection at a national level. As such, the CPS, TRCS, and other associations carrying out relief work and educational campaigns represented something of a middle-ground position on child welfare in the new republic. Such organizations relied on both the formal sanctioning of the state and benefited from municipal and republican financial credits, taxes, and funds. On the other hand, many of the operating costs were covered by the donations of benevolent individuals (many of them politicians and bureaucrats themselves) and through fund-raising campaigns among the Turkish people.

As I illustrate in this chapter, semi-voluntary, philanthropic organizations increasingly came under fire from both those supporting individual-oriented, privatized forms of giving and those who sought greater levels of state intervention into the daily lives of poor children and their families. I examine unfolding debates on the nature of the so-called child question and how a variety of groups in the early years of the Turkish republic proposed to best resolve the issue. Such a focus on struggles to define and attempts to systematically address child welfare offers a deeper understanding of contestation and control among elites, while it simultaneously extends our understanding of the lives of everyday poor in early republican Turkey.[3] Within a range of institutions charged with providing for children's needs, professionals often espoused contradictory explanations and solutions for the variety of ills that many children faced in Turkey during the 1920s and 1930s.[4] At stake was the question of what kind of relationship the state would have toward society—in this instance how and in what ways the state should be responsible for providing resources and care to poor families and, especially, to poor children.

I first outline some of the social conditions faced by poor children in the 1920s and 1930s, thus establishing a contextual background for understanding the debates that would emerge regarding the child question. Outlining the work of the TRCS and the CPS, I discuss the reliance on semi-voluntary, philanthropic associations for providing aid to poor children in the new republic. The latter part of the chapter is devoted to outlining the lines of contention regarding the scope, nature, and ways to solve the social problems linked to the child question. I discuss a range of critiques that were made in the media and memoirs of reformers regarding who was responsible for the persistence of child poverty and how it could be eliminated.[5] For reformers and policy makers, the question of what kind of nation–state would be crafted was of paramount concern, and as I show in this chapter, the unfolding of debates around the child question points to key fractures in the meaning of modernity, state, and society in a Turkish context.

From Children of the Martyrs to the Child Question

Well before the founding of the Turkish republic in 1923, the residents of Istanbul were no strangers to the issue of poverty. By the mid-1890s the Ottoman state endeavored to address officially issues of vagrancy and public health concerns through opening Darülaceze, an urban poor house that was to provide food and shelter to between five hundred and one thousand people. As Nadir Özbek has shown, the state shelter was multipurpose and intended to provide services for children and the elderly, as well as those adults of working age defined as indigents or vagrants.[6] Abdülhamid II furthered his interests in providing for disenfranchised children of the empire when he founded Darül Hayr-i Âli, an orphanage that operated between 1903 and 1909.

It was not until the Young Turk government was established in 1908, however, that the state undertook the management of a number of schools and orphanages.[7] According to Stanford Shaw, the Committee of Union and Progress founded orphanages throughout the Anatolian and Eastern Thracian provinces. Often Ottoman authorities took over buildings from foreign missions or hospitals and converted them into orphanages. They were "sometimes run by government officials, but most often by the Red Crescent organization based in Istanbul, helped by the privately organized and financed Protection of Children Society *(Himaye-i Etfal Cemiyeti)*."[8] Throughout the nineteenth and early twentieth centuries, local bureaucrats and minority communities segregated orphanages along ethnic or religious lines. In the late Ottoman period, facilities for minority communities such as the Greeks and Armenians outnumbered those serving Muslim populations. Anna Welles Brown reports that in Istanbul prior to the establishment of the Turkish republic there were no fewer than twenty-five Armenian orphanages, eight Turkish orphanages, three or four Greek orphanages, two Jewish orphanages, and two Russian orphanages. Outside of Ottoman Turkish arenas a number of minority and international institutions provided social services to needy children, primarily based on a given child's ethnic or religious background.[9] Hospitals, schools, and orphanages established by Greek, Armenian, and Jewish communities provided services for children, on a par with, if not greater in scope than, Ottoman Turkish efforts.[10]

Of the Turkish orphanages, seven were run by the Ottoman Turkish government and one was funded by the CPS.[11] Aside from such institutionalized forms of assistance, as in the case of Ottoman Salonica (discussed by Eyal Ginio in chapter 8 of this volume), children could be "adopted" into households in a practice known as *evlatlık* or *evladlık*. Such adoptions were commonly initiated among relatives and neighbors, and by the twentieth century could be facilitated through more formal means by organizations such as the CPS.

In the decade preceding the formation of the Turkish republic, physical dislocation and disruption of family networks throughout Anatolia and Thrace were everyday problems. The Balkan Wars, World War I, and the War of Independence were waged at terrible human costs.[12] C. Claflin Davis, a participant in a sociological *Pathfinder Survey* of Istanbul in the early 1920s, remarked that Istanbul, in particular, became a haven for refugees seeking assistance and relocation to other regions and countries after World War I. After the Allies gained control of Istanbul, many more refugees of varied nationalities fled to the city to seek asylum. Prohibitive costs of immigration abroad as well as lack of work within the city, began to precipitate a humanitarian crisis.[13] It was within somewhat overlapping national and international arenas that a discourse on establishing a "modern" child welfare system arose.[14]

With the end of World War I and the War of Independence, the new governing republican bureaucrats and professional elites turned their attention to assessing the costs of more than a decade of protracted military conflict and social upheaval and to constructing a nation–state. Transition from empire to nation–state in early republican Turkey was a profound process. It implied further transforming state *and* society along lines that had gained ascendancy in Europe in the previous century. The ramifications of nation–state building reverberated in the reformulation of the bureaucracy, military, religious institutions, education, and medicine at an institutional level and in campaigns to reshape the individual as national subject and family as a hearth for inculcating the modern citizen.[15]

Many scholars and laypeople of the era noted the tremendous loss of population in the decade that preceded the founding of the republic. Moreover, they acknowledged that many children, widows, and families without able, working adults, lived in dire conditions. Clearly nation–state building would mean assisting a beleaguered populace, particularly if those governing hoped to craft a new kind of citizen. Although poverty and dislocation were familiar issues for much of the populace in 1920s- and 1930s-era republican Turkey, the manifestation of want in the bodies of children was an increasingly poignant symbol of the need for reconstruction and a reinvestment in the idea of future prosperity.

Even as the republic was being established in 1923, child welfare activists accelerated local and national efforts to combat homelessness, chronic hunger, and other symptoms of endemic poverty. In the name of the new nation, many reformers lobbied for more comprehensive intervention, both by local individuals and families who were well off and by the new state. The challenges of postwar reconstruction combined with the effects of global depression beginning in 1929 created even greater challenges to the poor and working-class families in the 1930s. Journalists and those working in public assistance noted an increase in the number of hungry and

street-bound children in the 1930s. It is difficult to locate reliable figures that demonstrate a causal link between the intensifying discourse on child poverty and actual
numbers of children in need because of postwar reconstruction and the depression.
In the mid-1930s at the height of the economic crisis in Turkey greater numbers of
children under the age of fourteen *were* entering the industrial workforce,[16] for example, and a large number of elementary school children in Istanbul were identified
as chronically hungry and in need of clothing and adequate housing.[17]

In the media and among professionals the child question was portrayed as one
of the most important social problems of the day, linked to the broadest concerns
of economy and policy, on the one hand, and intimate practices of family life, on
the other hand.[18] In Turkey, key issues included high infant and child mortality rates;
the large number of orphaned, abandoned, or poor children; malnourishment;
disease; child labor; homelessness; begging; child abuse; child abandonment; child
prostitution; and delinquency. Though not always explicitly laid out in newspapers and journals of the day, debates about child welfare were closely linked to
questions of women's position and relative well being within society. Doctors stressed
that a woman's prenatal and postnatal health directly influenced the health of her
infant child and pressed to expand the number of maternity clinics. Real or imagined increases in the rate of child abandonment or infanticide were supposed to be
direct reflections of a mother's ability to care for her child. The plight of working
mothers who had to leave children at home unattended or to quit their work if their
children fell seriously ill reflected the interweaving of child and maternal welfare.

Thus, by the 1930s, despite some period of normalization of daily life throughout the republic, child poverty and its attendant social ills persisted. With the onset
of global depression, state and local efforts to recover from considerable wartime
losses suffered a substantial setback. The visibility of poor children in Istanbul,
Ankara, and other Turkish cities daily reminded policy makers, reformers, journalists, and those in the helping professions that they had yet to achieve the promise of
the new republic for the majority of families. Recalling Salim Ahmed's words from
the beginning of this chapter, if Turkey's children were its greatest asset—the nation
itself—then poor children were a visual reminder of what had yet to be achieved. If
indeed Turkey's future rested in the minds and bodies of its children, then the country had far to go to secure its status as a sovereign and powerful nation–state.

Child Welfare in the New Republic—A Patchwork
of Decentralized Efforts

Shortly after the establishment of the Turkish Republic, important parliamentari-
ans and President Mustafa Kemal (Atatürk) himself promised to assist organizations
willing to promote a pronatalist campaign and measures to assure infant and child

survival. Pronatalist policies of the Young Turk period (1908–1918) were extended into the early republic.[19] The child, viewed as a citizen-in-the-making, symbolized a nation–state embarked on a progressive march toward future prosperity and greatness.[20] Republican officials promised public assistance for children and families, particularly in cases of families with many children. The official stance on the importance of the child for future nationhood was also visible in the efforts to create a national primary education system.[21] Under a newly reformed Ministry of Education, the republican reformers endeavored to train new teachers, build schools, and create a comprehensive elementary school curriculum.[22]

Throughout the 1920s and 1930s, efforts to address the child question were largely decentralized and not well coordinated across state and private domains. Work could be carried out simultaneously by local or national private philanthropic associations *(hayırlı cemiyetler/müesseseler)*, local municipal administrations, and at the state level by the Ministry of Education, Ministry of Health and Social Assistance, and Ministry of Justice. Perhaps the two most visible institutions to address directly the needs of orphans and the children of the poor were the CPS and the TRCS. The CPS and the TRCS benefited from varying levels of municipal and national governmental support, though formally they were regarded as private associations officially recognized by the state.[23] Other groups such as the Mother's Federation *(Anneler Birliği)*, the Turkish Women's Federation *(Türk Kadınlar Birliği)*, local branches of the people's houses *(halk evleri)*, and branches of the Turkish Republican People's Party took up the cause of child poverty.

To an extent yet to be determined by research, local mosques and the *imaret* (soup kitchen) system continued to play a significant role in poor relief at a local level. In reading the popular media and official sources, the place of Islamic forms of giving and poor relief in the urban landscape of the early republic rarely are addressed explicitly. We know from scholarship on the early republic that a process to secularize state and society was accelerated by Kemalist reformers. Although chapters in this volume by Miriam Hoexter (7), Miri Shefer (6), Yasser Tabbaa (5), and Mine Ener (9) emphasize the centrality of the mosque and religious forms of charity in earlier eras, it is less clear what effect the reorganization of the administration of the *evkaf* (endowments), the abolition of *tarikat* (Sufi orders), or transformations of the mosque–*medrese* (college) complexes had on the daily lives of the poor who had relied on such institutions to subsist (particularly in times of crisis). In undermining the legitimacy of older forms of giving and divesting resources from these institutions that had served as soup kitchens, medical clinics, and provided temporary housing for widows and their children, for example, the very resources that most disenfranchised children or women would have initially requested services from were compromised significantly.[24]

When Islamic practices were cited, generally it was to encourage donors to divert their alms from individuals to organizations like the CPS or the TRCS. An example from the 1920s illustrates the attempt to shift giving from recognizably religious institutions or individuals to public charities. Süleyman Nazif implored Turkish citizens to help the children of those who had fought in World War I and the Turkish War of Independence: "Give! You need to give to those children who do not have anyone other than you, in order to show your appreciation and assure your future protection." Nazif cited a newspaper account mentioning fifteen families who were preparing to make a pilgrimage to Mecca, stating

> If I knew who these families were, I would tell them that instead of going to King Husein and Ibn Al Saud's lands, which are colonized by the British, they should think again and visit Kâbetullah located in their hearts. If they were to offer the money to orphans of the martyrs who had saved them from the insulting boots [of the British colonizers], their earned merit would be much higher. . . . April 23, the freedom that came to us on that day, is the most important holiday for our nation. May Allah bless those who have remembered donating to the Children's Protection Society by wearing this rosette.[25]

Here Nazif weds religious, anticolonialist, and nationalist sentiments in his request for readers to remember the Children's Protection Society.

In another example, renowned pedagogue, Professor Abdulbaki (Gürpınar), author of *Religious Lessons for the Children of the Republic*, praised almsgiving but advised schoolchildren to give "their small donations" they might have intended for individual poor people to "public charitable societies like the Red Crescent, the Children's Protective Society, and the Aviation Society" instead.[26] Helping organizations and the state thus sought to redirect highly personal or religious acts of charity toward more generalized, secularized institutions.

The Turkish Red Crescent Society and the Children's Protection Society

Modern welfare for government officials was epitomized by expanding governmental programs for health, education, and social assistance and promoting the importance of private organizations to help fill gaps not covered by the state. In this section I focus on the Red Crescent Society and the Children's Protection Society because they were the most broadly based and institutionally recognized associations working on behalf of children during the Young Turk and early republican eras. These two associations were the most visible in public discourses on how to address child poverty and children's health, and both played a fundamental part in child welfare initiatives on local and national levels. Of the two, the Children's Protection Society gradually became recognized as the most significant organization working for the overall welfare of children. The scope and influence of the CPS surpassed that of the TRCS, as did the intensity of the critique directed toward the CPS for not sufficiently meeting the needs of children and poor mothers.

The Turkish Red Crescent Society

The work of several Ottoman historians of the Tanzimat and Young Turk eras illuminates the early history of the Ottoman Red Crescent Society (hereafter ORCS), the precursor to the Turkish Red Crescent Society (TRCS). The ORCS was first established just before the Russo–Ottoman War of 1877–1878 to provide support to soldiers on the battlefield or wounded in hospitals, as well as their families at home. Nadir Özbek argues that after the Young Turk Revolution in 1909, the ORCS "provided enormous opportunities for members of the new political elite to construct, express, and legitimize the new functions on which their identity was based."[27] An emerging corps of doctors educated in Europe comprised the backbone of this association, even as women increasingly participated in the efforts of the society. It is through the efforts of the Women's Auxiliary that we see early efforts to care for poor and orphaned children. In the 1910s the Women's Auxiliary established an industrial school for young girls and women in Istanbul as well as an orphanage in Edirne.[28]

Throughout World War I and the War of Independence, the ORCS continued to play an important role in relief efforts on the home front, providing food, clothing, and medicine to women and children affected by the war. After the establishment of the Turkish Republic in 1923, the TRCS took up postwar efforts for reconstruction and relocation of orphaned or displaced children and widows with children. Units of the Red Crescent spread throughout the republic, though the greatest concentration of these branches was in the Istanbul region and in western Anatolia and eastern Thrace.

By the 1930s, the TRCS had established itself as a key institution providing for the needs of the people. Throughout the early republic, one of the TRCS's chief concerns was to combat child hunger. In 1926, the Red Crescent initiated a campaign to feed lunch to undernourished or hungry elementary school students (*gıdasız talebeler*) several times a week. This campaign continued throughout the 1930s. Much of the annual budget for the TRCS was devoted to the task of providing lunchtime meals. In the 1932–1933 budget, for example, the Istanbul Red Crescent Society provided 4,197 elementary school children with 16,978 lira in food aid.[29] TRCS canvased local wealthy individuals and businesses for financial support, and received funds specifically for the hot-lunch project from local branches and general headquarters of the TRCS, from the provincial government, and from a portion of fees collected by ferryboats. In a related fashion, local branches of the TRCS regularly donated school clothing,

264 | *Kathryn Libal*

supplies, and other essentials to poor children, particularly during holiday times or before the beginning of the school year.

The Children's Protection Society

The Children's Protection Society was founded in the late Ottoman period by a group of doctors, businessmen, lawyers, and other bureaucrats who sought to advance the cause of children's health and welfare.[30] The onset of the Balkan Wars and World War I prompted various groups of doctors to establish a set of private institutions to help deal with the growing numbers of orphaned or homeless children. By March 1917, a group of prominent doctors, businessmen, and local dignitaries gathered in Istanbul to craft a mission statement and bylaws. Shortly thereafter the newly organized Children's Protection Society gained permission from the Young Turk government to become an officially recognized association.[31] The activities of the CPS during World War I and the War of Independence were marked by the immediate needs of caring for displaced children (whether by the effects of a loss of parent or relatives, direct conflict, famine, disease, or voluntary or forced migration). Children who either had no immediate family or relatives, or could not be supported within the family, neighborhood, or rural community were often sent to the CPS by local police, military, other able individuals willing to intervene, and occasionally by the children themselves.

In 1921 the CPS moved its administrative center to Ankara. Historians have yet to map the struggle that must have taken place over the decision to move the general headquarters, but the decision was tied to a growing understanding of the power shift from Istanbul to the nationalist stronghold in Ankara. After the declaration of the republic in 1923 the CPS continued to expand the scope of its efforts and to open new branches throughout the republic. The early republican era (1923–1938) thrust the CPS into the public limelight as one of the most important institutions providing for the needs of children nationally. Not only did the number of branches grow throughout the 1920s and 1930s, but also the mission of the CPS expanded to fit the needs of this period of postwar reconstruction.[32]

The CPS recognized an overwhelming need for assistance to children on all fronts and hoped to focus, in particular, on high rates of infant mortality that persisted throughout Turkey. CPS doctors thought that only through curbing the numbers of babies lost in the first few years of life could the Turkish state's goals for significant population growth be met. To promote the reduction of infant mortality rates, the CPS wrote and disseminated educational materials on child health, child care, and nutrition. They also published posters, pamphlets, monthly magazines, and broadcasted radio addresses on child health and child-care techniques in an effort to reach greater numbers of Turkish mothers and families. The CPS convinced the Ministry of Education to incorporate lessons on modern child-care techniques for girls in the national curricula, and the CPS opened their own training program for professional child-care assistants.

The CPS, like the TRCS, relied in large part on donations from private citizens. Funding in the 1920s and 1930s came from predominantly private sources, including a significant amount from expatriates in the United States who wanted to contribute to philanthropic organizations promoting child welfare.[33] In the late Ottoman Empire the state promoted selling special stamps to support the TRCS and the CPS. Such practices continued under the republican leadership. In the early 1930s the Istanbul municipality supported a regulation that would allow passengers on ferries, trains, and other forms of private transport to proffer tickets that were sold on behalf of the CPS instead of the ordinary tickets purchased for travel. In 1932, the Postal, Telegraph, and Telephone Administration was mandated by the Turkish parliament to set aside for the CPS a portion of fees earned from sending letters, telegraphs, and other forms of special delivery mail over a ten-day period during the month of Children's Holiday.[34] The CPS was also offered special opportunities by the state to acquire buildings for child-care centers/orphanages *(ana kucağı)* at subsidized rates. Overall, however, contributions made by the Turkish state (at the municipal, provincial, and national level) accounted for a relatively small proportion of the CPS annual budget. The CPS secured a small proportion of its annual budget from the state, but throughout the 1930s this appropriation was consistently cut.[35] Thus, CPS leaders had to devote considerable attention to raising funds in support of basic services and functions.

Who Should Take Care of the Children?
The State, Social Welfare, and Traditional Forms of Charity

Even though the CPS, the TRCS, and other voluntary organizations were key players in child welfare efforts in the early republic, reformers and writers of the day frequently asserted that such work was not extensive enough to effect real change. Tensions over the direction that child welfare initiatives should take were evidenced repeatedly in the print media during the 1930s. The CPS was often a target for criticism, from both those who felt charity was best practiced within neighborhoods or villages and those who felt only state-sponsored welfare programs would settle the child question. Considerable diversity in political perspective further complicated the "state-centered" approach. On the one hand, ultranationalist supporters promoted a higher level of state control to ensure a strong population to ward off the possible threat of other nation–states. On the other hand, supporters of socialist or communist platforms sought the leveling of class differences and social inequalities.

CPS officials responded to critics who supported localized, neighborhood-based charity by placing the work of child welfare within the context of broader reforms, emphasizing that the child question was as important as any of the many tasks that new Turkey faced, including industry, education, public works, finance, agriculture, and health. The child-centered social problems, however, could not be regarded as just political issues to be debated ideologically; the child question must be regarded "from top to bottom the concern of the whole country."

> The educated and enlightened elite who appear to challenge the problem in front of the country's people need to understand that the child question in Turkey cannot be solved with partial solutions, as if it was a simple matter. The tasks that will have to take place for the sake of children will not be successfully implemented [and solved] with the assistance of people of one or two neighborhoods.[36]

The CPS writer asks "Why must we try to see the problem of children only in terms of 'traditional charity' given to them? Why must we diminish the problem? Or make it disappear? Is the child question in Turkey only that of barefoot street children?" To CPS leaders, localized, neighborhood-based "traditional charity" could never be sufficient in the Turkey of the 1930s. They believed that acting as a "national organization" in the long-term would ensure success. The key obstacle to be overcome was inspiring Turkish society itself to recognize the inherent worth and importance of children for the nation–state, to inculcate the idea of "love of the child" *(çocuk sevgisi)*, and thus promote a sense of obligation and commitment toward children in the Turkish populace.

Calls for rekindling Turkish notions of neighborly care—of relying on face-to-face charity to help poor children and their families to get by (at worst) or achieve self-sufficiency (at best)—do not appear in the print media as often as another proposed solution to the child question. This more widely espoused position called for the creation of a fully funded state-run agency or bureau that would ensure child welfare for the Turkish populace. Appeals for setting up a state institution or bureau that would provide comprehensive child health and welfare programs appear time and again in popular newspapers and publications. This bureau would be more firmly rooted under the administration of the state than the existing CPS was. In the estimation of many pedagogues, health-care workers, and activist writers, and even leaders of the CPS itself, the CPS was unable even remotely to meet the needs of the urban poor. Reaching children in smaller towns and villages who were hungry, malnourished, or diseased was even more distant a prospect.

The fact that neither the state nor local philanthropic organizations were able to meet the basic needs of large numbers of children living in poverty was highlighted in the reports of journalist, writer, and activist Suad Derviş.[37] In the mid-1930s Derviş published a series of articles that exposed the dire living conditions of many children and working mothers. Through such narratives, Derviş called into question the efficacy of the new nation–state and its leaders. In one article published in *Cumhuriyet* in 1934, Derviş narrated a case in which a teenage brother unsuccessfully sought care for his younger sister, who was dying of tuberculosis. After exhausting local resources for assistance, he was directed to take his sister to an Istanbul hospital. A car was sent to pick up the sister and deliver her to a hospital; however, after determining that the girl had an advanced case of tuberculosis, the chief of staff informed them that the hospital had no space for the patient. Seeing their dismay, the doctor eventually suggested placing the sister in a basement room with two other people who were close to death. When the brother protested the squalor and poor treatment his sister was likely to receive, the chief of staff repeated that no other provisions could be made for the boy's sister and they would have to return home. What struck the teenage boy as most preposterous—the final offense—was that the hospital would not provide a ride back to their neighborhood. The children were "no longer the hospital's concern." The boy stated:

> I accompanied my sister back to Köprü by tramway. I did not have any money to hire an automobile. I *am* complaining. Aren't we people? Isn't the state required to care for us? . . . I am going to the Directorate of Health. I want to reprimand the director and say "Your patients are here." If I saw the governor, believe me I would explain our situation. Because we don't have parents, isn't the state supposed to act as our parents?

Through the boy's putative voice Derviş posed a question: Why did not the state provide such children with desperately needed medical attention? The younger sister was close to death, the brother, too, gravely ill. In conclusion, Derviş herself asks "Which institution is it that is obligated to look after children without mothers or fathers? I am writing to attract the attention of that institution with these lines."[38]

Other commentaries on the unmet needs of children were widely published in the mid-1920s and 1930s and reflect the sharpening of the politicization of child welfare and children's rights in the early republic. Sabiha Zekeriya (Sertel), a well-known writer, scholar, and feminist, published extensively on child welfare and children's rights issues. During Children's Week in April 1929, Sabiha Zekeriya published a list of rights that all Turkish children should enjoy. At the conclusion of the declaration, Sabiha Zekeriya called on the state to take a leading role in children's welfare. Speaking in the imagined collective voices of Turkish children, she concluded: "We want you to find a solution for our problems in this Children's Week that you have created for us. . . . We want equality, nutrition, development, and education that is the right of every human child. . . . We want new laws and a social organization that will provide us with the rights and the life that we lack."[39]

Conclusion

As we have seen, Sabiha Zekeriya's call for "new laws and a social organization" that would provide children with legal rights and basic assurances of welfare was echoed by a growing number of professional elites interested in seeing the state play a larger role in social welfare. The concern was shared, too, by other parties invested in the child question. They included leaders of the Children's Protection Society, who sought the means to expand and deepen their projects on behalf of Turkey's children. Such professionals were beginning to do more than hint at the need for radical institutional change: Their modernist vision supported a more full-scale investment in the institutions and organizations at the level of the state, which would in turn imply a more engaged and totalizing form of governmentality.[40]

Both socialists and more moderate reformers signaled the need for a more organized and systematic approach to child welfare that could be accomplished through the establishment of an overarching institution embedded within the state. Creating a bureau or division within the state apparatus that would be charged with securing children's welfare contrasted with the idea of reviving a spirit of generosity among local, wealthy individuals and revitalizing systems of mutual assistance at the microlevel of the neighborhood to deal with child welfare problems.

Reşat Kasaba summarizes the intent of many early modernist reformers as those who "envisioned for Turkey an organized, well-articulated, linear process of modernization through which the whole nation was going to move simultaneously and with uniform experience."[41] This idealization of modernization and all that it should entail for the Turkish nation–state has been canonized in the nationalist narrative of the early republic. The historical record concerning childhood in early republican Turkey reveals that many people of the day were keenly aware of the unevenness of development. Members of the elite and working class recognized that the processes of modernization and nation–state building were neither smooth nor uniform endeavors.

Critics of the CPS and the state argued from increasingly polarized positions about the nature of social and economic inequality and the "duty" of individuals, private organizations, or the state to intercede on the behalf of children. Thus, proponents of rekindling the spirit of traditional charity found themselves proposing solutions fundamentally opposed to those of a more radical wing of social reformers who desired a much more centralized and comprehensive welfare program administered by the state. On the liberal–traditional end of the spectrum, critics of philanthropic associations like the CPS argued that welfare measures could be better provided through rekindling local face-to-face relations and obligations between neighbors in urban areas and villagers in rural ones. From newspaper accounts and memoirs it is clear that such local-level giving did persist throughout the early republic. At the other end of the spectrum, socialists, like Sabiha Zekeriya and Suad Derviş, highlighted the disjuncture between the ideology of modernization, nationalism, and statehood and what in reality the new nation–state structure and its ruling elite were offering to "the people" and more specifically to children. Their more radicalized vision for Turkey's future shared much with Kemalist ideology and might be considered a critique of the degree to which the state had been able to meet its professed goals. In this instance, only through more completely integrating the modernizing, secular state's efforts for health and education with the broader context of child and social welfare would real progress on the child question be achieved.

Notes

I would like to acknowledge Beth Baron, Mine Ener, Clarissa Hsu, Ali İğmen, Reşat Kasaba, Seth Koven, Nadir Özbek, Irvin Schick, K. Sivaramakrishnan, and Nicole Watts for helpful comments and criticisms on different versions of this chapter. All errors of fact or interpretation are my own.

1. Salim Ahmed, "Çocuk Haftasında Çocuk Esirgeme Kurumu," *Cumhuriyet*, 24 April 1936, p. 6.

2. See the people's house journal, *Ülkü*, throughout the 1930s for more on efforts to bring elementary school education and regular medical care to children in rural Turkey.

3. My use of *elites* in this chapter refers to a varied group of people who played roles in policy making, governing, educating, and providing medical and social services for the Turkish populace.

4. This included a mix of governmental, semi-governmental (voluntary associations with close governmental ties), and private institutions.

5. I focus on Istanbul because public discourses on the child problem and child poverty concentrate on this urban center during the period in question. Future work could address the debates about child welfare in a comparative provincial or regional perspective.

6. See Mine Ener (chapter 9 this volume); Nadir Özbek (chapter 10 this volume) and "The Politics of Poor Relief in the Late Ottoman Empire, 1876–1914," *New Perspectives on Turkey* 21 (Fall 1999): 1–33. For an account that focuses on Abdülhamid II and orphans in the late Ottoman period, see Nadir Özbek, "II. Abdülhamid ve Kimsesiz Çocuklar," *Tarih ve Toplum* 31, no. 182 (Şubat 1999): 11–20.

7. Necdet Sakaoğlu relates that Abdülhamid II mandated the opening of Darül Hayr-ı Ali after a six-year-old orphan asked him to create such an institution; see his "Darüleytamlar," *İstanbul Ansiklopedisi* (Istanbul: Ana Basım AŞ, 1994), 2:558.

8. Stanford Shaw, "Resettlement of Refugees in Anatolia," *Turkish Studies Association Bulletin* 22, no. 1 (spring 1998): 68.

9. See, in particular, Ann Welles Brown, "Orphanages," in *Constantinople Today, the Pathfinder Survey of Constantinople*, ed. Clarence R. Johnson (New York: Macmillan, 1922),

227–257. Mabelle Phillips's essay on "Widowhood" in the same volume (pp. 287–321) also illuminates various state, private, and international assistance programs to provide poor relief for widows and families affected by the decade or more of military conflict.

10. By the mid-nineteenth century and particularly by the post–World War I period of occupation, the European and American missionary presence in Istanbul was pronounced (particularly by the American Red Cross Association, Near East Relief, and other American missionary–philanthropic enterprises). A social history of poor relief and aid to refugees in the late Ottoman Empire would be incomplete without addressing local (e.g., Ottoman Turkish, Greek, Armenian, and Jewish) and international work on child welfare, the interplay between these realms, and the increasing politicization of a notion of the 'child' as future citizen of the Ottoman (Turkish) state. See, for example, Nazif Öztürk, *Türk Yenileşme Tarihi Çerçevresinde Vakıf Müessesesi* (Ankara: Türkiye Diyanet Vakfı Yayinlari, 1995), 322–335.

11. Brown, "Orphanages," 235. The Children's Protection Society mentioned here refers to an earlier incarnation of the Children's Protection Society that is often not recognized in republican historical records. The Istanbul society (with its bylaws and practices) was later blended with an organization formed in Ankara under the same name in 1921. For more on the struggle to define an administrative "center" for the Children's Protection Society in the years just before the establishment of the Turkish republic, see Cüneyd Okay, "Osmanlı Dönemi Himaye-i Etfal Cemiyeti Üzerine Belgeler/Notlar," *Toplumsal Tarih* 52 (April 1998): 21–31.

12. See, for example, Justin McCarthy, "The Muslim Population of Anatolia, 1878–1927" (Ph.D. diss., University of California at Los Angeles, 1978); Frederic Shorter, "The Population of Turkey after the War of Independence," *International Journal of Middle Eastern Studies* 17 (1985): 417–441.

13. Although accurate figures are not available and estimates from the time period are also open to question, it is helpful to get a sense of the overall population of Istanbul and the approximate numbers of refugees who had poured into the city after the Great War. Davis reports that in April 1921, according to estimates of the Turkish Red Crescent Society, there were fifty thousand Muslim, forty thousand Russian (some of whom were Turks and other Muslim, Greek, Armenian, Georgian, Ukrainians, and Jewish), and four thousand Greek and Armenian refugees. The American Red Cross reports that it had helped 85,524 people by April 1921 (working primarily among Russian refugees). Davis provides a safe conservative estimate as being one hundred thousand refugees total. This total estimate, taken in the context of Istanbul population estimates, means that conservatively one in eight to ten people encountered in the city during the early 1920s suffered from dislocation and the social problems that accompany being a refugee (namely, joblessness, homelessness, and fractured family structure). See C. Claflin Davis, "Refugees," in *Constantinople Today, the Pathfinder Survey of Constantinople,* ed. Clarence R. Johnson (New York: Macmillan, 1922), 203.

14. See Shaw, "Resettlement of Refugees in Anatolia." See also, League of Nations, "Commission for the Protection of Women and Children in the Near East: Extract from the Minutes of the Thirty-fifth Session of the Council," *League of Nations IV Social* (A.32.1925.IV), 1–16.

15. Deniz Kandiyoti, "End of Empire: Islam, Nationalism, and Women in Turkey," in *Women, Islam, and the State*, ed. Deniz Kandiyoti (Philadelphia: Temple University Press, 1991), 22–47.

16. Hüseyin Avni noted that it was illegal for children under the age of fourteen to be employed in factories (under the 1930 Law on Public Health), though the state either lacked the will or ability to enforce the provision effectively; see his "Fabrikalarda Çocuk," *Yeni Adam* 105 (January 2, 1934): 5.

17. Neşet Halil Atay, "Istanbul İlk Mekteplerindeki 7000 Çocuk," *Gürbüz Türk Çocuğu* 97 (1934): 3–7.

18 The "child question" was frequently raised in the popular press and was a focus of medical and pedagogical journals throughout the 1920s and 1930s. For this chapter I primarily drew on articles published in the leading newspaper *Cumhuriyet* (1928–1937); the official publication of the CPS *Gürbüz Türk Çocuğu* (1926–1935); CPS publication *Çocuk Haftası* (1929–1930); the journal *Yeni Adam* (1934–1939); and the official national people's house publication, *Ülkü* (1933–1939).

19. See Zafer Toprak, "The Family, Feminism, and the State during the Young Turk Period, 1980–1918," in *Première rencontre internationale sur l'Empire Ottoman et la Turquie moderne*, ed. Edhem Eldem (Istanbul: Institut National de Langues et Civilisations Orientales; Maison des Sciences de l'Homme, 1990), 449–450.

20. At the center of discourses on the problem of the child was the specter of failing to raise children as future Turkish citizens. I address the ideological conflation of child and the future in the essay, "National Futures: Time and the Child in the Making of the Turkish Republic" (paper presented at the ninety-eighth annual meeting of the American Anthropological Association, Chicago, Ill., November 17, 1999).

21. See Henry Elisha Allen, *The Turkish Transformation—A Study in Social and Religious Development* (Chicago: University of Chicago Press, 1935). See also Jessica Selma Tiregöl, "The Role of Primary Education in Nation–State-Building: The Case of the Early Turkish Republic, 1923–1938" (Ph.D. diss., Princeton University, 1998).

22. Malnutrition among schoolchildren, according to the press, was a chronic problem.

23. Elsewhere I have written about the gradual increase in state involvement in the policies and practices of the Children's Protection Society in the 1920s and 1930s; see Kathryn Libal, "The Children's Protection Society: Nationalizing Child Welfare in Early Republican Turkey," *New Perspectives on Turkey* 23 (Fall 2000): 53–78.

24. My hunch is that further research on the micropractices of mosques during the early republican period would reveal that many poor people continued to rely on mosques and face-to-face private acts of charity to meet short-term and long-term needs. Such an analysis falls outside the limits of sources for this study but is a concern I plan to take up in the future.

25. Süleyman Nazif, "Unutmayın ve Verin," *Çocuk Haftası* (Istanbul: Milliyet Matbaası, 1929), 1:53.

26. Allen, *The Turkish Transformation*, 198.

27. Özbek, "The Politics of Poor Relief," 2.

28. Ibid., 26–28.

29. *Türkiye Hilaliahmer Cemiyeti İstanbul Merkezi 1934 Meclisi Umumisine Takdim Olunan Rapor ve Hesabat Cetvelleri* (Istanbul: Ahmet İhsan Matbaası, 1934), 8.

30. See Okay, "Osmanlı Dönemi Himaye-i Etfal Cemiyeti"; Mustafa Şahin, "23 Nisan ve Himaye-i Etfal," *Toplumsal Tarih* 40 (April 1997), 15–18.

31. Okay, "Osmanlı Dönemi Himaye-i Etfal Cemiyeti," 21–22.

32. *Türkiye Çocuk Esirgeme Kurumu Istanbul Merkezi 1938–1939 Yılı Kongresinde Okunan Umumî Rapor* (Istanbul: Kader Basimevi, 1940), 1–3; *Türkiye Çocuk Esirgeme Kurumunun Küçük Bir Tarihçesi, 1921–1939* (Istanbul: Resimli Ay Matbaası T. L. Şirketi, 1940).

33. Veysi Akın outlines Dr. Fuad Umay's fund-raising and public relations efforts in the United States in 1923; see his "Dr. Mehmet Fuad (Umay) Bey' in Amerika Birleşik Devletleri Seyahati," *Akademik Araştırmalar* 1, no. 2 (1996): 18–29.

34. (Kanun Numara) 1947 Çocuk Bayramı Münasebetile Nisanı Yirmisinden Otuzuna Kadar Posta Müraselâtile Telgraflara Şefkat Pulu Yapıştırılması Hakkında Kanun (11 Nisan 1932)," *Türkiye Cumhuriyeti Sicilli Kavanini Kanunlar* (Istanbul: Cihan Matbaası, 1933), 271.

35. See, for example, *On Beşinci ve On Altıncı Yıllar (1936–1937) İş Raporu* (Ankara: Basvekâlet Matbaası, 1938); *TÇEK İstanbul Merkezi 1938–1939 Yılı Kongresinde Okunan Umumî Rapor,* 1940, which provide summaries of earlier CPS congresses in addition to new results.

36. "Bir Yazı ve Tahlili," 21–22.

37. For more on Derviş's contributions, see Kathryn Libal, "National Futures: The 'Child Question' in Early Republican Turkey" (Ph.D. diss., University of Washington, 2001).

38. Suad Derviş, "Kimsesiz Çocuklarımızla Meşgul Bir Müessese Yok Mu?" *Cumhuriyet,* 14 April 1934, p. 6.

39. Sabiha Zekeriya, "Biz . . . ," *Çocuk Haftası* 1 (1930): 44.

40. Jacques Donzelot, *The Policing of Families* (1979; reprint, Baltimore: Johns Hopkins University Press, 1997).

41. Reşat Kasaba, "Kemalist Certainties and Modernist Ambiguities," in *Rethinking Modernity and National Identity in Turkey,* ed. Sibel Bozdoğan and Reşat Kasaba (Seattle: University of Washington Press, 1997), 16–17.

Part V

Welfare as Politics

CHAPTER FOURTEEN

Islamic Redistribution through *Zakat*

Historical Record and Modern Realities

TIMUR KURAN

Introduction

The year 1995 saw the publication of the proceedings of an international conference on *zakat* (alms) held five years earlier in Kuala Lumpur.[1] The weighty volume's main theme is that today's zakat systems have a negligible impact on poverty alleviation—the very task they were expected to accomplish more effectively than secular redistribution systems. One contributor after another observes that even in countries where income redistribution has recently taken on an explicitly Islamic character, Muslims are by and large failing to live by Islam's only principal requirement that is squarely economic: the duty, incumbent on all adult Muslims except the poorest, to pay zakat on an annual basis.

Another striking feature of these proceedings is their diversity in regard to the substance of the zakat requirement. In every country with a government-sponsored or government-operated zakat system (including Malaysia, Pakistan, and Saudi Arabia), rates, exemptions, collection methods, and disbursement patterns have varied over time; and variations across countries are sufficiently sharp to make one wonder whether the designers of the different systems were interpreting the same religion. Equally remarkable is the diversity of the reform proposals in this volume. Like the wider literature on zakat, it harbors substantial disagreement over the practical meaning of the zakat requirement.

This contemporary diversity mirrors that of the past. There has never existed a single source that offers an authoritative account of how zakat should be paid or disbursed. Accordingly, the system has never been applied consistently over either time or space. A source of intense controversy from the start, the application of zakat underwent transformations even during the Prophet Muhammad's own lifetime. Also, during Islam's first few centuries the application was never uniform. In view of this historical record, the current diversity in implementation is hardly surprising. Nor is it puzzling that the contemporary literature on zakat is riddled with inconsistencies and ambiguities.

Even the distributional failures of the existing zakat systems become intelligible once one recognizes that poverty alleviation is but one of the objectives that zakat was initially meant to serve. Indeed, and as this chapter will show, zakat was not designed solely, or even primarily, to redistribute wealth in the manner of a progressive tax scheme, or as an antidote to poverty in the manner of a welfare program. Although the Quran and the Sunna, the traditional sources of Islam, contain prescriptions consistent with using zakat to transfer wealth to the poor, the system's past applications are compatible with any number of other objectives, even redistribution in favor of the rich. In any case, the zakat requirement took shape in an economy far simpler than even the poorest modern economy. For all these reasons, one may safely say that this requirement cannot fulfill the ambitious goals that contemporary Islamists have assigned to it—unless, of course, it is radically reinterpreted.

Origins

Like many other Islamic institutions, zakat grew out of the ideals and practices of communities in the Middle East around the time the Prophet Muhammad began spreading his message. Tithing and almsgiving were practiced by the region's pagan, Jewish, and Christian tribes, and in several ancient languages cognate words carried meanings similar to that of zakat. For example, the Aramaic *zakutha* originally meant "purity," and both Jews and Christians used it to mean "virtuous conduct."[2] Although the traditional sources of Islam give no indication that early Muslims considered zakat a loan word from pre-Islamic cultures, they definitely employed it in a sense consistent with earlier usages. Upholding a pre-Islamic tradition, the Quran treats zakat as a purifier of property. The acceptance that zakat gained among early Muslims was probably facilitated by their familiarity with the principle of giving away part of one's property as a means of ritually cleansing the rest.

Familiarity with a general principle does not imply acceptance of any particular application. During Islam's initial expansion, zakat quickly turned into a duty to pay tribute to the Muslim polity, and this bred resentment among some new converts. The significance of the ensuing discontentment may be gleaned from a Quranic verse that threatens hypocritical payers with retribution: "[O]f the wandering Arabs there is he who taketh that which he expendeth for the cause of Allah as a loss. . . . The evil of fortune will be theirs. Allah is Hearer, Knower" (9:98–99).

Evidently, certain tribes were meeting their obligations not to achieve salvation but to avoid being raided and punished; treating zakat as a burdensome tax, they were ready to suspend their payments to the nascent Islamic state if they could do so with impunity. Major challenges were not long in coming. As soon as the Prophet died, many converts refused to make payments to his successor at the community's helm, Abu Bakr. Abu Bakr, though opposed by other prominent Muslims, insisted that paying zakat to the Muslim community's leaders constituted as important an Islamic requirement as professing belief in the unity of God. Accusing noncompliant groups of apostasy, he sought to enforce the zakat requirement through military means, with considerable but not complete success.[3]

The seventh-century disagreements over zakat were hardly limited to the legitimacy of centralizing collections. Another controversy concerned the specifics of the individual Muslim's obligation. In particular, believers who agreed to make payments to the Islamic leadership did not necessarily accept the criteria of assessment. Within two decades, even before the caliphate passed into the hands of leaders who had not known the Prophet personally, major exemptions were instituted in response to demands for limiting collections. Most significantly, by abolishing the earlier practice of taxing all assets, including "hidden wealth," the third caliph Uthman restricted the tax obligation to "apparent wealth." The definition given in this particular context to *hidden* is at odds with the word's literal meaning. Hidden wealth was considered to include, in addition to easily concealed gems, highly visible assets such as housing and slaves. Meanwhile, certain easily concealed sources of wealth, such as gold jewelry, were treated as apparent wealth. That the categorization was not based on a coherent set of principles suggests that it was driven by expedience rather than strictly religious criteria. Whatever the exact motivations at play, Uthman's reinterpretation effectively exempted the accumulated wealth of property owners. From then on, zakat revenue came primarily from agricultural output. The previous system had involved an official of the Islamic treasury assessing and collecting yearly dues on all kinds of wealth. Now, it appears, payments on many important forms of wealth were left to the individual Muslim's conscience.[4]

This was not the first radical change to the enforcement method. In the religion's earliest years, while the Muslim community was still based in Mecca, assistance to the poor was not yet regulated by the Prophet's fledgling government. Strictly voluntary in spirit, charity was enforced through pre-Islamic Arabian customs that required everyone of means to assist orphans, widows, the infirm, and the undernourished. As in all primitive "face-to-face societies"—small enough that everyone knows everyone else—wealthy individuals who failed to meet social norms of generosity were rebuked and even ostracized.[5] Significantly, in this period the term zakat was used more or less interchangeably with sadaqa, which has always referred to voluntary almsgiving. Only with the rapidly growing community's relocation to Medina *(hijra)* in C.E. 622 did zakat become a formal and compulsory transfer system. This is when Muslims were required to make periodic payments to Islam's common treasury, its "House of Wealth" *(bayt al-mal)* that financed the new state's activities.[6] From then on, Islam would distinguish between the religious obligation to pay zakat and the praiseworthy, yet ultimately voluntary, act of helping the poor through sadaqa. But the two terms are closely associated *throughout* the Quran. In fact, in a key verse that specifies the permitted beneficiaries of Islamic assistance (9:60) the term *sadaqa* is generally interpreted as referring to zakat.[7] Such terminological ambiguities concerning almsgiving and tithing testify to the profound changes that took place during the Prophet's own lifetime: the emergence of a hierarchical and coercive Islamic state out of a loosely administered face-to-face community regulated largely by social norms.

The Quran is silent on the enforcement of the zakat obligation and the disbursement of zakat funds. As such, it rules out neither the decentralized and voluntary system of the earliest Islamic years nor the centralized and obligatory system of the Prophet's final decade. This lack of specificity complicated the resolution of the disputes that turned deadly after the Prophet. During the apostasy wars that followed his death in 632, neither side could prove that the Quran unequivocally supports its own position. To compound the difficulty, each side was able to justify its position through historical precedent. Accordingly, Abu Bakr invoked the pacts that committed various tribes to make regular payments to the Prophet's treasury. For their part, the rebellious tribes held that Islam treated zakat as a matter of individual choice.

Disputes over the beneficiaries of zakat funds were tempered by verses of the Quran that specify eight categories of expenditure: the poor, the needy, zakat administrators, potential converts and Muslims who might yet renounce Islam, manumitted slaves, debtors, people fighting for God, and wayfarers (for example, 2:177, 2:215, 4:8, 9:60, 24:22). Yet the Quran says nothing specific about the division of resources among these categories. In principle, therefore, some narrow segment of society could claim the majority of all zakat funds. Another potent source of disagreement lay in the criteria for assigning people to one category or the other. Any warrior could demand assistance under the pretext that he was fighting for Islam. Likewise, even the wealthiest traveler could make a case for having the state treasury cover his expenses.

A disbursement rule that seems to have emerged under the fourth caliph Ali prohibited the use of one year's zakat revenues in some subsequent year.[8] Subsequently, at the end of the second Islamic century, the view emerged that each year's zakat fund must be divided equally among the eight designated categories of expenditure.[9] These rules point to the popularity of binding the hands of rulers who controlled disbursement decisions. Yet, there is no evidence that either the equal-division rule or the ban against intertemporal revenue transfers was ever enforced.

No one familiar with the politics of redistribution in large societies will find it unusual that the Islamic community never achieved unity over the collection or disbursement of zakat, except perhaps initially, before the number of converts passed a few hundred. Although generosity is a universal human trait, it is equally common to favor members of one's own locality or group over people with whom one interacts minimally. So the converts who resisted Abu Bakr's demands were not necessarily refusing to provide charity. Rejecting the centralization of taxation, many were simply expressing a preference for local redistribution without intervention from spatially distant authorities.

This interpretation conflicts with historical accounts that treat the early Islamic community as a paragon of brotherly unity. It is highly plausible that by today's standards early Muslims were very motivated to assist the disadvantaged. What is implausible is the notion that they treated all their fellow Muslims equally, having shed their tribal attachments as soon as they converted. The bloody conflicts of Islam's Golden Age—the initial period that ended with the death of the fourth caliph Ali—testify to the internal divisions that plagued the community as it expanded and became increasingly heterogeneous. Significantly, officials of the early Islamic state, including the caliphs themselves, were often accused of nepotism and favoritism. Three of the four "rightly guided" caliphs died at the hands of fellow Muslims—graphic proof of deep divisions over the control of resources.[10]

These divisions doubtless hindered the task of reaching a common understanding of how a zakat system would operate. But the problem of delineating zakat entails much more than the appropriate degree of centralization. Is zakat payable on income or wealth? Zakat was initially a wealth tax, and to this day it is generally defined as such. The zakat entry in the *Oxford Encyclopedia of the Modern Islamic World* defines it as a wealth tax imposed on Muslims of sufficient means.[11] But the decision to limit collections to a share of apparent wealth turned the obligatory levy into what we would now call an income tax. When the government takes a share of the annual output of a farm, it is taxing income rather than wealth.

Still another source of ambiguity rooted in Islam's formative period concerns whether a Muslim's annual duty to share with others ends with payment of the designated segments of wealth or income. Certain verses of the Quran give the impression that no further payments are required, although some add that one wins divine favor by making voluntary donations in the form of sadaqa. But others suggest that eternal punishment awaits anyone who accumulates wealth. An example: "They who hoard up gold and silver and spend it not in the way of Allah, unto them give tidings, O Muhammad, of a painful doom" (9:34). Readers of this verse might worry, like Christian ascetics of medieval Europe,[12] that unless they renounce worldly comforts they will incur God's wrath.

To confuse matters further, during Islam's formative period the meaning of the term *zakat* did not stay fixed. Under the Prophet and the first two caliphs, all taxes were called "zakat," including the 2.5 percent customs duties imposed on Muslim traders. However, under the third caliph the meaning of the term narrowed. Thereafter, customs duties generally came to be called "*maks*," and agricultural levies *'ushr* (tithe) or *kharaj*, depending on the payer's religion. In time, moreover, numerous specialized taxes were instituted, including taxes on houses *(hilali)* and brokerage charges on the sale of sheep *(samsara)*.[13] But terminological variations never ceased. In an eighth-century treatise of Abu Yusuf, a founder of the Hanafi school of law, taxes on livestock are called "sadaqa." Moreover, sadaqa itself signifies not voluntary charity but the individual Muslim's obligatory payment to the Islamic state, in other words, what was generally known as "zakat."[14]

Whether collected as 'ushr or zakat, the tax on agricultural goods normally corresponded to 10 percent of the total output. However, the rate fell to 5 percent if artificial irrigation had been used. Such differentiation rested on the principle that a farmer in need of artificial irrigation exerts more effort than one who gets by with nothing more than rainfall.[15] This effort-based differentiation principle may be contrasted with the principle of taxable capacity that underlies modern agricultural taxation systems in developed countries. These tax systems typically differentiate according to land productivity. The owner of an irrigated parcel usually pays a higher tax than that of an otherwise identical unirrigated parcel because the irrigation boosts his productivity. In practice, however, the effort-based principle was never followed consistently. Partly because of diverse exemptions, there were great variations across time and space.[16] Complicated rules emerged also for the tax on livestock. Animals in a person's possession for an entire year were taxed according to their kind, provided they had grazed freely and not been put to work. Exemptions on animals reflected their value in the desert economy of seventh-century Arabia: five camels, or twenty cattle, or forty smaller animals.[17]

Such rates clearly reflect some concern with equity across payers. But it is the rates rather than the underlying equity objective that grabbed attention. The rates themselves came to be treated as sacred, gaining precedence over the principle they were initially meant to serve. Had the zakat requirement spawned a widely accepted redistribution principle, in subsequent periods they could have been adjusted freely in accordance with changes in the sectoral distribution of taxable capacity, the extent of poverty, and collective spending priorities.

Impact on Inequality

As a practical matter, the principal beneficiaries of the Islamic state's resources were government officials, clerics, religious institutions, and ostensible descendants of the Prophet. The resources from which they benefited included zakat levies, although booty and the taxes of non-Muslims usually constituted far more important categories.[18] Just as the medieval European church enriched the clergy through tithes supposedly collected to provide for the poor,[19] so, after the first four caliphs, the Islamic state seems to have treated zakat as a fungible component of a broader revenue stream controlled by powerful social groups. Successive rulers spent zakat income as they saw fit, without feeling seriously constrained by the Quran. The poor and the needy were probably never completely ignored. Yet, within a few decades of zakat's emergence as a principal religious requirement, the state-sponsored formal zakat system had clearly lost its importance as a source of poverty relief.

Two economists claim that the formal zakat system of the first Islamic century was progressive: Its burden fell disproportionately on the rich, and its benefits accrued primarily to the poor.[20] Other contemporary writers go much further. "For about a thousand years," says a Pakistani promoter of Islamic economics, ". . . there was no accumulation of wealth in a few hands, no hoarding and no profiteering, as these had been tabooed in Islam . . . the state was responsible for providing a living wage or relief to every inhabitant . . . there were neither slums nor multimillionaires."[21] Such rosy interpretations rest, of course, on old precedents. The early Islamic period produced numerous stories of compassionate rulers. One of them has the second caliph 'Umar making the rounds of Mecca every night with a sack of flour on his back, to make sure that everyone has enough to eat.[22]

In the early Islamic centuries, the poor as a whole may well have benefited from the combination of formal and informal transfers made under the rubric of zakat. But in truth we have no way of knowing. The available sources have not been studied for quantitative indicators, and in any case relevant documentation is very limited. Although some written records on the Egyptian land tax have survived, practically no documentation exists on that of Arabia, Syria, or Iraq. Even less can be inferred about disbursements to needy beneficiaries, since no pertinent records are known, if indeed any were kept.[23] As for informal transfers made to meet the zakat obligation, they would not have generated records. For all these reasons, the claim that zakat had an equalizing effect during Islam's initial expansion must be received with caution.

It is certain, however, that the radical equalization alleged by some modern writers is a myth. We saw how, in Uthman's time, the wealthy were protected through broad exemptions. There are also indications that this period saw the defeat of campaigns for greater equality. Certain early sources mention Abu Dharr al-Ghifari, a companion of the Prophet who complained of inequality and considered zakat a barrier to meaningful redistribution; although the accounts of his popularity may be exaggerated, it appears that he led a movement that was eventually crushed by Uthman.[24] For later times, there is evidence of substantial zakat evasion. The theologian al-Ghazali (1058–1111) speaks of ruses that allowed one to fulfill the letter of the zakat obligation while violating its original spirit. For example, a man would make a gift to his wife at the end of the year and take it back through an offsetting gift a few days later. "This will be of no use in the hereafter," warns al-Ghazali.[25]

Additional evidence of resistance to paying zakat is that in certain places the duties of the *muhtasib* (market supervisor) included the enforcement of traders' zakat obligations.[26] Finally, over time the task of poor relief was left increasingly to pious foundations *(awqaf)* established by private individuals. Especially in the Ottoman Empire, but also in earlier states, massively endowed soup kitchens, hostels, and schools made far greater contributions to poverty alleviation than any zakat-based transfer scheme.[27] As for broader redistribution, the Islamic inheritance system, which divided estates among extended relatives, was certainly a more potent equalizing instrument than practices undertaken to meet the zakat requirement.

The poverty relief practices of Ottoman Aleppo may be offered as an illustration. In the eighteenth century, we learn from Abraham Marcus, "Aleppo had no state-organized social security system that automatically took care of those unable to support themselves." The poor turned to their families or to communal charity, which was entirely voluntary.[28] Numerous pious foundations, including soup kitchens and shelters attached to mosques, assisted the needy. In addition, individuals participated in poor relief through casual almsgiving. However, neither the local government nor the imperial administration in Istanbul exhibited a sense of obligation to maintain a social safety net—to say nothing of performing this task through a zakat system. Decentralized assistance did not eliminate poverty. As in other parts of the premodern world, including Western Europe, eighteenth-century Aleppo featured a large and seemingly irreducible underclass.[29]

Contemporary historians of the past millennium's Muslim-governed states pay enormous attention to the pious foundations established under Islamic law. To a lesser but still significant extent, they also examine inheritance practices. But one can read major works on the economic history of these states without encountering a single reference to zakat. This is partly, no doubt, because the historical sources say very little of relevance. As for the paucity of sources, it reflects the lack of official commitment to enforcing the zakat duty. Although minor exceptions may be found, evidently the standard pattern was for the state to leave decisions regarding zakat transfers to individuals. Voluntary payments made in a decentralized manner would have left no documentary traces.

The Purpose of Zakat

My focus thus far has been on zakat's capacity to reduce inequality and its fairness to payers and recipients alike because its modern proponents have emphasized these dimensions of the institution. Yet, historically, neither equity among zakat payers nor equity in redistribution was the dominant consideration. From the beginning, another important purpose of zakat, as its meaning in the Quran suggests, was to cleanse both the donor's wealth and himself. By relinquishing some of his wealth, the donor would purify what remained; he would also limit his greed, thus soothing his conscience.[30] This interpretation draws support from two sayings attributed to the Prophet: "Goods on which one has payed zakat cease being part of one's treasure"; and "Allah instituted zakat so that you can enjoy the rest of your wealth with a clear conscience."[31]

Merely giving is not enough. Even more important is that the donor give without expecting anything in return, solely as an expression of pious generosity. According to a very common interpretation, this means that the act of paying zakat forms its own reward. Provided the donor's intention *(niyya) is* good, the donation's effects are immaterial.[32] Thus interpreted, the system releases individual donors, and the community as a whole, from the burden of considering and, when necessary, reacting to its effects on inequality, poverty, employment, or employability. As long as donors are giving out of the goodness of their hearts, it hardly matters whether the recipients are rich or poor, good or bad Muslims, honest workers or lazy cheats.

The jurists who shaped Islamic law during Islam's initial few centuries touched, of course, on such questions as how poverty should be defined, who qualifies as needy, and the extent of a poor person's zakat entitlement.[33] But their answers did not create a consensus capable of channeling zakat resources toward the poor. Nor did they generate a widely felt obligation for wealthy individuals to seek out the poorest Muslims. In practice, as the Marcus study of Aleppo shows, voluntary zakat transfers could flow toward the most visible poor rather than toward the neediest. The rich could offer assistance to their own servants or to the beggars in their own neighborhoods and, without giving any thought to the challenges of overcoming the causes of need, consider their zakat duty fulfilled. This possibility explains, in part, why the Islamic world has never produced a major organized movement aimed at eliminating poverty.

Under a voluntary zakat system, we have seen, the bulk of the available zakat funds may accrue to the relatively unneedy—those we might categorize as "barely poor." But we have also seen that in principle all poor individuals are entitled to aid; while they should not expect to be made rich, except by the grace of God, they need not worry that their more fortunate brethren will deny them help.[34] Framing zakat assistance as a poor person's entitlement also serves to legitimize the Islamic order in the eyes of the underprivileged. "You might feel exploited," it says to the downtrodden, "but know that your community will never exclude or forget you."[35] A complementary advantage of defining zakat assistance as an entitlement is that it enables the poor to accept it without loss of dignity. As Marcel Mauss recognized in relation to gifts in general,[36] and countless students of the welfare state have observed in relation to modern poverty relief,[37] unreciprocated transfers wound the recipient's pride.[38] By this logic, zakat transfers to the poor, insofar as they are considered a right that flows from membership in the community of Muslims rather than largesse from the rich, will harmonize relations among the economic classes.

So zakat is as much a political instrument as an economic one. Through its effects on the attitudes of both rich and poor, it serves as a social stabilizer. On the one hand, it counsels the rich not to feel obligated to eradicate poverty and never to feel guilty for being well-off. On the other hand, it dampens the resentments of the poor and moderates their demands. These features of the system might strike a modern reader as unduly pessimistic regarding zakat's potential. However, they were commonly acknowledged until recently, without any trace of apology. In a treatise published in 1921, Jamal al-Din al-Qasimi, a leader of a Syrian-led Islamic reform movement known as the *salafiyya*, advocated the establishment of a zakat system supported by obligatory payments from the rich. But he did not expect the system to eradicate material deprivation. In fact, he wrote that he could not even imagine a society without widespread poverty. While his ideal system would meet the basic needs of the poor, it also would awaken love of the poor and overcome feelings of envy.[39]

Instrument of Modern Redistribution?

Historically, then, zakat never became an agent of massive equalization. At best, it served as a vehicle for modest redistribution and political stabilization. Nevertheless, modern Islamists have viewed it as a powerful economic instrument—one that would promote not only psychological harmony and social peace but also fundamental economic equalization. Sayyid Mawdudi (1903–1979), the Indian Islamist who coined the term *Islamic economics*, advocated the reestablishment of an obligatory zakat system operated by the government.[40] He was convinced that this would improve morality, lower poverty, raise productivity, and depress unemployment.[41] Sayyid Qutb (1906–1966), the Egyptian Islamist, also considered zakat a powerful economic instrument, although he differed from Mawdudi in allowing for additional taxes to dampen class distinctions.[42]

Subsequent proponents of economic Islamization have varied in their characterization of zakat's potential effects. At least one writer argues that the benefits of zakat extend to the prevention of "famines and floods."[43] Less sweepingly, others hold that zakat lowers unemployment, poverty, and material inequality, and that these effects peak within a fully Islamic socioeconomic system harboring a "filter mechanism" that motivates Muslims to behave as good Muslims.[44] What is beyond dispute in Islamist circles is that zakat constitutes Islam's most basic instrument for redistribution. Moreover, Islamist writers consider it self-evident that the redistribution in question is equalizing—that is, from rich to poor.

The optimism of the modern promotional literature on zakat is based on the belief that it served as a powerful equalizer over much of Islamic history. Only with forced Westernization, it is thought, did this sacred institution degenerate and fall into disuse. The following passage from the earlier-mentioned entry in the *Oxford Encyclopedia of the Modern Islamic World* offers a representative account in this vein:

> *Zakat* was formerly applied in all Muslim territories and respected as an Islamic obligation. Because the general populace viewed *zakat* as a religious and moral duty, Muslim authorities had no problems in collecting it. With the advent of colonialism and the introduction of systems of government that excluded religious doctrine, authorities in most Muslim states largely abjured Islamic codes of law, including *zakat*.[45]

The last colonial regimes of the Islamic world gave way to independent states almost half a century ago. Is the time ripe, then, for reinstituting the redistribution system that ostensibly worked so well? Scores of writings try to make this case, going to great lengths to specify the practical implications of a restoration. Thus, each of these provides a long list of rates and exemption limits. These invariably come from classical Islamic sources, so they turn out to be those applied during Islam's first few centuries in the territories over which Islamic rule was established early on.[46]

Following are a few examples of the provisions these writings cite as elements of a modern zakat system. A person who owns up to twenty-four camels is to pay one goat for every five camels. On horses, the zakat rate is 2.5 percent of the value. Nothing is due on mules and elephants, the former because they "do not breed," and the latter because they "breed seldom or after a long time."[47] The rate on farm output depends on whether the land is irrigated: 5 percent if the land had to be irrigated by the owner and 10 percent otherwise.[48] Finally, the rate on gold and silver holdings is 2.5 percent of any amounts beyond the exemption limits *(nisab)* stipulated by the Prophet: for gold, 7.5 tolas (3 ounces) and for silver, 52.5 tolas (21 ounces).[49] As of 2000, these limits allow a Muslim to possess about $915 worth of gold and $275 worth of silver without having to pay zakat.

The promotional literature on zakat provides more such details, which are meant both to spell out the zakat system's concrete provisions and to demonstrate its power to redistribute wealth from rich to poor. No observer knowledgeable about the economies of the modern Islamic world will fail to notice that the writings avoid reference to some of the most important contemporary forms of wealth and income. Although none says that contemporary forms of wealth are exempt, one is hard-pressed to find details concerning stocks, bonds, vacation homes, collectibles, retirement accounts, or savings for a child's education, to mention just a few of those that now carry major significance. Likewise, for all the specifics they provide on agricultural income, they avoid commentary on income derived from the industrial and service sectors—neither of which is negligible in any contemporary economy. The exemption limits, too, will strike a modern reader as decidedly out of date. Why should the zakat duty of a silver holder differ from that of a gold holder?[50] And what is the exemption limit on platinum holdings, not to mention that on platinum futures?

In regard to beneficiaries, every contemporary promoter of zakat makes reference to the eight categories enumerated in the Quran. There is agreement that these cannot be modified. But the ancient controversy over dividing the zakat fund into eight lives on. The majority wish to allow the spending ratios to be varied in accordance with evolving social needs. Some add that in a society without slavery it is senseless to reserve resources to the liberation of slaves. In other respects, however, these writings seem out of touch with modern life. In many sources one searches in vain for commentary on whether the fund may support the Red Crescent or recreational programs for the handicapped.

Much of the promotional literature assumes, in effect, that improving the distribution of income and achieving social justice are simply procedural matters. To improve our existing social system, many writers suggest, one must follow the redistribution norms established by the early Muslims on the basis of the revealed truths of the Quran and the exemplary conduct of the Prophet. This proceduralism may be contrasted with situationism—the principle that the morality of an act depends on the state of the environment. Under situationism the morality of driving on the highway at the legal speed limit depends on the prevailing weather conditions: A driving speed acceptable on a sunny day would amount to recklessness during a snowstorm. Likewise, the morality of using a country's scarce resources to build a steel factory depends on that country's comparative advantage in trade. If those resources would yield higher returns in textiles, and textiles can freely be exchanged for steel, the pursuit of self-sufficiency in steel will result in waste. Whereas proceduralism supports the enforcement of prefabricated rules and regulations, situationism accepts, modifies, or rejects established directives according to circumstances and always relies on reason to interpret their spirit. The former says, "The zakat obligation on the output of an irrigated farm is 5 percent"; the latter says, "The zakat obligation on the output of an irrigated farm is 5 percent *if* conditions *a, b,* and *c* hold."[51]

The conditions that define a situationist obligation are obviously subject to variation across time, space, and context. So a situationist interpretation of the zakat requirement would be dynamic rather than static. It would not confer sacredness on any particular formulation adopted by the early Muslims. Treating as fixed only the goal of having the wealthy fund social relief programs, it would consider the rates implemented in seventh-century Arabia as illustrative of fundamental principles whose practical implications are subject to change. The Islamist writers who consider the zakat obligation a static duty do not concede that it entails sacrificing equality for the sake of procedural correctness. On the contrary, they maintain that the procedural approach would dramatically curtail inequality. Of course, that is hardly self-evident. The distributional impact of a system that entails taxing only certain kinds of wealth and income will depend on characteristics of the economy. If most income is derived from sources unknown in early Islam and a significant share of wealth is held in forms that developed only in modern times, zakat revenue might be too low to put even a dent in inequality.

In fact, it is not even certain that the contributors to an unreformed zakat system would belong exclusively, or even mainly, to the wealthy class. Consider Bangladesh's small farmers who depend on the monsoons. As a rule, they are very poor; few, if any, belong to their country's economic elite. Yet, under the classical system that proceduralist writers wish to resurrect, 10 percent of the output of such farmers would flow to a centralized zakat fund. Equally troubling from the standpoint of inequality reduction is that the classical system does not necessarily subject its beneficiaries to a means test. People of above-average wealth may be given support if financial incentives are necessary to secure their attachment to Islam. Likewise, a wealthy person is perfectly eligible for support if he is fighting for Islam or on a journey. Any preacher, however prosperous, is entitled to subsidies on the ground that he is serving Islam.

These observations rest on elementary logic. So it is not surprising that the potential consequences of an unreformed zakat system have troubled Islamists at least since the days of Sayyid Qutb. Nor is it surprising that Islamists, following Qutb's example, have increasingly been combining orthodox rhetoric with innovative proposals for fine-tuning the distributional effects of traditional zakat. The Islamic economist F. R. Faridi has advocated the establishment of an "Islamic tax system" that would coexist with a traditional zakat system. If the government determines that zakat-based transfers are benefiting the rich at the expense of the poor, it can use taxes to lessen, offset, or even reverse the resulting redistribution.[52] Suppose that zakat transfers $100 from poor farmer A to rich industrialist B, and that this outcome conflicts with the goal of inequality reduction. By imposing a tax of $150 on B and subsidizing A by the same amount, the government can achieve a net transfer of $50 for the benefit of the poor farmer. Consequently, it can claim that zakat is being implemented in its original form but without having to accept any of its consequences.

Faridi's proposal, like many others,[53] implicitly acknowledges that zakat is less well suited to a postindustrial economy than to the relatively primitive economy of the first Islamic state. It effectively concedes three points: First, the scope of the original system is far too limited to curb inequality and poverty; second, the original rates scarcely reflect the characteristics of a modern economy; and third, the beneficiaries of a zakat system may well be wealthier than its contributors. It also concedes that improving the distribution of wealth involves applying human judgment against a backdrop of continuously changing circumstances.

Why insist, then, on reviving the original zakat system as though its effects were fixed? Why not recognize squarely that the distributional goals of Islamic economics require policies similar to secular transfer policies currently in use throughout the world, including many predominantly Muslim countries? To return to the previous example, Faridi's distributional objective could be met more simply through a transfer system that takes $50 from B for the benefit of A. But remember that the purpose of zakat has never been limited to redistribution; from the beginning, it has been considered a purifier of wealth, a source of inner comfort for donors, and an instrument of religious solidarity. Insofar as these other objectives continue to carry weight, one may favor a zakat system even if it produces undesirable distributional consequences. Recall, too, that a person's wealth rank has never been the sole criterion for determining whether he is to be a zakat recipient. Subsidizing the pilgrimage of a wealthy person or supplementing the salary of a preacher is perfectly compatible with the original zakat system.

The history of zakat, along with its longstanding inclusion among Islam's five pillars, helps explain the present commitment to its revival in spite of its inadequacy as an antipoverty instrument. However, one cannot make sense of this commitment simply by reading a random sampling of the literature that advocates the system's restoration. Islamic economics exudes confidence that even in a modern economy zakat will dampen inequality; and this claim only grows bolder as the literature seeks to match neoclassical economics in technical sophistication and emphasis on quantification.

An Historical Perspective on Contemporary Shortcomings

The weaknesses of the promotional literature have not prevented the establishment of government-operated zakat systems. More than a dozen countries now have some form of an official zakat system. As the proceedings of the Kuala Lumpur zakat conference make abundantly clear, these systems exhibit huge differences, which mirror variations in the past. Another element of historical continuity is that none of the prevailing systems has had much impact on poverty. Finally, the distributional effects of these systems have not necessarily been to transfer resources from rich to poor. Malaysia's zakat system, though it is now being modified, has brought about perverse redistribution. Pakistan's heralded system has promoted transfers within the middle class, and its impact on poverty has been minimal.[54] Clearly, the optimistic projections of the past few decades have failed to materialize. There is no evidence that the zakat systems currently in operation combat poverty more effectively than relief systems lacking an Islamic identification.

From an historical perspective, these observations are unsurprising. No period of Islamic history offers evidence of a drastic reduction in poverty through zakat.

Early on, zakat became a highly politicized institution, and powerful groups interpreted both the requirement to make zakat payments and the entitlement to receive zakat assistance in self-serving ways. Consequently, the system quickly lost legitimacy, except as an abstract ideal. Moreover, governments subsequently did little to enforce zakat. Although voluntary zakat transfers never ceased, there is nothing to suggest that these have had major economic significance. Moving forward in time, we find that the Europeans who colonized large parts of the Islamic world did not try to enforce or revive zakat. But it is wrong to claim, as some writers do, that European imperialism damaged a system that had been working effectively. Well before the colonial period, the zakat requirement was being evaded or defied to the point where it was a dead letter practically everywhere.

The original Islamic community in seventh-century Arabia might have had a zakat system compatible with the standards of today's zakat advocates. However, it does not follow that the system implemented then would have similar distributional effects today. Making herdsmen and farmers bear the brunt of a modern society's zakat burden could actually have the perverse effect of increasing inequality. Only if the scope and rates of zakat were thoroughly overhauled might zakat serve a major role in curbing inequality and poverty.

Against the opposition of a shrinking minority of die-hard traditionalists, the reform process has already begun. Despite a rhetoric of continuing commitment to ancient details, which serves the interests of wealthy Islamists who are reluctant to tamper with economic structures that serve them reasonably well, several countries have started to modernize zakat. This experimentation has added to the variety of precedents.

The zakat system could be standardized by turning all levies into ad valorem taxes payable in money by Muslims of sufficient means. Such a solution would maintain parity among the obligations of people in different occupations and among different forms of wealth, in the face of changes in relative prices. But for anyone committed to economic Islamization, this move would also have a drawback: weaker links to early Islamic practices. Indeed, as zakat took on the colorings of a modern transfer system, its Islamic symbolism would get blunted, possibly setting the stage for questions as to whether a modern economy needs it.

Notes

1. Ahmed Abdel-Fattah El-Ashker and Muhammad Sirajul Haq, eds., *Institutional Framework of Zakah: Dimensions and Implications* (Jeddah: Islamic Development Bank, 1995).

2. Suliman Bashear, "On the Origins and Development of the Meaning of *Zakat* in Early Islam," *Arabica* 40 (1993): esp. 84–85; Franz Rosenthal, "Sedaka, Charity," *Hebrew*

Union College Annual 23 (1950–1951): esp. 421–423; Mahmood Ibrahim, *Merchant Capital and Islam* (Austin: University of Texas Press, 1990), 19, 76; W. Montgomery Watt, *Muhammad at Mecca* (Oxford: Oxford University Press, 1953), 165–169; C. Snouck Hurgronje, "La *Zakat*" (orig. Dutch ed., 1882), *Oeuvres choisies*, ed. G.-H. Bousquet and J. Schacht (Leiden: E. J. Brill, 1957), 152–153.

3. M. A. Shaban, *Islamic History: A New Interpretation* (Cambridge: Cambridge University Press, 1971), 1:19–27; Ibrahim, *Merchant Capital*, 99–109; Fred McGraw Donner, *The Early Islamic Conquests* (Princeton: Princeton University Press, 1981), 82–90; Elias Shoufani, *Al-Riddah and the Muslim Conquest of Arabia* (Toronto: University of Toronto Press, 1973), 10–47, 71–106. For an interpretation that puts greater emphasis on religious factors, see Bashear, "Origins," 99–113.

4. Ibrahim, *Merchant Capital*, 140; Shaban, *Islamic History,* 1:118–119. From the available historical sources we can identify neither the full range of goods defined as hidden wealth, nor all the controversies surrounding the dramatic reinterpretation believed to have occurred soon after the Prophet's death. What is clear is that regimes that followed the original Islamic state tended to exempt from regular taxation those assets believed to have been redefined as "hidden." It is plausible, therefore, that a radical reinterpretation took place under Uthman and also that the political elites of the time by and large welcomed the shift.

5. M. Bravmann, "Surplus of Property: An Early Arab Social Concept," *Der Islam* 38 (1963): 28–50; Joseph Schacht, "Zakat," *Encyclopedia of Islam,* 1st ed. (Leiden: E. J. Brill, 1934), 3:1202–1204. For the logic of redistribution norms in primitive societies and numerous examples similar to those of early Islam, see Richard A. Posner, "A Theory of Primitive Society," in his *The Economics of Justice* (Cambridge: Harvard University Press, 1981), chap. 6.

6. Claude Cahen, "Bayt al-Mal, History," *EI²*, 1:1143–1144.

7. Jonathan Benthall, "Financial Worship: The Quranic Injunction to Almsgiving," *Journal of the Royal Anthropological Institute,* n.s., 5 (1999): 29–31.

8. Frede Løkkegaard, *Islamic Taxation in the Classical Period* (Copenhagen: Branner and Korch, 1950), 93.

9. Snouck Hurgronje, "La *Zakat*," 164.

10. On this period's turbulence, see Marshall G. S. Hodgson, *The Venture of Islam: Conscience and History in a World Civilization* (Chicago: University of Chicago Press, 1974), 1:187–217; Shaban, *Islamic History,* chaps. 2–4; Ibrahim, *Merchant Capital,* chaps. 5–7.

11. Abdallah Al-Shiekh, "Zakat," *Oxford Encyclopedia of the Modern Islamic World* (New York: Oxford University Press, 1995), 4:366–370.

12. On the origins and practices of Christian asceticism, see Jean Delumeau, *Sin and Fear: The Emergence of a Western Guilt Culture, 13th–18th Centuries,* trans. Eric Nicholson (New York: St. Martin's Press, 1990), esp. chap. 16.

13. W. Björkman, "Maks," *EI²*, 6:194–195; A. Grohmann, "'Ushr," *Encyclopaedia of Islam,* 1st ed. (Leiden: E. J. Brill, 1936), 4:1050–1052; Claude Cahen, "Kharadj," *EI²*, 4:1030–1034.

14. Abu Yusuf, *Kitab al-kharaj,* trans. A. Ben Shemesh as *Taxation in Islam* (Arabic original c. 790; Leiden: E. J. Brill, 1969), 3:134–140.

15. Schacht, "Zakat," 1204.

16. Løkkegaard, *Islamic Taxation*, 120–125.

17. Schacht, "Zakat," 1204.

18. Løkkegaard, *Islamic Taxation*, 163. See also Baber Johansen, *The Islamic Law on Land Tax and Rent* (London: Croom Helm, 1988), esp. 19.

19. Jacques Le Goff, *Medieval Civilization, 400–1500*, trans. Julia Barrow (French original, 1964; Oxford: Basil Blackwell, 1988), 290–293; Robert B. Ekelund et al., *Sacred Trust: The Medieval Church as an Economic Firm* (New York: Oxford University Press, 1994), chap. 2.

20. Ahmad Oran and Salim Rashid, "Fiscal Policy in Early Islam," *Public Finance* 44 (1989): 75–101.

21. Ikram Azam, *Pakistan and Islamic Economics* (Lahore: Amir Publications, 1978), 97. The author attributes the passage to a 1952 book by S. A. Siddiqi.

22. Benthall, "Financial Worship," 30.

23. Personal communication with Fred Donner, May 12, 1997.

24. Maxime Rodinson, *Islam and Capitalism*, trans. Brian Pearce (French original, 1966; New York: Pantheon, 1973), 25–26; Snouck Hurgronje, "La *Zakat*," 161–162; Ibrahim, *Merchant Capital*, 145–148.

25. Abu Hamid al-Ghazali, *Revival of the Religious Sciences*, issued as *Imam Ghazali's Ihya Ulum-id-Din*, trans. Fazul-ul-Karim (Aratic original c. 1100; Lahore: Sind Sagar Academy, 1978), 34–35.

26. Yassine Essid, *A Critique of the Origins of Islamic Economic Thought* (Leiden: E. J. Brill, 1995), 141.

27. Timur Kuran, "The Provision of Public Goods under Islamic Law: Origins, Impact, and Limitations of the Waqf System," *Law and Society Review* 35 (2001): 301–357. See also Bahaeddin Yediyıldız, *Institution du waqf au XVIIIᵉ siècle en Turquie: étude socio-historique* (Ankara: Editions Ministère de la Culture, 1990).

28. Abraham Marcus, "Poverty and Poor Relief in Eighteenth-Century Aleppo," *Revue du monde musulman et de la Méditerranée* 55–56 (1990): 171–179, quote at 171.

29. Ibid., esp. 172.

30. Benthall, "Financial Worship," 29–30; Snouck Hurgronje, "La *Zakat*," 150; Norman A. Stillman, "Charity and Social Service in Medieval Islam," *Societas* 5 (1975): 106–107.

31. Snouck Hurgronje, "La *Zakat*," 150.

32. Essid, *A Critique of the Origins of Islamic Economic Thought*, 201–202.

33. Michael Bonner, "Definitions of Poverty and the Rise of the Muslim Urban Poor," *Journal of the Royal Asiatic Society* 6 (1996): 335–344.

34. Certain early Muslim writers sought to soothe the poor also by proposing that they would be the "first to enter heaven." See Bonner, "Definitions of Poverty," 341–343.

35. Josep-Antoni Ybarra, "The *Zakat* in Muslim Society: An Analysis of Islamic Economic Policy," *Social Science Information* 35 (1996): 643–656; Benthall, "Financial Worship," 35; Stillman, "Charity," 115.

36. Marcel Mauss, *The Gift: Forms and Functions of Exchange in Archaic Societies* (1925; reprint, New York: Norton, 1967).

37. See, for example, Charles Murray, *Losing Ground: American Social Policy, 1950–1980* (New York: Basic Books, 1984), chaps. 14, 16.

38. The point has also been made by Benthall, "Financial Worship," 36.

39. David Dean Commins, *Islamic Reform: Politics and Social Change in Late Ottoman Syria* (New York: Oxford University Press, 1990), 87–88.

40. See Timur Kuran, "The Genesis of Islamic Economics: A Chapter in the Politics of Muslim Identity," *Social Research* 64 (1997): 301–338.

41. Sayyid Abu l-A'la Mawdudi, *Let Us Be Muslims*, ed. Khurram Murad (Urdu original, 1940; Kuala Lumpur: Noordeen, 1990), chaps. 19–23, esp. 220.

42. Sayyid Qutb, *Social Justice in Islam*, trans. John D. Hardie (Arabic original, 1948; New York: American Council of Learned Societies, 1970), 133–138, 267–270.

43. Naseem Quazi, "Economic Morality in Islam," *Hamdard Islamicus* 16 (winter 1993): 93.

44. M. Umer Chapra, *Islam and the Economic Challenge* (Leicester: Islamic Foundation, 1992), esp. 225–226, 270–275.

45. Al–Shiekh, "Zakat," 368.

46. See, for example, Shaikh Mahmud Ahmad, *Economics of Islam*, 2nd ed. (Lahore: Sh. Muhammad Ashraf, 1952); Mohammad Abdul Mannan, *Islamic Economics: Theory and Practice* (Lahore: Sh. Muhammad Ashraf, 1970), 284–302; Afzal-ur-Rahman, *Economic Doctrines of Islam*, vol. 3 (Lahore: Islamic Publications, 1976), chaps. 14–18; Abdur Rahman Shad, *Zakat and 'Ushr* (Lahore: Kazi Publications, 1986). These books have all been reprinted many times, and Islamist bookstores with an English-language section tend to keep them in stock.

47. Ahmad, *Economics of Islam*, 91; Afzal-ur-Rahman, *Economic Doctrines*, 3:218–224.

48. Ahmad, *Economics of Islam*, 90; Afzal-ur-Rahman, *Economic Doctrines*, 3:206–207.

49. Ahmad, *Economics of Islam*, 89; Afzal-ur-Rahman, *Economic Doctrines*, 3:225–226.

50. The early Muslims tried to fix the ratio between the price of gold and that of silver, but they were ultimately unsuccessful. See W. Barthold, *İslâm Medeniyeti Tarihi*, ed. Fuad Köprülü (Russian original, 1918; Ankara: Türk Tarih Kurumu, 1963), 25. The exemption limits set by the Prophet probably reflected the price ratio that prevailed in his own milieu.

51. The clash between proceduralism and situationism has a long history in Islamic thought, as recognized by Majid Khadduri in his *The Islamic Conception of Justice* (Baltimore: Johns Hopkins University Press, 1984), chap. 6. For general insights, see Geoffrey Brennan and James M. Buchanan, *The Reason of Rules* (New York: Cambridge University Press, 1985), chap. 7; Joseph Fletcher, *Situation Ethics: The New Morality* (Philadelphia: Westminster Press, 1966), chap. 1.

52. F. R. Faridi, "A Theory of Fiscal Policy in an Islamic State," in *Fiscal Policy and Resource Allocation in Islam*, ed. Ziauddin Ahmed, Munawar Iqbal, and M. Fahim Khan (Jeddah: International Center for Research in Islamic Economics, 1983), 27–45. For another statement in favor of allowing corrections of the redistribution effected through zakat, see Chapra, *Islam and the Economic Challenge*, 274. "If the *zakat* proceeds are not sufficient," writes Chapra, "it is the unavoidable responsibility of the society to find other ways of attaining the desired goal."

53. For a broader critique, see Timur Kuran, "On the Notion of Economic Justice in Contemporary Islamic Thought," *International Journal of Middle East Studies* 21 (1989): 171–191.

54. See Timur Kuran, "The Economic Impact of Islamic Fundamentalism," in *Fundamentalisms and the State: Remaking Polities, Economies, and Militance*, ed. Martin E. Marty and R. Scott Appleby (Chicago: University of Chicago Press, 1993), 318–325; idem., "Islamic Economics and the Islamic Subeconomy," *Journal of Economic Perspectives* 9 (Fall 1995): 163–165.

CHAPTER FIFTEEN

Charity's Legacies

A Reconsideration of Ottoman Imperial Endowment-Making

AMY SINGER

Why Reconsider *Waqf*?

It would hardly be controversial to argue that throughout its history the most powerful formal vehicle for voluntary charitable and philanthropic endeavors in the Islamic world was probably the endowment, or *waqf*. As a form of charity, alms *(zakat)* had primacy of place as one of the five obligations of every Muslim. Zakat was assessed annually, at fixed rates, and due in cash or in kind. However, its universal nature did not allow any one person to be recognized as an outstanding contributor. The institutionalization of zakat after the death of Muhammad was not uniformly successful and was even undermined at times by the proliferation of state levies.[1] In contrast, the voluntary character of waqf, combined with its possibilities for social recognition, fiscal advantage, family benefit, and political profit, reinforced the attraction of this mode of formal giving.[2]

Large-scale beneficent undertakings might seem by their nature to be relatively immune from criticism. On the surface, endowments seem uniformly praiseworthy, created to sustain institutions that served the broader public. Their benefits to the spiritual, social, material, intellectual, and hygienic condition of the wider population offer no obvious target for rebuke. That they might also benefit the founder and his or her family is neither unusual in a donation nor necessarily blameworthy. Very few charitable or philanthropic acts are entirely selfless; rather, most donors profit from their own contributions, whether the benefits are spiritual or eschatological, or bring them social status, political legitimacy, and acclaim as social or cultural patrons. Endowments that primarily benefited their donors might be regarded as akin to contemporary family trusts. And yet, historical writing about waqfs moves easily from praise to blame in assessing the roles of endowed institutions and the people connected to them.

Ottoman endowment-making, especially at the elite and imperial level, is extremely well recorded. In addition to documentary evidence, chronicles, critical memoranda, and other forms of literary evidence all have something to say on the subject. The critiques of endowments vary, at times connected to discussions of Ottoman imperial decline, the reform of the empire, or the modernization of Muslim societies generally. Some critics suggest that the prevalence of waqfs in the Middle East impaired the development of agriculture and the reform processes and was detrimental to the evolution of the modern Middle East.[3] It is for these reasons that it is appropriate to reconsider the practice of waqf in the Ottoman Empire, as this empire defined politically the largest part of the Middle East immediately prior to the modern era and well into it.

A reassessment of waqf illustrates how the critiques of endowments are themselves problematic. They come from the observations of contemporaries, Ottomans and outsiders alike. Thus far they have not been systematically evaluated and little further empirical research has been done to test their specific claims. The question is: How did these negative perceptions of waqf develop and when? What prompted and sustained the critical attitude toward beneficent endowments that ultimately led to their being severely curtailed if not outright eliminated in the modern states of the Islamic world, in states that preserve Islamic law in various aspects of national law? What were the effects of these critiques on the appreciation of waqf in a historical context, of the legacy of this form of charity? Finally, despite the criticism voiced against waqf, is there room for a reconsideration of these legacies?[4]

I would like to claim in this chapter that the immediate contribution and the legacy of Ottoman imperial and elite waqf-making to the contemporary ex-Ottoman provinces is far more complex than the predominantly negative critique suggests. Although one may identify deleterious effects of waqf-making, some equally positive influences were established by this tradition that must be taken into account in attempting an overall assessment. Until now, the positive aspects of waqf were often idealized or reified when they were not ignored. Moreover, beyond a calculation of the favorable or harmful nature of waqf in the short and long term, it is perhaps more important to recognize the profound influence the institution has had in shaping Ottoman and post-Ottoman societies. This chapter is an initial consideration of the negative manner in which waqf and its legacies have been discussed. It presents a preliminary survey, necessarily incomplete, of opinions and judgments about waqf. It then posits a number of realms in which waqf-making has made a more constructive long-term contribution. This chapter articulates some important directions for new research, and questions certain long-held assumptions about this fundamental institution.

The Motivations to Endow

Waqf-making is a voluntary charitable act *(sadaqa)* by an individual. It is intended as a means to gain the proximity or favor of God *(qurba)*. The Quran enjoins people to "be good to your parents, and your kin, and to orphans, and the needy."[5] "Offerings *[sadaqat]* are meant for the indigent and needy, and those who collect and distribute them, and those whom you wish to win over, and for [redeeming] the captives and those who are in debt, and in the cause of God, and the wayfarers."[6] Waqf is not specifically mentioned in the Quran, but it is referred to as *sadaqa mawqufa* (an endowed charitable act) in very early Muslim texts, thus establishing the connection to the Quranic injunctions regarding sadaqa.[7] It seems to be as old as Islam, practiced by modest as well as substantial property owners. Gradually, it became a widespread tool among Muslims, and from the ninth and tenth centuries on, the use of endowments to create large public buildings and services was widely adopted by rulers, viziers, and people of great wealth and standing.[8]

Briefly, to make a waqf, the founder declared that a revenue-yielding property would be endowed, that the ownership of it would be alienated to God, and its revenues would support a particular purpose: the running of a mosque or school, the upkeep of a bridge or fountain, or stipends for scholars, students, orphans, and so on. The beneficiaries could include specific individuals as well. Waqf functionaries, including the appointed line of managers, were assigned salaries and could be appointed from the family of the founder.

Over time, those who wrote about waqfs came to divide them into two groups: public, beneficent *(khass, khayri)* and private, family *('amm, ahli)*—The defining factor in this characterization was the initial beneficiary of the waqf, either some public institution such as a mosque or public kitchen or successive members of the founder's family. The origin of the distinction is unknown, but it is a false one with respect to the nature of waqf. All endowments name the poor, or the poor of some specific place, as the ultimate beneficiaries once the original purpose has vanished—destroyed or died out (as it could within a generation or two.) This was to ensure that the purpose of a waqf be perpetual, to match the permanent endowment of the properties. As a result, ahli endowments have the same legal and religious status as the khayri. At some point, however, the distinction between khayri and ahli became so routine and emphatic that modern writers frequently refer to the two types as though they had always existed and were legally distinct.[9]

By and large, the founding of public endowments has more often earned praise than criticism. In general, both contemporaries and later commentators lauded the endeavors of rulers, ministers, and other powerful men and women who donated large sums and properties to build mosques, schools, hospitals, public kitchens, bridges, fountains, and other structures or institutions that benefited the wider community. A list of a person's good works was a familiar element in their written biography.

The assessments of so-called family waqfs, founded for the immediate benefit of the founders and their families, have often been less charitable. They were frequently regarded as suspiciously self-serving, not quite adhering to the spirit of beneficent enterprise, even though permissible according to the letter of the law and sustained by the Quranic prescriptions to care for family members.[10] Critics pointed out that these endowments were used to rob rightful heirs of their portions or to divert capital to persons who would otherwise inherit less or not at all, such as slaves and women.[11] Moreover, founders (even sultans) who endowed agricultural lands to both kinds of endowment, sometimes did so illegally, as they often came to "possess" them by usurping state lands, extending revenue collecting or usufructory *(tasarruf)* rights to take over the basic substance of ownership *(raqaba)*. Criticism also adhered to those who created charitable endowments but named themselves and their heirs to positions as salaried managers, teachers, and other beneficiaries or functionaries. These latter endowments were of a mixed type: sustaining family members while at the same time giving assistance or benefit to others.

From the time of the first Ottoman principality *(beylik)* in the fourteenth century, until the waning years of the empire, the men and women of the Ottoman imperial household (chiefly the sultan and ranking women in the imperial harem[12]) established endowments of all types to settle, develop, and sustain their domains and the subject populations. Founding waqfs was one strategy employed to reinforce the legitimacy of the dynasty, to promote the development of cities and regions, and to supply public services to the subject populations. The Ottomans also preserved many of the endowments made by their predecessors in the Muslim lands they conquered in Anatolia and the Arab provinces.[13]

As with other customs and practices, the waqf-making of the imperial household was replicated throughout society, though on a scale compatible with the means of each founder. A founder could endow any property she or he held fully and freely *(mulk)*, but only such properties. Viziers, governors, officers, religious figures, merchants, and others established endowments all over the empire. Sometimes these people created their own waqfs and sometimes they added revenue-yielding properties or funds to existing ones, especially those for the residents, pilgrims and institutions of the two holy cities: Mecca and Medina. Provincial governors left behind waqfs as testaments to their beneficence in the cities and regions they controlled.

It is clear that the motivations for creating endowments were many and the results served purposes not originally envisaged among the targets of charitable giving. The motivation as stated in the endowment deed *(waqfiyya)* was usually limited to qurba, although sometimes a desire to contribute to the well-being *(maslaha)* of Muslims was also attributed to the founder. In contrast, unstated reasons for founding waqfs included the protection of assets from confiscation, personal glorification, avoidance of inheritance laws, promotion of urban development, and the search for political legitimacy or social status. Along with their intended benefits, endowments could also result in the enrichment of family members or prominent religious figures, the alienation of state lands, the deterioration of endowed properties, the corruption of employees and the diminished motivation of beneficiaries to seek real work.

The Critiques

While observers might acknowledge the pious impulse that was recorded in the endowment deeds as the inspiration for waqfs, they also leveled various critiques against large donors. Imperial donors were not always lauded for the exorbitant sums they spent on endowments if, in this way, they had only added to the financial burden of the state without contributing anything to its coffers. In the year 1581, the historian Mustafa Ali commented in his *Counsel for Sultans*:

> For, the Divine Laws do not permit the building of charitable establishments with the means of the public treasury, neither do they allow the foundation of mosques and *medreses* [colleges] that are not needed. Unless a sultan, after conducting a victorious campaign, decides to spend the booty he has made on pious deeds *(hayrat u meberrat)* rather than on his personal pleasures, and engages to prove this by the erection of [public] buildings.[14]

Safiye Sultan, wife of Murad III (1574–1595) and mother of Mehmed III (1595–1603), was criticized for the expense incurred by her project to build an enormous mosque complex in Eminönü in Istanbul. Its construction was halted upon the deaths of Safiye and her son. Subsequently, the undertaking was remembered as an "act of oppression" because of the harsh manner in which the Jews were expropriated and expelled from Eminönü to make the site available. The endowment of Ahmed I (1603–1617) at Atmeydanı (Hippodrome) in the center of Istanbul drew criticism similar to that aimed at Safiye, as he had achieved no conquests that could finance his huge mosque complex.[15]

Fifty years later, Safiye's unfinished project in Eminönü was taken up by Turhan Sultan, mother of Mehmed IV (1648–1687). Turhan was more successful in creating a climate of public opinion that approved the completion of the Yeni Cami mosque complex. Though her son had no military gains to his credit, she had the project portrayed as a kind of conquest because the area had to be cleared again of its largely Jewish population, now viewed as an obstacle. As a result, Turhan's expropriations were characterized as "just," in comparison with Safiye's "oppression."[16]

It appears, then, that even large-scale imperial charitable projects had to conform to certain norms. Even though one might wish to see such endowments as the responsibility of the imperial household—part of their obligation to provide for the subject populations—waqf-making was also considered a privilege, at least in the sixteenth and seventeenth centuries. This privilege could be earned by proving oneself a successful conqueror, whether bringing booty to the state coffers as did the first eleven sultans (and some thereafter) or by portraying one's acts as those of a defender of the faith, as did Turhan Sultan.

A different kind of criticism is represented by Koçi Bey, a Christian slave recruit *(devşirme)* who served inside the Topkapı Palace, becoming the confidant and man-in-waiting to Murad IV (1623–1640). In 1630 he presented a *Risale* (treatise) to the sultan wherein he analyzed the problems of the Ottoman state and proffered his suggestions for their solution. The Risale was also submitted to Murad's successor Ibrahim I (1640–1648).[17]

In addressing the topic of waqfs, Koçi Bey thought that only those supporting charitable and religious institutions could be considered legitimate. He maintained that endowments made by the commanders of the early sultans should be considered valid, although in his opinion, far too much imperial land had been alienated by grants of ownership *(temlik)* to high-ranking members of the ruling class during the two centuries preceding his own. In this way, vast tax revenues had been lost to the state as the lands were converted into waqfs by these people, often for the benefit of their families and not the community of Muslims *(amme-i Muslimin)*. The missing revenues, according to Koçi Bey, should have gone to pay the janissaries and other troops, who regularly complained and made trouble over salaries. He argued that these revenues should be reclaimed for the state by confiscating lands from illegitimate endowments.

Koçi Bey also criticized the enormous advantages and powers accumulated by the chief black eunuch of the imperial palace *(darüsseadet ağası)*, as a result of his serving as supervisor of all imperial endowments and all those belonging to Mecca and Medina as well. He gave appointments as managers to his own people or sold them outright and collected and kept all surplus revenues *(zeva'id)* of the endowments. Ordinarily, these surpluses were intended for the maintainance and improvement of the endowed properties, not for the enrichment of the supervisor.

In his critique, Koçi Bey made a de facto distinction between those endowments benefiting the community of Muslims and those benefiting a founder's family, implicitly questioning the legitimacy of the latter type. He ignored the fact that the nonimperial waqfs of the early Ottoman commanders and many others were often mixed in type from their inception, benefiting the founders and their families, at the same time that they sustained some more general charitable undertaking. Nonetheless, Koçi Bey's criticism does not find fault with endowments as such but rather with the management of them and with the improper granting of imperial lands that ultimately depleted the treasury.

It is important to note that in none of the criticisms from the sixteenth and seventeenth centuries I have presented is the basic institution of waqf called into question. Corruptions and improprieties were identified and condemned to be corrected, not as a prelude to diminishing or even eliminating waqfs altogether. The people who founded or managed them were to blame for things that went wrong and they could be replaced.

Other criticisms were made. The revenue-yielding properties suffered as, in the absence of "proper" owners, no one invested in their upkeep and improvement. Waqf managers *(mütevelli)*, collecting and distributing the revenues from endowed properties as well as making appointments to the positions funded by the endowments, had enormous opportunities for corruption. In addition, waqf properties could be leased only for short periods, usually of one to three years, yet managers were persuaded to grant consecutive leases simultaneously in multiples of three to encourage tenants to invest in the properties. The long-term leases were ultimately harmful to some properties because they set a fixed rent that could not be changed later to reflect market values. Moreover, such leases might ultimately be translated into outright ownership when tenants took advantage of local upheavals or corrupt officials. These properties included built structures and agricultural lands alike, to the detriment of all.[18]

Over time the waqfs were also said to undermine the social fabric because they distributed pensions or sinecures to people—often members of the 'ulama (scholars)—and thus kept them dependent and unproductive. The extent to which the 'ulama both controlled and were supported by the waqfs meant that these institutions were the chief basis of their fiscal strength. Several leading figures of the Ottoman administrative and ruling elite also benefited extraordinarily from waqfs. Men like the head of the corps of judges and scholars *(şeyhülislam)*, the commander *(ağa)* of the janissaries, the chief black eunuch of the palace, the grand vizier, and others were named supervisors of endowments founded by various members of the different elites they headed. Over time, the number of endowments in the hands of this small group increased, providing each with a solid financial base and corresponding political power as the distributors of numerous remunerative positions. Each man was also strengthened vis-à-vis the sultan, particularly during the reigns of weaker men.[19]

The chief black eunuch was well placed to profit from the surplus revenues of endowments. He had been assigned the supervision of the imperial foundations in A.H. 1006/C.E. 1598 to reduce the abuses by individual managers. Despite Koçi Bey's criticisms of the seventeenth century, responsibility for many other imperial endowments was given to this powerful palace servant in 1128/1716.[20] Thus, not surprisingly, when they came, the first reforms of waqf management were aimed at reducing the control of the chief eunuch and the abuses he perpetuated. Mustafa III (1757–1774) and his grand vizier Ragip Mehmed Paşa were the architects of this reform, effective until the reign of Mustafa's successor Abdülhamid I (1774–1789). The chief eunuch then recovered his powers, though he now had to compete with the newly established Ministry for Waqf Affairs *(Evkaf-i Hümayun Nezareti)*. This ministry first came into its own only in the nineteenth century; in the meantime, it was marginally successful at creating an alternative authority to manage endowments.[21]

The Reforms

It was in the nineteenth century that radical reforming measures were finally aimed at waqfs. Instead of particular instances of corruption, the reforms initiated a wholesale renovation of the management of endowments, removing power from the hands of local managers as well as the supervisor and men like him who had held broad authority over many endowments by virtue of their other appointments. In 1826, Sultan Mahmud II consolidated most of the imperial endowments and those of state officials under the auspices of the Ministry for Waqf Affairs.[22]

Just as the elimination of the janissaries in that same year had removed the chief internal military threat to the sultan, so the removal of waqf management to the Ministry worked to undermine the fiscal strength of the strong men of government and the learned religious men throughout the empire. In effect, the Tanzimat reforms broadened the powers of the ministry and granted it authority for collecting waqf revenues. The revenues were then redistributed by the ministry as annual budgets to individual endowments. At the time, these measures presumably received much support from the Westernizing reformers and foreign observers, who looked to reduce the influence of the religious classes altogether.[23]

The criticism implicit in these reforms of waqf management was aimed at the power of traditional groups in Ottoman society. Religious men of every class lost income and power as the responsibility for collecting revenues was taken from them and as the sums of money budgeted to the institutions for salaries and upkeep were reduced. These measures were a necessary part of the general reform being undertaken in the Tanzimat era. The janissaries and the 'ulama provided some of the staunchest opponents of reform. With them removed or weakened, the reformers could more easily proceed to introduce innovations in military, educational, and judicial organization and content.

In addition to criticism originating inside the former Ottoman states and societies during the period of Ottoman rule, those outsiders who examined Muslim states and societies have contributed to a negative assessment of endowments. The attitudes of these writers, largely historians and colonial administrators, seem to be based primarily on contemporary local sources as well as the writings of other foreign observers. The negative portrayal of endowments was, for the most part, neither challenged nor investigated but rather reproduced. Other criticisms arose as a result of the critics' own flawed interpretations or ignorance of Islamic laws and/or of local languages and practices.[24]

The article on waqf in the first edition of the *Encyclopaedia of Islam* is a useful example of an authoritative and negative portrayal of endowments that has been cited repeatedly. Due to the stature of the *Encyclopaedia of Islam* and to the fact that *wakf* in Latin characters comes at the end of the alphabet, so that the second edition of the article only appeared with the new millennium, this earlier article remained the most accessible description of the institution in Western languages for seventy years. It is also based not only on traditional Muslim sources of law but also on the scholarship dealing with waqf produced at the end of the nineteenth and beginning of the twentieth centuries. Written under the influence of works dealing with the modernization of the Middle East, the establishment of new nations and the confrontation of major problems of agricultural and land reform, the article naturally reflects the perception of waqf as a hindrance, if not an outright obstruction to development. By calling waqf "the Dead Hand," a translation of the French *mortmain*, waqf was also mistakenly associated with everything negative in that European institution.[25]

An additional critique of waqf can be found in H. A. R. Gibb and Harold Bowen's *Islamic Society and the West*, another highly influential work.[26] While explaining the intricacies of waqf law and the various legal variants allowed for in management, Gibb and Bowen condemn the institution, emphasizing how devastating the condition of being waqf was to property, both agricultural and built.

> Although it was the duty of the central administration, aided by the local *Kadis*, to see that all *wakf* properties were kept productive and in full repair, the almost inevitable fate of *wakf* lands was to be starved, under-cultivated, and finally left derelict. . . . *Wakf* lands, however, probably suffered less from these abuses than *wakf* property in buildings. The experience of many centuries and in all countries proved that *wakf* properties rapidly fell into ruin.[27]

It is unclear on what basis Gibb and Bowen make this all-embracing claim. Nor do they indicate how the fate of waqf properties compared with that of other properties in any given time and place.

Although much research exists on individual waqf institutions as they were founded, essentially demonstrating their usefulness and contribution, not very often is there work that undertakes to study the soundness of a particular endowment over time. In part, this is because many studies of waqfs base themselves primarily, if not entirely, on the texts of the endowment deeds and not on records describing the subsequent functioning of any given institution. (The former survive in far greater numbers than the latter.) One of the few studies of a single waqf's functioning over time is by Miriam Hoexter, and her research is practically unique in its extent and calculation. Hoexter's discussion of the endowments for Mecca and Medina *(awqaf al-Haramayn)* in Algiers is based on a meticulous investigation of the account books of this huge endowment, actually comprising many proper-ties endowed separately over several hundred years. Hoexter shows conclusively that this waqf was run carefully, with purchases or sales of properties made to strengthen the total endowment, keeping pace with general fluctuations in the price trends of different kinds of lands and buildings.[28] This suggests that endowments were man-aged, in some cases at least, with the same considerations that governed the larger market in property. A similar conclusion has been put forward by Oded Peri in his study of waqf-making in Jerusalem in the late eighteenth century.[29]

These few studies aside, little has been said to mitigate the negative view of endowments as long-term propositions. Large individual institutions may have continued to earn praise over time. However, the long-term assessment of waqfs by historians and observers of this and previous centuries has been altogether less than enthusiastic. The operation and management of all forms of waqf have been con-demned in turn for the enduring harmful effects they inflicted on properties endowed to support institutions, as well as on the people associated with them—employees and beneficiaries alike. The older critique of a flawed but reparable institution shifted in the nineteenth and twentieth centuries to a critique of an out-moded institution, one no longer necessary or else incompatible with the workings of a modern bureaucratic state. Yet the legacy of waqf-making is a mixed one at the very least. Much work remains to be done before its specific effects on property ownership and development can be separated from those of other economic, so-cial, natural, and political factors. Meanwhile, it bears noting that this legacy includes many remarkable contributions as well. It is these that are examined in the concluding section of this chapter.

The Legacies of Charity

The Süleymaniye complex in Istanbul and the Hasseki Sultan *'imaret* (public kitchen) in Jerusalem are only two examples of a vast legacy created by the tradi-tion of waqf-making in the Ottoman Empire. As part of the ongoing Ottoman imperial project, Hurrem Sultan, wife of Sultan Süleyman I, founded an 'imaret in Jerusalem in the mid-sixteenth century. In this specific case, the 'imaret provided much-needed distributions of food, supported by a range of endowed agricultural properties and a double bath built especially for this purpose in Jerusalem.[30] At the same time, it was the culminating achievement of Hurrem's own public endow-ments, established in tandem with the magnificent Süleymaniye complex of her husband in Istanbul. His enormous undertaking created spaces for prayer, study, healing, and the distribution of aid, and set up a bath and markets to house the revenue-earning activities that sustained them.[31] The two waqfs together were a joint proclamation of imperial piety, power, and beneficence, aimed at the populations of both center and provinces, emphasizing the commitment of the Ottomans to the holy places of Islam as well as to their imperial capital.

While the foundations of Süleyman and Hurrem epitomize Ottoman imperial waqf-making, dozens of other endowments were made by sultans and the members of their households, throughout the era of Ottoman rule.[32] The sum total of these endowments not only established the monuments of the Ottoman past, but they also constructed or reinforced matrices and practices that define contemporary Turkey, as well as many of the Ottoman successor states in the Balkans and the Middle East. Still existing today, some buildings established as endowments retain their original functions, while some have been maintained but altered their use, and others have disappeared entirely. The permanent legacy of Ottoman waqf-making is apparent in the physical, intellectual, economic, social, and cultural realities of these lands. Moreover, the Ottoman habit of waqf-making is part of a larger tradition of sadaqa in Islamic societies, a tradition that has long fostered a culture of philanthropic activity little appreciated or mentioned in the larger history of charity. By emphasizing this tradition and sustaining it through numerous endowments of their own, the Ottomans preserved and replicated this form of elite patronage.

Physical Legacy

The physical legacy of waqf-making is the most striking and obvious, and it is inseparable from the others. Among the largest of the imperial Ottoman complexes *(külliye)*, the Fatih and Süleymaniye in Istanbul were built in the fifteenth and sixteenth centuries, respectively.[33] Each one added enormous, impressive buildings to the city. At the same time these buildings fostered the development of whole neighborhoods by providing a spiritual, social, and economic nucleus in the institutions established. The waqfs also created built spaces that entailed a particular expansion of the urban fabric surrounding them. The placement of walls, gardens, and roads defined form and functions within the various neighborhoods of cities. These spaces continue to configure contemporary cities, with the monuments still serving as hubs for the different quarters.[34] They preserve open and green spaces, determine routes of access and traffic patterns, and provide that most essential institution, clean public toilets.

In the Haseki neighborhood of Istanbul, named for the complex of Hurrem Sultan there, the Haseki hospital continues to function as a large public hospital whose logo is a portrait of the lady founder. The flow of ailing people to and from this place (though the present hospital is one hundred meters away from the original building) has continued since its founding in the mid-sixteenth century, defining one constant human aspect of the city.[35] Other hospitals, such as that of the Bayezid II complex in Edirne, have not fared so well, in part because long ago Edirne lost the prestige it had as the second Ottoman capital and a major city on the principal route to the European provinces of the empire. The impressive building and its medical school stand alone on the outskirts of the town, a site that must be visited deliberately by all but those who live in the nearby quarter, also removed from the main town. Of late, however, this old hospital space has been repaired to house a museum of Ottoman medicine. Concerts are held in the hexagonal building that once sheltered the mentally ill, where they too were treated to musical performances as part of their therapy. Thus, now again people come to the Bayezidiye, though no longer for medical care.[36]

At Eyüp, the tomb of the Prophet's companion Abu Ayyub al-Ansari at the top of the Golden Horn in Istanbul, pilgrims stream steadily through the site as they seek his intercession, or that of one of the other notable figures buried there. As with the Haseki hospital, the shrines of Eyüp and its kitchen have created enduring patterns of human movement in the city space. They also defined the use of that space. The tomb of Eyüp attracted others to make their final resting places in the same area, such that today the surrounding area comprises an enormous cemetery.[37] In addition to the tomb and the mosques near it sits the complex of Mihrişah Valide Sultan, mother of Selim III. Among the buildings she established in 1796 is an enormous public kitchen, which continues to feed some fifteen hundred people daily and supply food to several other distribution points throughout the city. Like the public kitchen in Jerusalem, that at Eyüp preserves a long-established social commitment.

Much of the physical, constructed achievement of the Ottomans and their subjects, perhaps with the exception of domestic space, was created for or by endowments. These physical remains have been so continually identified with the Ottomans that they even became the victims of nationalist policies, either eradicated specifically in an effort to erase the memory of an Ottoman past (Balkans), discarded in the search for remnants of the "true national past" (Israeli archaeology), or simply ignored for lack of interest or funds.[38]

Intellectual Legacy

The waqfs also created an intellectual legacy through the schools and libraries they supported. The large complexes often included one or more colleges, primary and specialized schools, and sometimes a medical school. These were the principal venues for reproducing and transmitting knowledge through teaching and the copying of important texts.[39] Teachers and students alike were supported by endowment funds dispensed as salaries and stipends. Through them, generations of teachers, scholars, judges, and bureaucrats were trained in Islamic sciences. Medical schools were one place for training doctors.[40]

In addition to the schools, which had their own collections of manuscripts, libraries were founded. Their holdings today comprise a wealth of religious, legal, literary, aesthetic, and historical works. They chronicle the intellectual endeavors of the Ottomans and their predecessors, offering testimony to the rich and varied culture of the Ottoman world. Their study increases our understanding of the works themselves, of their authors, of the nature of learning, and of the evolution of the fields of law and jurisprudence. In addition, the presence of these manuscripts in Turkey and the other former Ottoman lands draws a continual traffic of scholars from around the globe. To study manuscripts, for example, they come to Istanbul to the former 'imaret of the Bayezid II complex, to the former college of the Süleymaniye (both now libraries), and to the library of Grand Vizier Mehmet Ragip Paşa. It should be noted that a similar kind of traffic exists to and from the buildings themselves by those drawn to the study of architecture and art. Once again, patterns of human movement and, in addition, intellectual exchange, are being shaped by endowments made under the Ottomans.

Economic Legacy

No less important a legacy was the economic impact of the endowments. To support the purpose for which any waqf was created, revenue-producing properties were endowed for it. They included baths, markets, houses, and manufactories in cities, and agricultural properties of every type. Thus, in addition to building mosques, schools, and so forth, the waqfs added a range of other structures to the cityscapes around the empire. Each physical addition further shaped the urban fabric into which it was placed, changing patterns of human traffic, water flow, the movement of goods and location of services, interrupting light and adding sound.

Markets of every size gave a home to money changers, craftsmen, and the merchants of foodstuffs, clothing, household goods, weapons, animals, gold, and hundreds of other necessary and luxury goods. To these came people of every class, some to buy and sell, others to look, bargain, steal, or beg. Especially under the Ottomans, cash endowments provided a source of ready money, alongside the professional moneylenders, for those who needed to borrow.[41] Many of the old commercial spaces, such as the Kapalı Çarşı, Mısır Çarşısı, the silk market in Bursa, the various Selçuk *taşhan*s (stone inns or waystations) around Anatolia and the Suq al-Qattanin in Jerusalem (Mamluk but repaired under the Ottomans), to name only a fraction, continue to exist alongside the modern shopping centers, office buildings, and banks, thus perpetuating patterns and styles of exchange. The flow of people to and from the markets fluctuates to rhythms that shift by the hour,

day, week, and season, continuing to shape fundamentally the life of many contemporary cities.

Another institution of the urban economic fabric, also important for its physical and social aspects, was the bath *(hamam)*. Baths provided a vital service for men
and women of a range of classes who came to wash there and also to socialize.
The unmistakable windowed domes—single or double—regularly punctuated the
skyline of most cities, a counterpoint to the minaret–dome cluster of the mosques.
The founders of the baths were required to ensure that the water supply to the town
was increased in sufficient measure to allow the baths to operate, thus entailing the
construction of additional pipes, cisterns, or wells. Fees paid for entry and for various services offered at the baths supported the place and the numerous people who
worked there. The traffic of men and women was segregated either in space to
different sides of a double bath, or in time, according to the hours assigned the two
sexes. Baths still in operation today maintain one of these patterns.

Social Legacy

The social legacy of the waqfs is inseparable from the other legacies. As mentioned
before, the buildings themselves had a direct influence on the communities in
which they were constructed or which grew up around them. The physical spaces
created by endowed buildings constituted places of intersection for men, women,
and children of every class, and they still do. Whether their use is preserved or
changed, the buildings—mosques, baths, public kitchens, medreses, markets—
continue to fix the location of important social events and processes

Social practice was often maintained over hundreds of years in places such as
Hurrem Sultan's public kitchen in Jerusalem, which is now an orphanage and vocational school, yet still serves meals to local people. Even though its chief purpose
has changed, the building remains a beneficent institution dispensing assistance.
Other public kitchens continue to function or have been returned to use, like
that of Bayezid II (fifteenth century) in Amasya or the Ahmediye (eighteenth
century) in Üsküdar. The college of Çorlulu Ali Paşa (eighteenth century) in Istanbul is a hospice for university students, as well as a tourist market.[42]

Some historians have argued that the enormous scope of social services provided by the funds of private individuals through the waqfs removed an incentive
from the government or state to provide such services. However, this seems mis-
construed. First, the actions of private individuals such as sultans and viziers can
hardly be divorced from those of the state in the premodern era because the state
was the sultans and the viziers to a large extent. Second, the evolution of waqf
management over time, particularly in the nineteenth century, saw the state taking over the running of most large public endowments, creating branches of
government under which they could be subsumed in an effort to remove them

from the hands of powerful individuals. In this way, the large public waqfs became the precursors of modern state-provided social services. Alongside these services, however, there were and continue to be private charitable organizations, funded from the donations of private individuals and constituting yet another piece of the waqf-molded practice.

In addition to the effect on individuals, one may ask whether there was a more communal legacy from the large individual endowments. The Süleymaniye employed several hundred people, supported at least one thousand with daily food handouts, and drew its revenues from dozens of villages. Little is known of the extent to which the identities of any or all of these people were shaped by their connection to the waqf. Was any measure of solidarity evoked by this connection, and for how long did it last?

Cultural Legacy

Finally, as suggested earlier, the waqfs created important cultural legacies. In former Ottoman lands outside Turkey, structures that were emblematic of an earlier Ottoman presence were preserved or ignored, destroyed or repaired according to the prevailing attitudes toward the Ottomans or sometimes more practical considerations. These buildings more often than not originally belonged to endowments, sometimes made by local governors appointed to Ottoman posts. Yet some structures have become so engulfed by contemporary identity politics that the nuances relating to their founders have evaporated, along with the possibilities for their reuse.

More crucial for modern Turkey as the successor to the core of the Ottoman empire, waqf-making created and sustained a culture of philanthropic endeavor. This culture has been studied to a certain extent in the context of political, artistic, and professional patronage. But it has not been widely recognized or studied in the broader framework of research on charity.

Both among people of wealth and those of modest means in Turkey, giving and giving visibly are common and shared characteristics. Beggars cobble together daily meals through minute gifts from passersby, while others roam a fixed route through commercial neighborhoods or the large markets, each one sustained by a round of visits to his or her "family" of merchants. One tradition demands that upon leaving a hospital the person cured and his or her relatives must give generously to the first person they encounter who asks for assistance. And there is no need to detail the thousands of individual acts of generosity performed after the devastating earthquake of August 1999. The story of the grocer who loaded the entire contents of his shelves into a truck and drove off to distribute them to the victims is only one of many.

Among the wealthiest, some donors are more conspicuous than others. Many are no less hesitant to have their names attached to the institutions they endowed than their predecessors. The Aziz Nesin Foundation, established by the famous Turkish writer, works to help support and educate needy children. And certainly the new Koç University and Sabancı University, founded by two of Turkey's leading entrepreneurial and industrial families, are in many ways the contemporary parallels to the Fatih and Süleymaniye medreses.[43] It is the economic elite that has replaced the sultans and princes as premier benefactors, with the personal even rivaling government sources of assistance. This is in the best of Ottoman traditions.

Charity as a social practice is embedded in post-Ottoman culture, producing many endeavors honestly aimed at improving the welfare of broad or specific groups in society. Yet, like any form of patronage, philanthropy at the elite level is inherently an act of control and an effort at replication and socialization by the elite. As in Ottoman, so in contemporary societies, the shape and function of buildings, the production of aesthetic goods, the setting of academic curricula, or the distribution of food and clothing within the framework of charity are all driven by the vision(s) of a monied elite as to how society should be. The Ottoman legacy, like philanthropic practices elsewhere, reinforced the elite sense of a right to implement its vision(s) of society.

Conclusion

The claim in this chapter is not that the Ottomans were unique in evolving a rich philanthropic tradition, nor that they were only interested in philanthropy. The Ottoman tradition of waqf-making was chosen because it is extremely accessible for study. Rather, the emphasis here is that the roots of the contemporary Turkish culture of philanthropy are planted deep in the Ottoman past, particularly in that of waqf-making on a large and generous scale. To date, this tradition has been admired for what it accomplished in the past and perhaps for the buildings it left behind for the present. Waqf-making itself has not been credited with any long-term positive contribution; quite the opposite. At the very least, this assumption might be investigated more carefully. Further, the history of charity in the ex-Ottoman lands of Europe, Asia, and Africa needs to take into account this Ottoman legacy.

Notes

This research was supported by the Israel Science Foundation founded by the Israel Academy of Sciences and Humanities.

    1. U. Haarmann, "Islamic Duties in History," *Muslim World* 68 (1978): 8–15; Marshall G. S. Hodgson, *The Venture of Islam* (Chicago: University of Chicago Press, 1974), 2:124; J. Schacht, "Zakat," in *Encyclopedia of Islam*, 1st ed. (Leiden: Brill, 1931) (hereafter

EI¹). Also see Timur Kuran's chapter (14) in this volume for an assessment of zakat historically as well as in contemporary Muslim states.

2. Informal and incidental giving, on the other hand, may have had cumulative or momentary importance, but this is very difficult to evaluate because historical evidence is unsystematic and anecdotal.

3. See the discussion of this in W. Heffening, "Wakf," *EI¹*, 4:1100–1102.

4. One interesting study that has not yet been attempted is a comparative investigation of what becomes of waqfs and waqf-making with the founding of each of the modern states of the Islamic world.

5. *Al-Qur'an. A Contemporary Translation by Ahmed Ali*, rev. definitive ed. (Princeton: Princeton University Press, 1988), 2:83.

6. *Qur'an*, 9:60.

7. Robert D. McChesney, *Charity and Philanthropy in Islam: Institutionalizing the Call to Do Good* (Indianapolis: Indiana University Press, 1995), 8. See Peter Charles Hennigan, "The Birth of a Legal Institution: The Formation of the Waqf in Third Century A.H. Hanafi Legal Discourse" (PhD. diss., Cornell University, 1999) on the first written compilations of legal practice regarding waqf.

8. On the early development of waqf, see Claude Cahen, "Réflexions sur le *waqf* ancien," *Studia Islamica* 14 (1961): 37–56; J. Schacht, "Early Doctrines on Waqf," in *Fuad Köprülü Armagani* (Istanbul: Osman Yalçın Matbaası, 1953), 443–452; Norman A. Stillman, "Waqf and Charity in Medieval Islam," in *Hunter of the East: Studies in Honor of Clifford Edmund Bosworth*, vol. 1, *Arabic and Semitic Studies*, ed. I. R. Netton (Leiden: Brill, 1999).

9. The irrevocability of waqfs is most characteristic of the Hanafi *madhhab* (school of law). Robert McChesney points out that there are important social and economic differences between the two types of waqf, not to mention significant differences of scale; yet at the same time, he emphasizes that there is no distinction in law between the two; see R. D. McChesney, *Waqf in Central Asia: Four Hundred Years in the History of a Muslim Shrine, 1480–1889* (Princeton: Princeton University Press, 1991); idem., *Charity and Philanthropy*, 12.

10. For example, *Qur'an*, 2:83, 2:220.

11. John Robert Barnes, *An Introduction to Religious Foundations in the Ottoman Empire* (Leiden: Brill, 1987), 42.

12. Leslie Peirce claims that after the sons of Osman and Orhan, princes were no longer permitted to endow public institutions, as part of the curbs placed on their power and prominence altogether. On this see Leslie P. Peirce, *The Imperial Harem: Women and Sovereignty in the Ottoman Empire* (New York: Oxford University Press, 1993), 20–21.

13. This is reflected in the Ottoman survey registers *(tapu tahrir defterleri)* as executed in most provinces from the time of their conquest. On these registers see O. L Barkan, "Daftar-i khakani," and S. Faroqhi, "Tahrir" and "Tapu" in *EI²*, 2:81–83, 10:112–113, and 10:209–210, respectively. See also D. Behrens-Abouseif, *Egypt's Adjustment to Ottoman Rule* (Leiden: Brill, 1994), 146–149.

14. *Mustafa Ali's Counsel for Sultans of 1581,* ed., trans., notes Andreas Tietze (Wien: Österreichische Akademie der Wissenschaften, 1979), 54, 146.

15. Lucienne Thys-Şenocak, "The Yeni Valide Mosque Complex at Eminönü," *Muqarnas* 15 (1998): 63–66.

16. Ibid., 68.

17. The following discussion of Koçi Bey is based on his memorandum to Murat IV (r. 1622–1640) (*Koçi Bey Risalesi*, ed. Ali Kemal Aksüt (Istanbul: Vakit Kütüphanesi, 1939). *Risale*, as well as the discussions, can be found in C. H. Imber, "Koči Beg," *EI*²; 5:248–250; Barnes, *An Introduction to Religious Foundations*, 61–65.

18. Barnes, *An Introduction to Religious Foundations*, 51–56.

19. Ibid., 43.

20. I. H. Uzunçarşılı, *Osmanlı Devletinin Saray Teşkilatı* (Ankara: Türk Tarih Kurumu, 1984), 178–179.

21. On the Evkaf-i Hümayun Nezareti, see Barnes, *An Introduction to Religious Foundations*, 68–69

22. Ibid., 73.

23. On the Tanzimat and waqf, see B. Yediyıldız, "Vakıf," *İslam Ansiklopedisi* 13:163–167.

24. J. N. D. Anderson, "The Religious Element in Waqf Endowments," *Journal of the Royal Central Asian Society* 38 (1951): 294–297. For a discussion of how the French and British ignorance about waqf in Algeria and India contributed to several generations of flawed scholarship on the topic, see David S. Powers, "Orientalism, Colonialism, and Legal History: The Attack on Muslim Family Endowments in Algeria and India," *Comparative Studies in Society and History* 31 (1989): 535–571.

25. W. Heffening, "Wakf."

26. H. A. R. Gibb and Harold Bowen, *Islamic Society and the West*, vol. 1, *Islamic Society in the Eighteenth Century* (London: Oxford University Press, 1957), pt. 2, 165–178.

27. Ibid., pt. 2, 177–178.

28. Miriam Hoexter, *Endowments, Rulers, and Community: Waqf al-Haramayn in Ottoman Algiers* (Leiden: Brill, 1998).

29. Oded Peri, "Political Trends and their Impact on the Founding of Waqfs in Jerusalem at the End of the Eighteenth Century" *Cathedra* 21 (1981): 73–88. (Hebrew)

30. See S. H. Stephan, "An Endowment Deed of Khâsseki Sultân, Dated 24th May 1552," *Quarterly of the Department of Antiquities in Palestine* 10 (1944): 170–194, for the waqfiyya of this ʿimaret. For an extensive discussion of its founding and meaning, see Amy Singer, *Constructing Ottoman Beneficence* (Albany: State University of New York Press, 2002).

31. Gülru Necipoğlu, "The Süleymaniye Complex in Istanbul: An Interpretation," *Muqarnas* 3 (1985): 92, 96, 98–99, 112–113.

32. There is no exhaustive list of imperial Ottoman endowments. A preliminary appreciation for their number may be gained by reading Godfrey Goodwin, *A History of Ottoman Architecture* (Baltimore: Johns Hopkins University Press, 1971).

33. See Goodwin, *A History of Ottoman Architecture*, 121–131, 215–219.

34. Halil Inalcik, "Istanbul: An Islamic City," *Journal of Islamic Studies* 1 (1990): 1–23.

35. Nimet Taşkıran, *Hasekinin Kitabı* (Istanbul: Yenilik Basımevi, 1972).

36. Goodwin, *A History of Ottoman Architecture*, 143–150. In September 1999, I visited Edirne and was given a tour through the renovated hospital by the museum director.

37. On Eyüp see ibid., 410–411, as well as "Eyüp, *Dünden Bugüne İstanbul Ansiklopedisi* (Istanbul: Kultur Bakanlığı ve Tarih Vakfının ortak yayınıdır, 1994), 3:245–250.

38. On the Balkans, see A. Riedlmayer, "Erasing the Past," *MESA Bulletin* 29 (1995): 7–11. Years of living in Israel, viewing the comparative ruin of Ottoman sites next to biblical and Roman excavations and reconstructions, make the priorities of the Department of Antiquities obvious. For a discussion of the bias among historians of art surveying the Arabic-speaking countries conquered by the Ottomans, see A. Raymond, "The Ottoman Conquest and the Development of the Great Arab Towns," *International Journal of Turkish Studies* 1 (1980): 84–101.

39. See George Makdisi, *The Rise of Colleges* (Edinburgh: Edinburgh University Press, 1981); Jonathan P. Berkey, *The Transmission of Knowledge in Medieval Cairo* (Princeton: Princeton University Press, 1992).

40. For the medical schools they contained, see Miri Shefer, "Hospitals in the Three Ottoman Capitals: Bursa, Edirne, and Istanbul in the Sixteenth and Seventeenth Centuries" (Ph.D. diss., Tel Aviv University, 2001).

41. On the cash waqfs as lending institutions, see Murat Çızakça, "Cash Waqfs in Bursa, 1555–1823," *Journal of the Economic and Social History of the Orient* 38 (1995): 313–354.

42. I saw the Bayezid II kitchen functioning in the summer of 1995. John Freely told me about the Ahmediye in the fall of 1999. On Çorlulu Ali Paşa, see John Freely, *Blue Guide to Istanbul*, 1st ed. (London: Ernest Benn, 1983), 164.

43. For these universities and something of the philosophy of their founders, see their Web sites: <www.ku.edu.tr> and <www.sabanciuniv.edu.tr>.

Conclusion

NATALIE ZEMON DAVIS

Charity has been a central thread in Islam since the days of the Prophet, and debates about its goals and practices have lasted just as long. The chapters in this
volume have charted that important history, bringing many new perspectives to
specialists in the Middle East and North Africa, to historians of Europe and the
Americas, and to students of philanthropy and welfare everywhere. In these concluding remarks, I want to suggest how the rich insights from this collection add
to, reformulate, or confirm current views of the history of charity and its relation
to poverty, as they have been generalized primarily from the western experience.

   Zakat, the annual giving of alms, was one of the earliest commands to each
believer and remained an essential marker of Islam over the centuries. The first
acute struggles after the Messenger's death were not against idolaters, as with the
biblical Jews, or holders of false doctrine, as with early Christians, but against tribes
who refused to pay zakat. Rejection of broad group charity was as dangerous a challenge as a competing prophet. Charity sustained Jewish and Christian societies, but
the Islamic example shows us how vital charitable donation can be in the very formation and conceptualization of a religious community.

   Whether as required yearly zakat or as diverse and unscheduled *sadaqa* (charity), charitable gifts brought religious benefit to the Muslim donor, as they did also
to the Jewish and Christian donor: in the Arabic phrase, he or she acquired "close-
ness to God" *(qurba).* But there are differences. The Muslim's proximity was
achieved even without the added benefit of prayers for the donor's soul, so often en-
joined from recipients in medieval and early modern Catholic wills. More generally,
the offering of zakat brought "purification" of the donor's greed and of the donor's
surplus property, allowing the rest to be retained without blame for another year.

   The notion of charity, then, was connected to an important idea of property.
However, purification was not being judged against a Christian ideal of common
ownership among the Apostles and their early followers. Individual Muslim holy
men might live without private goods, Sufi communities might adopt a style of

heroic asceticism, but those were choices, not a higher condition by which all ownership was judged. According to a celebrated *hadith* (tradition), Muhammad said that "we Prophets leave no heirs; we leave only alms behind us," but for others the Quran prescribed the rules by which property was to be inherited (4:11–13).

The acceptability of private property in various Islamic settings is described in several of the chapters in this volume. According to Ingrid Mattson (chapter 2), the early Sunni schools of law (*madhhabs*) disagreed among themselves about how need was to be assessed in distributing zakat—some with views that reduced the gap between rich and poor, others with views that widened it; but all were in accord on the importance of property to maintain family. Adam Sabra (chapter 4) has found that Muslim jurists in Mamluk Egypt debated the appropriateness of caliphs intervening in the grain market, not only because the market was in the hands of God, but also because the commercial property of merchants must be respected. To jump to the nineteenth century, the radical Egyptian social critic, Rifaʿ al-Rafiʿ al-Tahtawi, still affirmed the right of great landlords to their property, as we learn from Juan Cole's chapter (11). Influenced by the French Saint-Simonians and their labor theory of value, al-Tahtawi thought landlords might split profits from the soil fifty–fifty with their peasants, but their ownership remained unimpaired.

Michael Bonner (chapter 1) has reminded us, however, of an alternate ideal of property attributed to the Prophet in several traditional narratives, which justifies zakat and sadaqa on the grounds of the "return of wealth." "God has laid the obligation of alms on their possessions, to be taken from the rich among them and returned to the poor." As Bonner suggests, the injunction here is for the circulation of wealth, not from rich to rich, but from rich to poor. Wealth, at least surplus wealth, must keep moving. Alms move down the social scale and persons gain wealth and move up and give alms once again in a repeated cycle of exchange.

The notions of 'purification' and 'return' provide a distinctive Islamic way of conceptualizing the processes of charity. It calls to mind processes different from the Christian notion of 'perennial reciprocity' between rich and poor and the ideal of 'charity' as an expression of community love.

Zakat and sadaqa were the long-enduring categories under which Islamic societies have thought about charity and created institutions for its practice in the Middle East and North Africa. Of the institutional inventions, the most innovative was the *waqf*, the giving of property in perpetuity for a charitable use, "an eternal charity," as Miriam Hoexter (chapter 7) puts it, with both public and private beneficiaries. Described in many forms in these chapters, the waqfs are a prime example of the Islamic circulation of riches—to some extent socially, and surely across the reaches of time.

These institutions and practices set a cultural stamp on Muslim societies, including in its ways of relating obligatory and voluntary actions. A distinction not made explicit in the Quran, "obligatory" zakat was contrasted with "voluntary" sadaqa in the teachings of the schools of the law. In a treatise on visiting the sick, described by Miri Shefer, (chapter 6) the question of whether it was obligatory or not was central for a ninth/fifteenth-century jurist. Yet the voluntary–obligatory split seems less troublesome in Islam than in Western Europe. In the early Christian church, the fathers stressed the importance of inner feeling: As Saint Ambrose said, "What is given without a loving heart is altogether insufficient." Catholic tithing for the church fell only on peasant households, and beyond it there was no medieval alms tax. When regular taxes for poor relief were introduced in some places in early modern Europe, there was principled resistance by some critics, both Catholic and Protestant, on the grounds that charity must always be voluntary. In Islamic lands, the zakat had been required since the beginning, and the donation was not thought thereby to lose its value or be robbed of inner spirit: Purification could work through a tax. Where zakat fell into disuse in practice, it seems to have been due to administrative failure and fears of corruption, not to opposition to a charitable requirement always in place for each Muslim. Here volition and obligation could openly overlap or be mixed, as they are to some extent in all donations everywhere. The subterfuge, famously formulated by Marcel Mauss in regard to The Gift, of "in theory voluntary, in reality given and returned obligatorily" was less pressing.

Zakat and sadaqa could be contrasted just as well by other qualities, as Amy Singer has suggested in her chapter (15): a routinely scheduled gift as against a gift more particularly timed, a standard gift as against a crafted or initiated gift, a gift from a general community as against a gift from an individual. The Islamic case shows that there may be features of charitable gifting more important to donors than obligation–volition.

The world of donors in Islamic societies is amply opened for us by the chapters in this book. It was a busy world, even beyond the multitude of actions expected in paying zakat. Military leaders and wealthy merchants in seventh/thirteenth-century Cairo were summoned to feed the hungry during famines. Middle-level families in eighteenth-century Salonika, as recounted by Eyal Ginio (chapter 8), took in young girls from poor country families, fostered them, and in return drew on their domestic service: Though the relation sometimes led to exploitation and sexual abuse, the foster parents and their supporters constructed it as "a charity, a benevolent act." Among other donors in Salonika—and surely throughout the Middle East—were the dying, who left meals for the poor at their funerals. Looking ahead to early-twentieth-century Turkey in Kathryn Libal's chapter (13), we see the newly founded Children's Protection Society and the Turkish Red Crescent Society supported mostly by gifts from many individuals. Finally, as Mine Ener (chapter 9) has reminded us, much of charitable aid over the centuries is undocumented: the informal help given by extended families, neighbors, and guilds.

Women played a guiding role in the world of donors as well as men. The mosque complex founded by Hafsa Sultan, mother of Sultan Süleyman, with its college *(madrasa)*, soup kitchen and more, won her praise as "the queen of queens . . . the cream of august women . . . [and] the protector of male and female Muslims." Other wives and mothers of the imperial household founded awqaf of great importance, as Amy Singer shows in chapter 15, in the tenth/sixteenth and eleventh/seventeenth centuries. The initiative came from the women, even in cases of delicate and controversial policy, as with the Yeni Cami mosque complex in Istanbul, which involved relocating the Jews from the quarter. In the early twentieth century, women are visible as activists and innovators, giving support in the new Turkish Republic to the Children's Protection Society and the Turkish Red Crescent. In Egypt of the 1920s, Labiba Ahmad founded an institute and workshop to train poor girls and give them a good Islamic education. Drawing many other women to her cause, as Beth Baron shows in chapter 12, Ahmad pioneered in her use of publicity devices, both in print and in radio. Meanwhile in Istanbul of the 1920s–1940s, secularist women journalists Suad Derviş and Sabiha Zekeriya were calling for more radical solutions to the problems of working women and poor children.

As with charitable gifts everywhere, donors had multiple intentions, discussed throughout this book. Besides the primary religious goals—becoming closer to God, cleansing one's wealth, and sustaining the community of Islam—founders of awqaf might hope for prestige for themselves and for their families. Here was a way to sustain position and be remembered for centuries. Charitable institutions also created and consolidated ties between patrons and clients, in the neighborhood and further afield.

Charitable gifts had political importance as well, not only in the decisions of caliphs at times of famine, but also in the sultans' establishment of awqaf and their distribution of alms and meat on religious holidays. However individual the act of donation, the benefit accrued also to the sultan's rule as a caring father of his people. Significantly, as Mine Ener points out in chapter 9, the new donations and welfare actions of the nineteenth-century Egyptian state were always presented as "out of the charity of the khedive." Economic and population policy was still to be linked to Muslim religious obligation. In Nadir Özbek's chapter (10), we see how Sultan Abdülhamid II, his rule challenged by the Young Turks, dramatized his benevolence on a grand scale, subsidizing the circumcision of thousands of boys at "modern" hospitals at the same time as the circumcision of his own sons. Beneficiaries shouted "Long live the Sultan," announcing to him and to the wider public their loyalty to their benevolent ruler.

Charitable and welfare institutions also have an important role in defining boundaries of community and gender and in controlling and classifying populations. Western historiography has especially explored the European hospital in these regards: the multipurpose medieval hospital receiving the sick, travelers, devout Christians wishing to serve, old people; the leper hospital; the plague hospital; the hospital used to receive the insane, who previously had been left with their families or lodged in monasteries; the fearsome hospital to enclose and discipline the "undeserving" poor and set them to work rather than allowing them to beg or remain idle; the hospital to enclose prostitutes and other incorrigibles and reform their way of life. The European hospital was also a center for receiving and rearing foundlings and orphans and for the delivery of babies to mothers from poor families. These activities, some in place in medieval times, others early modern, gave people care and relief but also helped define class distinctions and reinforce norms of seemly and modest behavior.

Endowed Muslim hospitals in North Africa and the Middle East, richly described in the chapters of Yasser Tabbaa (5) and Miri Shefer (6), were less numerous than in Western Europe and drew boundaries very differently. Hospitals were primarily buildings—intended to be beautiful and airy—in which people with maladies were received, separated perhaps into different wards by illness, but not removed to independent quarantine hospitals. The personnel gave them custodial care, as well as medical care, more frequently and earlier than in the West. Insane persons seem to have been received in hospitals from an early time and were among beneficiaries specifically mentioned in waqf foundations. The healthy poor were not enclosed in endowed hospitals, and the giving of alms to beggars in the streets was considered a meritorious act. Wrongdoers, on occasion, were incarcerated in hospitals, according to Tabbaa, including those thought to be insane, but their numbers were small. Though hospitals sometimes had wings for women, poor mothers did not deliver their babies in hospitals but at home; foundlings and orphans were raised elsewhere. Hospital beds were also open to foreign Muslim travelers who took sick and had no other place to go.

Endowed Muslim hospitals, then, were less divisive in their social representation of the world and less judgmental about unacceptable conduct by the poor. Islamic societies of the tenth/sixteenth–eleventh/seventeenth centuries were beset neither by fear of plague-carriers (theories of contagion being absent, according to Miri Shefer [chapter 6]) nor by epidemics of witchcraft accusation and prosecution; perhaps their hospital functions are another expression of this lack of inquisitorial fervor.

In the nineteenth century, new state institutions centralizing poor relief were established in the Ottoman Empire starting first in Egypt. Curtailing or limiting the older charitable forms, as we see from Mine Ener's study (chapter 9), the state set up government hospitals, like the Civilian Hospital of Azbakiyya, which included a school for training midwives, an orphanage, and a foundling home. Shelters were brought into use for those poor unable to manage on their own. Begging was prohibited in Cairo, and the men and women identified as nonresident but able-bodied poor were deported to their home villages. The "deserving poor" from among their lot, as well as beggars found to be residents of the city, were confined in poor shelters. Even then, the poor, insane, the elderly, and the needy children were described as having a "right" *(haqq)* to services from the charity of the state, and, rather than being coerced, relatives are found petitioning for the admittance of their members to the state's institutions. As Michael Bonner (chapter 1) reminds us, the idea of the haqq, or claim of the destitute on the property of the community of believers, goes back to the early days of Islam. The new institutions may create a class of poor and vulnerable people dependent on the state, but the poor are still left with a conceptual tool by which to measure their entitlement.

The notion of haqq is also found in the other innovation of the late nineteenth and twentieth centuries, the charitable associations, which, as Juan Cole shows in chapter 11, had been called for earlier by the Egyptian reformer al-Tahtawi. Explored for Egypt by Beth Baron (chapter 12) and for the Turkish Republic by Kathryn Libal (chapter 13), these associations focused on the care, education, and reshaping of the young: the young women to be given vocational training and Islamic instruction by Labiba Ahmad's institute and the boys and girls to be assisted in numerous ways by the Children's Protection Society and the Turkish Red Crescent. Here, too, the goals of "awakened" Islamic-Egyptian young women or of healthy, instructed Turkish citizens-in-the-making did not erase a position from which the poor could make a claim to their educators. Speaking in the voice of Turkish children, Sabiha Zekeriya called in 1929 for a set of "rights" that they should enjoy: "We don't only want your nurturance. We want equality, nutrition, development and education that is the right of every human child. We want new laws and a social organization that will provide us with the rights and the life that we lack." Kathryn Libal suggests that Zekeriya's view is related "to an emerging international discourse on children's rights and the responsibility of states to assure healthy childhoods." It may also owe something to the long-enduring Islamic idea of haqq.

What of the geographical range and spatial boundaries of Islamic and Middle Eastern charitable institutions and services? As in the Christian West, they appear to have an urban focus, perhaps even more so. Europe had some rural institutions: some medieval hospitals in the countryside, rural parish relief in early modern England and France, reorganized in England by the nineteenth-century Poor Laws. In Middle Eastern contexts, the poor in the countryside appear to have been helped over the centuries primarily by their relatives or their neighbors in informal and customary ways. Al-Hasan ibn Muhammad al-Wassan (Leo Africanus), in his travels through Morocco in the early tenth/sixteenth century, mentions hospitals and services for the poor only in large or small towns; in villages and hamlets, hospitality to strangers, rich or poor, was left up to individual notables. In nineteenth-century Egypt, when insane people were found in rural areas, they were brought for care to the new hospital in Cairo. In the early years of the Turkish

Republic, alarm was raised about the health and school needs of village children, but neither the funding nor the trained personnel were available to make much change. Perhaps there is a hidden story here still to be researched. Timur Kuran (chapter 14) has reminded us that fairly early on "the Islamic state seems to have treated zakat as a fungible component of a broader revenue stream kept in the service of powerful social groups," but it may have been distributed in some formal ways in the countryside from which much of it had been initially collected.

Islamic charitable institutions appear open both to the local residents and to foreign arrivals. As Saint Ambrose had told fourth-century Christians that after God, a man should love first his family—parents, children, wife, and members of his household—and then strangers, so the great jurist al-Shafiʻ told Muslims that zakat should go first to the needy nearby. Maintenance obligations *(nafaqa)* also made a man responsible first for his extended family and his slaves, as Ingrid Mattson (chapter 2) points out. The important research of Miriam Hoexter (chapter 7) has shown how the beneficiaries of waqf endowments were often "specific solidarity groups," persons to whom the donor felt attached; they might well be local, such as the inhabitants of one's neighborhood or Sufi confraternity. Nevertheless, these chapters also reveal the presence of immigrants and foreign travelers in endowed hospitals. Authorities in nineteenth-century Cairo received newcomers to the city in the state charitable institutions if they were considered worthy of care. Long-term traditions of hospitality, economic needs, and the initial Muslim prescription for recipients of zakat—including needy travelers—combined to allow this relative openness.

Mark Cohen (chapter 3) has provided a precious portrait of how need was assessed for the many immigrants and travelers in the Jewish community of Fustat in eleventh- and twelfth-century Egypt. What to do when *halakha* (Jewish ritual law) decreed that "the poor of your household have priority over the poor of your city, and the poor of your city have priority over the poor of another city"? Some wayfarers complained bitterly about their lot, but the Jewish elders usually found ways to get information about newcomers, connect them somehow to local Jews, and give them aid.

In their mixture of natives and newcomers among recipients of charity, Middle Eastern societies may be roughly similar to those in Europe. There may be something distinctive, however, in the geographical spread of donation in the Middle East, in the spaciousness of the Islamic charitable imagination, constantly stretched by pilgrimage and distant holy sites. Mosque complexes, hospitals, and soup kitchens were founded by Ottoman sultans and their relatives in dispersed cities of the empire, even though, as Eyal Ginio (chapter 8) has remarked, they passed over provincial towns such as Salonika. Especially one is struck by Miriam Hoexter's account (chapter 7) of the waqf founded in Algiers in the eleventh/seventeenth-century, which for more than 160 years sent 1,100–1,500 gold dinars with every pilgrimage caravan to be distributed to the "poor" of Mecca and Medina. Individual European Christians, of course, made donations to religious establishments when they went on pilgrimages, say, to Rome and to Jerusalem, but a regular gift of this magnitude seems unusual. Did the spatial sense of Dar al-Islam somehow invite this long-distance loyalty more strongly than the Christian? (The Jewish geographical sensibility may be more like the Islamic: The Jews of Hamburg were making periodic contributions to Jews of the Holy Land in the early seventeenth century.) The present-day debate, recounted by Timur Kuran (chapter 14), over zakat transfers across the borders of nation–states—from wealthy lands to poor lands—illustrates the tension between a tradition of breadth across the one religious community and the claims of modern polities.

Did the charitable practice of Muslims extend to those who were not followers of the Prophet? From the earliest days, the benefits of zakat could legitimately go to potential converts to Islam, but what of others? Miri Shefer (chapter 6) cites some evidence of an eleventh/seventeenth-century hospital in Istanbul that received non-Muslims, though in most instances, Jews, Coptic Christians, and other religious groups had their own establishments. Valid endowments could be made by Muslims for non-Muslims who were poor; and Miriam Hoexter (chapter 7) has found Christian captives among the regular beneficiaries of the Waqf al-Haramayn in Algiers. Some non-Muslims were accepted into the state shelters of nineteenth-century Cairo. This porousness on the outer boundary of charity in Islam would be worth exploring further.

The recipients of charity and welfare in Islamic lands have appeared often in the pages of this book. They were very numerous over the centuries, but, as in Europe and the Americas, they were by no means all economically poor. From the beginning, prescriptive and normative literature laid out several categories of persons worthy of alms, from slaves deserving of manumission and destitute persons to those serving or fighting for the cause of Islam. Every form of donation showed this range among the beneficiaries. Hospital beds were sometimes filled with persons of means, including wealthy travelers who had fallen sick, as well as the poor. The endowment lists in twelfth/eighteenth-century Algiers and Salonika had religious personnel, from learned prayer leaders and readers of the Quran to caretakers of the mosques, as their major category. The "poor" of Medina and Mecca receiving gold from Algiers ranged from freed female slaves to men with slaves in their households. The students supported at the madrasas were from families both rich and poor. Even the soup ladled out to hundreds from the huge cauldrons in the Jerusalem soup kitchen did not go only to indigent persons.

The innovations in the nineteenth century shifted this pattern somewhat in regard to social origin, gender, and age. Mine Ener's archival evidence (chapter 9) from the foundling center and orphanage of Cairo's Civilian Hospital shows they were used by the needy—whatever advantages these programs brought to the general population. Moreover, women were especially important among those being directly assisted, as mothers, as widows, and as old people. In twentieth-century Cairo, Labiba Ahmad's initiatives are aimed at helping poor girls become responsible Islamic women. This focus contrasts with the earlier distribution of alms and other benefits in Islamic lands, where men were the primary recipients. To be sure, the wives, sisters, and children of men on, say, a waqf list would clearly benefit as well, and widows, orphan girls, and women sufis were given sadaqa in their own right. But symbolically and practically, the men, as the religious scholars and leaders, were conceived as the more likely recipients. In Europe, from medieval times on, women were figured as the vulnerable gender—the widow with her orphans, the prostitute to be reformed—and this gender sign was simply strengthened with the new welfare forms of the nineteenth century. In North Africa and the Middle East, so these chapters suggest, the nineteenth century represented a shift.

The recipients emerge from the pages of this book as adept in making their way in the world of charitable donation. Those men hoping for zakat knew what important patrons to address themselves to so as to qualify. The foreign Jews in eleventh- and twelfth-century Fustat knew how to describe themselves to satisfy the Jewish authorities that they were "the poor of [their] household." Those in twelfth/eighteenth-century Medina and Mecca soliciting their alms from the Haramayn of Algiers knew how to cast themselves so as to be included on the distribution list. The poor of nineteenth-century Cairo knew the right formulas to use at the Central Police Station when bringing in a foundling or baby abandoned by her parents and whose grandmother could not pay for her wet nurse.

Lifesaving information about the possibilities for alms and welfare—about where and how to get them—evidently circulated among the poor and other would-be recipients. It would be interesting to know how their different relations to charitable institutions affected their self-perception. How widespread was the notion that the poor have a claim, a haqq, to aid? Haqq appears somewhat different from Christian canon law and Western social notions of the right of the poor to be fed. What sense of status did it allow those seeking alms or help? Did beneficiaries of waqfs see themselves as part of a long-term patron–client relation? Which is more characteristic: the youthful servants, fostered in a Salonika household, suing their masters for pay and accusing them of sexual abuse, or the Istanbul mother keeping her young child in Abdülhamid's poorhouse, so approving was she of the sultan's "compassion," even after she had found a post as domestic servant? Most likely, both reactions are part of the story.

These questions suggest the doors opened by the chapters in this volume for further research. I will suggest two further possibilities. First is the question of general gift theory, drawn on by Michael Bonner (chapter 1), Nadir Özbek (chapter 10), and Timur Kuran (chapter 14) to advance their discussion. Bonner has shown how the Prophet's insistence on zakat built upon and reshaped the competitive gift exchange and banqueting of the Arab tribes of his day. Özbek has stressed the obligation created by gifts to underscore the quest for power underlying Abdülhamid's policies of public donation. Kuran has asked whether framing zakat as an entitlement for members of the Muslim community would not moderate the loss of pride felt by recipients of "unreciprocated transfers."

Indeed, the theories and practices of gift exchange in Islamic societies might provide a useful frame for the whole subject of charity. What were the underlying beliefs about giving and reciprocity, about giving, receiving, and returning? Do they follow the Maussian pattern? What was a good gift and what a bad gift? (Franz Rosenthal opened this subject a number of years ago with a penetrating essay on gifts and bribes in Islamic thought.) The uses and meanings of charitable gifts might be understood afresh if placed alongside other forms of giving and other debates about gifts. Already Ingrid Mattson (chapter 2) has shown us how much can be clarified about the obligations of zakat by seeing them next to the obligations of maintenance.

Second is the question of the "look" of charity. Amy Singer (chapter 15) has reminded readers how the buildings, gardens, and fountains brought into being through endowments have shaped distinctive landscapes throughout Islamic lands. Elsewhere, Singer has commented on the elaborate calligraphy used for the documents founding waqfs. Here beauty is associated with the charitable act. But what of the performance of charity itself? The words, postures, and gestures of giving and receiving in the many scenes we can imagine? The personnel at the soup kitchen and the hungry—in queues? in crowds? silent? pleading? The formal giving of alms to a reader of the Quran? The informal handout to the beggar at the door? The reception of the sick person at the hospital? Of the beggar in a Cairo shelter?

Nadir Özbek (chapter 10) has given us a start on the performance of charity with his description of Sultan Abdülhamid's grand circumcision ceremonies. In the absence of a long and sustained tradition of pictorial representation of charity and poverty, such questions might have to be answered indirectly from literary texts, memoirs, travel accounts, and the like. But they may lead us into a new vision of the paths opened by the Prophet's claim that charity must circulate through the whole community of Islam.

Contributors

Beth Baron is professor of history at City College, City University of New York, and cofounder and codirector of the Middle East and Middle Eastern American Center at the CUNY Graduate Center. Her publications include *Women in Middle Eastern History: Shifting Boundaries in Sex and Gender*, edited with Nikkie R. Keddie (New Haven: Yale University Press, 1991), *The Women's Awakening in Egypt: Culture, Society, and the Press* (New Haven: Yale University Press, 1994), *Iran and Beyond: Essays in Middle Eastern History in Honor of Nikki R. Keddie*, edited with Rudi Matthee (Costa Mesa: Mazda, 2000), and *Egypt as a Woman: Gender, Culture and Nationalism* (Berkeley: University of California Press, forthcoming).

Michael Bonner is associate professor of medieval Islamic history in the Department of Near Eastern Studies, the University of Michigan, Ann Arbor, where he is also director of the Center for Middle Eastern and North African Studies. He is the author of *Aristocratic Violence and Holy War: Studies in the Jihad and the Arab-Byzantine Frontier* (New Haven, Conn.: American Oriental Society, 1996) and of articles on poverty and the poor in the early Islamic Middle East.

Mark R. Cohen is professor of Near Eastern studies at Princeton University. His research has focused on the position of Jews in Islamic countries and communal relations. His books include *Jewish Self-Government in Medieval Egypt: The Origins of the Office of Head of the Jews, ca. 1065–1126* (Princeton: Princeton University Press, 1980) and *Under Crescent and Cross: The Jews in the Middle Ages* (Princeton: Princeton University Press, 1994). He is now completing a monograph on poverty and social welfare in the Jewish community of medieval Egypt.

Juan R. I. Cole is professor of history at the University of Michigan, Ann Arbor, where he is editor of the *International Journal of Middle East Studies*. His research has focused on the modern cultural, religious, and social history of Egypt, Iraq,

Iran, and Muslim South Asia. His publications include *Colonialism and Revolution in the Middle East: Social and Cultural Origins of Egypt's 'Urabi Movement* (Princeton: Princeton University Press, 1993) and *Modernity and the Millennium: The Genesis of the Baha'i Faith in the Nineteenth-Century Middle East* (New York: Columbia University Press, 1998).

Natalie Zemon Davis, one of the foremost historians of early modern France and Europe, is Henry Charles Lea Professor Emerita of History at Princeton University and adjunct professor in the Department of History at the University of Toronto. Her many books include *The Return of Martin Guerre* (Cambridge: Harvard University Press, 1983), *Women on the Margins: Three Seventeenth-Century Lives* (Cambridge: Harvard University Press, 1995), and *The Gift in Sixteenth-Century France* (Madison: University of Wisconsin Press, 2000).

Mine Ener is assistant professor of history at Villanova University. Two of her many published articles are "Getting into the Shelter of Takiyat Tulun," in *Outside In: On the Margins of the Modern Middle East*, ed. Eugene Rogan (London: I. B. Tauris, 2002) and "Prohibitions on Begging and Loitering in Nineteenth-Century Egypt," *Die Welt des Islams* (1999): 319–339. Her book, *Managing Egypt's Poor and the Politics of Benevolence*, will be published by Princeton University Press.

Eyal Ginio is lecturer in the Department of Middle Eastern Studies at the Hebrew University of Jerusalem, where he received his Ph.D. in 1999. His publications include "'Every Soul Shall Taste Death': Dealing with Death and the Afterlife in Eighteenth-Century Salonica," *Studia Islamica* 93 (2001): 113–132; "Childhood, Mental Capacity, and Conversion to Islam in the Ottoman State," *Byzantine and Modern Greek Studies* 25 (2001): 90–119; "Piracy and Redemption in the Aegean Sea during the First Half of the Eighteenth Century," *Turcica* 33 (2001): 135–147.

Miriam Hoexter is associate professor in the Department of Middle Eastern Studies at the Hebrew University of Jerusalem. She has published numerous articles on the social history of Ottoman and colonial Algeria, Ottoman Palestine, and the Islamic endowment institution *(waqf)*, *Endowments, Rulers and Community: Waqf al-Haramayn in Ottoman Algiers* (Leiden: Brill, 1998), and, in cooperation with Shmuel N. Eisenstadt and Nehemia Levtzion, *The Public Sphere in Muslim Societies* (Albany: State University of New York Press, 2002).

Timur Kuran is professor of economics and law and King Faisal Professor of Islamic Thought and Culture at the University of Southern California, where he served as chair of economics for several years. He is the author of *Private Truths,*

Public Lies: The Social Consequences of Preference Falsification (Cambridge: Harvard University Press, 1995) and of many publications on Islamic economic history, contemporary Islamism, and economic trends in the Middle East.

Kathryn Libal completed her Ph.D. in 2001 at the University of Washington, Seattle, with a dissertation entitled "National Futures: The 'Child Question' in Early Republican Turkey." She is currently a lecturer in women's studies and international studies at the University of Kansas.

Ingrid Mattson earned her Ph.D. at the University of Chicago in 1999, with a dissertation entitled "A Believing Slave is Better than an Unbeliever: Status and Community in Early Islamic Society and Law." In 1998 she became professor of Islamic studies at the MacDonald Center for Islamic Studies and Christian-Muslim Relations at Hartford Seminary (Connecticut), where she is also associate editor of *The Muslim World*.

Nadir Özbek, after completing his Ph.D. at Binghamton University in 2001, is assistant professor at the Atatürk Institute for Modern Turkish History, Boğaziçi University, Istanbul. He has published "The Politics of Poor Relief in the Late Ottoman Empire: 1876–1914," *New Perspectives on Turkey* 21 (1999): 1–33; "Poor Relief in the Ottoman Empire, 1839–1918," *Toplum ve Bilim* 83 (1999–2000): 111–132 (Turkish); and "Welfare State Reconsidered: Social Policy in the Late Ottoman Empire and Modern Turkey," *Toplum ve Bilim* 92 (2002): 7–33 (Turkish).

Adam Sabra is assistant professor of history at Western Michigan University. A Princeton Ph.D., he is the author of the pathbreaking *Poverty and Charity in Medieval Islam: Mamluk Egypt, 1250–1517* (Cambridge: Cambridge University Press, 2000).

Miri Shefer is lecturer in the Department of Middle Eastern and African History, Tel Aviv University, where she received her Ph.D. in 2001. Her publications include "Being Sick and Pretending to Be Sick in the Ottoman Empire in the Sixteenth and Seventeenth Centuries," *Zmanim* 73 (2001–2002): 60–70 (Hebrew); and "Medical and Professional Ethics in Sixteenth-Century Istanbul: Towards an Understanding of the Relationships between the Ottoman State and the Medical Guilds," *Medicine and Law* 21 (2002): 307–319.

Amy Singer is associate professor in the Department of Middle Eastern and African History, Tel Aviv University. She is the author of *Palestinian Peasants and Ottoman Officials: Rural Administration around Sixteenth-Century Jerusalem* (Cambridge:

Cambridge University Press, 1994) and, most recently, of *Constructing Ottoman Beneficence: An Imperial Soup Kitchen in Jerusalem* (Albany: State University of New York Press, 2002).

Yasser Tabbaa has published *Constructions of Power and Piety in Medieval Aleppo* (University Park: Pennsylvania State University Press, 1997) and *The Transformation of Islamic Art during the Sunni Revival* (Seattle: University of Washington Press, 2001). He is completing a full-length study of medieval Islamic hospitals, architecturally and institutionally.

Index

SUNY series in the Social and Economic History
of the Middle East
Donald Quataert, editor

Thabit A. J. Abdullah, *Merchants, Mamluks, and Murder: The Political Economy of Eighteenth Century Basra.*

Ali Abdullatif Ahmida, *The Making of Modern Libya: State Formation, Colonization, and Resistance, 1830–1932.*

Rifa'at 'Ali Abou-El-Haj, *Formation of the Modern State: The Ottoman Empire, Sixteenth to Eighteenth Centuries.*

Cem Behar, *A Neighborhood in Ottoman Istanbul: Fruit Vendors and Civil Servants in the Kasap Ilyas Mahalle.*

Michael Bonner, Mine Ener, and Amy Singer, eds., *Poverty and Charity in Middle Eastern Contexts.*

Palmira Brummett, *Ottoman Seapower and Levantine Diplomacy in the Age of Discovery.*

Palmira Brummett, *Image and Imperialism in the Ottoman Revolutionary Press, 1908–1911.*

Ayse Burga, *State and Business in Modern Turkey: A Comparative Study.*

Guilian Denoeux, *Urban Unrest in the Middle East: A Comparative Study of Informal Networks in Egypt, Iran and Lebanon.*

Beshara Doumani, ed., *Family History in the Middle East: Household, Property and Gender.*

Hala Fattah, *The Politics of Regional Trade in Iraq, Arabia, and the Gulf, 1745–1900.*

Samira Haj, *The Making of Iraq, 1900-1963: Capital, Power, and Ideology.*

Issa Khalaf, *Politics in Palestine: Arab Factionalism and Social Disintegration, 1939–1948.*

M. Fuad Koprulu, *The Origins of the Ottoman Empire,* translated and edited by Gary Leiser.

Zachary Lockman, ed., *Workers and Working Classes in the Middle East: Struggles, Histories, Historiographies.*

Heath W. Lowry, *The Nature of the Early Ottoman State.*

Donald Quataert, ed., *Manufacturing in the Ottoman Empire and Turkey, 1500–1950.*

Donald Quataert, ed., *Consumption Studies and the History of the Ottoman Empire, 1550–1922, An Introduction.*

Sarah Shields, *Mosul Before Iraq: Like Bees Making Five-Sided Cells.*